Common
LISPcraft

Common
LISPcraft

ROBERT WILENSKY

UNIVERSITY OF CALIFORNIA, BERKELEY

W•W•NORTON & COMPANY
New York   London

ISBN 0-393-95544-3

W. W. Norton & Company, Inc.,
500 Fifth Avenue, New York, N.Y. 10110

W. W. Norton & Company Ltd.,
37 Great Russell Street, London WC1B 3NU

3 4 5 6 7 8 9 0

For my family and friends

Contents

Contents

Contents

vi

Contents

Contents

Preface

1. The LISP Language

LISP is one of the oldest programming languages in active use today. The LISP language was first conceived by John McCarthy and his students in the late 1950's. The name *LISP* is an acronym for *LISt Processing,* a reference to the fundamental structure underlying most LISP programs and data. Its main use, both then and now, is in the field of artificial intelligence.

LISP is one of the few older languages to have survived the transition to the current era of computing. Since its initial inception and implementation, the LISP language has undergone considerable evolution. Many new features have been added, implementations have been dramatically improved, and interfaces markedly upgraded. Whole programming environments have been created and integrated into the language. LISP has even been given hardware support in the form of high performance LISP machines.

These developments were often in response to drawbacks in the early conception and implementations of the language. As a result, many of the reasons underlying the reluctance of some to accept LISP are no longer valid today. Nevertheless, LISP still maintains a vestige of its past reputation as an interesting but impractical language. Recent improvements in computer technology, together with the availability of some of the finest software development environments in existence, have done much to change this attitude. The LISP community currently appears to be undergoing a period of rapid expansion.

One difficulty with LISP is trying to define exactly what the LISP language is. Unlike many other languages, there is no such thing as standard LISP. Rather, LISP has evolved in a number of different directions. This has resulted in a whole family of LISP languages. While these share many basic features, they differ from one another in substantial ways. Among the most widely used dialects of LISP today are *MacLISP,* a version of LISP developed at MIT, and *INTERLISP,* developed at Bolt, Beranek and Newman and Xerox Palo Alto Research Center. Versions of these dialects currently run on various special purpose LISP machines. *Portable Standard LISP* is another dialect designed to be easily transportable across different machines. The *Scheme* dialect of LISP, invented by Sussman and Steele at MIT, contains a rather different interpretation of a number of basic concepts than that found in most other versions of the language.

A previous version of this book, **LISPcraft**, which is still available separately, was based on a dialect of LISP called *Franz LISP*. Franz LISP is closely related to MacLISP, and was developed at the University of California at Berkeley. It is available under Berkeley UNIX* and a number of other operating systems. Among the reasons for its selection was the fact that it was and still is widely available to students, mostly due to the widespread presence of UNIX in the university environment.

2. Common LISP

Recently, there has been an attempt to standardize many of the innovations that have entered into the different LISP dialects. The result of this attempt at synthesizing LISP variations is called *Common LISP*. There are a number of ways in which Common LISP departs from previous efforts to build LISP systems. Most significantly, Common LISP is defined as a *language,* rather than as an implementation of LISP. In most other instances, new LISPs came into existence as the need arose to have a LISP that ran on a certain machine or under a certain operating system. In contrast, Common LISP is defined as a set of specifications that could be realized in different ways. With the advent of Common LISP, it is now possible to talk about an actual LISP language without having to talk about a specific implementation.

Common LISP implementations are only now becoming available. However, they are becoming available for a wide variety of machines and operating systems. While variations and incompatibilities are likely to creep in, the possibility of painlessly moving a LISP program from one machine to a quite different machine is now rather realistic. Students may now learn something approaching a standard, and not have to relearn a great deal as they move to a different environment.

Of course, this is not to say that Common LISP is the perfect resolution of all the incompatibilities that exist among LISP dialects. Indeed, while the language is on the whole a rather significant achievement, to some degree it has been designed by a committee. Some issues appear to be treated inconsistently. Some of the particular decisions that were made are questionable. For example, users accustomed to a certain environment will be dismayed to find that input in Common LISP is normally converted to upper case. Some of the terminology is poor, so much so that I developed new terminology in its stead. For example, the terms "binding" and "special form" are used in a confused and confusing fashion in Common LISP; a different terminology for talking about variables and special functions has been instituted here in its place. Also, some critics have accused Common LISP of being too complex a language, making efficient implementations difficult. As the programmer's credo goes "A feature is worth a thousand words, or 2K bytes." Common LISP is not a small language.

We also have no guarantee that Common LISP will be enthusiastically or universally accepted by the LISP community. Indeed, this community is known to suffer considerably from the "not invented here" syndrome. Nevertheless, the need for standardization is compelling enough that industry, the government, and even universities and research centers appear to be headed in the Common LISP direction.

Common LISP is not perfect, but is sure to continue to progress in response to a large user community. No individual may ever be completely satisfied by the result, but the community at large is certain to benefit.

3. Scope and Aim of *Common LISPcraft*

This book is designed to give the reader a working knowledge of Common LISP. No formal description of the language is attempted. Rather, the book emphasizes pragmatic considerations. In addition to explaining the basic features of LISP, programming language idioms, elements of various programming styles, and the actual use of the language are given equal attention. It is the experience of this author that such items contribute just as much to the characteristic flavor of a programming language as do the core features of that language.

While issues of programming style are addressed, an effort has been made not to be chauvinistic. Instead, certain useful programming language styles are suggested to the reader for consideration. Comments about good and bad programming style are given throughout. These generally derive from observations of LISP programming practice rather than from stylistic prejudices.

LISP is used largely as a programming language for artificial intelligence research. However, this bias is not substantially reflected in this book. The language rather than its applications is emphasized here. After familiarizing himself with the essentials of the language, the reader may want to consult other texts that feature artificial intelligence issues more prominently.

While this document is self-contained, it does not exhaust or fully describe every aspect of Common LISP. The reader may consult *Common LISP: The Language* by Guy L. Steele, Jr., the bible of specification for all Common LISPs. In addition, a manual for the particular implementation of Common LISP will contained implementation details that cannot be contained herein.

4. Format

Programming in a computer language is a skill like any other: Proficiency does not come without practice. The best programming language text will not promote fluency in a language unless the reader uses the language as he goes along. With this in mind, this book has been designed as an interactive session with the LISP interpreter. To get the most out of this book, the reader should participate in the dialogues given below by running LISP, typing in the expressions as they appear, and noting the responses given by the LISP system.

Equally important are the exercises at the end of each chapter. These are designed not only to develop a facility for LISP programming, but to acquaint the reader with some details of Common LISP that cannot be adequately covered in the text. Solutions to the exercises are available from the publisher under separate cover.

This book should be viewed more as a travel guide than a textbook. Without the accompanying exploration, real learning is not possible. The reader should first familiarize himself with the basic features of the language as described in the initial chapter of this text. This should supply the reader with enough knowledge and safety equipment to handle any situations that are encountered by straying off the tour suggested in subsequent chapters.

The reader is encouraged to take the time to make as many side trips as possible. Not everything the reader encounters in his explorations will make sense at first. Nevetheless, a good way to get to know a country is to get off the beaten path. Do not neglect the main attractions, however. There is usually a reason that there is so much interest in them.

Bon voyage!

Acknowledgments

My understanding of Common LISP, and of many issues in programming languages, was greatly aided by Paul Hilfinger. He was generous with both his time and insights. In particular, his comments on recursion led to the presentation I adopted in Chapter 6.

I benefitted continually from numerous conversations with Richard Fateman, who also pointed out many errors in earlier manuscripts. James Larus also provided useful feedback on Common LISP.

Peter Pirolli sparked my desire to rewrite my chapter on recursion. He also made many detailed suggestions that I attempted to incorporate. The idea of presenting iteration before recursion was his, and, I think, resulted in a considerable improvement.

This book would not have been possible (or necessary) without the development of the Common LISP language. This involved a large number of people at many institutions across the nation. The existence of Common LISP is a tribute to their collective technical accomplishments, but even more so to their willingness to place the general welfare above their individual prejudices.

The result of this collective effort was crystalized in *Common LISP: The Language* by Guy L. Steele, Jr. Steele's book forms the basis for this one, and for any other books on Common LISP, for that matter. Steele and his colleagues deserve our thanks for creating so clear a document for so difficult a task.

The preparation of this book would have been impossible without the help of my secretary, Sharon Tague, who successfully defended my time against all intruders, domestic and foreign.

Finally, I want to thank Diana Currie, who served as a patient sounding board, as well as a source of helpful suggestions, good advice, and most of my motivation and encouragement.

Common
LISPcraft

Chapter 1

Getting Started

1.1. Introduction

In this chapter we encounter the basic elements of LISP. These include the primary data structure of LISP, called the *s-expression*. They also include the LISP *interpreter,* which constitutes the heart of any LISP system. The LISP interpreter performs computations on s-expressions through a process called *evaluation.* We examine this process, and describe how it applies to different kinds of s-expressions. Along the way, the major categories of s-expressions, called *lists* and *atoms,* are discussed.

We encounter our first LISP functions in this chapter. These are largely concerned with arithmetic computation. We also learn how to store the value of a computation for subsequent use, and how to recover from an error. By the end of this chapter, the reader will be familiar with the syntax of LISP, and be able to specify and understand complex computations.

1.2. The LISP Interpreter

LISP is normally used as an *interpreter.* Think of an interpreter as a kind of glorified handheld calculator – you type in arguments and an operation to perform on them. The "calculator" does the operation and prints out an answer. To begin a session with the LISP calculator on most computers, we first need to start up a LISP process. This is generally done by issuing the command to your operating system to run LISP. LISP will identify itself and signal that it is ready to accept an input:

Generic Common LISP
->

The arrow is LISP's signal that it is waiting for an input.

Standardization Note: The exact command to start a LISP process may vary from one operating system to another. Moreover, on a LISP machine, one is normally in communication with a LISP interpreter, so no additional command is required.

There is no standardization of prompts in Common LISP. Rather than an arrow, some entirely different prompt may be used. Some LISP implementations issue no prompts at all.

Now we are ready to ask the LISP calculator to perform an operation for us. LISP accepts commands in a somewhat different form from most handheld calculators. First, we begin the command with a parenthesis. Next, we specify the name of an operation we would like to perform. Then we give the arguments we want to use. We finish the whole thing off with a final parenthesis. For example, if we want to compute "8+3" using our LISP calculator, we type the following:

        -> (+ **8 3**)
        11
        ->

In this example, we only typed the expression in parentheses; the arrows and the answer were output by LISP.

Standardization Note: In many implementations of LISP, the user types a carriage return to signal that the command is complete. Other implementations will go to work as soon as they see the closing parenthesis. Also, some implementations will output additional blank lines along with the result.

+ is the name for the addition operator in this LISP; **8** and **3** are the arguments to this operator. There are lots of other operators like + in LISP (a full enumeration of them can be found in Appendix A). Unlike +, operators in LISP are not always one character long, nor are they generally composed of peculiar symbols. However, all the operators in LISP work pretty much the same way. For example, if we want to multiply 8 by 3, we can type

```
-> (* 8 3)
24
->
```

LISP programmers sometimes call commands like these *s-expressions,* which stands for *symbolic expressions.* This is a very general term, applicable to just about anything one can say in LISP. This terminology is used because, unlike our examples so far, LISP is normally used for things other than numeric computation. However, the basic form of all symbolic expressions will be similar to what we have already seen. In fact, you have already learned most of the syntax of LISP!

For the time being, we will stick with numeric examples because they will be easier to relate to other programming experience you are likely to have had.

1.3. Evaluation

The symbolic expressions given above are also called *lists.* A list is just a sequence of objects inside a pair of parentheses. As we indicated above, LISP assumes that the first element of the list is an operator. It assumes that the rest of the list contains arguments to this operator. LISP applies the operator to the arguments. This process of taking a symbolic expression, or list, and performing a computation based on it is called *evaluation.* The result of evaluating an s-expression is called, naturally enough, the *value* of that expression. In our first example, we typed in the list (+ **8 3**); LISP evaluated this s-expression by assuming that + is an operator to be applied to the arguments **8** and **3**. The result of this evaluation was the value **11**. When it had finished evaluating this s-expression, LISP printed out the resulting value on the terminal.

1.3.1. Evaluating More Complicated S-expressions

Suppose we want to compute something a bit more complicated. For example, suppose we want to know the value of "8*(3+7)". On a handheld calculator we would probably add 3 to 7 first, and then multiply the result by 8. To do the equivalent computation in LISP, we would type the following expression:

```
-> (* 8 (+ 3 7))
80
->
```

Note that this expression looks just like the last expression we evaluated, except that here the second argument is itself an expression. When LISP evaluates an expression, it evaluates the arguments to the operator *before* it applies that operator to the arguments. So when LISP tries to apply * to the second argument above, it notices that this argument is itself an expression and evaluates it. The result of this evaluation is used as the argument for subsequent computation. In the example above, LISP evaluates (+ **3 7**) to produce the result **10**. Then it multiplies the argument **8** times **10** to get the final result.

We see from this example that s-expressions, or lists, can contain elements that are themselves s-expressions or lists. We can nest this construction as much as we like, that is, put lists inside lists inside lists, and so on. LISP will evaluate every expression according to one simple rule:

The LISP Evaluation Rule: *Look at the outermost list first. Evaluate each of its arguments. Use the results as arguments to the outermost operator.*

In this manner, we can use LISP to compute expressions of arbitrary complexity. For example, to compute "(8+3)*(4+(9*2))", we would type

```
-> (* (+ 8 3) (+ 4 (* 9 2)))
242
->
```

While this expression looks complicated, it is easy to see what it means to LISP. In accordance with the rule just given, LISP first tries to evaluate the entire expression. That is, it tries to apply * to its two arguments. Since each of these arguments is itself a list, LISP has to evaluate each one before it can perform the multiplication.

The first argument is (+ **8 3**). Evaluating this is simple – LISP merely applies + to **8** and **3** and gets **11**. However, the second argument is (+ **4** (* **9 2**)). This itself contains an argument that is a list, namely, (* **9 2**). Thus to evaluate the second argument of the entire expression, LISP must first evaluate its complex argument. This evaluation is itself straightforward – LISP applies * to **9** and **2** and gets **18**. Now the expres-

4

sion that contains this multiplication can be evaluated. The other argument in this expression is **4**, so LISP applies + to **4** and **18** and gets **22**.

LISP has now completed the evaluation of the two arguments of the entire expression. The outermost expression is now ready to be evaluated. The result of the evaluation of the first argument was **11**, so LISP applies * to **11** and **22** and gets **242**. This result is then printed out on the terminal.

LISP will not be bothered by such nesting. But you might be. Although they are perfectly legal, it becomes difficult to read heavily nested s-expressions. Writing them often leads to errors involving *unbalanced parentheses* (an old joke among LISP hackers is that LISP really stands for "Lots of Irritating Single Parentheses"). There are ways around this problem, involving the use of good indentation and editors that help you write LISP. These help, but nevertheless, most people consider it to be bad programming style to use many deeply nested s-expressions.

LISP Evaluates Everything

In these examples, we said that LISP evaluates complex arguments in order to apply an operator. Actually, LISP tries to evaluate *all* its arguments, even simple ones like **8** and **3**. But what does it mean to evaluate a number? The answer, in LISP, is that numbers evaluate to themselves. That is, any time LISP tries to evaluate **8**, the answer is always **8**; when it tries to evaluate **3**, the answer is always **3**.

This is just a convention. It makes LISP more uniform, because we can say that LISP expressions evaluate their arguments without having to make exceptions for numbers and other things we are going to see later on. One way in which this uniformity is manifest is that we can ask LISP directly to evaluate an **8** or a **3**. That is, we can type the following:

```
-> 8
8
-> 3
3
->
```

In sum, numbers are really s-expressions too. They are just very simple ones that always evaluate to themselves.

Expressions Always Return a Value

Another general rule about LISP that has been true so far is that expressions always return a value. When we evaluate the innermost argument of a complicated expression, the result is a value that is used by the next stage of our computation. Eventually, a value is returned from the evaluation of the whole expression. LISP prints this value back to the user.

1.4. Arguments to Functions

Our examples above all contain two arguments. There is nothing sacred about two, however. For example, **1+** is a LISP operator that takes a number and adds 1 to it, as in

```
-> (1 + 8)
9
->
```

Some LISP operators, such as +, can take a variable number of arguments. For example, we can do the following in LISP:

```
-> (+ 7 8 9)
24
->
```

Since we do not normally talk about operators when more than two arguments are involved, we should more properly call things like + *functions*. We will use this terminology from now on.

The function + is somewhat unusual in that it will handle any number of arguments. Most LISP functions require a fixed number of arguments. For example, look what happens if we supply the incorrect number of arguments to **1+**:

```
-> (1 + 8 9)
```

Error: Incorrect number of args to 1+

Debug 1>:

LISP caught our error and printed out a message. However, the familiar -> prompt is gone, replaced by a mysterious **Debug 1>:**. This is LISP's way of communicating with us after an error. The **Debug 1>:** indicates that we are in a program called a *debugger*. If we were debugging a real program, we would use the debugger to interactively debug our program. We will discuss LISP debugging facilities in detail in Chapter 11. However, we will not bother with this for now. Instead, we would simply like LISP to forget the error ever happened and put us back where we were. In this implementation of Common LISP, we can do so by typing the following:

Debug 1>: quit

−>

We have now left the debugger and returned to where we were before. The place where we were is called the *top level* of LISP. Think of the top level as the place where LISP has finished all pending evaluations and is waiting for new input from the user.

Standardization Note: The exact nature of the debugger is not part of Common LISP per se. Rather, this is left up to the creators of various Common LISP implementations. For example, there is no Common LISP standard specifying the nature of the prompt to be displayed after an error. Nor is there standardization of the commands the debugger will accept. In some implementations, the user normally does not type a command at all; rather a special key is reserved just for this purpose. For example, on a Symbolics LISP machine, the user types the key "ctrl-meta-abort" to exit the debugger. The reader must determine how the equivalent of **quit** has been realized in the local LISP implementation. Experiment, check the implementation manual, or consult a local expert.

LISP is somewhat unusual in that virtually everything gets done by executing a function. In fact, there is really no more to LISP than that. All the complexity of LISP comes from the particular functions LISP provides and the details of how various types of functions are treated by the interpreter.

Supplied Arguments and Actual Arguments

Since LISP has a tendency to evaluate the arguments to a function, we sometimes have need to distinguish between the objects supplied to a function, and the objects that the function operates on. For example, consider the expression (* **8** (+ **3 7**)). The objects supplied to the function * are **8** and (+ **3 7**), but LISP evaluates these to produce the objects **8** and **10**, respectively. These are the objects that actually get multipled together.

We will refer to the objects present in a call to a function as the *supplied arguments*. We will call their values, upon which the computation is performed, as the *actual arguments*. Thus (+ **3 7**) above is an argument *supplied* to *, while **10** is the corresponding *actual* argument. We will use the undifferentiated term *argument* to refer to either the supplied argument or the actual argument. In most situations, it will be clear from the context which object is being referred to.

1.5. Symbols

So far, we have seen how to perform arbitrarily complex numerical computations in LISP. But we have not seen any way to store the results of such computations. We need something to fill the role played by variables in other programming languages. LISP provides a similar service through the use of *symbols*. Symbols look like variables, although symbols have other uses as well. Typical examples of symbols are **foo**, **baruch**, and **long–variable–name13**. Just as one can assign a value to a variable in most programming languages, one can assign a value to a symbol in LISP.

Most programming languages provide a special notation for assignment, e. g., an assignment arrow or an equal sign. However, LISP does no such thing. Instead, LISP uses its routine workhorse, the function. LISP has a special function which assigns the value of one of its arguments to the other argument. This function goes under the rather peculiar name of **setq**. For example, to accomplish the equivalent of "x ← 5" in LISP, we do the following:

```
-> (setq x 5)
5
->
```

It does not look like much has happened. But we can now query LISP about the value of **x**:

```
-> x
5
->
```

The use of **setq** has caused LISP to remember a value for **x**. Another way of saying this is that symbols are also s-expressions that LISP tries to evaluate when we type them in. The value of a symbol in LISP is the value assigned to that symbol by some previous assignment operation.

We can use a symbol wherever we expect an s-expression to appear. For example, having previously assigned a value to **x**, we can do the following:

```
-> (+ x 8)
13
-> x
5
->
```

Note that using a symbol as an argument to a function does not ordinarily change its value, unless that function is something specially designed for that purpose, like **setq**.

What would the value of a symbol be if it were not explicitly assigned a value by a call to a previous assignment function? Let us find out by asking LISP to evaluate some previously unmentioned symbol:

-> money

Error: Attempt to take the value of an unassigned variable: MONEY

Debug 1>:

Attempting to evaluate the symbol **money** caused an error. In particular, LISP complained that **money** is an *unassigned* symbol, i. e., that it was never assigned a value. As we can see, LISP considers this to be an error. We can return to the top level in order to proceed.

But there appears to be an inconsistency here. We said before that LISP tries to evaluate arguments before applying a function. When we evaluate a **setq**, the symbol whose value we are changing may not be defined. If LISP treated **setq** like any other function, then should not LISP try to evaluate its first argument, and thereby cause an error? For example, if we type in **(setq x 5)**, should not LISP try to evaluate the argument **x**, and generate an error because **x** has not yet been assigned a value ?

In fact, it should. The only reason this does not happen is because LISP treats **setq** differently from the other functions we have seen so far. In particular, **setq** does not cause its first argument to be evaluated (the second argument is subject to normal treatment). For example, we can type

```
-> (setq x (+ 4 5))
9
-> x
9
->
```

Here LISP evaluated the expression constituting the second argument to produce the actual argument **9**. However, the argument **x** was passed directly to **setq**. Thus **setq** operated on the actual arguments **x** and **9** to produce the desired assignment.

Special Functions

LISP treats **setq** differently from the other functions we have seen because **setq** is an instance of a *special function.* Whereas LISP causes the arguments to an ordinary function to be evaluated, LISP may handle the arguments of each special function rather idiosyncratically. Fortunately, there are only a small number of special functions in LISP. We will see a more systematic treatment of functions in subsequent chapters.

Unless explicitly stated otherwise, assume that all the functions we describe are ordinary functions, and evaluate all their arguments.

Note that when we assigned **x** a value using **setq**, LISP also printed out that value. That is, the expression **(setq x 5)** returned the value **5** *in addition to assigning* **x** *the value* **5**. This is important in that we can use the value returned by **setq** to continue the computation. Consider the following example:

```
-> (+ 2 (setq x (* 3 4)))
14
-> x
12
->
```

This may look strange at first, but let us apply our rule of LISP evaluation: LISP tries to evaluate arguments first, so first it evaluates **2** to **2**. The second argument then gets evaluated. This is a **setq**, so to evaluate it, LISP only evaluates its second argument. This causes the * function to be applied to **3** and **4**, and the value **12** is computed. Then **setq** is applied to **x** and **12**. **setq** sets **x** to **12** and also returns **12** as its value. + is now applied to **2** and **12**, and the answer **14** returned. Since **x** was changed in the process, we can query LISP for its value afterwards.

This sort of construct is not too desirable from a programming-style vantage point. We have caused a side-effect (i. e., changing the value of a symbol) right in the middle of an expression, and this can be confusing. So even though this is legal, it should be used with caution. Later on we will see some techniques that will help us structure our code to avoid such expressions.

Function Names and Symbols

The names that we use to denote functions in LISP, e. g., *, +, 1+ and **setq**, do not constitute a separate class of object. Rather, these are symbols, just like **x**, **y**, and **foo**. As far as LISP is concerned, the only difference between the first group of symbols and the second is that members of the former group are known to LISP as denoting some function, while those of the latter are not. For example, watch what happens when we try to use the symbol **bodily** where LISP expects a function name:

> -> (bodily 1 2)

> **Error: Symbol has no function definition: BODILY**

> **Debug 1>:**

LISP objected to this because it does not know about any function named **bodily**. We can return to the top level to go on.

Other than the fact that they denote functions built into LISP, there is nothing at all special about the symbols +, 1+, etc. (Of course, symbols like + and 1+ may look rather unconventional. In many programming languages, variables and function names cannot contain non-alphanumeric characters like +; nor can they begin with a digit, like 1+. In comparison, LISP is remarkably broadminded in what it deems an acceptable symbol.) For example, we can assign values to these symbols just as we can to less prominent symbols:

> -> (setq 1+ 17)
> 17
> -> 1+
> 17
> ->

Since 1+ appears in an argument position in the call to **setq**, LISP completely ignores the fact that the symbol 1+ is normally used to refer to a function. Instead, the symbol **1+** is assigned a value, as would any other symbol passed to **setq** in this manner. Afterwards, we see that **1+** evaluates to the value it has just been assigned, just like a "normal" symbol would.

But what about **1+**'s ability to act as a function? Let us see if it is still reliable:

```
-> (1+ 3)
4
->
```

Assigning **1+** a value has absolutely no effect whatsoever on its role as a function name.

Thus symbols serve the dual roles of function identifiers and variable specifiers in LISP. And it is possible to use symbols for both roles simultaneously, as the above example demonstrates. In principle, symbols can have multiple roles in LISP, because the LISP interpreter can determine the role served by a particular symbol from its context. We have already seen how this is done: If we ask LISP to evaluate a list that begins with a symbol, LISP interprets that symbol as naming a function; if we ask LISP to evaluate just the plain symbol, LISP interprets that symbol as referring to a variable. So LISP is not confused by expressions like **(setq 1+ 17)**: it knows that **setq** is meant to be used to refer to a function because it occurs in the beginning of the list; it knows that **1+** is intended as a variable because it occurs elsewhere.

However, expressions such as **(setq 1+ 17)** are generally bad programming practice. While it is perfectly acceptable LISP, it tends to be confusing to us humans to use the same symbol for more than one purpose. The programmer is probably better off picking a name that is not already serving another purpose.

Since the interpretation of a symbol is clear from context, LISP programmers tend to talk in an informal way about the roles played by symbols. In the above example, a LISP programmer might refer to the *variable* **x**, since the symbol **x** is used here to designate a variable; similarly, LISP programmers would refer to the *function* **setq**, since the symbol **setq** is used here to name a function. This is actually a kind of shorthand. It saves the programmer the trouble of saying "the variable named by the symbol **x**", or "the function named by the symbol **setq**". These formulations may be technically more accurate. But they are much too painful for everyday use.

(By the way, the variables denoted by the symbols * and + happen to serve a special function in Common LISP. This function has nothing to do with their role as arithmetic functions. Their use as variables, as well as that of every other Common LISP symbol used in a similar manner, is described in Appendix B. Changing or accessing the value of any of these symbols may have unexpected results. The user is therefore cautioned against doing so inadvertently.)

Atoms

So far, we have encountered three different kinds of LISP objects: symbols, numbers, and lists. LISP imposes an additional layer of organization upon these objects. Namely, we use the term **atom** to refer to just about any LISP object that is not viewed as having parts. In particular, numbers and symbols are both considered to be atoms; lists are not. In fact, symbols are sometimes referred to as *literal atoms,* a term that emphasizes their common heritage with other primitive LISP elements.

1.6. Leaving LISP

If at any point you should wish to terminate your current session with the LISP interpreter, most LISPs have some function that will do so. Such a function is often called **exit**. This is a function of no arguments which terminates the current LISP process. Thus executing

> -> **(exit)**

will return the user to the operating system interface from which the LISP process was originally created.

Standardization Note: There is no standard Common LISP function for returning to the operating system. In fact, on LISP machines, no such function exists as there is no notion of a separate operating system. You must determine the details of your local system yourself.

---

exit kills the current LISP process, so if you want to play with LISP some more, you will have to create a new process, as we did in the beginning of this chapter. This new process will not know about any of the things you did in your previous session, for better or for worse. For example, if we **setq** the values of some symbols in one session and then **exit** LISP, the next LISP process we create will be oblivious to these assignments:

```
-> (setq x 4)
4
-> (exit)
```

Now let us create a fresh LISP process:

```
Generic Common LISP
-> x

Error: Attempt to take the value of an unassigned variable:
X

Debug 1>:
```

1.7. Summary

We have encountered the following types of LISP objects:

(1) *s-expressions,* which encompass everything we have seen, including both lists and atoms,

(2) *lists,* which are sequences of s-expressions inside matching parentheses,

and

(3) *atoms,* which are s-expressions that LISP treats as whole things. There are two kinds of atoms, *numbers* and *symbols* (sometimes called *literal atoms*). The latter fill the roles of both variables and function names.

We communicate with a LISP *interpreter,* which tries to *evaluate* each s-expression we type in. After evaluation, the interpreter prints the value it computed. We refer to this aspect of the LISP system with which we communicate directly as the *top level* of LISP.

Evaluation is done according to the following rules:

(1) Numbers evaluate to themselves.

(2) Symbols evaluate to the last value assigned to them.

(3)   Lists are evaluated by interpreting the first element as a function name, and the rest of the list as arguments to that function. The arguments are (usually) evaluated, and the function applied to the resulting values. The value returned by the function is the value of the list.

We have seen the following functions:

(1)   Arithmetic functions like +, **1**+, and *. Some of these accept any number of arguments, and some, a fixed number. They all cause all their arguments to be evaluated.

(2)   The special function **setq**, which assigns its first argument, which should be a symbol, the value of its second argument.

(3)   The system function **exit**. This is a function of no arguments that terminates the current LISP process. The name of this function, and its very existence, is highly implementation-dependent.

Exercises

(1)   Write s-expressions to compute each of the following:

(a) $3^2 + 4^2$

(b) $(3*17) + (4*19)$

(c) $12^3 + 1^3 - (9^3 + 10^3)$

(2)   All the numbers we have encountered in this chapter have been whole numbers. These are referred to in Common LISP as *integers*. Common LISP allows several other types of numbers. For example, Common LISP allows you to specify manipulate fractions. **1/2**, **2/3**, and **44/100** are all valid numbers in Common LISP. These are referred to as *ratios*. The term *rational* is used to refer to numbers that are either integers or ratios.

Common LISP also supports a form of real numbers. These are called *floating point numbers*. Floating point numbers are designated using decimal points or scientific notation. For example, **18.3**, **0.07**, and **6.02252E23** are all floating point numbers.

Common LISP actually supports several forms of floating point numbers. These are called *short*, *single*, *double* and *long* floating point numbers. They are listed here in order of increasing precision.

Standardization Note: The exact precision of each type of floating point number is implementation-dependent.

The user can specify these precise types by using the symbols **S**, **F**, **D** and **L** (or their lowercase equivalents), respectively, in place of the usual exponent indicator **E**. For example, **3.141592653589793238400** represents a double floating point approximation to π.

Common LISP supports complex numbers as well, although we will not bother with them here.

The numerical functions discussed in this chapter work on all types of numbers, not just integers. Familiarize yourself with floating point and rational numbers by doing some computations on them using the functions we encountered in this chapter. In particular, note what happens when numbers of different types appear together in a computation.

Standardization Note: Most other LISPs support integers and floating point numbers. However, not all formats of floating point numbers are universally present. Ratios and complex numbers are also not generally available in other LISPs. In addition, some LISPs distinguish between small and large integers. The smaller ones are called *fixnum*s and the larger, *bignum*s. Common LISP also makes this distinction, the division between the two being implementation-dependent. Common LISP is designed to hide this distinction as much as possible, whereas it is often prominent in other LISPs.

---

(3)   Write an s-expression that computes the average of the following numbers: 83, 83, 85, 91, 97. How might we write this s-expression so that the answer is expressed as a floating point number?

(4)   The function **sqrt** returns the square root of its argument. Use this function to write LISP s-expressions that find the roots of the equation $x^2 - 11x - 1302 = 0$.

(5) Compute 1!, 2!, 3!, etc., efficiently by storing the latest result as the value of a symbol (recall that n! = n(n−1)(n−2)...1).

(6) Does LISP distinguish between upper and lower case symbol names? Try assigning values to symbols with names like **foo**, **FOO**, and **Foo** to see if these are the same or different. Determine whether function names like **setq** are also sensitive to case.

(7) In our description of LISP evaluation, we never explicitly asserted anything about the *order* in which the arguments to a function are evaluated. For example, if we ask LISP to evaluate an expression like (+ (∗ **3 4**) (∗ **5 6**)), LISP could either evaluate (∗ **3 4**) first, or evaluate (∗ **5 6**) first. That is, LISP might evaluate arguments to a function from left to right, or from right to left.

In all the instances in this chapter, the order of argument evaluation has no effect on the result of the computation. However, in general, the order of evaluation is significant. Therefore, *LISP guarantees that arguments are always evaluated in the same order.*

Under what circumstances does the order of evaluation of arguments to a function make a difference? Use this insight to devise a test to determine which order LISP uses to evaluate function arguments.

Chapter 2

Symbolic Computation

2.1. Introduction

So far, we have treated LISP as if it were a sort of interactive FORTRAN or PASCAL, doing arithmetic operations and storing some results by assigning them to symbols. Of course, LISP was not designed particularly for these operations, but for *symbolic operations.* Symbolic operations are rather abstract manipulations of LISP data structures. Because they are so abstract, symbolic operations might seem a bit meaningless at first. Not to worry. Later on we will apply them in useful ways.

In this chapter we introduce the fundamental symbolic operations of LISP. These are primarily methods of putting s-expressions together and taking them apart. In the process of exploring symbolic computation, we examine the structure of lists more closely. We learn about some pervasive LISP concepts such as the *empty list,* and how to prevent evaluation of s-expressions when it is necessary to do so.

2.2. More on Lists

The basic symbolic operations involve manipulations of lists. Therefore, let us first familiarize ourselves with lists a bit more. Consider the list **(a b c)**. This is a list of three elements, namely, the symbols **a**, **b**, and **c** (we refer to the number of elements in a list as its *length,* so we might call this a list of length three). Now consider the following list: **(a (b c) d)**. How many elements does this list have? The answer is, also three. The first element is the symbol **a**, the second the list **(b c)**, and the third the symbol **d**. It just so happens that the second element of this list is itself a list. But the original list is still a list of length three.

As we can observe from these examples, we need to be careful not to confuse the various "levels" within a list. LISP distinguishs the elements of a list from the elements of its elements. Thus the symbol **b** is *not* an element of the list **(a (b c) d)**, while the list **(b c)** *is* the second element of this list. When we refer to "the next element of a list", we are referring to the next item at the same level; this may be either an atom or a list, depending upon the particular datum. So the next element of the list **(a (b c) d)** after the element **a** is the list **(b c)**; the next element after this one is the symbol **d**. The embedded list **(b c)** has two elements, the symbols **b** and **c**, and there is no next element after **c** in this list.

Let us consider some more "tricky" examples to get the hang of things. Consider the list **(((x)))**. What is the length of this list? You are right if you answered one. This is a list of one element, namely, the list **((x))**. This in turn is also a list of one element, the list **(x)**, which is also a list of one element, the symbol **x**.

What about the list **((a b))**? Also a list of length one. It contains only one element, the list **(a b)**. This element, of course, is a list of length two. This example demonstrates that lists can contain elements that themselves have more elements than the list that contains them.

Note that the LISP objects **((a b c))** and **(a b c)** are very different. The first is a list of one element, the list **(a b c)**. The latter is a list of three elements, the symbols **a**, **b**, and **c**. Now consider the lists **(a)** and **(a a)**. These are also quite different. The first is a list of one element, and the second a list of two elements, both of which happen to be the same symbol. The lists **(a b)** and **(b a)** are both the same length, but they are different lists because their elements appear in different orders.

In sum, lists must look alike to be equivalent lists. That is, they must have exactly the same elements in the same order to be considered the same.

2.3. Taking Things Literally

We are just about ready to begin some symbolic operations. Symbolic operations will appear just like arithmetic functions, or any other LISP function for that matter. We will specify a symbolic operator or function in the beginning of a list, and its arguments will be found in the rest of the list. LISP will apply the function to its arguments as before. The only difference here is that the arguments, and resulting value, will be general s-expressions (i. e., lists or atoms) rather than numbers.

But there is a problem. Whenever we have previously entered a list into LISP, LISP tried to evaluate it. For example, if we type the list (+ **2 3**), LISP evaluates this by applying + to **2** and **3**. However, if we want to perform symbolic operations on lists, somehow we will have to get them to be arguments to functions without them first being evaluated. To see why this is a problem, consider what would happen if we just typed (**a b c**) directly to the LISP interpreter. In fact, let us try this:

> **-> (a b c)**

> **Error: Symbol has no function definition: A**

> **Debug 1>: (reset)**

> **->**

What happened? LISP tried to interpret the first element of the list as a function, and the rest of the list as its arguments. But LISP does not know about any function called **a**, so it gave us an error message.

A similar thing would happen if we tried to supply the list (**a b c**) as an argument to some function. LISP will eventually try to evaluate the list, and will give an error message when it tries to interpret the first element as a function.

This problem is reminiscent of the "Who's on First" comedy routine made famous by Abbot and Costello. In this routine, Costello is trying to find out from Abbot the names of the players on a baseball team. Unfortunately, the names of first, second and third basemen are "Who", "What" and "I don't know", respectively. So their conversation goes like this:

> Costello: Who's on first?
> Abbot: That's right.
> Costello: What's right?
> Abbot: "Who" is the first baseman.
> Costello: That's what I'm trying to find out!
>   Look, does your first baseman have a name?
> Abbot: "Who"
> Costello: The first baseman.

Abbot: That's right.
Costello: Look, what's the name of the first baseman?
Abbot: No, "What" is on second.
Costello: I don't know!
Abbot: He's on third.

Costello is confused because he cannot see that the utterances "Who", "What" and "I don't know" should not be interpreted in ordinary manner. Rather, they are meant as uninterpreted expressions. The problem is that Abbot has no convenient means to tell Costello not to interpret these words. Hence Costello ends up with a rather different meaning from the one Abbot intended.

This is exactly the problem we are having with LISP above. We want LISP to take the list (a b c) literally, rather than evaluate it. That is, we would like some way of overcoming LISP's tendency to evaluate everything we give it. This is done in LISP, as you may have guessed by now, through the use of a special function. This function is called **quote**. **quote** is a function of one argument, which is *not* evaluated. **quote** simply returns this argument as its value.

For example, let us type **(quote (a b c))** directly to LISP and see what happens:

```
-> (quote (a b c))
(A B C)
->
```

LISP evaluates this list as it would any other. It considers the first element to be a function and the rest to be arguments. In this case, because the function is **quote**, LISP does not evaluate the argument, but merely applies **quote** to it. **quote** returns the argument as its result.

Note also that the expression LISP returned contains only upper case characters, while the one we typed contains only lower case. Typically, Common LISP converts all lower case characters to upper case when they are read in. So case differences should not be important in most situations.

Standardization Note: The treatment of case varies widely among LISP systems. In some LISPs, the default is to distinguish upper case from lower case unless told otherwise. In Common LISP, it is possible to enforce this distinction, but the default is to convert to upper case

---

quote may appear to be a rather uninteresting function, since it does nothing. But in fact, the need to prevent LISP from evaluating something arises so often that a special syntax is provided for **quote**ing expressions. Rather than writing the cumbersome **(quote (a b c))**, LISP allows you to write **'(a b c)**. That is, we preface the s-expression with the "single quote" or "apostrophe" character (be sure not to use the similar looking "backquote" character ', as this has a rather different interpretation).

This is just syntactic sugar – the two expressions are identical as far as LISP is concerned.

We can apply **quote** harmlessly to anything. For example:

```
-> '(a b c)
(A B C)
-> 'a
A
-> '6
6
->
```

The last example might strike you as superfluous. It is. **6** would evaluate to **6** anyway, so putting in the **quote**, while legal, is wasteful and should be avoided.

Let us use **quote** in a more useful example:

```
-> (setq x '(a b c))
(A B C)
-> x
(A B C)
->
```

Here we assign **x** the value **(a b c)**. Remember, **setq** causes only its second argument to be evaluated. Since this is quoted, the argument evaluates to the list **(a b c)**. This list becomes the actual argument to **setq**, which then assigns it to the first argument. We could now use this value in a subsequent symbolic computation.

LISP Values Are S-expressions

Note that values in LISP are arbitrary s-expressions. That is, they are exactly the same sort of object that we ask the LISP interpreter to evaluate for us. This may take a little getting used to at first, since values and programs look identical in LISP. For example, we could assign a symbol a value that looks just like an s-expression we would normally ask the interpreter to evaluate:

```
-> (setq x '(+ 3 4))
(+ 3 4)
->
```

Here we assign **x** the value **(+ 3 4)**. LISP did not evaluate this value, because **quote** prevented it from doing so. Instead, it treated **(+ 3 4)** just like it were any random data object. We might just as well have typed **(how are you)** as far as this example is concerned.

This example illustrates that expressions that contain functions like + or **setq** have a special meaning to LISP only when they are evaluated. Otherwise, they are inert data objects with the same status of any other LISP s-expression.

We can also assign a symbol a value that is itself a symbol. For example:

```
-> (setq x 'y)
Y
-> x
Y
-> (setq a 'a)
A
-> a
A
```

In the first example, we assign **x** the value **y**, and in the second, we assign **a** the value **a**. (There is nothing wrong with assigning a symbol itself as a value, although there are not too many cases where we have a good reason to do this.)

As is the case for lists, the values that we assigned these symbols are themselves real live LISP s-expressions. For example, the **y** assigned to **x** above is a real LISP symbol, and could have a value assigned to it as well. And, if we had a LISP function that, unlike **setq**, caused its first argument to be evaluated before attempting an assignment, then we could change the value of the symbol **y** indirectly by going through **x**.

In fact, the function **set** does just this. **set** is like **setq**, except it causes its first argument (as well as its second) to be evaluated. It then performs an assignment on the resulting actual arguments. For example, suppose **x** had **y** assigned to it as above. Then we could do the following:

```
-> x
Y
-> (set x 'z)
Z
-> y
Z
-> x
Y
```

set causes both its arguments to be evaluated, so **x** is evaluated to **y** and **'z** to **z**. These are passed to **set**, which then assigns the second actual argument to the first, i. e., **y** is given the value **z**. We then check this by asking LISP to evaluate **y**. LISP obligingly returns **z**.

But what happened to **x**? We check this at the end and find that it still has the value **y**. The call to **set** did not affect **x** at all.

If this example strikes you as a little confusing, you are in good company. Although it is perfectly legal and sometimes necessary, such uses of LISP are relatively rare and always a bit hairy. We almost always know the actual symbol whose value we want to change, so there is no need to have the extra level of indirection. In practice, most calls to **set** would look like the following:

```
-> (set 'x '(a b c))
(A B C)
-> x
(A B C)
->
```

Here we want to assign the symbol **x** some value. Therefore, we quote **x**, and **set** causes this argument to evaluate to **x**.

Since this construction occurs so frequently, LISP allows a special shorthand for it, namely, **setq**. **setq** is named for **set quote** since it combines these two functions into a more practical package. Now that we know this, we will rarely see **set** again. It is important that you understand the above examples, though, so you understand how LISP works.

Forms

We have now seen symbolic expressions that are evaluated by the LISP interpreter, as well as symbolic expressions that we protect from evaluation. There is a useful terminological distinction worth introducing at this point.

When a symbolic expression is intended for evaluation by the LISP interpreter, it is sometimes referred to as a *form*. Thus we can say that the LISP interpreter evaluates forms, which are symbolic expressions; other symbolic expressions may be manipulated by various LISP functions, but in ways other than evaluation.

We will now examine what some of these other manipulations may be.

2.4. car and cdr

Now that we know how to use **quote**, we are ready to do some symbolic operations on lists. As mentioned above, symbolic operations on lists consist primarily of taking lists apart and building them up. Let us consider taking lists apart first. LISP provides two basic functions for this, called **car** and **cdr** (the latter is usually pronounced "could-er"). These names have to do with the machine upon which LISP was first implemented and, unfortunately, now have no mnemonic value.

Both **car** and **cdr** are functions of one argument. These are ordinary functions, so their supplied argument is always evaluated. In addition, it should evaluate to a list. **car** returns the first element of this list. **cdr** returns the list with its first element missing, that is, the list that results from taking the argument and removing its first element. For example:

```
-> (car '(a b c))
A
-> (cdr '(a b c))
(B C)
```

In both cases, the argument supplied evaluates to the list **(a b c)**. **car** returns the first element of this list, the symbol **a**. **cdr** returns the list that results from removing the first element, namely, the list **(b c)**.

car and cdr are Non-destructive

car and **cdr** do not actually change the lists on which they operate. Consider the following evaluations:

```
-> (setq x '(a b c))
(A B C)
-> x
(A B C)
```

```
-> (car x)
A
-> x
(A B C)
-> (cdr x)
(B C)
-> x
(A B C)
->
```

Since these functions cause their argument to be evaluated, **(car x)** results in **car** being applied to **(a b c)**. But this does not change the value of **x** in the slightest. Similarly for **cdr**.

Thus when we say that **cdr** returns a list with its first element removed, we are speaking figuratively. **cdr** does not really remove an element from anyone's list; it merely returns as its value a list that looks like the list one would get from crossing off the first element of the list constituting the actual argument to **cdr**.

Let us consider some more examples:

```
-> (cdr '(a b))
(B)
-> (car (cdr '(a b)))
B
```

Taking **cdr** of the list **(a b)** returns the list **(b)**, the list that results from scratching out the first element of **(a b)**. Remember, this is a completely different creature from the symbol **b**. To get at the second element of the original list, we have to compose two functions, as in the second example. Let us see why this works. To evaluate the second expression, LISP first evaluates the argument. The argument in this case is a call to the function **cdr**. To evaluate this call, LISP first evaluates this function's argument. This is **'(a b)**, which evaluates to **(a b)**. LISP then applies **cdr** to this value, and **cdr** returns **(b)**. Then **car** is applied to this result. **car** always returns the first element of its actual argument, in this case, **b**.

Parentheses Are Important

A few "extra" parentheses are very important to LISP, even if they may not seem so significant to us humans. For example, what would you suppose the **car** of **((a b))** would be? Try to determine this from what you have learned so far. Now let us ask LISP to see if you are right:

26

```
-> (car '((a b)))
(A B)
```

You get one brownie point if you got this answer and not **a**. This answer can be seen to be correct if we consider the structure of the list **((a b))**. This is a list of one element, the list **(a b)**. **car** always returns the first *element* of a list, not the first *atom* it can find. The first *element* of the list **((a b))** is the list **(a b)**, so **car** returns this as its value.

What function could we apply to **((a b))** to return the symbol **a**? Since **car** of this list returns **(a b)**, and since the first element of this value is the symbol **a**, then the **car** of the **car** of **((a b))** should get us what we want. Let us try this and see:

```
-> (car (car '((a b))))
A
->
```

Now let us consider taking the **cdr** of **((a b) (c d))**. What value should this return? Choose your answer, and now let us test it:

```
-> (cdr '((a b) (c d)))
((C D))
->
```

Go to the head of the class if you chose this value, and not **(c d)**. Why is this answer correct? Because **((a b) (c d))** is a list of two elements, the list **(a b)** and the list **(c d)**. **cdr** returns the list that results from crossing off the first *element* of a list. If we cross off the first element of **((a b) (c d))**, we are left with the list of one element **((c d))**, which is the value **cdr** returns.

This might be clearer if you consider taking the **cdr** of a list like **((a b) (c d) (e f))**. This is a list of three elements, the lists **(a b)**, **(c d)**, and **(e f)**. **cdr** removes the first element, and therefore should return a list consisting of the other two:

```
-> (cdr '((a b) (c d) (e f)))
((C D) (E F))
->
```

How could we get the list **(c d)** from the list **((a b) (c d))**? **cdr** of this list returns **((c d))**, a list whose first element is the list we seek. Since the first element of a list is returned by **car**, it should suffice to take the **car** of the **cdr** of the original list:

```
-> (car (cdr '((a b) (c d))))
(C D)
->
```

What if we composed these functions in the opposite order? That is, instead of taking the **car** of the **cdr**, suppose we took the **cdr** of the **car**. Well, the **car** of **((a b) (c d))** should be its first element, namely, the list **(a b)**, and the **cdr** of this list should be the list **(b)**. Let us check:

```
-> (cdr (car '((a b) (c d))))
(B)
->
```

What would happen if we tried executing **(cdr (car '(a b)))**? You are right if you think this would be a mistake. Since **(car '(a b))** evaluates to **a**, taking **cdr** of this value amounts to taking **cdr** of a symbol. But **car** and **cdr** were meant to apply only to lists, so this would be an error.

Standardization Note: Some LISPs use **car** and **cdr** of a symbol for implementation-dependent hacks. Even in such LISPs, however, it is a bad idea to write code that depends heavily on being able to take the **car** or **cdr** of a symbol, as the code is likely to be obtuse and difficult to transport to other LISP systems.

Something like this example might be valid if we have a more complicated list, though. For example

```
-> (cdr (car '((a b c) (d e f))))
(B C)
-> (car (car '((a b c) (d e f))))
A
-> (car (cdr '((a b c) (d e f))))
(D E F)
-> (car (car (cdr '((a b c) (d e f)))))
D
-> (cdr (car (cdr '((a b c) (d e f)))))
(E F)
-> (car (cdr (car (cdr '((a b c) (d e f))))))
E
->
```

You should go through each of these examples and be sure you understand why it returns what it does.

2.5. cadr, etc.

As you no doubt have noticed, code containing long strings of **car**s and **cdr**s, like the ones in the examples above, is hard to follow. Most LISP programmers consider this bad programming style and try writing their code to avoid such long sequences. However, since the need to do this sort of computation sometimes occurs, LISP provides a slightly more convenient way of composing **car**s and **cdr**s. This is done by providing built-in functions corresponding to sequence of **car**s and **cdr**s. For example, **cadr** is a LISP function equivalent to taking the **car** of the **cdr**:

```
-> (car (cdr '((a b c) (d e f))))
(D E F)
-> (cadr '((a b c) (d e f)))
(D E F)
->
```

Common LISP allows you to use functions whose names contain a sequence of up to four **a**'s and **d**'s. For example, **(cadadr x)** is equivalent to **(car (cdr (car (cdr x))))**, and **(cddaar x)** is equivalent to **(cdr (cdr (car (car x))))**. Thus, the following two lines of code compute the same thing:

```
-> (car (cdr (car (cdr '((a b c) (d e f))))))
E
-> (cadadr '((a b c) (d e f)))
E
->
```

While the second item above is terser (and possibly more efficient) than the first, it is no less cryptic. Good LISP programmers use these functions sparingly as well.

Standardization Note: The length of the sequence of **a**'s and **d**'s permitted in a **car/cdr** combination function may be different in other LISPs.

Finally, just to reinforce the point that programs and data are the same sort of stuff in LISP, consider the following computation:

```
-> (car '(cdr '(a b c)))
CDR
->
```

What is going on here? The argument supplied to **car** evaluates to the list **(cdr '(a b c))**. This happens to be a valid s-expression for evaluation, but LISP could not care less about that in this context. The argument has already been evaluated, and LISP just passes along the result. **car** treats the resulting value like any old list, and returns its first element, which happens to be the symbol **cdr**.

The example is tricky only because the actual argument to **car** looks like something that would ordinarily be evaluated. The **quote** prevents it from being evaluated in this example, though, so the argument acts just like any other piece of passive data. Take away the first **quote**, and the expression would have a radically different meaning:

```
-> (car (cdr '(a b c)))
B
->
```

Here the evaluation of the argument supplied to **car** causes the s-expression containing the **cdr** to be evaluated also. This returns **(b c)**, which becomes the actual argument to **car**. **car** then returns the first element of this list.

Programs and data are made out of the same stuff in LISP. A **quote** here or there may be all that determines whether something will be treated as one or the other.

2.6. The Empty List

Note that when we take the **cdr** of a list, the resulting value is always one element shorter than the argument. **(cdr '(a b c))** returns **(b c)**, a list of length two, and **(cdr '(b c))** returns **(c)**, a list of length one. But what would **(cdr '(c))** return? If we followed this logic, we would expect something like **( )**, a list of length zero. Let us try it and see:

```
-> (cdr '(c))
NIL
->
```

Relax. LISP really did compute a list of length zero. However, rather than print a list of length zero as ( ), LISP always prints this as the symbol **nil**.

nil means the empty list in LISP. To see that this is really the same thing as ( ), the list of no elements, let us type '( ) directly into LISP and see what happens:

```
-> '( )
NIL
->
```

LISP evaluated this expression to ( ), and then printed out this value. But since LISP always prints out the empty list as **nil**, we get the result shown above.

Actually, we did not need to quote the empty list. This is because, by convention, the empty list always evaluates to itself. So we have

```
-> ( )
NIL
-> nil
NIL
->
```

nil serves several important functions in LISP. In fact, it is so important that LISP will not let you change its value. That is, trying to **setq nil** to something will cause an error.

Objects like **nil**, whose value cannot be changed, are sometimes referred to as *constants*. Numbers are constants, since they always evaluate to the same thing (themselves). Quoted expressions are also considered constants, since it is clear what they will evaluate to.

2.7. cons

Just as **car** and **cdr** take lists apart, **cons** builds lists up. **cons** is a function of two arguments. The second argument should always be a list. **cons** returns as its value the list obtained by taking the second argument and sticking the first one in front of it. For example:

```
-> (cons 'a '(b c))
(A B C)
->
```

cons constructed a new list by taking the second actual argument, **(b c)**, and inserting the first actual argument, **a**, as its first element. **cons** returns the new, composite list **(a b c)** as its value.

A good way to think of **cons** is as a sort of inverse function of **car** and **cdr**. **cons** will always produce a list whose **car** is the first argument to the **cons**, and whose **cdr** is the second argument. Thus

```
-> (setq x (cons 'a '(b c)))
(A B C)
-> (car x)
A
-> (cdr x)
(B C)
->
```

Here we save the value **cons** produces, and then take **car** and **cdr** of this value. The results are the same as the values of the original actual arguments to **cons**.

A few other examples will help to give you the feel of this:

```
-> (cons 'a '(b))
(A B)
->
```

Here we simply **cons** the symbol **a** onto a list of length one and get a list of length two.

What would happen if we **cons** the list **(a b)** onto the list **(c d)**? Decide your answer, and now let us check:

```
-> (cons '(a b) '(c d))
((A B) C D)
->
```

The answer is not **(a b c d)** because **cons** blindly sticks its first argument into the front of the list that is its second argument, without caring whether its first argument is an atom or a list. How can we get the list **(a b c d)** starting with the list **(c d)**? This would require two **cons**'s, as follows:

```
-> (cons 'a (cons 'b '(c d)))
(A B C D)
->
```

The innermost **cons** returns **(b c d)**, and the outermost one prefixes **a** to this value.

What if we start with a list of two elements, like **(a b)**, and want to put each of its elements in the front of the list **(c d)** to produce **(a b c d)**? Then we would have to use some sequence **car**s and **cdr**s to access each element of the first list, and then **cons** them onto the second. For example, if **x** has the value **(a b)**, we could access **b** by getting the value of **x**, and taking the **car** of its **cdr**; we could **cons** this value onto the list **(c d)** to get **(b c d)**. Then we could access **a** by taking the **car** of the value of **x**, and produce the desired result by **cons**ing this value onto the value built up so far. Thus we have the following:

```
-> (setq x '(a b))
(A B)
-> (cons (car x) (cons (cadr x) '(c d)))
(A B C D)
->
```

The second s-expression is a typical LISP construct. Make sure you understand what it is doing. In essence, it uses **car** and **cdr** to tear apart an s-expression, and **cons** to stick the pieces back together.

What happens when we **cons** something onto the empty list? For example, suppose we **cons a** onto **nil**. Since **nil** represents the list of no elements, i. e., **( )**, **cons** should make a list whose only element is **a**, i. e., the list **(a)**. Let us try and see:

```
-> (cons 'a nil)
(A)
->
```

cons is Non-destructive

As is the case for **car** and **cdr**, **cons** does not change its arguments. Consider the following:

```
-> (setq x 'a)
A
-> (setq y '(b c))
(B C)
-> (cons x y)
(A B C)
-> x
A
```

```
-> y
(B C)
->
```

Thus **cons** builds a list out of its arguments, but does not change them in any way.

consing Requires Storage and Is Expensive

car and **cdr** do not have to create anything because they return as their value a piece of a structure that is already there. For example, **cdr** of **(a b c)** returns **(b c)**, which is actually a piece of the longer list. However, unlike **car** and **cdr**, **cons** has to return a list that is not there to begin with, and thus must create something new.

But this creation must require some new storage. Where does this storage come from? The answer is that LISP dynamically allocates storage for lists as the need arises (e. g., in response to calls to **cons**). When it runs out of room, LISP garbage-collects unused **cons** cells, as they are called, and reuses them. Since garbage collection is generally regarded as an expensive operation, the effective average cost of using **cons** is quite high. For example, an efficient LISP implementation may execute a **car** as a single machine instruction, taking, say, a microsecond. But the effective cost of a single **cons**, when garbage collection is considered, might be a millisecond.

Of course, one cannot avoid **cons**ing up lists altogether. But remember that functions that build lists tend to be more expensive than comparable functions that just manipulate existing lists. Use the former frugally.

Standardization Note: Considerable effort has been given of late to producing LISP systems in which the cost of garbage collection is minimal. In such a system, the cost of doing a **cons** is proportionally cheapened. You will need to examine your local implementation to determine just how efficiently it performs garbage collection. However, the chances are very great that creating lots of garbage on your system will be costly.

2.8. List Construction Functions

We can use **cons** to build up arbitrarily complicated s-expressions from scratch. For example, to get the lists **(a b c)** and **(a (b c) d)**, we would do the following:

```
-> (cons 'a (cons 'b (cons 'c nil)))
(A B C)
-> (cons 'a (cons (cons 'b (cons 'c nil)) (cons 'd nil)))
(A (B C) D)
->
```

Since this is cumbersome, LISP provides us with some more convenient list-building tools. **list** is a function that takes any number of arguments, and builds a new list containing each actual argument as an element. **append** is a function that takes any number of arguments, which should all be lists, and creates a new list by sticking all the elements of these lists together. So

```
-> (list 'a 'b 'c)
(A B C)
-> (list 'a '(b c) 'd)
(A (B C) D)
-> (append '(a b) '(c d) '(e f))
(A B C D E F)
->
```

LISP contains many other more specialized functions to help construct lists. As you become more proficient in LISP, you will want to consult Appendix A to see what other list construction functions may be pertinent to your needs.

At this point, you may be wondering what all this symbolic manipulation could possibly have to do with anything. Why should anyone care that we can take lists of meaningless symbols, and produce yet longer lists of meaningless symbols, even if we can do it elegantly? Of course, in a real application, our symbols might not be quite so meaningless. For example, instead of random **a**'s and **b**'s, the elements of a list might correspond to the words of an English sentence, and another list might denote some sort of analysis of this sentence. The values of symbols may represent repositories of information that are useful in making such an analysis.

Unfortunately, at this point we can only be suggestive, as we have not yet built up enough machinery to solve any "real world" problems you are likely to have. We will enrich our repertoire in the next few chapters to remedy this situation. For a little while, though, we will have to be satisfied with some rather abstract-looking computations.

2.9. Summary

In this chapter we have encountered the basic elements of symbolic computation:

(1) **quote** is used to prevent the interpreter from evaluating an s-expression. **(quote (x y z))** can be abbreviated as **'(x y z)**.

(2) **car** is a function of one argument, which should be a list. **car** returns the first element of this list as its value.

(3) **cdr** is a function of one argument, which should be a list. **cdr** returns the rest of this list after removing its first element.

(4) There are a set of functions called **cadr, caar, cadar**, etc. Each function is equivalent to some sequence of **car**s and **cdr**s, with each **a** indicating a **car** and each **d** indicating a **cdr**.

(5) **cons** is a function of two arguments, of which the second should be a list. **cons** returns a list whose value looks like the list one would get by inserting the first argument at the front of the second argument.

(6) **list** and **append** are list-building functions. They both take any number of arguments. **list** returns a list whose elements are its actual arguments; **append** returns a list whose elements are the elements of its actual arguments, which should all be lists.

(7) **nil** is the empty list, the list of no elements. **nil** is identical to ( ), although LISP always prints out the empty list as **nil**. By convention, the empty list always evaluates to itself.

(8) **set** is an infrequently used function that causes both its arguments to be evaluated. The first actual argument should be a symbol. **set** assigns the first actual argument the second actual argument.

(9) A *form* is a symbolic expression intended for evaluation. A *constant* is a form whose value is predetermined. Some special symbols like **nil** are constants, as are all numbers and quoted expressions.

Exercises

(1) Find the sequences of **car**s and **cdr**s that return **x** when applied to the following s-expressions:

    (a) **(a b x d)**

    (b) **(a (b (x d)))**

    (c) **(((a (b (x) d))))**

(2) Construct the lists used in Exercise 1 using only symbols and calls to **cons**.

(3) The function **length** returns the length of its argument, e. g., **(length '(a b c))** returns **3**. Use **length** to check your assessment of the lengths of the lists in Exercise 1.

(4) Assign **x** the value **(a b c)**. Use this to produce the list **(a b c a b c)**.

(5) Write the expression **''(a)** using **quote** rather than **'**. What data type is the expression **' a**?

(6) Assign **x** the value **y**. Now, without mentioning **y** explicitly, assign the value **(1 2 3)** to **y**.

(7) What is the difference between the following s-expressions:

    (a) **(car (setq x '(a b c)))**

    (b) **(car '(setq x '(a b c)))**

(8) Evaluating **(caadadr '(a '(b (c))))** returns the value **b**. So does evaluating **(caadr (cadr '(a '(b (c)))))**. If we evaluate the second part of this expression, i. e., **(cadr '(a '(b (c))))**, we get **'(b (c))**. But evaluating **(caadr '(b (c)))** returns **c**. Explain this.

Chapter 3

Defining Our Own Functions

3.1. Introduction

We now have the machinery to construct some heavy-duty expressions. However, it is a futile exercise to write down a complex s-expression, evaluate it once, and never use it again. Rather, we would prefer to do what is done in all programming languages: Write a stored program that takes a few inputs, and produces some output, and which we can use repeatedly.

In this chapter, we describe LISP's facility for allowing the user to create stored programs. This is done in LISP by allowing the user to create his own functions. We examine LISP's function calling scheme in some detail, with particular attention paid to the treatment of program variables. We also show how to save function definitions in files for repeated use.

3.2. User-Defined Functions

In LISP, we achieve the equivalent of a stored program by creating a new function. User-defined functions will be used just like the functions that come with LISP. That is, once a function is defined, we can put it in the beginning of a list, in front of a few arguments, and LISP will apply the function to those arguments. For example, suppose **addthree** were a function we defined that takes one argument, and adds three to it. Then we could type expressions like the following:

```
-> (addthree 7)
10
-> (setq x (addthree 19))
22
->
```

and so on. We could use this function in LISP wherever we could use those functions that were native to LISP. In effect, we have extended LISP by adding a new function to its repertoire.

All we need to know is how to create a new function. Well, how do we do anything in LISP? We have some function tailored to that need. So to define new functions, we have a LISP function that produces new functions. This function is called **defun**, for "define function". **defun** takes as its arguments the name of the function to be defined, a list of formal parameters (which should all be symbols), and some bodies of code (which are just s-expressions). **defun** is a special function, and does not evaluate any of its arguments. It merely associates the formal parameter list and bodies of code with the function name for future reference.

Standardization Note: In other LISPs, the basic function-defining function may have a different name, and a somewhat different syntax. **de**, **def** and **defineq** are other common names for a function-defining function.

Let us take as an example the simple function we mentioned above, **addthree**. Here is how we can use **defun** to create this function:

```
-> (defun addthree (x) (+ x 3))
ADDTHREE
->
```

The name of the function is **addthree**, so that appears first in the definition. Then comes the formal parameter list. We intend for **addthree** to be a function of only one argument (namely, the value to which we wish to add three), so the list contains only one symbol. I picked the uninspired name **x** here. Finally, we have the body of code that expresses the work the function is to perform. In this case, the body is an s-expression that adds three to the value of **x**.

Note that the call to **defun** returned as its value the name of the function it defined. We do not normally use functions like **defun** for the value they compute, but rather for their side-effects (in this case, creating a new function). Nevertheless, **defun** is a LISP function, and obediently returns some value.

Having used **defun** to create **addthree**, we can now use **addthree** as advertised above. Thus we have

```
-> (addthree 11)
14
->
```

To evaluate an expression that contains a user-defined function such as this one, LISP takes the following steps:

(1)   It retrieves the function definition associated with the function name by the call to **defun** that defined the function. In the case of **addthree**, the function definition retrieved consists of the parameter list **(x)** and the body of code **(+ x 3)**.

(2)   It evaluates the forms supplied as arguments to the function. In the example above, the only form supplied is **11**, which happens to evaluate to itself.

(3)   It assigns the resulting values to the symbols in the function's formal parameter list. In our example, the only element of the formal parameter list was **x**, which was assigned the value **11**.

(4)   Lastly, LISP evaluates the code of the function. In our **addthree** example, the code is **(+ x 3)**. Since **x** was just assigned the value **11**, this piece of code evaluates to **14**. This value is returned as the value of the call to **addthree.**

More generally, a call to **defun** looks like this:

```
(defun fname (v1 v2 ... vn)
    (...body of code 1...)
    (...body of code 2...) ...)
```

The formal parameters, **v1** to **vn** in this example, are just a (possibly empty) list of symbols. Each body of code is just any old s-expression.

If we defined **fname** this way, then we could call **fname** as follows:

    (fname arg1 arg2 ... argn)

LISP would evaluate this call in the following manner:

(1)   The function definition of **fname** is retrieved.

(2)   All the forms supplied as arguments to the function call, **arg1** to **argn**, are evaluated to produce the actual arguments.

(3)   Next, each formal parameter in the function definition is assigned the corresponding actual argument. **v1** is assigned the value of **arg1**, **v2** the value of **arg2**, and so on.

(4)   Lastly, LISP evaluates each body of code in turn, from left to right. The value of the last body is returned as the value of the call to **fname**.

Normally, the bodies of code will contain references to the formal parameters of the function. So a good way to think about a function call to a user-defined function is as follows: *Evaluating a call to a user-defined function is like evaluating its bodies of code with the formal parameters initialized to the corresponding actual arguments.*

Since the arguments supplied to user-defined functions are always evaluated, we can supply arbitrarily complicated s-expressions as arguments. For example:

    -> (addthree (* 4 (1– 7)))
    27
    ->

Here the argument to **addthree** evaluates to **24**, so this value gets passed to **addthree** as the actual argument.

Let us examine another simple example. Suppose we want to write a LISP function that takes two values and averages them. Such a function will require a formal parameter list containing two symbols, one for each value; its body will add these values together and then divide by two:

    -> (defun average (x y) (/ (+ x y) 2))
    AVERAGE

```
-> (average 7 21)
14
-> (average 9 31)
20
->
```

When we call the function **average**, say, by evaluating **(average 7 21)**, LISP evaluates the arguments, and assigns the resulting actual arguments to the corresponding formal parameters. In this case, **x** gets the value **7** and **y** the value **21**. Then LISP evaluates the body, and returns the resulting value as the value of the call to **average**.

Now let us look at some user-defined functions that do some symbolic computation. If you do not like the order of arguments that **cons** requires, we can define our own function that accepts arguments in the opposite order:

```
-> (defun xcons (l e) (cons e l))
XCONS
-> (xcons '(b c) 'a)
(A B C)
->
```

In this example, we used **l** and **e** as formal parameters, intending these names to be mnemonic for "list" and "element", respectively.

Let us trace through the evaluation of **(xcons '(b c) 'a)**:

(1)   First, the function definition of **xcons** is retrieved.

(2)   LISP then evaluates arguments. In this case, it evaluates the argument **'(b c)** to **(b c)**, and the argument **'a** to **a**.

(3)   Then we assign formal parameters. The formal parameter **l** is assigned **(b c)**, the first actual argument, and **e** is assigned **a**, the second actual argument.

(4)   Finally, LISP does the real work. It evaluates the bodies; in this case, there is only one, **(cons e l)**. This evaluates to **(a b c)**, because **e** has the value **a** and **l** the value **(b c)**. This value is returned as the value of the call to **xcons**.

Now let us write a function that expects as input a list of two elements, and returns as its value a list of the list of each element:

```
-> (defun list-of-lists (x)
        (list (list (car x)) (list (cadr x))))
LIST-OF-LISTS
-> (list-of-lists '(a b))
((A) (B))
-> (list-of-lists '(1 2))
((1) (2))
->
```

Note that we entered the definition of this function on two separate lines. In general, LISP will allow you as many lines as you need to enter an s-expression.

We can compose these functions just like we can compose functions that came with LISP. For example:

```
-> (list-of-lists (xcons (cons 'c nil) 'd))
((D) (C))
->
```

Here the argument supplied to one user-defined function happened to involve another user-defined function. This function, in turn, was supplied an argument that involved a call to the built-in LISP function **cons**. This call produced **(c)**, which was subsequently passed to **xcons**. The call to **xcons** then evaluated to **(c d)**. **list-of-lists** received this value as its input, and then produced the ultimate result.

In general, we can intermix the use of user-defined and native LISP functions in any way we like.

3.3. The Treatment of Formal Parameters

LISP is careful to avoid conflicts between different variables that happen to be denoted by the same symbol. For example, suppose **x** is assigned a value on the top level of LISP, and then we call a function that uses **x** as a formal parameter. When that function returns, we will find that the value of **x** has not been modified. Thus, even though the definition of **addthree** uses a formal parameter called **x**, calling **addthree** will not cause the value of **x** to change outside of that function:

```
-> (setq x '(a b c))
(A B C)
```

```
-> (addthree 7)
10
-> x
(A B C)
->
```

The value of **x** outside of **addthree** would not be changed even if **addthree** explicitly changed the value of its formal parameter **x**, say, by calling **setq**.

In general, what happens to a formal parameter of a function does not affect code outside a call to that function. This is true if even we called our function from another function that used the same symbol as a parameter. Let us examine an example that illustrates this point. Suppose we defined a function **squared** that multiplies its argument by itself:

```
-> (defun squared (y) (* y y))
SQUARED
->
```

Now we can use **squared** to define a function that computes the length of the hypotenuse of a right triangle from the length of its sides (recall that this length is the square root of the sum of the squares of the sides):

```
-> (defun hyp (x y) (sqrt (+ (squared x) (squared y))))
HYP
-> (hyp 3 4)
5.0
->
```

Even though our two user-defined functions happened to use the same symbol as a formal parameter, LISP does not get confused. Changes to the value of a formal parameter are local to a function. Thus when we evaluate **(hyp 3 4)**, **x** is assigned the value **3** and **y** the value **4**. When the s-expression **(squared x)** within the function body of **hyp** gets evaluated, the formal parameter of **squared** gets assigned the value of **x**, which is currently **3**. This parameter happens to be named **y**. So the variable denoted by **y** in the call to **squared** now has the value **3**. But this **y** has nothing to do with the formal parameter **y** that appeared in **hyp**. This still has its original value of **4**. When we finish evaluating this call to **squared**, and return the value **9**, we find that the value of **y** in **hyp** is still **4**. Thus the subsequent call to **squared** with argument **y** evaluates properly.

Similarly, when **hyp** finishes, whatever changes it made to **x** and **y** will no longer be felt. From the point of view of the top level of LISP, this is just as if the values of neither symbols had been played with.

Because LISP does not allow parameters from one function call to interfere with those of another, you may use the same symbol as a parameter in as many definitions as you like. You need not fear that a parameter name will clash with a parameter name in another function, even if the functions call each other intimately.

One way to think about this is as follows: Each time a function gets called, LISP creates a new variable for each of that function's formal parameters. Within that function call, all references to a given formal parameter are interpreted as references to the variable created just for that function call. Although other function calls may involve parameters of the same name, LISP produces a new variable for each of them as well. Thus, none of the variables from difficult function calls can interfere with each other.

3.4. Free Occurrences, Special Variables and Global Variables

In this section, we discuss in more detail how variables work in Common LISP. It is not necessary to master all these details in order to write Common LISP programs. However, it is useful to know some of the terminology, and know that certain issues exist. You may want to read this section now, and refer back to it later should you encounter or write code that involves the situations described below.

3.4.1. Free and Bound Symbols

We have seen that changes to formal parameters have repercussions only within a call to their associated function. But what would happen if a variable appearing in a function definition is *not* a formal parameter of a function? For example, consider the following function, which first assigns the variable **sum** the sum of its arguments, and then returns their average:

```
-> (defun sum-average (x y)
      (setq sum (+ x y))
      (/ sum 2))
SUM-AVERAGE
-> (sum-average 29 13)
21
```

The function computes exactly the value we would expect it to. But what happened to the value of **sum**? Let us check its current value:

```
-> sum
42
->
```

Unlike formal parameters, changes to variables that are not formal parameters of a function can have repercussions outside of the call to that function. Even though **sum** was changed within **sum-average**, the value of **sum** at the top level of LISP reflects this alteration. If we call **sum-average** again, the top level value of **sum** will change again:

```
-> (sum-average 7 93)
50
-> sum
100
->
```

If **sum** had some value before the first call to **sum-average**, that value would have been lost.

A symbol used as a variable within a function, but which is not a formal parameter of that function, is said to be *free* within that function. For example, **sum** is free within **sum-average**. Symbols that are not free within a function are said to be *bound* in that function. Thus, saying that a symbol is bound in a function means exactly the same thing as saying it is a formal parameter of that function.

Changes to Free Symbols are Not Local to a Function

If a function changes the value of a free symbol, the repercussions of that change are not confined to that function. For example, whenever we run **sum-average**, the change it makes to **sum** persists after the call to **sum-average** has terminated. Similarly, a function that examines a free symbol will find whatever value has been assigned to that symbol by the last function that did so. Thus, changes to free symbols are not local to the functions they occur in. This is completely unlike changes to bound symbols (i. e., formal parameters), which are strictly local to a function.

Because of the non-local nature of free symbols, it is possible to use them to communicate between functions. For example, some other function can come along and determine the value of the last **sum** computed by **sum-average**, simply by examining the value of **sum**. Similarly, we might define a function whose detailed behavior depends on the value of the free symbol **switch**. We could then change the value of **switch**, in accordance with how we would like our function to behave.

However, the same non-local nature of free symbols that makes them useful also makes them dangerous. Since changes to free symbols are non-local, it is difficult to anticipate the consequences of such changes. In other words, it may be hard to understand what a program containing free symbols is actually doing. So you are advised to use free symbols only with great care. Indeed, a number of the additions to LISP incorporated into Common LISP were made so as to reduce the need for free symbols. However, many programmers still include them in their bag of tricks, and even the built-in functions of Common LISP exploit them to a considerable extent. Usually, programmers who use free symbols use some special spelling convention, for example, always including a * at the beginning and end of the name of a free symbol, just so they will remember to be extra careful. Eternal vigilance is the price of free symbols.

3.4.2. Global Variables

Just how pervasive is the change made to a free symbol? In our **sum-average** example, we saw that changing the value of **sum** within **sum-average** resulted in the value of **sum** being changed when we got back to the top level. The variable designated by a symbol at the top level of LISP is called a *global variable*. Global variables are independent of any function. They can be referred to directly on the top level of LISP, and can be referred to using free symbols in any number of different function calls.

This is in contrast to *local variables*, such as those associated with formal parameters. Local variables come into existence with a particular function call. They can be referred to only by the code of that function. And they tend to disappear forever when the function has terminated. Thus the bound symbols of **sum-average**, **x** and **y**, cause new local variables to be created each time **sum-average** is called; these can be referenced only by **sum-average**, and cease to exist when the call to **sum-average** has been completed. However, the free symbol **sum** refers to the same global variable through any number of calls to **sum-average**; the very same variable can be referred to by other functions, and by the user talking to the top level of LISP.

From what we have seen so far, a free symbol designates a global variable, and a bound symbol, a local one. That is, a free symbol, as well as a symbol appearing on the top level, refers to a global variable; a bound symbol

47

refers to a variable that only exists during and inside of a call to a given function.

3.4.3. Scope

But consider the following situation. Suppose a symbol were free in one function, but bound in another. Suppose further that the latter function calls the former. That is, we use a symbol as a formal parameter in one function, and this function calls another function in which that same symbol is free. The question is, which variable will that symbol refer to, the one associated with the formal parameter of the calling function, or the global variable beyond?

Let us make this more concrete. Suppose we created a function called **sum–average–caller** that calls **sum–average**. Moreover, suppose **sum–average–caller** uses the symbol **sum** as a formal parameter:

```
-> (defun sum-average-caller (sum x y)
        (sum-average x y) sum)
SUM-AVERAGE-CALLER
->
```

All **sum–average–caller** does is call **sum–average**, and then return the value of its own formal parameter **sum**. Now the question is, does the free occurrence of **sum** back in **sum–average** refer to the global variable **sum**, or to the variable associated with the formal parameter **sum** of **sum–average–caller**? If **sum–average** changes the formal parameter **sum** of **sum–average–caller**, then **sum–average–caller** will return the value of the average computed; when we return to the top level of LISP, the value of **sum** should be unchanged. On the other hand, if **sum–average** changes the global variable **sum**, then **sum–average–caller** will return the value we pass it for **sum**; the value of **sum** on the top level will be altered.

First, let us assign something to the value of the **sum** at the top level (i. e., to the global variable **sum**):

```
-> (setq sum '(a b c))
(A B C)
->
```

Now let us call **sum–average–caller** and see what happens (be sure to make up your mind about what should happen before peeking):

```
-> (sum-average-caller 0 55 65)
0
-> sum
120
->
```

The value of **sum** inside **sum-average-caller** was not changed, as is evidenced by the value **sum-average-caller** returned. However, **sum-average-caller** affected the value of **sum** at the top level.

All this means that local variables are *truly local to the code in which they appear.* That is, even though a local variable named **sum** existed at the time the free symbol **sum** was referenced by **sum-average**, this did not matter. The variable **sum** is local to the function **sum-average-caller**, so it could not be referenced by any other function.

The issue of which variable is referenced by the occurrence of a symbol in a program is sometimes referred to as *scoping.* You need only know the function definition to determine the scope of symbol in Common LISP. So this sort of a system for dealing with variables is known as *lexical scoping* (also called *static scoping).* In contrast to lexical scoping, *dynamic scoping* refers to a setup in which the most recently created variable of a given name is used as the reference for a symbol.

The formal parameters of Common LISP functions normally have *lexical scoping,* meaning that they can be referenced only by the code of the functions within which they are parameters. Had they had dynamic scoping, then the variables designated by a parameter can be referred to outside their functions. For example, changing the value of **sum** in **sum-average** *would* have changed the value of **sum**, the formal paramater of **sum-average-caller**, had dynamic scoping been in effect. But it would not affect the value of the global variable **sum**.

3.4.4. Special Variables

Because Common LISP uses lexical scoping, everything seems nice and simple. Parameters refer to variables that are strictly local to the text in which they appear; free symbols refer to global variables.

Unfortunately, this simplicity is shattered by one option provided in Common LISP. It turns out that it *is* possible to have variables in Common LISP that have dynamic scoping. That is, it is possible to have a parameter that is not strictly local to a function. Since this sort of parameter is not typical, Common LISP variables with dynamic scoping are called, not surprisingly, *special variables*. We can specify that the variable associated with a parameter is to be special through the use of a *declaration*. A declaration is a kind of function that is used to instruct a LISP system about the status of various entities. These are described in more detail in Chapter 20. We shall not concern ourselves with the details here.

Intuitively, a special variable is half-way between a local variable and a global one. It is as if a new variable is being introduced dynamically that intercepts references aimed at a global variable. If another special variable of the same name is created, it will intercept references to the previously introduced special variable. Any number of functions can reference the same special variable, just as they can a global variable. But there may be any number of different special variables with the same name around at the same time, each one "shadowing" the previously created one. And a change to a special variable will only affect the most recently introduced special variable.

The existence of special variables in Common LISP means that we need to be a bit more careful in describing which variable will be referenced by a free symbol in a function. A free symbol refers to the most recently created special variable of that name, if one exists, or to the global variable of that name, if no special variables of that name are to be had. A bound symbol that is not special refers to a variable that is strictly local to a call to that function; a bound symbol that is declared to be special refers to a special variable that is created when the function is called, but which can be referenced outside of the code of that function.

Note that we cannot really tell what variable is designated by a free occurrence of a symbol just by looking at the text. At run time, some function may call this one, and that function may use the same symbol as a special variable. In this case, the free symbol refers to the special variable set up by the calling function. On the other hand, by looking at a piece of code, we can sometimes tell where a formal parameter will be referenced: If it is not declared special, the parameter can only be referred to by the forms within the function of which it is a parameter. If it is declared special, it may be referenced by symbols that are not textually visible.

Standardization Note: Prior to Common LISP, most LISP systems used dynamic rather than static scoping as the default. If you are using some other LISP, you should check to see which form of scope your system uses. Even if you are using an implementation of Common LISP, you should examine the scoping regimen; not all implementors have adhered faithfully to this feature of the language.

3.5. Saving Functions in Files

By now some of the LISP expressions we are playing with have become awkward to type in at the keyboard. Besides, you now know enough to write some useful functions of your own that you may want to keep around for your next session with LISP. Rather than typing these functions in from scratch each time, LISP allows you to put your functions in a file, and then read them in. This way, you can use your favorite editor to enter and edit these functions, and load them in quickly each time you run LISP.

To make use of this facility, use an editor to create a file and put some LISP function definitions in it. Then the next time you run LISP, you can read in this file by using the function **load**. For example, suppose we put the definitions given above for **average** and **sum−average** in the file **utilities**. If we then want to use these functions during a subsequent session with LISP, we could do the following:

```
-> (load 'utilities)
[load utilities]
T
->
```

The functions that were in this file are now defined.

load goes through a file and reads and evaluates each expression in it just as if you typed it in yourself. You could put any LISP s-expressions in such a file and they will be evaluated. But you will generally only want to put in things like calls to **defun** and **setq**, which have some lasting effects.

Standardization Note: Many LISP systems have special conventions surrounding the naming of LISP files. For example, in some systems, it would be proper to call our file **UTILITIES.l**. When we typed **(load 'utilities)**, the LISP system would be smart enough to look for a file named **UTILITIES.l**. Other details of your local **load** implementation are worth investigating. For example, most LISPs also allow some loading to go on automatically. In such systems, each time a LISP process is started, it quietly checks for a file with some special name, such as **LISPINIT**. If it finds one, its contents are loaded. You can place your frequently used function definitions and **setq**s, etc., in this file, so your working environment will be ready for you each time you begin a session with the interpreter.

3.6. Summary

(1)   We can create our own functions using the special function **defun**. Once they are created, our own functions can be used just as if they came built into LISP.

(2)   Symbols designating variables within a function definition but which are not formal parameters of that function are called *free symbols*. In contrast, the formal parameters are sometimes referred to as *bound symbols*.

(3)   The formal parameters of LISP functions normally have *lexical scoping,* meaning that they can be referenced only by the code of the functions within which they appear. A parameter can be made to have *dynamic scoping* through the use of a *declaration*. A dynamically scoped parameter gives rise to a *special variable* when the function containing that parameter is invoked. Special variables can be referred to by free symbols in other functions.

(3)   Symbols used for their values at the top level of LISP are called *global variables.*

(4)   A free symbol refers to the most recently created special variable created from a parameter of the same name, or to the global variable designated by that symbol. Which variable a free symbol turns out to reference can be determined only at run time.

(5)   The function **load** can be used to read in files just as if their contents were typed in to the interpreter.

Exercises

(1)   Define a function that computes the area of a circle given its radius.

(2)   Given that yearly interest rates are 10%, write a function that computes the monthly payment on a loan of a given amount.

(3)   Write a version of the answer to Exercise 2 in which the interest rate is taken from a global variable. Test your function by using it for different interest rates.

(4)   The *Euclidean distance* between two points (x_1,y_1) and (x_2,y_2) is defined as $\sqrt{(x_1-x_2)^2+(y_1-y_2)^2}$. Suppose we represent a point (x,y) as a

two-element list. Write a function that takes two such lists as arguments, and returns the Euclidean distance between the points they represent.

(5) If you are distressed that the names **car** and **cdr** are non-mnemonic, you are now in a position to do something about it. Define functions **head** and **tail** that behave exactly like **car** and **cdr**, respectively.

(6) Write a function **switch** that accepts a two-element list and returns a list with these elements in the opposite order. E. g., **(switch '(a b))** returns **(b a)**.

(7) In the following definition, ***basis*** is a free symbol used to adjust values:

(defun normalize (v) (/ v *basis*))

Suppose we also had the following function:

(defun n–percentage (a b *basis*) (/ a (normalize b)))

If ***basis*** has the value **100.0** on the top level, what value will be computed by the expression **(n–percentage 50.0 100.0 125.0)**? Why? What would the value of this expression be if we declared ***basis*** to be a special variable in **n–percentage**?

Addendum – A Note on Terminology

Most descriptions of Common LISP, and of LISP in general, use a somewhat different terminology from the one used here to talk about variables and their associated values. Underlying this more traditional terminology is a different conception of what variables are and how LISP manipulates them. In particular, this conception holds that there is really only a single variable associated with a given symbol. When we enter a function, then, we do not create a new variable, but rather, *save* the value of the old one. Then we assign the old variable a new value, namely, the actual argument. The old value of the variable is *restored* when the function is exited.

The relationship between a parameter and its value during the course of a function application is called a *binding*. A binding is like a temporary variable created just for the course of a function application. But rather than say that a new variable is created for the application of a function, in this jargon we say that a new binding is created for a variable. Furthermore, we say that the formal parameter is *bound* to the actual argument, and that such a variable is a *bound* variable. For example, if **x** were a formal parameter of **fn**, and a call of the form (**fn** '**a**) occurred, we would say that a new binding is created for **x**, and that in this binding, **x** has the value **a**. Additionally, we could say that **x** is bound to **a**, and that in **fn**, **x** is a bound variable.

Note that, according to this terminology, a symbol on the top level of LISP never has a binding, since such symbols are not bound by any construct. That is, the variable **x** on the top level of LISP may have a value that will be saved and restored if a new binding is created for **x**. But it is not itself a bound variable.

Unfortunately, the distinctions just made tend to be used rather loosely. For example, in this convention, there is widespread confusion about whether a binding is itself a variable, or is associated with a variable. That is, is **x** in **fn1** really the same variable as the **x** in **fn2**, but with different associated bindings? Or are these two separate variables? If **x** is a free symbol in some function, does it refer to different variables depending on the context, or only to different bindings? The actual usage is quite inconsistent.

Even worse, though, is that the term "bound" has come to mean "having a value." Along these lines, a variable that has no value at all is said to be "unbound." For example, a typical LISP error message is that some symbol is an unbound variable. Of course, this terminology is horribly inconsistent with the use of these terms given above. For example, if we are allowed to use the term "bound" to describe a global variable with a value, then we can have a case in which a variable is "bound" (that is, it has a value) but has no "binding" (since it is not a parameter of a function). In addition, it is possible to bind a special variable, and then remove its value altogether (this requires using a certain function we have not yet seen). The resulting variable is "unbound" (i. e., it has no value), but still has a binding. Thus we have variables that are bound but have no binding and bound variables that are unbound.

Simple attempts to clean up this terminology are generally not successful. For example, we can simply refuse to say that a variable without any bindings is bound. But then we are committed to saying of a global variable with a value that it is not "bound", not "unbound", and has no "binding" (although, of course, it has a perfectly fine value).

The reason for this confusion, in my opinion, has to do with the fact that symbols, the designators of variables in LISP, are actually data objects, unlike identifiers in most programming languages. Implementations of LISP use symbols to implement variables, and these implementations may introduce some notion of binding to facilitate the association of different variables with the same symbol. Of course, such an implementation consideration should not play a prominent role in the terminology of the language itself.

The terminology adopted here is meant to rectify this situation. While it appears to be internally consistent, and, I think, much simpler, some traces of the other terminology remain in the names of some Common LISP functions. While we are waiting for official recognition, the terminology chosen here should serve as a clear description of what a LISP program actually does.

Chapter 4

Predicates, Conditionals, and Logical Operators

4.1. Introduction

To gainfully employ the functions we have encountered, we need to be able to arrange them into the LISP equivalent of programs. In particular, we would like to do something other than write "straight-line code" (code with no branching). To do so, we need some kind of conditional (i. e., "if...then...else..." type statement). In addition, we must have some way of testing s-expressions for various properties.

In this chapter we introduce LISP *predicates,* which are functions that test for various conditions. These predicates can be combined into more complicated tests using other functions called *logical operators.* We also discuss the basic LISP mechanisms for altering flow of control. Together with predicates and logical operators, the LISP flow of control mechanisms allow us to write arbitrary computations in LISP.

4.2. LISP Predicates

To alter the flow of control in any language, we must first have some way of testing a value for a particular property. Of course, we will do this in

LISP by having functions expressly designed to test for different things. Such a function is called a *predicate*. This is a term borrowed from logic. Predicates are just tests, that is, functions that return true or false. In LISP, false is indicated by **nil**, and true by any value other than **nil**.

As a convention, LISP often returns the atom **t** to mean true. **t** is special in that, like **nil**, it evaluates to itself and its value cannot be changed. However, **t** is generally not distinguished from other non-**nil** values. That is, most LISP functions will check to see that a value is either **nil** or non-**nil**; **t** is merely a convenient way of returning something other than **nil**.

One useful predicate in LISP tells whether or not an s-expression is an atom. This function, naturally enough, is called **atom**. So

```
-> (atom 'a)
T
-> (atom 8)
T
-> (atom '(a b c))
NIL
-> (atom (car '(a b c)))
T
-> (atom (cdr '(a b c)))
NIL
->
```

Similarly, the function **listp** determines whether something is a list (many LISP predicate names end in **p**, for "predicate").

```
-> (listp 'a)
NIL
-> (listp 8)
NIL
-> (listp '(a b c))
T
-> (listp (car '(a b c)))
NIL
-> (listp (cdr '(a b c)))
T
->
```

Is **nil** an atom or a list? This would appear to be an ambiguous case. We said above that **nil** is atom, but **nil** is also ( ), the empty list, and surely, this must be a list. Let us appeal to the LISP interpreter for a resolution to this dilemma:

```
-> (atom nil)
T
->
```

So **atom** claims that **nil** is an atom. What does **listp** think?

```
-> (listp nil)
T
->
```

listp also claims rights to **nil**. So **nil** seems to be treated as both an atom and a list, as far as these functions are concerned.

Actually, **nil** is a special case. It is often necessary to distinguish **nil** from other s-expressions, so LISP has a special predicate just for this purpose:

```
-> (null nil)
T
-> (null 'a)
NIL
-> (null '(a b c))
NIL
-> (null ( ))
T
->
```

null returns **t** if its argument is **nil**, and returns **nil** otherwise.

There is also a predicate called **consp** that returns true for every list other than **nil**, in case we want an easy way of determining if something is a non-**nil** list. We will talk more about this predicate when we discuss LISP internals in Chapter 15.

Standardization Note: Other LISPs may use a slightly different set of names for the predicates just described. However, all LISPs need to make these distinctions one way or another.

Another useful predicate is **equal**, which tests if two s-expressions look alike. For example:

```
-> (equal 'a 'b)
NIL
-> (equal 'a 'a)
T
-> (equal '(a b c) '(a b c))
T
-> (equal '(a b c) '(a (b) c))
NIL
->
```

In general, there are many predicates in LISP for determining if some data object is of a particular type. Then there are usually a number of predicates specific to that type. For example, consider predicates on numbers. **numberp** tests to see if its argument is a number. Thus we have

```
-> (numberp 6)
T
-> (numberp 'a)
NIL
->
```

Predicates like **zerop**, **oddp**, and **evenp** test for special types of numbers; predicates such as <, and > test if a specific relation exists between numbers.

There is also a very general Common LISP predicate for determining if a datum is of a given type. This predicate is called **typep**, and takes two arguments, an s-expression whose type is in question, and an s-expression that denotes a particular type. For example, another way to determine if something is a number is to do the following:

```
-> (typep 6 'number)
T
-> (typep 'a 'number)
NIL
->
```

Here the symbol **number** denotes the corresponding type. Common LISP supports a rather complex type specification scheme that we shall elaborate on in subsequent chapters. Suffice it to say here that the types of objects we have encountered, i. e., list, atom, symbol and number, are recognized by name by **typep**.

An interesting predicate specific to lists is **member**. **member** takes two arguments, the second of which should be a list. **member** checks to see if the first argument appears in the second argument. If so, **member** returns the part of the list at which the match first occurs. If not, **member** returns **nil**:

```
-> (member 'b '(a b c))
(B C)
-> (member 'x '(a b c))
NIL
-> (member 'y '(x (y) z))
NIL
-> (member '(a b) '(a b c))
NIL
```

Why doesn't **member** just return **t**, like the other predicates we have seen? Remember, LISP distinguishes only between **nil** and non-**nil** as far as true and false are concerned. Thus a value like **(b c)**, which is returned in the first example above, would be considered true, just as **t** would. However, the value **(b c)** is likely to be more informative. For example, if we want to know if a value occurs twice in a list, returning **t** would not help. But returning the rest of the list after the match would. In general, LISP tries to return something informative as the result of a predicate.

Note also that **(member 'y '(x (y) z))** returns **nil**. **member** only checks to see if the first argument is literally an element of the second. In this example, **y** is not an element of **(x (y) z)** (although it is an element of one of its members). We could write a LISP function that checked for "anywhere membership", but **member** happens not to do this.

There are plenty more predicates that come with LISP, but these will do for now. Again, you will want to stare at Appendix A when you have mastered the basics to see what else is available.

Of course, we could use **defun** to define arbitrary predicates of our own. For example, if we want a predicate that determines if the **car** of a list is an atom, we could do the following:

```
-> (defun car-atomp (x) (atom (car x)))
     CAR-ATOMP
-> (car-atomp '(a b c))
T
-> (car-atomp '((a) (b) (c)))
NIL
->
```

Actually, **car–atomp** is not exactly what we want. It blindly takes the **car** of its argument, and thus if we happen to pass it an argument that does not evaluate to a list, **car–atomp** will cause an error. In such cases, we would rather that **car–atomp** simply return **nil**.

What we would like to do here is to test to see if the actual argument is a list, and take its **car** *only* if this were the case. However, as yet, we have no way of writing such a function. We have seen how to use a predicate to determine whether some condition holds, but so far we have not seen any way to evaluate something conditionally, based on the outcome of a test. To do so, we need to introduce a new construct.

4.3. Conditionals

Now we are ready to use predicates to make a choice. To do so, we need some equivalent of a conditional branch. Once again, LISP provides this facility through the use of an expressly designed function. In this case, the function's name is **cond**, for conditional. **cond** is similar to an "if...then...else..." statement, but is a bit more general. **cond** is a special function, and can have any number of arguments, which are sometimes called **cond** clauses . Each **cond** clause consists of a series of s-expressions. The first element of a **cond** clause is treated as a condition to be tested for; the rest of the clause consists of things to do should the condition prevail.

To evaluate a **cond** clause, LISP first evaluates its condition, i. e., the first element of the clause. *It evaluates the rest of the expressions in the clause only if the condition evaluates to true.*

For example, if we want to be sure that something is a list before we take its **car**, we could do the following:

```
(cond ((listp x) (car x)))
```

This is a **cond** of one clause, the s-expression **((listp x) (car x))**. The first element of this clause, **(listp x)**, is the condition of this clause. If this evaluates to true, only then will LISP evaluate the elements in the rest of the clause; in this case, there is only one additional element in the clause, the expression **(car x)**.

Let us assign **x** some value and see how this works:

```
-> (setq x '(a b c))
(A B C)
-> (cond ((listp x) (car x)))
A
-> (setq x 'y)
Y
-> (cond ((listp x) (car x)))
NIL
->
```

Like any other LISP function, **cond** returns a value. As we can see in this example, when the test in the **cond** clause panned out, LISP evaluated the next expression. It also returned the value of that expression as the value of the **cond**. When the test failed, the **cond** returned **nil**.

While the above example is perfectly legal, it does not make much sense to evaluate a **cond** on the top level of LISP. Rather, **cond**s are meant to be used inside function definitions, where the values they encounter will vary from application to application. For example, we can use **cond** to write a better version of the function **car-atomp**, which we tried to write in the previous section. Recall that **car-atomp** is supposed to return true only if the **car** of its argument is an atom. Above we noted that we had no way to ensure that we only take the **car** of an expression when it is legitimate to do so, i. e., when the expression is a list. However, with **cond**, it is easy to assure such conditional evaluation:

```
-> (defun car-atomp (x)
       (cond ((listp x) (atom (car x)))))
CAR-ATOMP
-> (car-atomp '(a b c))
T
-> (car-atomp 'z)
NIL
->
```

Here we use **cond** to determine if it is safe to take the **car** of the argument. If it is not, the **cond** simply returns **nil**, which is returned as the value of the function. Otherwise, the **cond** returns the value of **(atom (car x))**, whatever that happens to be.

4.3.1. More Complex conds

In this example, **cond** has the effect of an "if...then..." statement: We evaluate the latter part only if the former part tells us to. However, it is possible to use **cond** to make some more discriminations. In particular, **cond** allows us to specify as many **cond** clauses as we like. LISP will evaluate the test in the front of each one until it finds a test that returns true. Then it will evaluate the rest of that **cond** clause as above. If there are additional **cond** clauses after the one that is evaluated, they will all be ignored.

For example, suppose we want to write a function that behaves as follows: If it is passed a list, it **cons**es the atom **a** onto the front of it; if it is passed a number, it adds **7** to it; otherwise, it just returns **nil**. We can construct this function using a **cond** with two clauses:

```
-> (defun cond-example1 (x)
      (cond
         ((listp x) (cons 'a x))
         ((numberp x) (+ 7 x))))
COND-EXAMPLE1
-> (cond-example1 '(b c))
(A B C)
-> (cond-example1 9)
16
-> (cond-example1 'z)
NIL
->
```

Note that we indented the **cond** clauses to better reveal the structure of the function. This is good programming practice in general.

When we use **cond-example1**, the condition of the first **cond** clause is evaluated first. This will return true whenever the argument is a list. In this case, **a** is **cons**ed onto the front of the list. The resulting value is returned as the value of the **cond**, the other **cond** clause being ignored. However, if the argument is not a list, the condition of the first **cond** clause returns false, and the rest of that clause is ignored. The condition of the next **cond** clause is evaluated. This will return true whenever the argument is a number, in which case **7** is added to that number and the resulting value returned. If the conditions of both **cond** clauses evaluate to **nil**, we fall off the end of the **cond**, which then returns **nil**.

Thus far, each of our examples of **cond** clauses had only one expression to evaluate should its condition return true. However, LISP will allow any number of s-expressions after the condition of the clause. If that clause is reached and its condition evaluates to true, each expression after the condition is evaluated in order. The value of the last expression is returned as the value of the **cond**. For example, here is another version of the function we just wrote. Unlike the previous example, this one has the side-effect of setting the global variable **flag** to the value **list** or **number**, depending on its argument:

```
-> (defun cond-example2 (x)
     (cond
        ((listp x) (setq flag 'list) (cons 'a x))
        ((numberp x) (setq flag 'number) (+ 7 x))))
COND-EXAMPLE2
-> (cond-example2 '(b c))
(A B C)
-> flag
LIST
-> (cond-example2 9)
16
-> flag
NUMBER
->
```

cond-example2 looks just like **cond-example1**, except that here each **cond** clause has an additional expression in it. When the condition in either clause pans out, all the s-expressions following the condition are evaluated. In the case of each **cond** clause in **cond-example2**, the new expression causes the atom **flag** to be assigned a value before the expression producing the value of the **cond** is evaluated. Thus **cond-example2** always returns the same value as **cond-example1**, but in addition produces the side-effect of changing the value of **flag**.

Note that **cond-example2** may not do exactly what we want. For example, if we call **cond-example2** with an argument that is a number, say, it will assign **flag** a **number**. But if we call **cond-example2** again with the argument **'z**, neither clause is evaluated and **flag** will not be reset. Instead of this behavior, we might prefer to assign **flag** some other value, say **neither**, in the instance in which neither **cond** clause is used. Thus we would like a kind of catchall **cond** clause that always gets used if the other **cond** clauses are of no avail.

A standard way to do this is to begin a **cond** clause with the atom **t**. **t** always evaluates to **t**, which is non-**nil**, so any **cond** clause that begins with **t** will always be used if it is reached. For example, we can correct the problem with **cond-example2** as follows:

```
-> (defun cond-example3 (x)
      (cond
         ((listp x) (setq flag 'list) (cons 'a x))
         ((numberp x) (setq flag 'number) (+ 7 x))
         (t (setq flag 'neither) nil)))
COND-EXAMPLE3
-> (cond-example3 '(b c))
(A B C)
-> flag
LIST
-> (cond-example3 'z)
NIL
-> flag
NEITHER
->
```

cond-example3 has three **cond** clauses, of which the last begins with **t**. If neither of the first two clauses is used, the third one will be. This results in setting the value of **flag** to **neither**. Since we do not want to return this value as the value of the **cond**, we put another element in this clause. This is the value **nil**, which is the value we want **cond** to return in this instance.

4.3.2. The General Form of cond

We have now seen **cond** in all its glory. We can write out this general form as follows:

```
(cond (exp11 exp12 exp13 ... )
      (exp21 exp22 exp23 ... )
      (exp31 exp32 exp33 ... )
       .
       .
       .
      (expn1 expn2 expn3 ...))
```

Each list of expressions (e. g., **(exp11 exp12 exp13 ...)**) is one **cond** clause.

In general, to evaluate a **cond**, LISP examines the first **cond** clause. LISP takes the first element of this clause, and evaluates it. If it returns true (i. e., non-**nil**), LISP will continue down that clause, evaluating each expression, until it comes to the end. Then LISP returns the value of the last expression it evaluates as the value of the **cond**. The rest of the **cond** is ignored. On the other hand, if the first element of the clause evaluates to

false, LISP ignores the rest of the elements of that clause. It finds the next
cond clause and repeats the whole procedure. Eventually, either some
cond clause will pay off, or LISP will run off the end of the **cond**. If this
happens, the **cond** evaluates to **nil**.

In the general case above, LISP would first evaluate **exp11**. If it returns
true, LISP continues by evaluating **exp12** and then **exp13**, and so on, until it reaches the last expression of the clause. When it finishes evaluating
this expression, it returns its value as the value of the **cond**. On the other
hand, if **exp11** evaluates to **nil**, LISP skips the rest of its **cond** clause.
Then it evaluates **exp21**. LISP repeats this procedure until one expression
turns out to be true, or until it runs out of them.

There is one fine point about **cond** that is useful to know. It is perfectly legal to have a **cond** clause with only one expression in it. In this case, the
expression still serves as the condition of the clause. However, if the condition evaluates to true, LISP will return the value of the condition as the
value of the **cond**. For example, suppose we want **cond-example** to both
assign **flag** the value **neither** *and* return **neither** as its value, in the case
where it is passed neither a number nor a list. We could accomplish this
as follows:

```
-> (defun cond-example4 (x)
     (cond
       ((listp x) (setq flag 'list) (cons 'a x))
       ((numberp x) (setq flag 'number) (+ 7 x))
       ((setq flag 'neither))))
COND-EXAMPLE4
-> (cond-example4 '(b c))
(A B C)
-> flag
LIST
-> (cond-example4 'z)
NEITHER
-> flag
NEITHER
->
```

The last **cond** clause here consists of only one expression,
(setq flag 'neither). Since this expression is in the condition position, if
we reach this clause, the expression will be evaluated. It will always return
a non-**nil** value (namely, the value **neither**), so this value will be returned
as the value of the **cond**.

Some LISP programmers avoid this feature of **cond**, claiming that it makes code less transparent. For example, they would put a **t** in the beginning of the third **cond** clause above. The resulting **cond** has exactly the same effect, but its logical structure is more apparent.

One way to conceptualize a **cond** is as a generalized "if...then...else...". I will write out the general form of **cond** below, with italicized English words annotating the expressions they precede:

> (cond (*if* **exp** *then do* **exp** *also do* **exp** ...)
>   (*else if* **exp** *then do* **exp** *also do* **exp** ...)
>   (*else if* **exp** *then do* **exp** *also do* **exp** ...)
>   .
>   .
>   .
>   (*else if* **exp** *then do* **exp** *also do* **exp** ...))

While **cond** allows any number of clauses with any number of expressions to be evaluated, in practice, most useful **cond**s are relatively simple. For example, **adjoin** is a handy Common LISP function that **cons**es an element onto a list only if that element is not already in that list. We can write our own simple version of **adjoin** using **cond**:

```
-> (defun our-adjoin (e l)
      (cond
         ((member e l) l)
         (t (cons e l))))
OUR-ADJOIN
-> (our-adjoin 'b '(a b c))
(A B C)
-> (our-adjoin 'b '(x y z))
(B X Y Z)
->
```

our-adjoin uses **member** to first check if the list assigned to **l** contains the element assigned to **e**. If so, then the list is simply returned. Otherwise, the value of **e** is **cons**ed onto the value of **l** and the resulting list is returned as the value of **our-adjoin**.

In this example, **cond** is used as an "if...then...else" construct. This probably represents the prototypical use of **cond** in actual programming situations.

4.3.3. Other Conditionals

cond is the traditional and universal LISP conditional function. However, sometimes the full glory of **cond** is not necessary for the particular programming task at hand. In these cases, a simpler function may make one's code clearer.

To meet this need, many LISPs have introduced a special function that resembles a more conventional "if...then...else" construct. In Common LISP, this function is called **if**. The general form of **if** is (**if** *test then-action else-action*). To evaluate an **if**, LISP first evaluates *test*. If it evaluates to non-**nil**, then the *then-action* argument is evaluated and the resulting value returned as the value of the call to **if**; otherwise, LISP evaluates the *else-action* form and returns the resulting value. If the *else-action* form is omitted, then nothing is done and the call to **if** returns **nil**.

For example, we can write a slightly simpler definition of the function **our-adjoin** if we use **if** instead of **cond**:

```
-> (defun our-adjoin (e l)
      (if (member e l) l (cons e l)))
OUR-ADJOIN
```

There are several other conditional functions in Common LISP that resemble common programming language constructs. These include the special functions **when**, **unless**, and **case**. You may want to bear these in mind should your current set of conditionals seem inappropriate for a given task.

4.4. Logical Operators

Suppose we want to check if an s-expression evaluates to an even number between 50 and 100. We can use the predicates **evenp**, >, and < to check the various parts of this condition, and compose them using a **cond**. For example, the following function would do the job:

```
-> (defun even-50-100 (x)
      (cond ((numberp x)
              (cond ((evenp x)
                      (cond ((> x 49)(< x 101)))))))))
EVEN-50-100
-> (even-50-100 17)
NIL
```

```
-> (even-50-100 88)
T
-> (even-50-100 89)
NIL
-> (even-50-100 102)
NIL
-> (even-50-100 '(a b c))
NIL
->
```

Needless to say, the function works, but it is just about impossible to read. In general, it is bad practice to imbed a conditional within another conditional for reasons of readability. However, with what we have at our disposal, we would have no other choice.

Fortunately, LISP, like most programming languages, provides an easier way to compose predicates. This is through the use of *logical operators*. Logical operators take truth values as arguments, and return truth values as results. The most commonly used logical operators are **and**, **or**, and **not**.

not is the simplest, returning **t** if its argument is false, and **nil** if it is true. For example, if we want to check to see if the value of **x** is not an atom, we could do the following:

> -> (not (atom x))

This will return true exactly when (**atom x**) returns false.

(Note – Since true and false are non-**nil** and **nil**, respectively, **not** has exactly the same behavior as **null**. These are really two different names for the same function, provided to help make programs more readable. You should use **null** if you conceptualize its argument as a (possibly empty) list, and **not** if you conceptualize its argument as a truth value.)

and and **or** each take any number of arguments, which are evaluated one after the other. In the case of **and**, the evaluation goes on until some argument evaluates to **nil**, in which case **and** returns **nil**; if it reaches the end without any argument evaluating to **nil**, **and** returns the value of its last argument (which by now would be guaranteed to be non-**nil**). For example, to determine if **x** were both even and less than 100, we could type

> (and (evenp x) (< x 100))

or works similarly, stopping before the end only if some argument evaluates to true. If any does, **or** returns the value of that argument; otherwise it returns **nil**.

For example, if we want to know if the value of **x** is either a number or **nil**, we could write

> (or (null x) (numberp x))

This expression would return true if either of the predicates within it return true.

4.4.1. Using **and** and **or** for Flow of Control

Since **or** and **and** are guaranteed to stop evaluating their arguments as soon as they know what the result is going to be, they are useful for flow of control as well as for their logical value. For example, suppose we want to know if the first element of the list **l** is a number. If we just do a **(numberp (car l))**, this would cause an error if **l** evaluates to an atom. But we can check for this first:

> (and (listp l) (numberp (car l)))

Since **and** evaluates the first argument before looking at the second, the expression above will never take the **car** of **l** unless the first condition is true, i. e., unless **l** is a list, in which case the **car** should be safe.

In this example, we used **and** instead of **cond** to effect a conditional evaluation. Using **cond** for this purpose would be only slightly less elegant:

> (cond ((listp l) (numberp (car l))))

However, as we saw at the beginning of this section, **cond** becomes awkward if the composition is more complex. Let us use logical operators to write a version of **even–50–100** and compare it to the one above that uses **cond**:

```
-> (defun even-50-100 (x)
       (and (numberp x) (evenp x) (> x 49) (< x 101)))
EVEN-50-100
->
```

Clearly, using **and** is much simpler and more expressive for this purpose.

4.5. Summary

(1) *Predicates* are functions that check to see if a certain condition prevails. LISP uses **nil** to mean "false" and non-**nil** to mean "true". The special atom **t**, which always evaluates to itself, is used as a convenient way to return a non-**nil** value.

(2) Some commonly used LISP predicates are **atom**, **listp**, **null**, **numberp**, **equal**, **evenp**, **oddp**, >, <, **zerop**, and **member**.

(3) Predicates can be conveniently composed into more complex predicates using *logical operators*. The most common logical operators are **not**, **and**, and **or**. **and** and **or** cease evaluation when they have determined a result; hence they are useful for flow of control as well as for their logical properties.

(4) Predicates are commonly used inside **cond**s, which allow conditional evaluation of s-expressions. A **cond** consists of any number of **cond** clauses, each of which consists of a condition and a series of things to do. LISP evaluates each condition until it finds one that prevails; then it evaluates the rest of the expressions in that **cond** clause, returning the value of the last one as the value of the **cond**.

If a simpler form of conditional is desired, the function **if** can be used. This special function evaluates its first argument. It evaluates and returns the second if and only if the first evaluated to non-**nil**; otherwise, it evaluates and returns the third argument, if one is present.

Exercises

(1) What values do the following expressions return?

(a) **(not (atom '(a b c)))**

(b) **(member '(y) '(x y z))**

(c) **(and (setq x 4) (not (numberp x)) (setq x 5))**

(d) **(or (setq x 4) (not (numberp x)) (setq x 5))**

(e) **(equal ( ) 'nil)**

(2) Write a LISP predicate that determines if its argument is an odd number greater than a million.

(3) Write a LISP predicate **multiple–member** that returns true if its first argument occurs at least twice in its second.

(4) Write a LISP function that averages its two arguments, first checking to see that they are numbers; if they are not, have the function return **nil**.

(5) Write a LISP function that checks to see if two numbers are sufficiently close to one another to be counted as identical for some purpose. "Sufficiently close" will mean that the two numbers are within the value of **∗tolerance∗** of one another, where **∗tolerance∗** is a free symbol.

Chapter 5

Iteration in LISP

5.1. Introduction – Recursion versus Iteration

The functions we have written so far have been rather simple. They all compose built-in LISP functions or previously written user-defined functions, possibly using a conditional function to influence flow of control. However, in programming, we often need to perform some operation an arbitrary number of times. For example, we cannot currently write a function that does something to each element of a list of arbitrary length, because we have no way to express such an indefinite notion. What we need is some LISP construct that enables us to do something an indefinite number of times, each time varying the objects that we manipulate.

We can accomplish this aim by introducing some LISP constructs designed specifically to promote indefinite repetition. The explicit use of constructs for repetition is called *iteration*. To accommodate iteration, LISP has several built-in functions that enable the user to write an explicit loop. We discuss these functions in this chapter.

None of the functions described in this chapter are really necessary to do what we want, however. Instead, we can accomplish the equivalent of indefinite repetition through the use of *recursion*. A function is said to be *recursive* if it refers to itself in its definition. In the next chapter, we will see how recursive functions can be designed to perform the equivalent of the iterative operations shown here.

Older versions of LISP tended not to support iteration very much at all, and programmers were encouraged to use recursive techniques instead. In fact, some LISP "purists" frown on the introduction of iteration to LISP. This position has generally softened today, and most LISPs and LISP programmers include both recursive and iterative techniques in their repertoire. After examining both techniques, the reader should decide for himself which techniques are most appropriate for which problems.

5.2. Structured Iteration

Common LISP provides both "structured" and "unstructured" iterative constructs. By "structured" iteration, I mean iteration in which no explicit "gotos" are required. "Unstructured" iteration requires some explicit branching statement to effect the flow of control.

The general structured iterative construct of Common LISP is a special function called **do**. This is similar to a **while** statement in other languages. The Common LISP **do** function allows the user to specify the following aspects of iteration:

(1)   Some code that is to be executed repeatedly.

(2)   A condition upon which the iteration should be terminated.

(3)   A value to be returned upon termination.

(4)   Any number of new variables to be used for the duration of the iteration. These are referred to as *index variables* (and more informally, simply as **do** variables).

(5)   Initial values for the index variables.

(6)   Values to be assigned the index variables each time an iteration is performed.

For example, here **do** is used to write a version of the LISP function **length**, which returns the number of items in a list:

```
-> (defun do-length (l)
     (do ((ll l (cdr ll)) (sum 0 (1+ sum)))
         ((atom ll) sum)))
DO-LENGTH
-> (do-length '(a b c))
3
-> (do-length 3)
0
-> (do-length '(a (b c)))
2
->
```

The first item after **do** is a list of index variable *specifiers*. A specifier is simply a list which supplies **do** with information about a variable. In the case above, there are two specifiers, **(ll l (cdr ll))** and **(sum 0 (1+ sum))**. The first element of each specifier should be a symbol; it designates an index variable for the **do**. The next element is a form whose value is used to initialize the index variable when the **do** is begun. The final element is a form whose value is assigned the index variable each time the iteration is performed. So the specifier **(sum 0 (1+ sum))** states that there should be an index variable **sum**, and that its initial value should be **0**; moreover, each time the iteration is performed, **sum** is to be assigned the value of **(1+ sum)**. Thus the overall effect of this specifier is to cause the creation of a variable named **sum**, have it initialized to zero, and have its value incremented by 1 each time a repetition is performed.

The next item in the call to **do** is a kind of exit clause. This is similar to a **cond** clause. The first expression in the clause acts as a test. It is evaluated, and the **do** will exit if and only if the test evaluates to an atom. If and when it does, then the expressions following the test are also evaluated, and the value of the last one returned as the value of the call to **do**. In the example above, the **do** will return whenever **ll** is an atom, and it will always return the value of **sum**.

If the test is not met, then the index variables are updated and the whole process is repeated. The repetition occurs continually until the test is met.

For example, when we evaluate **(do-length '(a b c))**, the index variables **ll** and **sum** get initialized to the values of **l** and of **0**, respectively. Thus, **ll** is assigned the value **(a b c)**, and **sum** the value **0**. Then the test, **(atom ll)**, is evaluated. This turns out to be false, so we reassign the index variables and try again. In the reassignment, **ll** is assigned the value of **(cdr ll)**, which is **(b c)**, and **sum** is assigned the value of **(1 + sum)**, or **1**. The test is examined again, and still not met. This time through, **ll** is assigned the value **(c)**, and **sum** the value **2**. The test fails again; **ll** is assigned the value **nil** and **sum** the value **3**. This time the test succeeds, and the value of **sum** is returned. Thus the value computed is **3**.

Note that in this example, there is no "meat" to the call to **do**. That is, there is no code to execute each time through the loop. All we did was update variables, and examine the test. **do** is actually more general than this. It has the following general format:

(**do** ((*var1 val1 rep1*) (*var2 val2 rep2*) ...) *exit-clause form1 form2* ...)

The element right after the **do** is a (possibly empty) list of index variable specifiers. When the **do** is evaluated, a new variable is created for each of the *vari*. (By "*vari*" I mean all of *var1*, *var2*, etc. We will use this notation throughout.) These index variables persist for the duration of the call to **do**. Next, all the *vali* are evaluated; each *vari* is assigned the value of the corresponding *vali*. Since all the *vali* are evaluated first, no *vari* is changed until after all the *vali* have been evaluated. The *repi* are ignored for the time being.

Then *exit-clause* is examined. If the entire *exit-clause* is **nil**, then the **do** returns immediately with the value **nil**. If it is non-**nil**, then it should be of the form (*test test-form1 test-form2* ...). In this case, *test* is evaluated. If it evaluates to non-**nil**, then the *test-formi* are evaluated in order, and the last one is returned as the value of the **do**. If *test* evaluates to **nil**, then the *test-formi* of *exit-clause* are ignored. Instead, the *formi* of the **do** are evaluated in order. Then the *repi* are evaluated, and the *vari* are assigned these values. This process is then repeated starting with the examination of the *exit-clause*.

Thus the general form of **do** allows any number of forms to be evaluated each time through. For example, we could have written the definition of **do−length** this way:

```
(defun do−length (l)
    (do ((ll l) (sum 0))
        ((atom ll) sum)
        (setq ll (cdr ll))
        (setq sum (1 + sum)))))
```

Here we omitted the repeated forms from the variable specifiers. In this case, **do** will not automatically change the values of the variables on each repetition. (If an initialization form is omitted, by the way, the variable will be initialized to **nil**.) Instead, the code of the **do** does this explicitly. Of course, since **do** has the built-in "automatic reassignment" mechanism, it would be silly to write a definition this way. In fact, the original definition is typical of the use of **do**, in that all the work is done via the automatic reassignment facility.

Here is another example that illustrates the power of the automatic reassignment feature of **do**. The following function returns the reversal of its argument:

```
-> (defun do-rev (l)
      (do ((x l (cdr x))  (res nil (cons (car x) res)))
          ((null x) res)))
DO-REV
-> (do-rev '(a b c))
(C B A)
```

Here the **do** initially assigns **x** the value of **l** and **res** the value **nil**. Each subsequent pass through the **do** assigns **x** successive **cdr**s of this list, and **cons**es the leading element of **x** onto **res**. The test terminates the **do** when there is no more list, and causes the value of **res** to be returned. Again, there are no *formi* in this example. All the work is done is the repeated assignment of the index variables.

By the way, the index variables of **do** are treated just like formal parameters of a function. That is, they are accessible only from the code of the **do** that creates them. Thus we need not worry about accidental variable name conflicts. In fact, in our definition of **do-length**, we need not have used the new name **ll** as the index variable. Had we used the name **l** again, the resulting code would function identically. The index variable **l** would have been initialized to the value of the formal parameter **l**; subsequent changes to **l** in the **do** would have affected only the index variable **l**, and not the formal parameter of the same name.

5.2.1. Other Structured Iteration Functions

Common LISP has several variants on the **do** theme. One is a special function called **do***. **do*** is just like **do**, except that each *vari* is assigned the value of each respective *vali* or *repi* before the next one is evaluated. That is, it is fine in a **do*** if the expression *val4*, say, contains a reference to *var3*, because *var3* will have been assigned a value by the time *val4* is evaluated. This would not be proper in a **do**, as there, none of the *vari* is assigned a value until after *all* the *vali* are evaluated.

The functions **dolist** and **dotimes** are simpler, specialized versions of **do**. **dolist** allows for simple iteration over the elements of a list, and **dotimes** allows for iteration for every integer up to a specified value. A call to

dolist looks like this:

> (**dolist** (*var list-val return-val*) *form1 form2 ...*)

Upon evaluation, *list-val* is evaluated, and should evaluate to a list. Then *var* is assigned the first element of this list. Then each *formi* is evaluated. *var* is assigned each successive element of the value of *list-val*, and all the *formi*s are reevaluated for each assignment. At the conclusion, the value of *return-val* is returned (*return-val* is optional; the value **nil** will be returned if it is omitted.)

Similarly, **dotimes** has the following form:

> (**dotimes** (*var stop-val result-val*) *form1 form2 ...*)

This is evaluated similarly to **dolist**, except that *var* is initialized to **0**, and incremented by one each time through. This is continued until *var* reaches the value of *stop-val*, at which point the value of *return-val* is returned.

5.3. prog

The various **do** functions provide a means to write structured, iterative code. However, sometimes it is desirable to write less structured iteration. The basic LISP unstructured iteration function is called **prog** (short for "program"). **prog** lets you write code that looks more like traditional programming language constructs, with statements, branches, and so on. **prog** has fallen from favor of late, probably due to the influence of structured programming advocates on the design of LISP. Nevertheless, it is still part of Common LISP. And, arguably, there are some cases in which a **prog** may be more desirable than a structured construct. In any case, **prog** is unarguably of historical interest.

Let us illustrate **prog** by using it to write another function that computes the length of a list:

```
-> (defun prog-length (l)
      (prog ((sum 0))
        again
          (cond ((atom l) (return sum)))
          (setq sum (1+ sum))
          (setq l (cdr l))
          (go again)))
PROG-LENGTH
```

```
-> (prog-length '(a b c))
3
-> (prog-length 3)
0
-> (prog-length '(a (b c)))
2
->
```

The first argument in a **prog** is always a list of *local variable specifiers.* These are just like the index variable specifiers of **do**, except that there is no element specifying a value for automatic repetition. Indeed, this must be done manually in the body of the **prog**. The local variables of the **prog** are sometimes called **prog** variables. Upon evaluating a **prog**, LISP creates a new variable for each symbol in the local variable list, and initializes it to the value of the form appearing in the specifier. In this case, a call to **prog** creates a new variable named **sum**, and initializes it to **0**.

The next s-expression in this **prog** is an atom, namely, the atom **again**. (This is the next expression in the **prog**, although I indented it differently to make it stand out.) **prog**s just ignore atoms when they appear; we will see their significance in a minute.

The next s-expression in the **prog** is a **cond** of one clause. LISP simply evaluates this expression. In fact, after the initial list of local variables, LISP will start evaluating the remaining non-atomic s-expressions in the **prog**, one after the other.

However, the **cond** contains a reference to the function **return**. To interpret a **return**, LISP evaluates its argument and exits from the **prog**; the value of the **prog** will be the value of the argument to **return**. In this case, if the **return** is executed, the **prog** will return the value of **sum**. It is legal to use **return** only inside of a form like a **prog**, as we are doing in this example.

If the **cond** clause does not pan out and the call to **return** is not evaluated, we just continue evaluating the s-expressions in the **prog**. The next couple of s-expressions change the assignments of the atoms **sum** and **I**, respectively. Then we encounter a call to the function **go**. LISP looks at the argument to **go**, which is not evaluated, and looks in the **prog** for an atom of this name. In this case, LISP looks in the **prog** for an atom named **again**. LISP resumes evaluating the expressions in the **prog** starting at the expression immediately after the atom designated by **go**. In our example, the computation would continue with a reevaluation of the **cond**. Like **return**, it is only legal to call the function **go** from inside a form like a **prog**.

Suppose we applied the function **prog–length** to an argument, as in
(prog–length '(a b c)). It would behave as follows: First, the formal
parameter **l** of **prog–length** would be assigned to the actual argument, i. e.,
(a b c). Then we enter the **prog**. Since **sum** is local to the **prog**, a new
variable corresponding to **sum** is created and initialized to **0**. The symbol
again is ignored. Next, we test to see if the value of **l** is an atom. It is
not, so we go on. We assign **sum** the value **1** (i. e., its old value plus 1),
and **l** the value **(b c)** (the **cdr** of its old value). We then jump to the expression immediately following the atom **again**, i. e., the call to **cond**. **l** is
still not an atom, so we assign **sum** the value **2** and **l** the value **(c)**. We
jump to the **cond** again; the condition is still not met; we assign **sum** the
value **3** and **l** the value **nil**, and jump to the **cond** once more. This time,
the value of **l** is an atom, so the **return** gets evaluated. We leave the
prog, returning the value **3**. Of course, when we exit the **prog**, the variable named **sum** that existed during the **prog** becomes unavailable; if we
had another variable named **sum** outside the **prog**, it would now be in
force. The value of the **prog** is returned as the value of the call to
prog–length.

5.3.1. The General prog

The structure of a general **prog** is as follows:

> **(prog** ((*var1 val1*) (*var2 val2*) ...) *exp1 exp2* ...)

The first argument to **prog** is a (possibly empty) list of local variable
specifiers. Then come any number of s-expressions. When LISP enters a
prog, it goes through the following steps:

(1)   It creates new variables for all the *vari*. Then it evaluates all the *vali*,
      and assigns the results to the corresponding *vari*. The *vali* are actual-
      ly optional; if one is omitted, the lone symbol designating the vari-
      able may appear without the enclosing list. In this case, the variable
      will be initialized to **nil**.

(2)   Then it examines the first s-expression. If it is an atom, it ignores it
      for now. If it is list, it evaluates it.

(3)   What happens next depends on the expression just evaluated:

      (a) If the expression includes something of the form (**go** *symbol*),
      LISP looks for an atom among the **prog**'s s-expressions by the name
      symbol. It continues execution by evaluating the s-expression im-
      mediately following that atom (not finding such an atom is an error).

(b) If the expression includes the form (**return** *form*), LISP evaluates the s-expression *form,* and exits the **prog** returning the value of this s-expression as the value of the **prog**.

(c) If neither a **go** nor a **return** transfers control, **prog** evaluates the next s-expression in the list. If there is no next s-expression, because we have reached the end of the list of expressions in the **prog,** we exit the **prog** with value **nil**.

As an illustration, let us write our own version of the function **member** using **prog**:

```
(defun prog–member (e l)
    (prog ()
      label1
        (cond ((atom l) (return nil))
              ((equal e (car l)) (return l))
              (t (setq l (cdr l)) (go label1)))))
```

We did not need any local variables here, so we just supplied an empty list. Next, we inserted a label where we wish to loop back later on. Then comes a **cond** to do the work. The **cond** first checks to see if there is any list left to search, and if so, checks if it begins with the desired object. If not, it chops off the first element of this list and jumps back to the beginning.

Note that, as is the case for the formal parameters of any function call, changing the value of **l** does not change the argument supplied in the call to this function, so no harm is done to the calling code. That is, if **x** were assigned the value (**a b c**), and (**prog–member 'b x**) were evaluated, the value of **x** would remain (**a b c**), even though the value of **l** would change several times during execution.

There are usually several ways to write essentially the same code using **prog**. For example, we could just as well have written the following:

```
(defun another–prog–member (e l)
    (prog ()
      label1
        (cond ((atom l) (return nil))
              ((equal e (car l)) (return l)))
        (setq l (cdr l))
        (go label1)))
```

I prefer this version because it has somewhat less nesting. Also, it is good programming style not to bury a **go** or a **return** deeply within a **prog**.

Standardization Note: Some LISPs cannot handle calls to **go** or **return** if they occur too far from the surface of a **prog**. Deeply nested **go**s or **return**s should work in a correctly implemented version of Common LISP, however.

By the way, the functions **go** and **return** are actually legal within a **do** or **do∗**; the structure iteration functions just allow you to implement explicit iteration without explicit branches or return statement.

5.4. Other Iterative Forms

There are a number of simpler variants of these more general iterative forms. Some of these are useful for very particular kinds of iteration. Others do not really alter flow of control at all, but merely allow you to execute some expressions one after the other in sequence.

For example, the function **loop** takes any number of expressions, and evaluates them repeatedly, from left to right. **loop** never terminates unless it is explicitly exited by a call to **return**.

There are a number of LISP functions that do simple sequencing. **prog1** takes any number of s-expressions, evaluates them in order, and returns the value of the first one. For example, **prog1** is useful for simulating the popping of a stack, where you return the first element of a list and set that list to its **cdr**. Thus

> **(prog1 (car stack) (setq stack (cdr stack)))**

returns the first element of the list **stack,** without having to first save this element temporarily as the value of a variable.

prog2 is just like **prog1**, except that it always returns the value of its second s-expression (**prog2** exists primarily for historical reasons). **progn** is similar, returning the last expression it evaluates.

A similar form of sequential execution has been incorporated into other aspects of LISP. As we discussed previously, LISP allows multiple bodies of code in function definitions, which are evaluated one after another. At one point, LISP did not have this facility, so these simpler forms of **prog** were very useful. They are used less frequently now that LISP supports functions with multiple bodies of code.

Another idea related to iteration is called *function mapping.* We talk about this concept in Chapter 8. There are also some rather non-standard flow-of-control functions in LISP, which are discussed in Chapter 16.

Finally, the functions we have examined in this chapter are not really basic to Common LISP. Instead, they can be thought of as combinations of more primitive and abstract functions. The reader may eventually want to consult the definitions of **block**, **tagbody**, and **return–from** to learn about these underlying constructs.

5.5. Summary

(1) *Iteration* refers to the implementation of indefinite repetition by an explicit construction. Common LISP has several built-in functions that accommodate iteration. In particular, structured iteration can be accomplished using **do**, and unstructured iteration using **prog**.

(2) The special function **do** allows one to provide *index variable specifiers.* These specify variables local to a call to **do**; they also provide the initial values of these variables, as well as update values for them. **do** also allows an exit clause, and a set of forms to evaluate during each iteration. **do∗** is just like **do**, but interprets its index variable specifiers sequentially while **do** interprets them in parallel.

(3) The **prog** special function allows the user to declare local variables, to branch to explicit labels, and to exit directly from any point in the **prog**. Branching and exiting are accomplished with the functions **go** and **return**, respectively.

(4) Less elaborate forms of iteration are effected using the functions **loop, dolist,** and **dotimes**. Simple sequences can be accomplished by **prog1, prog2,** and **progn**. The latter do not allow the use of **go** or **return**, just the evaluation of a number of expressions.

Exercises

(1) Write a **do** and a **prog** version of a function **power–of–two** that computes the nth power of 2. E. g., **(power–of–two 8)** returns **256.**

(2)   Write a **do** and a **prog** version of the LISP function **remove**.
remove removes all occurrences of an element from a list. For example, **(remove 'b '(a b c b d))** returns **(a c d)**.

(3)   Write a **do** and a **prog** version of the LISP function **assoc**. **assoc**
"looks up" a value in a list of lists, and returns the first list it finds
whose first element matches the desired value. For example,
(assoc 'y '((x a) (y b) (z c))) returns **(y b)**.

(4)   Write a **do** and a **prog** version of a function that computes factorials.
(Recall that n! means n(n-1)...2x1.)

(5)   Write a **do** and a **prog** version of the function **pairlis**, which makes a
list of the sort **assoc** uses out of two lists of items to be paired with
one another. For example,

        (pairlis '(a b c d) '(1 2 3 4))

returns

        ((a 1)(b 2)(c 3)(d 4)).

(6)   Write a LISP function that computes *perfect numbers.* A perfect
number is defined as a number whose proper divisors sum to that
number. For example, 6 is a perfect number because the sum of the
proper divisors of 6, namely, 1, 2, and 3, is equal to 6; 28 is a perfect
number because the proper divisors of 28 are 1, 2, 4, 7, and 14,
which add up to 28. You may write this as a function that finds all
perfect numbers between a range of two numbers given as arguments.

(7)   Write a version of the LISP function **intersection** that computes the
set intersection of two lists. The set intersection of two lists is the list
of elements that occur in both lists. For example,
(intersection '(a b c d) '(c a b)) returns **(a b c)**. Note that we ignore
the order of elements in a list as far as set intersection is concerned.
In addition, in your version of **intersection**, an element should appear only once in the result, even if it appears repeatedly in the arguments.

Chapter 6

Recursion

6.1. Introduction

The iterative functions described in the previous chapter provide quite a bit of programming versatility. However, none of these is strictly necessary. Instead, we can accomplish the equivalent of indefinite repetition through the use of *recursion*. Recursive functions are those that use themselves to perform components of the total task in which they are engaged. Unlike iteration, there are no "recursive constructs" in LISP. Rather, recursion is a style that requires no additional LISP machinery. We will examine recursive programming in this chapter, and contrast the recursive style with the iterative style introduced previously.

6.2. The Fundamentals of Recursion

Many novice programmers have difficulty comprehending recursion at first. Actually, recursion itself is a rather transparent phenomenon, as I hope to demonstrate shortly. It is merely the particular instances of recursion that we require for certain computations that are tricky. Unfortunately, these tricky examples of recursion are generally the ones novices first encounter. It is not surprising then, that people often find recursion difficult to comprehend.

So let us begin with something entirely different. Imagine the task of programming a robot to follow a recipe. That is, imagine we had a robot that
could perform some physical actions, and suppose that we had integrated
the robot with our computer so that special LISP functions caused the
robot to perform certain motions. For example, the function **move–arm**
might cause the robot to move its arm in a manner specified by the arguments to this function. We might use such functions to write the more elaborate functions necessary for the task at hand. For example, we might
write functions called **mix** and **stir**, etc., in terms of these low-level functions, so that it would be easy to program our recipe-interpretation task.

Now a recipe might look like this:

```
(recipe omelet
   (put–in–bowl (eggs 3))
   (stir–bowl)
   (put–on–stove skillet)
   (light stove)
     .
     .
     .                           )
```

Our recipe interpretation program might contain a subroutine called
interpret–step. **interpret–step** might just be a big conditional that
figured out how to perform a step of a recipe. For example, it might look
something like the following:

```
(defun interpret–step (step)
   (cond ((equal (car step) 'stir–bowl)
            (get 'mixer)
            (dip–bowl 'mixer)
            (turn–on 'mixer)
            (wait 5)
            (turn–off 'mixer)
            (put–aside 'mixer))
          ((equal (car step) 'put–in–bowl)
            (get 'bowl)
            (lift (cadr step))
            (move–arm–over–bowl)
            ...                           )
            .
            .
            .                               )
```

(Actually, this could be accomplished in a variety of more elegant ways. You might want to examine the function **case**, for example. Other techniques for writing more elegant versions of this sort of code will be discussed in later chapters.)

The definition of our master recipe-following function, which we can call **interpret–recipe**, can be defined simply as the repeated application of **interpret–step** to each step of the recipe. This might look something like the following:

```
(defun interpret–recipe (recipe)
    (dolist (step (cddr recipe)) (interpret–step step)))
```

Recall that **dolist** is an iterative construct that, in this case, will assign **step** successive values of **recipe**, and then evaluate **(interpret–step step)** for each assignment.

Now consider the following situation. Suppose one of the steps of our recipe specified another recipe. For example, if our recipe was for a cake, the final step of the recipe might be to ice the cake using icing prepared by following a recipe for icing. That is, we might have a step of a recipe that looked like the following:

```
(prepare–recipe (recipe icing (get 'chocolate) ...))
```

To interpret this kind of instruction, we would have to add the following clause to the **cond** in **interpret–step**:

```
((equal (car step) 'prepare–recipe)
    (interpret–recipe (cadr step)))
```

The resulting program will now handle "embedded recipes" without any problem.

But did you notice that the function we just specified, **interpret–recipe**, is a recursive function? It is recursive because, in the middle of evaluating a call to **interpret–recipe**, we may encounter an embedded recipe, and call **interpret–recipe** again without ever having exited from the original call. However, you probably found **interpret–recipe** to be a rather straightforward idea, and you would be surprised if LISP had some trouble executing it. In fact, the function seems so straightforward, it is hard to believe it is recursive!

So what is it that makes recursion difficult for beginners? To get the usual uncomfortable feeling normally associated with recursion, imagine the following. Suppose that the first step of a recipe were another recipe. Suppose that the first step of that recipe were another recipe, and so on, for quite a few levels. The function **interpret–recipe** we described above would handle such a recipe just fine. However, it becomes difficult for us humans to follow what is going on. In fact, this sort of difficulty is exactly the difficulty that many novices experience in learning recursion.

We can see from this example that there is nothing really magic or conceptually challenging about recursion per se. It just becomes difficult to think about deeply nested recursions. Fortunately, we generally need not do so. As in the case above, we had to specify only the basic idea: LISP takes care of keeping track of what is going on.

Writing recursive functions is simple once you get the hang of it. The hard part of writing a recursive function is noticing the *recursive relation* within the problem. By this I mean that we can reduce a problem to some computation that involves a smaller version of the same problem. For example, in **interpret–recipe**, the recursive relation is that we can follow a recipe by interpreting each step, and that we can interpret a step by either executing that step directly, or, if it is a recipe, by following that recipe. Thus our conception of following a recipe is defined in terms of following a recipe. Following a recipe within a step is a bit smaller task than following the entire recipe, so the recursion makes sense. That is, making just chocolate icing is simpler than making a chocolate cake with chocolate icing, no matter how complicated making chocolate icing may be.

So the basic idea behind recursion is to think of the task we are doing as being composed of some computation that involves a smaller version of the same problem. This is not so much a programming technique as a way of thinking about a problem. What is surprising about recursion is that so many things that we may not initially have thought of as involving recursion can be thought of this way.

Once the basic conception of a problem as a recursive relation has been done, programming it is easy. About the only thing to be cognizant of is the following. Since a recursive approach tries to define a solution to a problem in terms of a simpler version of that problem, the recursive calls to a function must get simpler and simpler, until some "grounding" condition is reached. This grounding condition should not involve calling the function again. For example, in our recipe program, we eventually bottom out by reaching some step that does not involve interpreting a recipe. The same must be true for every well-defined recursive function.

So we must make sure our program will reach some grounding case, and will recognize this case when it reaches it. Since our recursive program never knows in advance on which call this is going to happen, it must check each call to see if it has reached such a grounding condition. It will call itself recursively only if this is not the case.

To summarize, we have the following components to recursive programming:

(1) Breaking down the task at hand into a form that involves simpler versions of the same task.

(2) Specifying a way to combine the simpler versions of the task to solve the original problem.

(3) Identifying the "grounding" situations in which the task can be accomplished directly, without decomposing it further.

(4) Specifying checks for these grounding cases that will be examined before the recursive steps are taken.

6.3. Some Examples of Recursive Thinking

As an example, let us write a recursive version of the function **length**, called **recursive–length**. Recall that **length**, which we implemented iteratively in the previous chapter, computes the length of a list.

First, we must express the idea of length as a recursive relation. This is the hard part, because most of us are probably not used to thinking about length this way. It takes a bit of practice to be able to come up with recursive relations for a problem on one's own. In this case, we can observe that the length of a list is one more than the length of its **cdr**. This is a sensible way of viewing length, since the **cdr** of a list is shorter than that list. It is a recursive relation, because we are talking about the length of an entire list in terms of length of a slightly smaller list.

We can translate this idea into a piece of code directly. If **l** is the formal parameter of **recursive–length**, then the length of **l** can be computed by evaluating the following:

(1 + (recursive–length (cdr l)))

That is, we merely add 1 to the length of the **cdr** of **l**, as our recursive relation suggests.

However, this cannot be the entire definition of **recursive–length**. The reason for this is that the recursive relation we stated above is somewhat incomplete. In particular, it does not correctly describe the length of a list of no elements. The length of the list **nil** is zero. But the **cdr** of this list is **nil**, also a list of length zero, and not a list of length one less than zero. This is just a special case that we must take into account in stating our recursive relation. A more accurate version might be this: "The length of a list is one more than the length of its **cdr**, unless the list is empty, in which case its length is zero."

We can express this in a conditional, and complete an accurate version of **recursive–length**:

```
(defun recursive-length (l)
    (if (null l) 0 (1 + (recursive-length (cdr l)))))
```

All this version does is check for the grounding case before making the recursive step.

Virtually every recursive function is similar to this one in the following respect. There is a basic recursive relation, with a special case or two. The special cases usually deal with some degenerate condition, e. g., the input being zero for some numeric function, or **nil** or an atom for some list manipulation function. The program to compute the function usually consists of a basic recursive step encoding the basic recursive relation, preceded by some checks for the grounding situations corresponding to the special cases of the recursive relation.

Note also that the recursive relation is biased towards thinking about lists in terms of **car**s and **cdr**s. By this I mean that we also could have defined the length of a list as being one more than the length of the list created by removing the last element from that list. This is correct, but difficult to realize in LISP, because we have no convenient way of taking a list apart in such a manner. There is nothing intrinsic about recursion or lists that make this true; it is just that LISP happens to give us functions that traverse lists in a particular manner. So it best to think of recursive relations in terms of the first element of a list and the rest of a list, for easy translation into LISP code.

Another Example

Let us apply this methodology to another example. Suppose we want to write our own version of **member**. Remember, the function **member** checks to see if an element is contained in a list. Let us call our version of this function **recursive–member**. To write this as a recursive function, we must first try to think of the problem in terms of a recursive relation. One recursive relation that captures the idea of membership adequately is the following. An element is a member of a list if it is the first element of the list, or if it is a member of the rest of the list. Be sure you understand this recursive relation before you go on. If you understand it, writing the corresponding recursive function will present no problem.

In LISP, we might express the first part of this relation, for an element **e** and a list **l**, using the following test:

    (equal e (car l))

That is, **l** contains **e** if its first element is **e**. We can express the second, and recursive, part using the following test:

    (recursive–member e (cdr l))

That is, **e** is a member of **l** if it is a member of the tail of **l**.

We can put these together using **or**:

    (or (equal e (car l)) (recursive–member e (cdr l)))

Remember, **or** will not evaluate the second form if the first one evaluates to true, so this expression will use the recursive step only if the first, non-recursive step fails.

The only problem about using this form as the body for the function **recursive–member** is that it fails to take one degenerate case into account. Namely, if **l** happens to be the empty list, then **e** cannot be a member of it. Because the code above does not check for this case, if we used it when **l** were **nil**, it would try to determine if **e** were a member of the **cdr** of **nil**. Since the **cdr** of **nil** is **nil** in Common LISP, the computation would never cease.

We can remedy this problem simply by inserting a check for **nil** first. We can do this using **and**, and get the following definition:

```
(defun recursive–member (e l)
    (and l (or (equal e (car l))
               (recursive–member e (cdr l)))))
```

This works because **and** will only go on to the next form if the previous form evaluates to non-**nil**.

Alternatively, we can use **cond**:

```
(defun recursive-member (e l)
   (cond
      ((null l) nil)
      (t (or (equal e (car l))
            (recursive-member e (cdr l))))))
```

Both of these definitions are valid, but neither of them is exactly like the version of **member** that comes with LISP. This is because **member** is guaranteed to return the portion of the list from the point of the match, not just a truth value. It is easiest to modify the **cond** version to do this:

```
(defun recursive-member (e l)  ; our own version of member
   (cond
      ((null l) nil)                      ; any list left?
      ((equal e (car l)) l)               ; make the test
      (t (recursive-member e (cdr l)))))  ; do recursive step
```

Note that I commented some of the lines of **recursive-member** using the LISP comment character ; (semicolon). LISP simply ignores the rest of a line after a semicolon.

Standardization Note: The use of semicolon as the comment character is close to universal across LISP dialects, although some exceptions persist.

The first **cond** clause of **recursive-member** ensures that we exit the function when the value of **l** is the empty list. If not, the next **cond** clause checks to see if the value of **e** is the same as the first element of **l**. It returns **l** in this case, meeting the condition that **member** return the rest of the list from the point of the match. These two **cond** clauses represent the "grounding" situations of this recursion. These are the situations in which our function has encountered some condition that allows it to return a value.

If neither of these situations is the case, the final **cond** clause is used. This clause calls the function **recursive-member** again. This part of the definition constitutes the characteristic "recursive step" of the function. Note that this time **recursive-member** is passed **e** and **(cdr l)**. **(cdr l)** contains one less element than **l**. So in effect, we are asking **recursive-member** to do a slightly easier job this time.

Each time the recursive step is taken, **recursive–member** gets passed a shorter list. This cannot go on indefinitely. **recursive–member** will eventually be called with **l** assigned to **nil**. Its first **cond** clause will catch this and cause the process to terminate.

Let us trace through a call to **recursive–member** to see how it works. Before doing so, remember that tracing through a recursive function is confusing, much more confusing than writing one. We go through the exercise here to illustrate the computation that is performed, and so you get some idea of what the resulting flow of control is like. But do not think that keeping track of exactly what is going on during a recursive call is necessary to think about while you are programming.

Suppose we evaluate the expression (**recursive–member 'b '(a b c)**). As with any other function call, the formal parameters get assigned the actual arguments, so in this case, **e** gets assigned the value **b** and **l** the value (**a b c**). Next, we evaluate the function body. **l** is not **nil**, so the first **cond** clause is not used; the **car** of **l** is not **equal** to **b**, so the second **cond** clause is not used either. The final **cond** clause begins with **t**, so it is used. This calls the function **recursive–member** again. LISP does not handle this call differently than it would any other function call. It evaluates the arguments supplied, and assigns the resulting values to the formal parameters of the function called. That is, **e** evaluates to **b**, and (**cdr l**) to (**b c**); the parameters of **recursive–member**, **e** and **l**, are assigned these values, respectively. Of course, LISP created new versions of these parameters when it began this function call, as it always does upon calling a function.

At this point we have entered **recursive–member** again with **e** assigned the value **b** and **l** assigned the value (**b c**). **l** is still not **nil**, so that clause is ignored. However, the **car** of **l** is **equal** to **b**, so the condition of the second **cond** clause is met. We have now reached a "grounding" situation, and we begin our climb back up the recursion ladder. LISP evaluates the rest of the expressions of this **cond** clause, in this case, the lone expression **l**. It returns this value as the value of the **cond**. Since **l** is currently assigned the value (**b c**), this value is returned from the **cond** and, subsequently, as the value of the most recent call to **recursive–member**. This most recent call to **recursive–member** occurred in the final **cond** clause of the previous call to **recursive–member**. We have now finished evaluating that **cond** clause. It returns the value returned by its call to **recursive–member**, namely, the list (**b c**). This value is returned as the value of the **cond**, and thereby, as the value of the original call to **recursive–member**.

Even in this simple example, tracing through a recursive function call is a bit confusing. However, all recursive functions conform to a simple regimen. A recursive function first checks to see if it has reached some "grounding" situation. A "grounding" situation is one in which the function either computes some desired element or runs out of things to try. These are usually derived from the special cases of our recursive relation. If it has not encountered such a situation, then the function calls itself on a slightly simpler version of the same problem. This step is derived from the basic recursive relation. Since the problem to which the function is applied gets simpler each time, the function will eventually encounter a grounding situation. Thus the computation will terminate eventually.

There is one more flourish we might want to add to **recursive–member**. **recursive–member** first checks for **nil**, and then, if **l** is non-**nil**, tries to take its **car**. This would result in an error if a user mistakenly used a non-**nil** atom as the second argument. A good way to fix this bug is to change the call to **null** to a call to **atom**. Since **nil** is an atom, using **atom** will catch all the cases that using **null** would catch; in addition it would prevent a hard error if the second argument turned out to be some other atom.

6.4. Recursion and Parameters

Recall that each call to a function in LISP creates a new variable for each of formal parameters of that function. Therefore, having a function call itself does not result in any confusion of the parameters in the various calls to a function. We did not exploit this feature in our previous example, but it is a crucial part of recursion.

For example, suppose we want to write a function that computes n!. Recall that n! is defined as $n(n-1)(n-2)...1$, so that $3! = 3*2*1 = 6$, $5! = 5*4*3*2*1 = 120$, etc. As before, let us first derive a recursive relation to express the idea of factorial. From the definition just given, we might note that the factorial of n is equal to n times the factorial of n–1. This is true because the factorial of n–1 would be $(n-1)(n-2)...1$. If we multiplied this by n, we would get $n(n-1)(n-2)...1$, which is the definition of the factorial of n.

Thus, we could express the basic recursive relation using the following code:

```
(* n (factorial (1- n)))
```

That is, to compute the factorial of n, compute the factorial of n–1, and then multiply it by n. Computing the factorial of n–1 is easier than computing the factorial of n, so the computation seems sound. However, as before, we now have to worry about the grounding condition. In this case, we will eventually try to compute factorial of 1, which in turn will cause our function to try to compute factorial of 0, and then factorial of –1, and so on. Fortunately, there is a convention that 0! is defined as 1. Now we need only check for this special case before we embark on the recursive step, leading to the following definition:

```
-> (defun factorial (n)
      (cond ((zerop n) 1)
              (t (* n (factorial (1– n)))) ) )
FACTORIAL
-> (factorial 3)
6
-> (factorial 6)
720
->
```

factorial first checks to see if the value of its parameter **n** is **0**. If so, it returns **1**. This is the grounding situation of this recursion. If **factorial** has not reached a grounding situation, it calls **factorial** again, this time asking it to compute the factorial of **n**–1. As is always the case for a recursive step, this computation constitutes an application of the recursive function to a simpler version of the original problem.

When this simpler computation is complete, **factorial** multiplies the result by **n** to obtain the factorial of **n**. For this process to work, LISP must ensure the integrity of the value of **n** within a given call to **factorial**. However, since each call to **factorial** creates a new version of the variable **n**, changes to **n** in one call to **factorial** have no effect on the value of **n** in any other call to **factorial.** In general, when we return to one function call from another in Common LISP, we can be sure that all our formal parameters are the way we left them. In other words, evaluating calls to recursive functions does not present a special problem to the LISP interpreter.

6.5. A Common Recursive Bug

Introducing recursive programming also introduces a new source of potential problems. For example, consider what happens if we call **factorial** with a negative number, or with some non-integer value. Each time **factorial** is called, its argument is decremented by one. But a negative or non-integer argument will never become 0 in this process. Thus LISP will foolishly call **factorial** over and over again until it computes a number whose magnitude is too large for the machine to handle, or until it runs out of room to nest more recursive calls. Either way, the program runs for a long time and then blows up. For example:

> **-> (factorial -1)**

> **Error: Control Stack overflow**

> **Debug 1>:**

LISP called **factorial** so many times that it ran out of room to keep track of new function calls. Some internal stack used to implement function calls bumped into a wall, and LISP had to abort the computation.

Standardization Note: Of course, various implementations will give somewhat different error messages.

We could patch **factorial** to prevent this particular error from happening. However, in the course of writing and debugging a recursive function, such travesties are bound to occur. When your program causes a stack overflow or some similar error, there is a good chance that you have an improper termination condition in a recursive function definition.

If your function is doing some particularly complex computation, it may take quite a while for an error to occur. If you get suspicious and are tired of waiting, most operating systems and associated LISPs will allow you to interrupt the computation. For example, here I interrupt an errant call to **factorial** by typing CTRL-c, the interrupt character that I use:

> **-> (factorial 0.1)**
> **Interrupt:^C**

> **Debug 1>:**

LISP shows the interrupt and then behaves just as if an error occurred. We can go back to the top level, or use some of the debugging techniques described in Chapter 11.

Standardization Note: The particular method of interrupting a LISP computation will vary from implementation to implementation and machine to machine.

6.6. More Complex Recursion

A more elegant use of recursion appears in the definition of the LISP function **subst**. This is a function of three arguments; the first is substituted for the second in the third, i. e., **(subst in out struct)** substitutes the value of **in** for the value of **out** wherever it appears in the value of **struct**. Unlike **member**, **subst** does its work on all levels, not just at the top one. For example, **(subst 'a 'b '((a b c) b c (d c b a)))** returns **((a a c) a c (d c a a))**.

To write our own version of **subst** using recursion, let us first try to specify a recursive relation. To do so, we observe the following: If we are trying to substitute **in** for **out** in **struct**, then if **out** matches the **car** of **struct**, the correct substitution replaces the **car** of **struct** with **in**. If not, then the correct substitution replaces the **car** of **struct** with a correctly substituted **car** of **struct**. In either case, the correct substitution replaces the **cdr** of **struct** with a correctly substituted **cdr**. For example, to substitute **x** for **a** in **(a b a)**, we should first replace the **car** of the list with **x**, and replace the **cdr** with the correctly substituted **cdr**, i. e., with **(b x)**. Similarly, to substitute **x** for **a** in **(c b a)**, it is correct to leave the **car** alone, but to replace the **cdr** with the correctly substituted **cdr**.

This is a good recursive relation because both the **car** and **cdr** of a list must be smaller than the list, so each subproblem (i. e., substituting the **car** and substituting the **cdr**) is simpler than the original problem (i. e., substituting the whole list).

We can use this recursive relation to compute a substitution by first computing the substitution on the **car**, then computing it on the **cdr**, and then pasting the two results together. Thus we have the following recursive step:

```
(cons (if (equal out (car struct))
          in
          (our-subst in out (car struct)))
      (our-subst in out (cdr struct)))
```

Here we use the fact that conditionals in LISP return a value, so that the first argument to **cons** will return the value of **in** if a substitution should be made, and will return a properly substituted **car** if it should not. In any case, the resulting value will get **cons**ed onto a properly substituted **cdr**.

If you find the embedded conditional unappealing, you could have just as easily written the code with the conditional on the outside, although the resulting code will be a bit redundant:

```
(if (equal out (car struct))
    (cons in (our-subst in out (cdr struct)))
    (cons (our-subst in out (car struct))
          (our-subst in out (cdr struct)))))
```

If you prefer to use **cond**, you can write the following:

```
(cond
    ((equal out (car struct))
     (cons in (our-subst in out (cdr struct))))
    (t (cons (our-subst in out (car struct))
             (our-subst in out (cdr struct)))))
```

Unlike our previous examples of recursion, this task requires two recursive steps. One step recurses down that **car** of a list, and another recurses down its **cdr**. This is necessary here because we need to do the substitution at all levels of the list. Had we not recursed down the **car**, we would have specified a function that performed the substitution only on the top level of the list.

In general, we can think of the "single recursion" technique of the previous examples as a method for marching down the elements of a list (sometimes called "**cdr**ing down a list", for obvious reasons). In these cases, we do not care to examine the constituents of these elements. We can think of the "double recursion" used in **subst** as a technique for **cdr**ing down a list *and* simultaneously examining the contents of each element of that list. Again, there is nothing really special about either of these cases. They are just typical of the kind of tasks we often find ourselves doing in LISP programming.

While the code specified above encodes the basic recursive relation for substitution, we still have to worry about the special cases. In particular, **struct** may have an atom for its value. This can occur in one of two ways. We may recurse down the **car** until we encounter an atomic element of a list. For example, if our list were (**a b c**), and **a** did not match the element we are trying to eliminate, our code will try to substitute on the **car**. In this case, the **car** is the atom **a**. Alternatively, while recursing down the **cdr**, we may run off the end of the list. In this case, we will end up trying to do the substitution on **nil**.

In either case, we merely wish to return the element we were passed. Another way of saying this is that the substitution of an atom is that atom, regardless of what we are trying to substitute "in it"; likewise, the substitution of an empty list is the empty list. While these are conceptually two different special cases, we can handle both of them at once because **nil** happens to count as an atom in LISP. So we can write the following complete function:

```
(defun our-subst (in out struct)
   (if (atom struct)
      struct
      (cons (if (equal out (car struct))
               in
               (our-subst in out (car struct)))
            (our-subst in out (cdr struct)))))
```

This accounts for both worrisome special cases because the recursion will be attempted only if the list is in fact a non-empty list; if it is either empty or not a list, then that value is returned.

If you prefer not to see the nested conditionals, then a **cond** version of this function is recommended:

```
(defun our-subst (in out struct)
   (cond
      ((atom struct) struct)
      ((equal out (car struct))
       (cons in (our-subst in out (cdr struct))))
      (t (cons (our-subst in out (car struct))
               (our-subst in out (cdr struct))))))
```

There is yet another way to write this function recursively. Let us examine the **cond** version of our function for a moment. Note that the second **cond** clause sort of "peeks ahead" at the first element of list in order to decide whether it should do the substitution or take the recursive plunge on the **car** of the list. Suppose instead we postponed this decision a bit. On the next step, our function will attempt to do the substitution on the **car** of the list. Suppose at this point we check if the entire item passed as the list to be substituted *is* the same as the value we want to replace. If this is so, then we need only return the value to be substituted in its stead.

This may not be obvious at first, because we are actually changing the definition of substitution here. Previously we said that substituting **in** for **out** in **struct** should be **struct** when **struct** is atomic. Now we are saying that substituting **in** for **out** in **struct** should be **in** if **struct** happens to be the same as **out**. Using this notion of substitution, we can write the following recursive definition:

```
(defun our-subst (in out struct)
  (cond
    ((equal out struct) in)
    ((atom struct) struct)
    (t (cons (our-subst in out (car struct))
             (our-subst in out (cdr struct))))))
```

Note that here, we must check for equality before checking to see if we bottom out. This is because our new definition may substitute an atom with the replacement value if the atom matches the item we are trying to eliminate.

This version of **subst** will get rid of the entire third argument if it matches the second, i. e., **(our-subst 'a 'b 'b)** will return **a**. This is the price we pay here for a somewhat simpler piece of code. Apparently, most programmers do not object to this notion of substitution, since most LISP systems, including Common LISP, use a definition of **subst** that is compatible with this one.

6.7. Programming Notes

Programming Is an Iterative Process

Note that in this example, we considered changing the definition of what we were doing in order to write a more elegant or efficient piece of code. This is typical of many programming tasks, because it is hard to specify in advance exactly what we want.

In addition, we did not write the entire function at once, but wrote important pieces of it first. Only then did we consider the finer points. For example, we wrote the code for the basic recursive step first. Then we worried about the special cases. Moreover, as we worried about them, we may have changed our previous code. For example, it was easy to write the basic recursive step of **our-subst** using **if**. But as we began checking for special cases, the use of **cond** became more appealing.

Not only did we not pick the final solution at our first attempt, but the solutions that I proposed in writing these simple examples had errors in them. Of course, I did not show all my failed attempts at creating these examples. But they certainly did occur. For example, the initial versions of **our-subst** that I attempted did not check for all the special cases correctly. I wrote an erroneous function, and discovered that I made an error only when I tried out the function. Then I had to do some debugging to figure out what went wrong. Only then did I realize that there was a grounding condition I had neglected.

The final product of a programming task almost never is a direct reflection of the process that composed it.

For example, I recommend writing a recursive function by first writing down the basic recursive step. This ends up being "inside-out" programming, if we look at where this step ends up in our final code.

It is important to realize that even very experienced programmers write code this way. Programming is rarely a single-pass process in which correct code for a specified problem is directly generated. Instead, it is an iterative process. We move from a conception of a problem to a rough sketch of the solution, to a more detailed but probably erroneous solution, back to a somewhat different sketch after debugging, or even back to redefine the entire conception of the task we are carrying out.

When to Use Recursion

We have spent some time in this chapter demonstrating that any notion that intuitively involves iteration may be thought of as a recursive relation. For example, the idea of counting the elements of a list may at first seem like an iterative idea. But we could also think of it in terms of recursion. Once we have done so, we can easily write a recursive program for it.

However, the fact that we can do so does not mean that we always should. For example, consider the mathematical sequence known as Fibonacci numbers. This is the sequence one gets by adding together the last two numbers of the sequence, beginning the sequence with two 1's. So one gets the sequence 1,1,2,3,5,8.... It is easy to express each element of this sequence as a recursive relation. Namely, the nth Fibonacci number is the sum of of the n-2 and n-1 Fibonacci number. The special cases are simply that the first Fibonacci number is 1 and the second Fibonacci number is also 1.

We can now write a program that computes Fibonacci numbers using this relation:

```
(defun fib (n)
    (cond ((or (equal n 1) (equal n 2)) 1)
          (t (+ (fib (1- n)) (fib (- n 2)))))))
```

Correct as this program is, it is horrendously inefficient. For example, to evaluate **(fib 100)**, our program first computes **(fib 99)** and **(fib 98)**, and then adds the two together. However, to compute **(fib 99)**, our program computes **(fib 98)** and **(fib 97)** and adds these together. That means that our program computes **(fib 98)** twice, once when it is trying to compute **(fib 100)** and again when it is trying to compute **(fib 99)**. In fact, we will repeat this behavior over and over again, needlessly performing a computation that we have already performed.

There are a number of solutions to this problem. One is that we might be lucky enough to have an interpreter or compiler that was smart enough to realize what was going on, and arrange the actual computation not to recompute duplicates. Such systems are few and far between. Until they are standard, we will have to think about the computations that result from our code, and try to arrange our code so that these are efficient. In this case, we might try to use a bit of mathematics to derive a formula for computing Fibonacci numbers that did not involve recursion at all.

In any case, we should remember that recursion is just one way to think about a problem. Sometimes it is useful and efficient. Other times it is awkward and inefficient. The programmer should give these issues careful consideration, and not blindly chose one technique or the other.

6.8. A Recursive Trace

As an exercise, let us trace through a call to our latest version of **subst**. In particular, let us examine what happens when we evaluated the form **(our-subst 'a 'b '(c b a))**. Be forewarned that tracing through a call to a recursive function is confusing. The power of recursion comes from *not* having to consider explicitly all the various details of the flow of control when we write the code. Instead, we just specify the basic structure of the problem and let LISP take care of the rest. Thus the definition of **our-subst** is quite simple, but the computation it performs is quite complex. We will look at that computation here to get a better understanding of the computation that a call to a recursive function may trigger. However, it is important to realize that one need not (in fact, better not) be concerned about all these details when one is programming.

When we first enter **our-subst**, its parameters get assigned as shown in Figure 6.1.

Typing in the given form causes **our-subst** to be called with its parameters assigned as shown. Since we will have need to refer to a number of different calls to **our-subst** in this exposition, I have adopted a naming

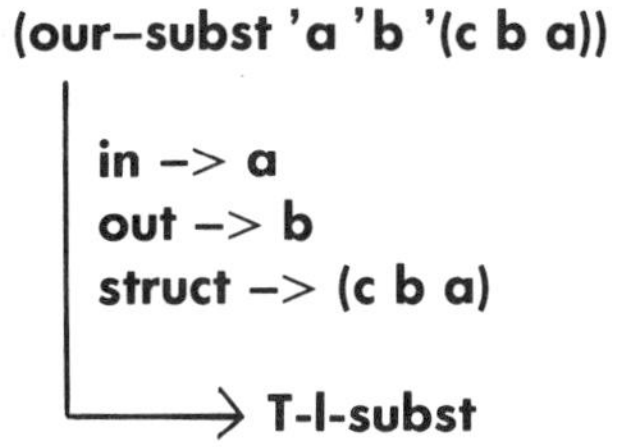

```
(our–subst 'a 'b '(c b a))

  │   in –> a
  │   out –> b
  │   struct –> (c b a)
  │
  └────────> T-l-subst
```

Figure 6.1: The initial function call is made.

convention for them. I will call the initial call to **subst** "T-l-subst", for "top level call to **subst**". There are two recursive calls to **our–subst** within **our–subst**. I will refer to one as "car-subst" and the other as "cdr-subst". I will use a number to indicate how many times each of these calls has been made.

The initial call to **our–subst** causes its last **cond** clause to be evaluated. **our–subst** is called again, resulting in the situation shown in Figure 6.2.

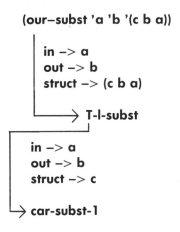

```
(our–subst 'a 'b '(c b a))

  │   in –> a
  │   out –> b
  │   struct –> (c b a)
  │
  └────────> T-l-subst

  │   in –> a
  │   out –> b
  │   struct –> c
  │
  └─> car-subst-1
```

Figure 6.2: The first recursive step is taken.

Note that we have not yet exited from the initial call to **our–subst**. The values of the versions of **in**, **out**, and **struct** within "T-l-subst" are of course undisturbed by other calls to **our–subst**, so that evaluation of "T-l-subst" can continue when "car-subst-1" is finished. "car-subst-1" actually finishes right away: **b** is not **equal** to **c** but it is an atom, so "car-subst-1" returns **c**.

The value **c** computed by "car-subst-1" is returned to "T-l-subst", i. e., the original call to **our–subst**. Back there, we were evaluating the first argument supplied to a **cons**, and now it is the second argument's turn. This is again a call to **our–subst**. We now have the situation depicted in Figure 6.3.

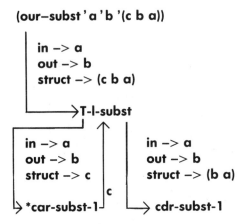

(our–subst 'a 'b '(c b a))

    in –> a
    out –> b
    struct –> (c b a)

       T-l-subst

in –> a   **in –> a**
out –> b   **out –> b**
struct –> c   **struct –> (b a)**

             c
*car-subst-1   **cdr-subst-1**

Figure 6.3: The first recursive step finishes; another begins.

In this figure I use the asterisk to indicate that the call to **our–subst** termed "car-subst-1" has been completed. The value it returned to "T-l-subst" is also shown.

In the execution of "cdr-subst-1", the third **cond** clause is again reached, causing yet another call to **our–subst**. This is shown in Figure 6.4.

At this point, there are three pending calls, "T-l-subst", "cdr-subst-1", and "car-subst-2". Note that the initial list passed to **our–subst** contains only atoms, so we will not travel down any of its elements. That is, all "car-subst" calls will return immediately, so our example does not really exploit the full power of the recursion built into **our–subst**.

Thus "car-subst-2" also finishes right away, returning **a**. This step does the actual substitution for which the whole function is designed. The other calls to **our–subst** simply build up a new list to house the substituted version of the argument.

Now we enter **our–subst** yet again, resulting in the configuration shown in Figure 6.5.

Next we reach the third **cond** clause again, and make a call to "car-subst-3", which immediately returns **a**. This is returned to "cdr-subst-2", which now calls "cdr-subst-3". The resulting state of affairs is shown in Figure 6.6.

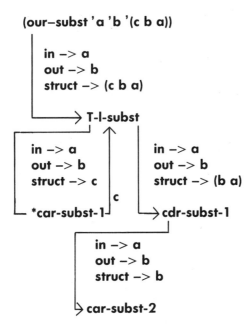

Figure 6.4: A recursive step within a recursive step.

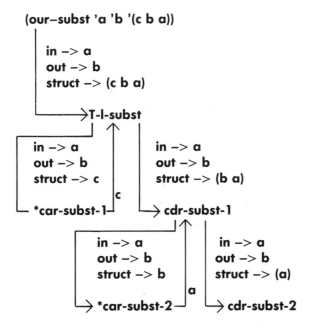

Figure 6.5: A substitution is made and recursion continues.

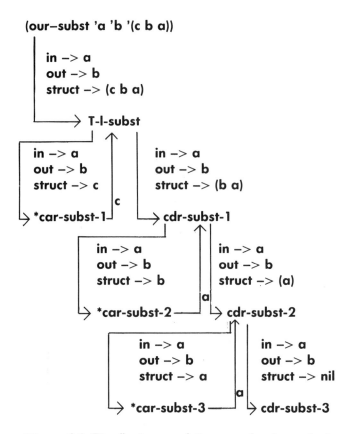

Figure 6.6: The final rung of the recursion is reached.

"cdr-subst-3" returns **nil** right away. We now return to "cdr-subst-2", which is in the middle of executing a **cons**. The other actual argument to this call to **cons** was already computed to be **a** by "car-subst-3", so "cdr-subst-2" returns **(a)** to "cdr-subst-1". This call was also in the middle of computing a **cons**. The first actual argument to this call to **cons** was computed to be **a** by "car-subst-2", so "cdr-subst-1" returns **(a a)**. "cdr-subst-1" was called by "T-l-subst", which was also in the middle of computing a **cons**. The first argument to this call to **cons** was computed to be **c** by "subst-car-1". So "T-l-subst" can now run to completion, returning **(c a a)**.

We summarize the overall flow of the computation in Figure 6.7.

Fortunately, it is harder to follow the flow of control through recursive functions than it is to write them. It is important to go through the exercise once, though, so that you understand what is actually going on.

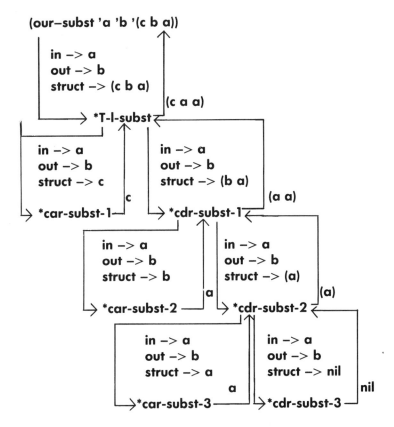

Figure 6.7: The recursive computation is complete.

Note that a function need not call itself directly for it to be recursive. For example, if function **a** calls function **b**, and function **b** calls **a** again, this is also considered to be a form of recursion. Thus a recursive function is one whose execution will result in another call to that function before the initial call is complete. It makes no difference whether or not there is an intervening series of function calls.

6.9. Iteration Versus Recursion

Consider the following programming task. The function **reverse** takes one argument, a list, and returns a list with the same elements but in the reverse order, i. e., **(reverse '(a b c))** returns **(c b a)**. To do this iteratively, we use a local variable to help build up the reversed list as we **cdr** down the original:

```
(defun iterative-reverse (l)
   (do ((ll l (cdr ll))
        (result nil (cons (car ll) result)))
       ((null ll) result)))
```

We build up **result** as we peel off each element of the original list, and return the value of **result** when we run out of elements from the original list.

However, writing a recursive version of **reverse** is a bit tricky. We could write a function that reversed the **cdr** of the list, and then stuck the **car** on the end. The problem with this is that, in LISP, it is harder to add an element to the end of a list than to the beginning. In fact, with what we know so far, we would have to rebuild the whole list each time, and that would require a lot of **cons**es! (Think about how to do this if you are not sure why this is so.)

A more efficient way to use recursion would be to have a function that was called with a partially reversed list and with part of the original list. This function would move one element from the original list to the beginning of the partially reversed list, and then call itself again with these arguments. Eventually the original list would become **nil**, and the recursion would terminate. Such a version of **reverse** would look like this:

```
(defun reverse-2 (original revdlist)
   (cond ((null original) revdlist)
         (t (reverse-2 (cdr original)
                       (cons (car original) revdlist)))))
```

The only problem here is that **reverse-2** is a function of two arguments, and we really want **reverse** to be a function of a single argument, the list to be reversed. The way to accomplish this is to create another function, of one argument, which calls **reverse-2** passing along its argument and a second argument of **nil**:

```
(defun recursive-reverse (l) (reverse-2 l nil))
```

For my part, the iterative version of **reverse** is more transparent than the recursive version.

In addition, iteration is often more efficient than recursion. For example, the iterative versions of **reverse** do not require entering a function over and over again, as does the recursive version. The overhead of calling a function may be considerable, in both time and storage, so the iterative version is liable to require fewer resources. Some LISP interpreters are smart enough to minimize the overhead of certain types of recursive calls so that their efficiency is comparable to that of iterative methods. But in many cases on many LISPs, iteration will be more efficient than recursion.

6.10. Summary

(1) *Recursion* is a method for doing indefinite repetition that does not require any additional LISP constructs. Recursion involves having a function call itself during its execution. Because of LISP's normal tendencies to create new versions of formal parameters for each function call, having a function call itself does not require any special machinery.

(2) To write a recursive function, we must first specify a *recursive relation*. This is an expression of a solution to a problem in terms of a smaller version of the same problem. We can then code the recursive step of the function from this recursive relation.

(3) The general form of a recursive function is as follows: First, check for "grounding" situations. Then take the recursive step. A common error in writing a recursive function is an improper check for the "grounding" situations. In this case, a call to the function is liable to cause a long computation ending in an error.

(4) Much of the time, recursion is used to **cdr** down a list. We can use *double recursion* to both **cdr** down a list and recursively examine the contents of each of the list's elements.

(5) In writing recursive functions, and in programming in general, we rarely know exactly what we want, nor write it correctly the first time. Programming is an iterative process that involves successive refinement of both our code and the notion of the task we are accomplishing.

Exercises

(1) Write a recursive function that returns 1 where each element of a list is non-**nil**, and 0 where the elements are **nil**. For example, **(nonnil '(a nil (b) (nil) 2))** should return **(1 0 1 1 1)**.

(2) Write a recursive function **power-of-two** that computes the nth power of 2. E. g., **(power-of-two 8)** returns **256**.

(3)   Write a recursive function **count–atoms** that counts the number of atoms that appear at all levels of an s-expression. For example, **(count–atoms '(a (b c) (d (e) f)))** returns **6**.

(4)   Write a recursive version of the LISP function **remove**. **remove** removes all occurrences of an element from a list. For example, **(remove 'b '(a b c b d))** returns **(a c d)**.

(5)   Use recursion to write your own version of the LISP function **assoc**. **assoc** "looks up" a value in a list of lists, and returns the first list it finds whose first element matches the desired value. For example, **(assoc 'y '((x a) (y b) (z c)))** returns **(y b)**.

(6)   A common mistake involving recursion takes the following form. Suppose we want to write our own version of the Common LISP function **if**. We might try to do this as follows:

```
-> (defun our–if (condition then–action else–action)
        (cond (condition then–action) (t else–action)))
OUR–IF
-> (our–if (< 4 5) 'yes 'no)
YES
-> (our–if (> 4 5) 'yes 'no)
NO
->
```

our–if seems to work. But what might happen if we use **our–if** inside a recursive definition? For example, suppose we wrote **factorial** in terms of **our–if**:

```
-> (defun factorial (n)
        (our–if (zerop n) 1 (* n (factorial (1– n)))))
FACTORIAL
->
```

What would happen if we used this version of **factorial**? Why?

(7)   Write a function **sub–splice** which is like **subst**, but which "splices in" its first argument for the second. For example, **(sub–splice '(1 2) 'b '(a b c))** returns **(a 1 2 3)**; **(sub–splice '(1 2) 'b '(a (b c) d))** returns **(a (1 2 c) d)**. Decide which is simpler, a recursive or iterative version of this function. Implement the simpler version.

(8) Suppose we represented a *matrix* in LISP as a list of lists. For example, **((a b) (c d))** would represent a 2x2 matrix whose first row contains the elements **a** and **b**, and whose second row has the elements **c** and **d**. Write a function that takes a matrix as input, and outputs its transpose. For example, **(transpose '((a b) (c d)))** should return **((a c) (b d))**.

(9) Do all recursive functions have an iterative, non-recursive version? Consider the functions **subst** and **count–atoms** described previously.

Chapter 7

Property Lists

7.1. Introduction

So far, we have treated LISP symbols just like they were identifiers in other programming languages, even though we claimed that they are different. One important difference is that symbols can have something called *properties*. Think of the properties of a symbol as being like the properties of a real world object. For example, a chair can have a color, a weight, a height, and so on. A given chair might be blue, weigh 40 pounds, and be 3 feet tall. To describe an object, then, we need *properties,* like **color**, **weight** and **height**, and *property values,* like **blue**, **40** pounds and **3** feet.

Properties of symbols in LISP are based on this idea. In this chapter we describe the LISP notion of properties, and introduce property manipulation functions. Then we give some programming examples to illustrate their utility. Finally, we use properties to help demonstrate how different symbols are from more familiar programming language entities.

7.2. The Basics

A symbol can have any number of properties, each of which can have its own value. We can query LISP about a given property of a given symbol using the function **get**. Without having done anything to assure that a particular symbol has some specific property, we will get the value **nil**. For example, we can ask LISP about the **color** of the symbol **chair3** as follows:

```
-> (get 'chair3 'color)
NIL
->
```

Since we did nothing previously to create a **color** property of **chair3**, **get** returns the default value **nil**.

To give properties of symbols values in Common LISP, we must use the special function **setf**. This is a rather general "setting" function (hence the name) used for many different kinds of assignments in LISP. We will discuss **setf** more fully later. To use **setf** to change the value of a property of a symbol, though, we do the following:

```
-> (setf (get 'chair3 'color) 'blue)
BLUE
->
```

That is, we supply as our first argument to **setf** the form we would like to use to get the value of the property of a symbol; the second argument specifies the value we would like this property to have. **setf** assures that a subsequent call to **get** requesting the specified property of the specified symbol will return the designated value. In addition to making this assurance, **setf** returns the property value as the value of the call.

We can now access this value using **get**:

```
-> (get 'chair3 'color)
BLUE
->
```

A symbol can have any number of properties. For example, we can specify another property of **chair3**:

```
-> (setf (get 'chair3 'owner) 'john)
JOHN
->
```

Now when we ask LISP about the **owner** of **chair3**, it will give us an informed answer:

```
-> (get 'chair3 'owner)
JOHN
->
```

Standardization Note: Most versions of LISP other than Common LISP have functions called **putprop** and **defprop** that are specifically designed to specify the value of a property. A call of the form (**putprop** *name value property*) causes the property *property* of *name* to have the value *value*. **putprop** evaluates all its arguments; **defprop** is just like **putprop** except that it is a special function and evaluates none of its arguments.

These functions were not included in Common LISP to encourage greater reliance on **setf** as a general assignment function.

LISP maintains all the properties and associated values together on a *property list* associated with each symbol. The property list is an actual LISP list, consisting of alternating properties and corresponding values. For example, the property list of **chair3** is now (**owner John color blue**). The user rarely has need to retrieve or replace the entire property list of a symbol (although there are functions that allow this). Rather, the set of property lists is often thought of as a simple kind of data base: **setf** is used to insert into this data base and **get** to query it.

We mentioned above that, if there is no property corresponding to the one you specify when you do a **get**, **get** will return **nil**. As a result, **get** will *not* distinguish between a property whose value is **nil**, and a nonexistent property:

```
-> (setf (get 'chair3 'animate) nil)
NIL
-> (get 'chair3 'animate)
NIL
-> (get 'chair3 'manufacturer)
NIL
->
```

Here we define the **animate** property of **chair3** to be **nil**. When we retrieve this value, we get **nil** back. However, we get exactly the same answer when we do a **get** on a property we have never mentioned before. The former case is likely to indicate that some feature is known not to be present (in this case, the chair is not an animate thing), while the latter is likely to be indicative of not knowing something (in this case, who the manufacturer is).

As a programmer, you should be careful to distinguish between these situations if the distinction is meaningful within the context of your program. One way to do so is to adopt a convention in which you always use a symbol other than **nil** to indicate a known but negative value. For example, we might have asserted **(setf (get 'chair3 'animate) 'negative)**, using **negative** rather than **nil** to designate the lack of a feature. Then the result of using **get** will no longer be ambiguous when **nil** is returned.

Yet another way to accomplish the same thing is to supply an additional argument to **get**. **get** requires only two arguments, a symbol and a property. However, it is possible to specify a third argument in a call to **get**. If this is done, the third argument is interpreted as the value to return should the search for the property fail. For example, if we had explicitly given the **animate** property of **chair3** the value **nil**, we could still distinguish between the two potentially ambiguous cases as follows:

```
-> (get 'chair3 'animate 'unknown)
NIL
-> (get 'chair3 'manufacturer 'unknown)
UNKNOWN
->
```

Here we supply a third argument that evaluates to **unknown**. In the first case, **get** finds the actual property value **nil**, so it returns this as its value. In the second case, however, **get** finds nothing. Rather than return **nil**, it returns the third argument, in this case, **unknown**. So our program can distinguish between these two cases even if we wish to use **nil** to mean a known negative value.

By the way, an argument that need not be specified to a function call is called an *optional argument*. So we might describe **get** as having two *required* arguments, as well as an *optional* third argument. As is the case for **get**, most LISP functions that tolerate optional arguments assume some default if the argument is not supplied. For example, with **get**, if we do not supply the optional third argument, it is as exactly as if we called the function supplying a third argument of **nil**.

We will examine optional arguments more closely in Chapter 12. In the meantime, it is sufficient to know that quite a few LISP functions accept such arguments.

Standardization Note: An optional argument to **get** is not universal to all dialects of LISP.

7.3. An Example

As an example of the use of property lists, consider the problem of main-taining a data base of information about the books in our library. For each book, we might want to use property lists to store its title, author, and publisher. We might use the global variable ***library*** to hold the list of all the books we know about. Then we can write a utility function to add a new book to the data base:

```
-> (defun add-book (bookref title author publisher)
       (setf (get bookref 'title) title)
       (setf (get bookref 'author) author)
       (setf (get bookref 'publisher) publisher)
       (setq *library* (cons bookref *library*))
       bookref)
ADD-BOOK
->
```

bookref will be assigned the symbol used to represent a book, e. g., **book1**, **book2**, etc. **add-book** just sticks its arguments on the property list of this symbol and adds that symbol to the library. For example:

```
-> (setq *library* nil)
NIL
-> (add-book 'book1
             '(war and peace)
             '(leo tolstoy)
             '(frumpdeedump press))
BOOK1
-> (add-book 'book2
             '(artificial intelligence)
             '(patrick winston)
             '(addison-wesley))
BOOK2
```

```
-> (add-book 'book3
             '(data structure techniques)
             '(tim standish)
             '(addison-wesley))
BOOK3
-> *library*
(BOOK1 BOOK2 BOOK3)
->
```

We can also define some functions that access this data base. For example, here is a function that retrieves items from the data base that have a certain characteristic:

```
-> (defun retrieve-by (property value)
     (do ((l *library* (cdr l))
          (result nil (if (equal (get (car l) property) value)
                          (cons (car l) result)
                          result)))
         ((null l) result)))
RETRIEVE-BY
-> (retrieve-by 'author '(leo tolstoy))
(BOOK1)
-> (retrieve-by 'publisher '(addison-wesley))
(BOOK3 BOOK2)
->
```

We might introduce any number of other properties to complete our library system. For example, we could use a property **status** to indicate whether the books were checked out or are on the shelf, another to indicate who has borrowed it if it is checked out, etc. We might also write functions to remove books from the data base, or for any other library "bookkeeping" that we needed.

7.4. The Significance of Property Lists

In the early days, people seemed to take the analogy between LISP properties and properties of real world objects rather seriously. Some people in artificial intelligence, for example, thought that using property lists in this manner might be a good way to represent the real world inside the machine. While there is some merit in this approach, representing real properties of real objects turned out to be more complicated than the naive version of properties that comes with LISP. The upshot of all this is that today people use properties as just another LISP programming language feature. Most AI researchers, for example, will use property lists to implement more complex theories, but do not attribute theoretical significance to property lists per se.

7.5. Property Lists and the Uniqueness of Symbols

The following example illustrates an important fact about LISP. Suppose we had the following session with the LISP interpreter:

```
-> (setq v 4)
4
-> (setf (get 'v 'color) 'black)
BLACK
-> (prog (v) (setq v 9) (return v))
9
-> v
4
-> (prog (v)
        (setf (get 'v 'color) 'red)
        (return (get 'v 'color)))
RED
-> (get 'v 'color)
???
```

When we enter the **prog** and declare **v** to be local, changes to the value of **v** will only last as long as we are in the **prog**. When we return to the top level of LISP, **v** is back to its previous value. However, what do you suppose happens to the old value of a property if we change it inside a **prog**? If you executed these lines of code, you have found that the last one returned **red**, not **black**! A change to a property is *not* local to a function definition or **prog**, even if the symbol designates a formal parameter or a local variable!

This seeming inconsistency is really quite consistent with the distinction we have made previously between symbols and variables. A single symbol in LISP may refer to different variables at different times. The same symbol may be used to designate a formal parameter in one place, a **prog** variable in another, and an index variable somewhere else. Indeed, each time such a piece of code is executed, a new variable corresponding to the symbol is created. However, each occurrence of the symbol is indeed an occurrence of the same symbol. Thus the symbol **v** inside a **prog** is the same symbol **v** as on the top level, and is the same symbol **v** as appears elsewhere in your code. If you change a property of this symbol **v**, you have changed a property of the symbol **v**, period. That is, a LISP property is an attribute of a symbol, not of a variable the symbol may designate.

Some people do not like this feature of LISP because it is so totally global, i. e., a change in some obscure part of a program can affect the behavior of the rest of the program. However, if you think of property lists as a data base, this may not seem so terrible.

7.6. Property Lists without Symbols

It is sometimes useful to use the idea of a property list even if you do not have an symbol around. For example, if you want to associate some data with some keys, and then look up the data by key, property lists are handy. But these keys and data may have nothing to do logically with properties of a symbol. Thus we may want to assert that John owns a Mercedes, Bill a Ford, and Mary a Porsche, using something like property lists. Then we could ask what kind of car one of them has using something like **get**. But these assertions are not logically the properties of any preexisting symbol.

To allow functions like **get** to be applied to such uses, Common LISP allows you to maintain property lists that exist apart from symbols. A property list not associated with a symbol can be searched for a property using the function **getf**; it can be updated using **setf**, as before, with the occurrence of **get** replaced by **getf**.

For example, we can use **getf** on such an "unattached" property list to implement the automobile example given above. First, we create a property list-like value:

> **-> (setq list–of–cars '(john mercedes bill ford mary porsche))**
> **(JOHN MERCEDES BILL FORD MARY PORSCHE)**

And now we can use **getf** to query it:

> **-> (getf list–of–cars 'bill)**
> **FORD**
> **->**

Unlike **get**, **getf** does not expect its first argument to be a symbol with a property list. Instead, it expects a property list to be supplied directly. Then it searches that property list for the specified property.

We can use **setf** to update unattached property lists as well. However, doing so will change the property list being worked on in a rather disturbing

119

way. For example, watch what happens when we add a new property to **list–of–cars**:

```
-> (setf (getf list-of-cars 'biff) 'jaguar)
jaguar
-> list-of-cars
(BIFF JAGUAR JOHN MERCEDES BILL FORD MARY PORSCHE)
->
```

The actual value of **list–of–cars** was changed, even though we did not explicitly reassign it. For this reason, use of such property lists is not recommended for amateurs. Read Chapter 15 on LISP internals to more fully understand the implications of this feature.

Standardization Note: Some dialects of LISP have a notion of a "disembodied" property similar to the "unattached" property lists shown here. Disembodied property lists can be accessed using **get** (rather than with a special function). However, they are decidedly strange creatures. For example, they usually contain an odd number of elements, the first element being ignored as far as **get** is concerned.

7.7. Summary

(1)   Every LISP symbol can have any number of *properties*. Each property has an associated value. The set of property and value associations for a particular symbol is called its *property list.*

(2)   We can access the property of a symbol using the function **get**. **get** takes two arguments. It interprets the first as the name of a symbol and the second as a property. It returns the value of that property of that symbol, or **nil** if there is no such property. A third, optional argument may be supplied to **get**; this is interpreted as the value to return if the symbol does not have the property requested.

(3)   We can create or change a property of a symbol using the function **setf**. We do this by supplying as a first argument to **setf** the call to **get** we would like to be able to make, and as the second argument, the value we would like this call to return.

(4)   Changes to property lists are totally global. They are not localized by entering function calls or **prog**s. This is because properties are functions of symbols, not of the variables that a symbol might refer to.

(5) A property list can exist that is not attached to a symbol. Such property lists are accessed using **getf** and updated using **setf**.

Exercises

(1) Define the function **putprop** that is specifically designed to update property lists. A call of the form (**putprop** *name value property*) causes the property *property* of *name* to have the value *value*.

(2) Use property lists to represent information about the cost and model numbers of a set of different makes of automobiles. For example, you might include that a Mercedes 380SL costs $45,000, a BMW 320i, $15,000, a Plymouth Volare, $8,000, and a Toyota Tercel, $6,000. Now write a function that, given a list of cars as input, returns the model of the least expensive car.

(3) A common use of property lists is to "mark" symbols for various purposes. For example, we can use "marking" to speed up the set intersection function we wrote as an exercise in the last chapter (recall that set intersection takes two lists, and returns the elements that they have in common). The idea is to go through one list of elements and "mark" them by putting something on their property lists. For example, we can set the **mark** property of each symbol to **t**. Then we can go through the second list, and collect only those elements whose **mark** property is **t**, and return these as the set intersection.

This function is fast because it requires running through each list only once, while the version you wrote at the end of the last chapter had to run through one list once for every element of the other list.

Write a version of set intersect that uses property lists as described above. Remember that we want elements to appear only once in the answer, no matter how many times they appear in the input.

If you are not careful, your version of this function may leave marks on symbols when it is finished. Then subsequent calls may mistake these old marks for current markings and give the wrong answer. Be sure that your version of set intersection does not behave this way.

Note that this hopped up version of set intersection is intrinsically more limited than the previous version. What is this limitation?

(4)   We can implement a sort of virtual property list using a technique known as *inheritance.* For example, suppose we stated that a canary was a bird, and that a bird has wings. We would like to be able to ask the question "Does a canary have wings?" and get a positive answer. One way to do this is to store these facts as properties. For example, we can assert **(setf (get 'bird 'wings) t)**, meaning that birds have wings, and **(setf (get 'canary 'bird) 'isa)**, meaning that a canary is a bird. This latter assertion is sometimes called an "isa–link".

We now need a special function **inherit–get**. **inherit–get** will get two arguments, just like **get.** It will try to do a **get** first, and if this succeeds, will return the value **get** returns. However, if **get** fails, **inherit–get** will use **get** to get the **isa** property of its first argument. If it finds one, **inherit–get** will examine the resulting value to see if it has the desired information. **inherit–get** will keep on going up this "isa hierarchy" until it finds the property requested or it runs out of isa-links.

For example, suppose we evaluated **(inherit–get 'canary 'wings)**. **inherit–get** will first try a **get** of the **wings** property of **canary**. When this returns **nil**, **inherit–get** will do a **get** of the **isa** property of **canary**. This returns **bird**. **inherit–get** then does a **get** of the **wings** property of **bird**, and gets the answer **t**. **inherit–get** returns this as its result.

In general, **inherit–get** may go through any number of iterations before it fails or finds an answer. For example, if we evaluated **(inherit–get 'canary 'alive)**, we would first check **canary**, and then **bird** for an **alive** property. These both fail, so we check the **isa** property of **bird** and find that it **isa animal**. This may not have the desired information either, so we move up the hierarchy again. The **isa** property of **animal** might be **living–thing**, which should carry the target information.

Write a version of **inherit–get** that works as described.

Chapter 8

Control Over Evaluation
and Function Application

8.1. Introduction

Property lists are one way in which LISP begins to look less like other programming languages. Another way in which LISP differs from many other
languages is in the flexible way the user can control the evaluation of forms
and the application of functions. So far, whenever we wanted to apply a
function to some arguments, we have had to put the function and arguments in a list. Then we must enter the resulting form to the LISP interpreter for it to be evaluated. But we have no way of applying a function to
some arguments under program control; similarly, we have seen no way for
a program to evaluate a form on its own.

We may want to do such things for a number of reasons. For example, if
we had some way to evaluate forms *within* a program, then our program
could store code as data, and retrieve and execute different pieces of code
in different situations. This would provide us with an alternative control
structure to the more conventional kind. Even more radically, we could
have a program that built up forms as it ran, and then evaluated these
forms dynamically. In effect, such a program would be writing code that it
then would execute.

Similarly, if we could apply a function to some arguments under program control, we would also achieve some additional flexibility. For example, we could then write functions that accepted other functions as arguments. Thus a single function accepting a function as an argument would be able to do many different things, depending on the function it was passed. Without such an ability, what a given function could do would be much more confining.

LISP provides both these additional levels of flexibility. In this chapter, we examine a number of ways in which LISP allows the user to apply a function to arguments under program control. In particular, we discuss LISP functions for applying a function to a single set of arguments, as well as functions that can apply a function repeatedly to any number of sets of arguments. These latter functions are called *mapping functions.* We also show how the user may evaluate forms dynamically, under program control.

8.2. Functions as Arguments

Suppose we want to write a function that determines the sum of the first **n** integers. We could write a straightforward version of this function as follows:

```
-> (defun sum-of-ints (n)
      (do ((i n (1- i))
           (result 0 (+ i result)))
          ((zerop i) result)))
SUM-OF-INTS
-> (sum-of-ints 5)
15
-> (sum-of-ints 10)
55
->
```

Now suppose we want to write a function that computes the sum of the *squares* of the first **n** integers. With what we have seen so far, we would have to write a function that would be completely distinct from the one we just wrote. And if we want to write a function that computes the sum of the cubes of the integers, or the sum of their square roots, we would have to write distinct functions for each case. This is annoying, since the logic of computing the sum of the squares, etc., is almost identical to computing the sum of the integers, and we would like to take advantage of this similarity.

124

To do so, we would have to be able to write a function **sum–loop** that computes the sum of an arbitrary function of the first **n** integers. **sum–loop** looks almost identical to **sum–of–ints**, except that instead of just adding **i** to **result**, **sum–loop** would first compute an arbitrary function of **i**. This arbitrary function would be supplied as an argument to **sum–loop**. For example, to compute the sum of the squares of the integers, we would supply **sum–loop** with a function that computes the square of its argument; to compute the sum of the square roots, we would supply it with the function **sqrt**. Thus, to compute the sum of the square roots of the first 10 integers, we would type **(sum–loop 'sqrt 10)**. It would be **sum–loop**'s job to apply **sqrt** to each integer from 1 to 10 and add up the results.

Our first attempt at writing the function **sum–loop** might look something like the following:

```
(defun sum–loop (func n)
   (do ((i n (1– i))
        (result 0 (+ (func i) result)))
       ((zerop i) result)))
```

Here **func** is meant to be a parameter that will be supplied a function as an argument. For example, if we evaluate **(sum–loop 'sqrt 10)**, **func** will be assigned the value **sqrt**. The idea is for **sum–loop** to apply this value to each integer, and collect the result.

However, **sum–loop** has an important bug in it. Can you find it? Look at the piece of code that purports to apply the function argument to **i**. What it actually says is to apply the function **func** to **i**. If **func** happens to have a function definition, LISP will use this definition to evaluate the form **(func i)**, just as it would any form that is a list beginning with a symbol. For example, if we had previously defined **func** to compute cube roots, applying **func** to **i** will always compute the cube root of **i**, regardless of what value we assign **func** when we call **sum–loop**. Of course, if **func** has no function definition, we will always get an error when we attempt to apply **func**, regardless of its assigned value.

This confusion results because we want to apply the *value* of **func** to an argument. But LISP looks at a symbol's function definition, not its value, when attempting to interpret that symbol as a function.

To write a proper version of **sum–loop**, we need some way of applying a function to an argument ourselves. That is, we would like to take a symbol whose value is a function, and apply that value to an argument. Right now, the only way we know how to apply functions to arguments is by putting the actual function name and arguments in a list and asking the interpreter to evaluate it. This will only work if we know in advance what the function is. This will not be the case if the function is supplied as an argument.

8.3. apply and funcall

To rectify this situation, LISP provides a set of functions that apply functions under user control. One such function is called **apply**. **apply** takes two arguments. The first argument should be a function, and the second, a list of actual arguments to that function. For example, let us use **apply** to apply the function **cons** to the actual arguments **a** and **(b c)**. We do this by supplying **apply** with one argument that evaluates to the symbol **cons**, and another argument that evaluates to the list of actual arguments to **cons**, in this case **(a (b c))**:

```
-> (apply 'cons '(a (b c)))
(A B C)
```

The above expression is equivalent to evaluating **(cons 'a '(b c))**. Note that we did not have to quote the individual elements of the list of arguments to **apply**. In fact, we had better not, because **apply** makes these values the actual arguments of the user-supplied function without further evaluation. Also, the second argument to **apply** should always be a *list* of arguments. For example, to use **apply** to apply **car** to the list **(a b c)**, I would have to type the following:

```
-> (apply 'car '((a b c)))
A
->
```

The second argument supplied here evaluates to **((a b c))**, the list of the single actual argument to **car**.

As another example, we can use **apply** to sum up all the numbers in a list. Note that it would be incorrect to evaluate a form like **(+ '(1 3 5 7))**, because + expects its arguments to be numbers, not lists. However, we can use **apply** to do just what we want:

```
-> (apply '+ '(1 3 5 7))
16
->
```

Here + is applied to all the arguments contained in the list. So this is just as if we typed (+ **1 3 5 7**).

In Common LISP, it is legal to use **apply** only on ordinary functions. Attempting to apply special functions like **setq** or **defun** will result in an error.

Standardization Note: Many versions of LISP allow one to **apply** other kinds of functions. The exact format and interpretation of applying functions other than ordinary functions will vary from LISP to LISP.

It is unusual to need to use **apply** on the top level of LISP, where the normal process of interpretation allows a simpler syntax. However, we could use **apply** to write a correct version of **sum-loop**:

```
-> (defun sum-loop (func n)
      (do ((i n (1- i))
           (result 0 (+ (apply func (list i)) result)))
          ((zerop i) result)))
SUM-LOOP
->
```

This function definition is identical to the previous, buggy version of **sum-loop**, except for one new piece of code. This code, **(apply func (list i))**, applies whatever function is assigned to **func** to the argument **i** (recall that **apply** requires a *list* of arguments, so we needed to put the value of **i** in a list to conform to this condition). Now that we have gone through all this trouble, let us play with **sum-loop** a bit:

```
-> (sum-loop 'sqrt 5)
8.382332347441762
-> (sum-loop 'sqrt 10)
22.4682781862041
-> (defun squared (x) (* x x))
SQUARED
-> (sum-loop 'squared 5)
55
-> (sum-loop 'squared 15)
1240
-> (defun cubed (x) (* x x x))
CUBED
```

127

```
-> (sum-loop 'cubed 5)
225
-> (sum-loop 'cubed 15)
14400
->
```

Take a moment to appreciate the power of this simple function. By taking advantage of the ability to pass functions as arguments, we have been able to separate out the control structure of a process from other aspects of the computation. The result is a simple procedure that can be used for many potential applications, each one requiring only the specification of an appropriate function argument.

Most LISPs have a few functions that are alternative versions of **apply**. For example, Common LISP has a function called **funcall**. This works like **apply**, except that **funcall** expects the arguments to its function argument to appear one right after another directly after the function argument, rather than in a list. For example, to **apply cons** to the arguments **a** and **(b c)**, we would type **(apply 'cons '(a (b c)))**. But to use **funcall** to do exactly the same thing, we would type **(funcall 'cons 'a '(b c))**.

funcall accepts as many arguments as its function argument requires. Like **apply**, it is legal to pass **funcall** only ordinary functions as arguments.

For example, if we wrote **sum-loop** with **funcall** instead of **apply**, the code would look like this:

```
-> (defun sum-loop (func n)
      (do ((i n (1- i))
           (result 0 (+ (funcall func i) result)))
          ((zerop i) result)))
SUM-LOOP
->
```

In this particular application, using **funcall** makes the code a bit simpler than would using **apply**, since we did not have to put the argument in a list.

Standardization Note: If you are using some LISP other than Common LISP, and you tried the original, buggy version of **sum-loop**, you might have found that it actually works. This is because of a seldom used feature of some LISPs. In some LISPs, the interpreter will try to use the *value* of a symbol as a function if the symbol has no function definition. In such a LISP, it is possible to do the following:

```
-> (setq x 'cons)
CONS
-> (x 'a '( b c))
(A B C)
->
```

Here **x** has no function definition, so LISP checks its value. Its value happens to be the function **cons**, so LISP applies this function to the arguments in the expression.

While this feature is not part of the Common LISP language, it is apt to be found in some implementations. In any case, it is a terrible idea to depend on this feature. Code depending on this feature will work quite differently if later on **x** is given a function definition. Hence it is much wiser to use **apply** or **funcall**.

8.3.1. The FUNARG Problem

Suppose that a function being passed to another function as an argument contains some free symbols. How to interpret these free symbols is a problematic issue. For example, a free symbol may refer to one variable in the context in which it is supplied as an argument, and to quite a different variable in the context in which that function is used. Which variable should we assume the user intended? The question of interpreting the free symbols of a function passed as an argument is sometimes called the *functional argument* or *funarg* problem.

In Common LISP, a free symbol of a function being applied within another function has the usual interpretation. That is, it refers to the last special variable created that is associated with the given symbol, or to the global variable associated with that symbol. In other words, they will ordinarily be interpreted in the context that exists when the function is applied.

It is possible to create a kind of function in which free symbols will always be interpreted in the context in which that function was *created,* rather than in the context in which it is *applied.* This means that subsequent changes to the variables associated with its free symbols will have no effect whatsoever on that function's performance. Such a function is called a *closure.* We will not discuss closures further here. Instead, we will give them special attention in Chapter 12.

8.4. eval

The functions **apply** and **funcall** give the user control over one aspect of evaluation, namely, function application. But what about giving the user control over evaluation itself? That is, suppose we want to write a function that is given a form as an argument, but evaluates that form itself, perhaps depending on some circumstances. A case where such a need arises is in writing a conditional evaluation function, such as **if**. Of course, **if** is already defined in Common LISP. But for the sake of an example, suppose we were given only **cond**, and had to write an **if**-like function ourselves. The syntax of a call to our version of **if** might be something like

> (**our–if** *test* ' *true-form* ' *false-form*).

(We need to use the quotes here to overcome LISP's inclination to evaluate arguments. If would be nicer if we knew how to write functions that do not cause their arguments to be evaluated. We will see how to do this in Chapter 12. Until then, we will have to bear with this awkwardness.)

For example, a call of the form

> (**our–if** (> *n* 3) '(– *n* 3) '(+ *n* 3))

would cause 3 to be added to or subtracted from the global variable *n*, depending on the value of that variable. Note that it is important to do the evaluation of the second and third arguments under program control. There may be a lasting side-effect from such an evaluation, and it would be correct to produce this side-effect only if the proper condition held. The first argument is supposed to get evaluated all the time, so it is safe to let LISP do this for us.

We might consider having **our–if** use **apply** to do its conditional evaluation. That is, we can evaluate a form like (– *n* 3) by applying its **car** to its **cdr**. But this would not work in general. For example, if the form contained a special function, such as **setq** or **cond**, **apply** will not be able to handle it. And of course, the form might be a variable or a constant, and using **apply** would not be appropriate for those cases either.

Fortunately, LISP provides a function that does just what we want. This function is called **eval**. **eval** takes one argument, which is evaluated. It should evaluate to a legitimate form. *LISP then evaluates this value again.*

For example, consider the following:

```
-> (setq x '(cons 'a '(b c)))
(CONS 'A '(B C))
-> (eval x)
(A B C)
->
```

Here we set **x** to the value **(cons 'a '(b c))**. When we evaluate the call to **eval**, **x** is evaluated, returning its assigned value. Then **eval** evaluates this expression, just as if we typed it into the interpreter directly.

As another example, consider the following:

```
-> (setq a 'b)
B
-> (setq b 'c)
C
-> a
B
-> b
C
-> (eval a)
C
->
```

To evaluate **(eval a)**, LISP first evaluates the argument supplied. This produces the value **b**. So **b** is passed to **eval** as the actual argument. **eval** now evaluates this value, just as if we typed it in for the top level of LISP to interpret. Since the value of **b** is **c**, the latter value is returned by **eval**.

We can also use **eval** to execute a piece of code we create on the fly. For example, consider the following:

```
-> (eval (cons '+ '(2 3)))
5
->
```

Here the argument to **eval** evaluates to the list **(+ 2 3)**. This is then passed to **eval**. **eval** treats its actual argument the same way the LISP interpreter would if we typed it in, so it returns the result **5**.

This particular usage of **eval** reveals a significant fact about LISP. Since the data to LISP, s-expressions, are of the same form as expressions of the language itself, it is perfectly possible to have LISP programs that write code as they run, and then execute this code later on. The example above is a rather trivial instance of this, but this feature can be exploited in much more dramatic ways.

Let us first use **eval** to write a function definition for **our–if**. Clearly, **our–if** should be a function of three arguments. We will assume that the first has already been evaluated enough, but that either the second or the third should be evaluated again depending on the value of the first argument. So we have the following simple definition:

```
(defun our–if (test true false)
    (cond (test (eval true))
          (t (eval false))))
```

Or, if you prefer

```
(defun our–if (test true false)
    (eval (cond (test true)
                (t false))))
```

Either of these will do what we want:

```
-> (setq *n* 5)
5
-> (our–if (> *n* 3) '(- *n* 3) '(+ *n* 3))
2
-> (setq *n* 1)
1
-> (our–if (> *n* 3) '(- *n* 3) '(+ *n* 3))
4
->
```

8.4.1. Context Problems with eval

eval should be used with some care. Whenever we evaluate a form using **eval**, we are likely to evaluate it in some context in which the form has a different meaning than we intended. For example, suppose our function **our–if** happened to contain a free occurrence of the symbol *n*. That is, suppose its definition were as follows:

```
(defun our–if (test true false)
    (setq *n* 1)
    (eval (cond (test true)
                (t false))))
```

(True, this is a bit contrived, but we could imagine a more complicated example in which the use of a free symbol by a function that also used **eval** were not so far-fetched.) Now if we evaluated the same form we used above, we would get a different result:

```
-> (setq *n* 5)
5
-> (our-if (> *n* 3) '(- *n* 3) '(+ *n* 3))
-2
->
```

We get this surprising result because the symbol *n* is evaluated in one context when the first argument is evaluated, and in another when the next argument is evaluated. That is, the first argument is evaluated in the context of the function call, in which *n* has the value **5**. However, the value of the second argument is evaluated in the context of **our-if**, in which *n* always has the value **1**.

We would get the same bizarre behavior if *n* happened to be a formal parameter of **our-if** and was declared to be special. This case is even more insidious, because it is more transparent.

In sum, our variation on **our-if** is a function that will work fine, unless one of its arguments just happens to contain the symbol *n*. The moral is that we need to be careful when using **eval** to be sure that we are evaluating an expression in the context in which we intend it to be interpreted.

Standardization Note: Some LISPs allow the user to specify a context within which to evaluate an expression, so that problems such as this one can be addressed directly. Common LISP does not encourage this practice. Instead, the philosophy seems to be to avoid constructions that create this danger. This is probably best, as context manipulation mechanisms are invariably awkward and implementation-dependent.

8.5. Mapping Functions

Suppose we want to do the same operation not just to a single set of arguments, but to several sets of arguments. For example, rather than just add x to y, suppose we also want to add a to b, c to d, and so on. LISP provides us with a convenient way to express such computations that involves passing functions as arguments. The technique is called *function mapping*.

The idea behind function mapping is the following. Suppose we had a function of one argument. Normally, we would simply apply this function to its argument. If we want to apply the same function to several different arguments, however, we put these arguments into a list. Then we instruct LISP to apply the function to each element of this list.

Of course, we need some way to instruct LISP to apply a function to each element of a list. We could write a **prog** or a **do** that does this for a user-supplied function. But LISP provides us with a built-in mechanism that both eliminates the need to write such a function and is usually more efficient to boot.

LISP accomplishes this by supplying the user with functions to do function mapping. The function mapping functions take functions as arguments. They also take as arguments *lists* of the actual arguments to those functions. Then the mapping function applies its function argument to each element of its argument list.

For example, suppose we want to add 1 to the values 100, 200, and 300. Rather than write three separate computations **(1+ 100)**, **(1+ 200)**, and **(1+ 300)**, I could use a mapping function to apply the function **1+** to the list of actual arguments **(100 200 300)**. One such mapping function is named **mapcar**. This can be used to perform the desired computation as follows:

```
-> (mapcar '1+ '(100 200 300))
(101 201 301)
->
```

Here we supplied **mapcar** with an argument that evaluated to the function **1+**, and an argument that evaluated to a list of arguments to this function. **mapcar** applied the function **1+** to each element of this list of arguments; it returned as its result the list of each resulting value.

Observe that **mapcar** allows us to perform a kind of indefinite repetition. In the example above, it only performed the equivalent of a fixed number of function applications. But suppose we call **mapcar** as follows:

```
-> (mapcar '1+ x)
```

x may be assigned a list of arbitrary length. Since each element of the list is treated as an argument to **1+**, evaluating the above expression may result in an arbitrary number of calls to **1+**.

If the function we wish to use repeatedly requires more than one argument, we can supply more than one argument list to **mapcar**. For example, suppose we want to add 1 to 100, 2 to 200, 3 to 300, and 4 to 400. Here we need two argument lists, the list **(1 2 3 4)** and the list **(100 200 300 400)**. Then we can use **mapcar** to apply + to these lists of arguments:

```
-> (mapcar '+ '(1 2 3 4) '(100 200 300 400))
(101 202 303 404)
->
```

mapcar evaluates all its arguments. Then it applies the first argument to the **car**s of each latter argument. So + gets applied to **1** and **100**. Then **mapcar cdr**s down the argument lists, and applies + again, this time to **2** and **200**, and so on. **mapcar** collects the results of these computations and returns them all in a list when it is finished.

As another example, suppose we want to know which elements in a list are atoms. We could write an iterative or a recursive function to do this, but it is easier just to use **mapcar**:

```
-> (mapcar 'atom '(a b c (x y) nil (a b) x y))
(T T T NIL T NIL T T)
->
```

atom is a function of only one argument, so there is only one list of arguments supplied to **mapcar**. **atom** is applied to each element of this list, and the resulting values are collected into a list and returned as the value of the call to **mapcar**.

8.5.1. The Various Mapping Functions

There are a number of different mapping functions in LISP. Each one goes down its lists of arguments, and applies a user-supplied function to consecutive sets of arguments. Mapping functions differ from one another in exactly how they go down a list and in what value they choose to return, but the basic idea behind all of them is the same.

mapc

Sometimes the values returned by **mapcar** are less interesting than the side-effects that transpire. For example, suppose we had a function **paint** that let us put a particular color value under the **color** property of a symbol:

```
-> (defun paint (object color)
       (setf (get object 'color) color))
PAINT
-> (paint 'wall4 'white)
WHITE
-> (get 'wall4 'color)
WHITE
->
```

Now suppose we wanted to "paint" a number of symbols. We could do so using **mapcar** as follows:

```
-> (mapcar 'paint
              '(barn house lenin)
              '(white blue red))
(WHITE BLUE RED)
-> (get 'barn 'color)
WHITE
-> (get 'house 'color)
BLUE
-> (get 'lenin 'color)
RED
->
```

paint is a function of two arguments, so we supply two argument lists to **mapcar**. This worked fine, but note that **mapcar** had to **cons** up the value **(white blue red)** in order to return this as its result. This is wasteful, since we have no use for this value in our example, and only throw it away after it is created. As we mentioned above, **cons**ing is expensive. So LISP gives us a mapping function that acts just like **mapcar** except that it does not bother much with a value. This function is called **mapc**. **mapc** always returns its *second* argument. (Do not waste your time trying to puzzle out the motivation for the names of mapping functions – there is not much of one. However, there is nothing to prevent you from creating your own version of these functions with better names, if you like.)

Standardization Note: In some LISPs, **mapc** returns **nil** rather than its second argument.

Let us use **mapc** for the example above:

```
-> (mapc 'paint
         '(barn house lenin)
         '(white blue red))
(BARN HOUSE LENIN)
-> (get 'barn 'color)
WHITE
-> (get 'house 'color)
BLUE
-> (get 'lenin 'color)
RED
->
```

Here we get the same side-effect as with **mapcar**, but save a little overhead by returning a less interesting value.

mapl and maplist

There is also a set of mapping functions that apply a function to the whole list given as an argument to the mapping function, and then to successive **cdr**s of these arguments. This is easier to do than to say. For example, **mapl** is the **cdr** equivalent of **mapc**, and **maplist** is the **cdr** equivalent of **mapcar**:

```
-> (maplist 'cons '(a b) '(x y))
(((A B) X Y) ((B) Y))
-> (maplist 'list '(a b) '(x y))
(((A B) (X Y)) ((B) (Y)))
->
```

In the first example, **maplist** first applies the function **cons** to the entire the argument lists, i. e., to **(a b)** and **(x y)**. (This is in contrast to **mapcar**, which would have applied the function to the first element of these lists, **a** and **x**, respectively.) The resulting value is **((a b) x y)**. Next, **maplist** applies **cons** to the **cdr**s of the two argument lists, namely, to **(b)** and **(y)**, to yield the list **((b) y)**. The **cdr** of each of these two values is **nil**, so **maplist** stops and puts the values it has computed so far in a list. This list is returned as the result shown above.

As you might imagine, these mapping functions are not used very frequently. In fact, it is hard to think of a non-contrived example of the use of **mapl**.

137

Standardization Note: In most LISPs prior to Common LISP, **mapl** is called **map**. In Common LISP, the symbol **map** is used to name a more elaborate function that applies to data types other than lists, and which returns an interesting value.

8.5.2. The apply-append Trick

It is often the case that we use a function to return a (possibly empty) list of objects that we wish to scrutinize further. If we end up using a mapping function to apply such a function to a list of arguments, we will get a list of lists of objects to further scrutinize. For example, an expression of the form **(mapcar 'find–candidates list–of–arguments)** may return a value like **((a b c) nil (d e) nil (f g h))**, where each element represents the result of each call to **find–candidates**.

A problem with this result is that it contains some list structure that only gets in the way of further computation. The results of each application of **find–candidates** are returned individually wrapped. In our subsequent computation, we would like to examine each item **a**, **b**, **c**, **d**, etc., in turn. But we do not care to know which elements were returned together. Thus we would like to get rid of the list structure that **mapcar** creates, and instead work on the list **(a b c d e f g h)**.

A clever way to do this is to **apply** the function **append** to the value **mapcar** returns. Recall that **append** expects any number of arguments, each of which is a list, and returns a single list containing all the elements of these lists. Since **apply** applies a function to a list of its arguments, **apply**ing **append** to the value **mapcar** returns will produce a single list of the form desired. Let us try an example:

```
-> (apply 'append '((a b c) nil (d e) nil (f g h)))
(A B C D E F G H)
->
```

Hence a construct of the form

(apply 'append (mapcar 'find–candidates list–of–arguments))

will return a list of all the candidates that **find–candidates** finds from each application to the arguments in **list–of–arguments**. This is a useful construct to employ whenever we want to use **mapcar** to apply a function that we expect to return a list, and when only the elements of that list are potentially interesting.

There are a few other mapping functions, but understanding them involves some appreciation of LISP internals. For this reason, we will discuss them in Chapter 15.

8.6. Summary

(1) LISP allows the user to supply functions as arguments to other functions. The user may then control function application himself. The functions **apply** and **funcall** can be used to apply a function to some arguments.

(2) **apply** takes two argument. The first should be a function, and the second, a list of actual arguments to that function. **apply** applies the function to the arguments and returns whatever value the function returns. The function **funcall** is similar to **apply**, but accepts the arguments to the function argument "in-line", rather than in a list. **funcall** accepts as many arguments as are needed for the function it is to apply.

(3) LISP allows the user to evaluate forms under program control. The function **eval** is used to evaluate a form explicitly.

(4) **eval** takes one argument, which is evaluated. Then it evaluates that argument again. Care should be taken when using **eval** to ensure that expressions are evaluated in the correct context.

(5) *Function mapping* is a technique for applying a function repeatedly to a series of arguments. There are a number of function mapping functions. Each takes one argument, which should be a function, and other arguments that should be lists. There should be as many of these lists as the function argument requires. A mapping function will sequence through the elements of these lists, repeatedly applying the function argument.

(6) The mapping functions differ from one another in how they sequence through the argument lists and in what value they return. **mapc** and **mapcar** apply their function argument to successive **car**s of their argument lists; **mapl** and **maplist** to successive **cdr**s. **mapcar** and **maplist** return the list of the values their function argument returns after each application; **mapl** and **mapc** just return their second actual argument.

Exercises

(1)   What are the values of the following expressions:

   (a) **(eval (list 'car '(cdr '(b c))))**

   (b) **(eval (list 'car ''(cdr '(b c))))**

   (c) **(eval (cons 'cdr '('(a b c))))**

   (d) **(apply 'cdr '((a b c)))**

   (e) **(mapcar 'list '(a b) '(c d))**

(2)   Write a version of the function **make–assoc–list** using mapping functions. Recall that this function makes a list of the sort **assoc** uses out of two lists of items to be paired with one another. For example, **(make–assoc–list '(a b c d) '(1 2 3 4))** returns **((a 1) (b 2) (c 3) (d 4))**. Compare this version to the iterative version you wrote for the exercise at the end of Chapter 5.

(3)   Write your own version of **mapcar**, or of any of the other mapping functions. Your version will have to be more limited than the actual LISP function, since we do not yet know how to write functions that accept a variable number of arguments, as does the real **mapcar**. So write your version assuming your function argument will always be a function of exactly one argument.

(4)   Use a mapping function to write a better version of the matrix transpose function described in the exercises in Chapter 6. Recall that we represented a matrix as a list of lists; the transpose of **((a b) (c d))** would be **((a c) (b d))**. (Hint – the most concise version involves **apply**ing a mapping function.)

(5)   Using mapping functions, rewrite the set intersection function described at the end of Chapter 5.

(6)   Suppose a function returns a list of true or false values, e. g., **(nil nil t nil t nil)**. Suppose we want to know if this list contains any non-**nil** value. Use **eval** in conjunction with a logical operator to make this determination.

(7)   One problem with the various mapping functions is that there is no way to stop them before they have run to completion. In many appli-

cations, we want to apply a function to arguments repeatedly until a certain condition is true. Therefore, many LISPs include some function applying functions that apply their function only as long as it is necessary to do so.

Common LISP contain four such functions. One such function that combines flow of control and function mapping is called **some**. This is a function of two arguments, a function and a list. It applies the function to successive elements of the list *until* the function returns non-**nil**. Then it returns a non-**nil** value. It returns **nil** otherwise. For example, **(some 'numberp '(a b 2 c d))** should return non-**nil**.

The function **every** is like **some**, except that it stops as soon as one of the function applications returns **nil**. **every** then returns **nil** as its value. If all the applications return non-**nil**, **every** returns **t**.

The functions **notany** and **notevery** behave analogously.

Try writing your own versions of these functions. However, make such that your version of **some** returns the elements of the list from the point at which the test is first met. Thus, **(our-some 'numberp '(a b 2 c d))** should return **(2 c d)**.

(8)   Define a function **subset** that takes two arguments, a function and a list. **subset** should apply the function to each element of the list. It returns a list of all the elements of this list for which the function application returns non-**nil**. For example, **(subset 'numberp '(a b 2 c d 3 e f))** returns **(2 3)**.

(9)   We can use **eval** and **apply** to implement a programming technique called "data-driven" programming. In this technique, we store functions along with data, and use the data to suggest which functions to use to manipulate the data.

For example, suppose we had a data base of assorted objects, each of which we want to display according to different rules. People in the data base might be identified by first and last names, books by title and author, cars by make, year, and model, etc.. We could put the code to do this inside a big **cond**, but then we would have to hack this code in order to extend our function to other types of data. A more elegant solution is to first write separate functions for each type of datum:

```
-> (defun car-display (datum)
      (list (get datum 'year)
            (get datum 'make)
            (get datum 'model)))
CAR-DISPLAY
-> (defun book-display (datum)
       (list (get datum 'title) 'by (get datum 'author)))
BOOK-DISPLAY
->
```

and so on. Now we attach one such function to the **display-fn** property of each datum:

```
-> (setf (get 'car13 'display-fn) 'car-display)
CAR-DISPLAY
-> (setf (get 'book7 'display-fn) 'book-display)
BOOK-DISPLAY
->
```

etc. Of course, we would need to define the other properties of these data as well.

Now we can write a generic display function, **item-display**. This function picks the display function off the property list of the item to be displayed, and applies it to that item. We can extend our displaying capability to new types of data items without modifying this function at all. Instead, we simply write a new display function for the new data type and put it on the property list of each item of that data type.

Write the function **item-display**, and use it to display a small data base of objects.

Chapter 9

Lambda

9.1. Introduction

Sometimes it is desirable to define functions that have no name. In this chapter we list some of the reasons for desiring such functions. We show how to implement nameless functions using something called the *lambda notation.* We reveal a fact we have been hiding until now, namely, that the lambda idea underlies all LISP functions. Knowing this fact, we examine some alternative ways of defining functions in LISP. We also present a use of lambda as a way to introduce local variables. Finally, we assess its overall significance.

9.2. Functions without Names

When we use functions as arguments to other functions, as we did in the previous chapter, the need sometimes arises to create a little function that will only be used once. For example, in the last chapter, we used the function **sum–loop** to compute the sum of the cubes of the first **n** integers. To do this, we had to create the function **cubed** that computes the cube of its argument. This simple function will probably never be used again. Even if the need to compute a cube arose elsewhere in our program, it is too easy just to write (∗ **x x x**) in line than to bother with calling the function **cubed**.

Sometimes a "use-once, throw away" function is created because it fits a very specialized need. For example, suppose we had occasion to determine whether any element of a list were a symbol with property **color** and value **red**. We could write an iterative or recursive version of a function that tests a list for this, but it is easier to let **mapcar** do the work. To do this, we first define a function that tests a single symbol for this property:

```
(defun red-symbol-p (a)
   (and (symbolp a)
        (equal (get a 'color) 'red)))
```

red-symbol-p first makes sure that it is looking at a symbol; then it gets that symbol's **color** property and checks if it is **equal** to **red**.

Now to apply this to a list, we use **mapcar**:

```
-> (setf (get 'b 'color) 'red)
RED
-> (mapcar 'red-symbol-p '(a b c))
(NIL T NIL)
->
```

One problem with this code is that **red-symbol-p** is a rather silly function: we are fairly certain never to see it again, and it is a shame to have to waste the storage required to permanently house a new function definition, and waste the time required to think up a name for it.

A solution to this problem is to create a function without a name. To see what this would mean, let us consider more closely what it means to be a function. As we learned in Chapter 3, when we define a function using **defun**, we need to specify a name, a formal parameter list, and some function bodies. **defun** just stores the parameter list and bodies with the name until it needs them during function application. The name serves as a way of associating a formal parameter list with the bodies, and of referring to these some time later on.

Obviously, we need the bodies of code to have a function, because they define what it is the function does. We need a formal parameter list because this specifies which symbols that appear in the code should be treated as formal parameters. But the function name is not really intrinsic to there being a function. If we had some way of associating a formal parameter list with the code directly, we could bypass the need to use symbols to associate these two together.

Putting this another way, the essence of a function is the code that it executes and the way in which it manipulates formal parameters. The function name is not an essential part of this concept, but rather a convenient way of referring to it. In most programming languages, the concept of a function name and the idea of what it means to be a function are closely tied together, so that if you define a function, you must give it a name. And thus far in LISP, this has been the case. However, if we are willing to give up the convenience of being able to refer to every function by name, it should be possible to distill the essence of a function and thereby produce nameless functions.

To produce such a disembodied function, we need some way of associating some formal parameters with a piece of code without having to give it a name. This is done in LISP with something called the *lambda notation*. The lambda notation is merely a way of telling LISP that some symbols in a chunk of code are meant to be parameters. To use this notation, the user creates a list that begins with the symbol **lambda**. The next element of this list is a list of symbols, and the subsequent elements, some forms. The whole business represents a function, where the list of symbols denotes the formal parameters and the forms, the bodies of code.

For example, suppose we want to make a nameless version of the function **red–symbol–p**. We need to tell LISP that **a** is a formal parameter of this function, and that the code is the single expression **(and (symbolp a) (equal (get a 'color) 'red))**. To do this using the lambda notation, we would write the following expression:

```
(lambda (a)
   (and (symbolp a)
      (equal (get a 'color) 'red)))
```

This whole expression denotes a function. The list **(a)** following the occurrence of **lambda** represents the function's formal parameter list; the expression after this denotes the function's single body of code. The entire expression constitutes a function, which, except for the fact that it has no name, is entirely equivalent to the function **red–symbol–p** defined above.

Expressions that look like this are called *lambda expressions.* Do not type a lambda expression into LISP to evaluate it, though, *because lambda expressions are not function calls.* It would be meaningless to try to evaluate a list like the one above, because **lambda** is not a function. Rather, the whole expression we just typed, **lambda**, formal parameter list, and all, is a function. That is, we can stick this expression wherever we are used to having symbols designating functions. For example, we are used to putting function names in the beginning of a list, and then following them with arguments. To apply **red–symbol–p** to the value **b** we would type **(red–symbol–p 'b)**. Since the lambda expression given above is entirely equivalent to **red–symbol–p**, we can apply it to **b** by putting it in the equivalent position in a form:

```
-> ((lambda (a)
     (and (symbolp a)
          (equal (get a 'color) 'red)))
   'b)
T
->
```

Take a deep breath and examine this expression. Remember, LISP tries to evaluate lists by assuming that the first element of a list is a function. In this case, the first element of the list is a lambda expression. That is okay with LISP, because it thinks lambda expressions are functions. Then, as before, LISP evaluates the supplied arguments to produce the actual arguments. In this case, the single argument **'b** evaluates to **b**. Now LISP applies the function to the latter value. How? It creates new variables for each formal parameter of the function, and assigns each variable the value of the corresponding actual argument. Then it evaluates the function body. It returns the resulting value as the value of the expression.

This is just what happens when we apply named functions that we create using **defun**. The only difference is that, when the function is created via **defun**, we specify the function name and LISP retrieves the previously stored parameter list and function bodies at function-application time. With the lambda notation, the formal parameter list and bodies are presented directly to the interpreter. Like **defun**, the lambda notation allows you to specify any number of bodies of code in a definition. Thus the lambda notation is entirely equivalent to using **defun**, but with one less level of indirection.

This business might strike you as a rather convoluted way of doing a simple thing. After all, could we not just have evaluated the expression **(and (symbolp 'b) (equal (get 'b 'color) 'red))** and skipped all this hairy stuff? Yes, we could have, in this case. But now let us go back to our **mapcar** example. Here we want to apply a function to a list, and with our lambda expression, we can do this as follows:

```
-> (mapcar
      '(lambda (a)
        (and (symbolp a)
              (equal (get a 'color) 'red)))
      '(a b c))
(NIL T NIL)
->
```

Remember, whenever you see a lambda expression, try to see a function. The expression above looks exactly like our original call to **mapcar** using **red–symbol–p**, except that here, the lambda expression appears where **red–symbol–p** was previously. The advantage of using the lambda notation is that it eliminates the need to create a permanently stored function named **red–symbol–p**. Instead, we create a "function essence" that is useful for expressing what we want to say, without having to dignify it by alloting it the name and permanent storage space granted to a more significant procedure.

Since the idea behind lambda is to abstract out the pure essence of what it means to be a function, some people also refer to the lambda notation as *lambda abstraction.*

Let us apply the lambda notation to a more compelling situation. Consider the function **sum–loop** that we defined in the previous chapter. As we mentioned above, **sum–loop** requires a function as an argument. Therefore, it became necessary to define little functions like **squared** and **cubed** just for the purpose of passing them to **sum–loop**. However, with the lambda notation, we can create these functions without going to so much trouble. For example, to define the function **cubed** in the last chapter, we did the following:

```
-> (defun cubed (x) (* x x x))
CUBED
```

Then we called **sum–loop**, passing it **cubed** as an argument, i. e.:

```
-> (sum–loop 'cubed 15)
14400
```

To do the same with the lambda notation, let us first express the lambda-expression equivalent of the function **cubed**. This would be the following expression:

```
(lambda (x) (* x x x))
```

Again, this is just the formal parameter list of the function and its function body preceded by the symbol **lambda**. Now, let us use this lambda expression in the call to **sum-loop**:

> -> (sum-loop '(lambda (x) (* x x x)) 15)
> **14400**

Using the lambda notation, we did not previously have to create a permanent function. Instead, we took the body of code we wanted to execute, (* **x x x**), and turned it into a function by putting it inside a lambda expression.

9.3. symbol-function and LISP Internals

The lambda expression is the basic internal mechanism with which functions are implemented in LISP. For example, when you use **defun** to define a function, **defun** actually builds a lambda expression from the arguments you give it and associates the lambda expression with a symbol. When you put that symbol in the beginning of a list to indicate a function call, LISP fetches the lambda expression and then uses it just as if it had appeared in the beginning of the list.

Thus if we could peek at the function definition that LISP stored with a symbol, we would see that it is actually kept as a lambda expression. In fact, the function **symbol-function** lets us do just this. **symbol-function** takes one argument, which should be a symbol. Then it returns the function previously associated with that symbol. For example, after defining **cubed** with **defun**, we can use **symbol-function** to see what LISP has actually attached to the symbol:

> -> (symbol-function 'cubed)
> **(LAMBDA (X) (* X X X))**
> ->

So the LISP interpreter is always dealing with lambda expressions when it comes to function application; we have been spared this detail until now because the use of **defun** for function definition insulates the user from having to specify lambda forms directly.

We can change the function definition associated with a symbol by using the special function **setf**, which we introduced in Chapter 7, in conjunction with function **symbol-function**. As before, we supply **setf** with the form we would like to use to access a value, and then with the value we would like returned. In this case, we supply **setf** with a call to

symbol–function, and with the lambda expression we would like as the definition of our function. For example, to define **cubed** using **setf**, we would type the following:

```
-> (setf (symbol-function 'cubed)
       '(lambda (x) (* x x x)))
(LAMBDA (X) (* X X X))
-> (cubed 3)
27
->
```

Using **setf** in this fashion is actually the most primitive LISP nechanism for defining functions. That is, the LISP function **defun** is itself defined in terms of **setf** and **symbol–function**. You may occasionally need to use these functions yourself, for creating your own function-defining function, for example. However, it is much more convenient to use **defun** for the everyday business of defining new functions.

9.4. Some More Examples

Let us better familiarize ourselves with lambda by considering some more examples. First, here is a function like **cons**, but which accepts its arguments in the opposite order:

```
(lambda (x y) (cons y x))
```

Now let us apply it:

```
-> ((lambda (x y) (cons y x)) '(b) 'a)
(A B)
->
```

The formal parameter list of this lambda expression contains two elements, **x** and **y**, so the lambda expression denotes a function of two arguments. We obligingly supply two arguments, **'(b)** and **'a**.

To emphasize that lambda expressions are just functions without names, consider what we would do if we want to create a named function of this function. Suppose we want to call it **xcons**:

```
-> (defun xcons (x y) (cons y x))
XCONS
-> (xcons '(b) 'a)
(A B)
->
```

Both forms are equivalent, except that using **defun** produces a permanent version of the function that we can use elsewhere in our code; the pure lambda expression is used only once, because there is no way to refer again to the function that it defines.

Now here is a lambda of no arguments that always returns the symbol **hello**:

```
(lambda ( ) 'hello)
```

Since this is a function of no arguments, there will be no other elements in the list when we apply it:

```
-> ((lambda ( ) 'hello) )
HELLO
->
```

The corresponding named function would be something like

```
-> (defun say-hello ( ) 'hello)
SAY-HELLO
-> (say-hello)
HELLO
->
```

9.5. The Function function

When you supply a function as an argument to some other function, so that the function needs to be quoted, it is considered good practice to use a special function designed specifically for this purpose. This function is called **function**. Here is the **mapcar** example we used above done over with **function**:

```
-> (mapcar
     (function
       (lambda (a)
        (and (symbolp a)
             (equal (get a 'color) 'red))))
     '(a b c))
(NIL T NIL)
->
```

This example will behave exactly as if we used **quote** instead of **function**.

You should use **function** to quote named functions as well as lambda expressions. For example, if we call the function **sum-loop**, and pass it the function **sqrt** and then the function **(lambda (x) (* x x x))**, we should quote these using **function**:

```
-> (sum-loop (function sqrt) 10)
22.4682781862041
-> (sum-loop (function (lambda (x) (* x x x ))) 15)
14400
->
```

While **function** seems to act like **quote** in these examples, it has some other properties that are useful when creating a new function. These will be discussed in Chapter 12. Besides, stylisticly, many programmers think the use of **function** makes their code clearer. In the examples in this chapter, the more esoteric aspects of **function** are not exploited, so no great harm would have been done if you had used **quote** in these cases.

In Common LISP, you can abbreviate **function** in a manner resembling the way in which we can abbreviate **quote**. The characters #' before an expression are interpreted just as if a call to **function** surrounded that expression. For example, here are some of the expressions shown above, using #' instead of **function**:

```
-> (sum-loop #'sqrt 10)
22.4682781862041
-> (sum-loop #'(lambda (x) (* x x x )) 15)
14400
->
```

The # notation will be discussed further in Chapter 14.

9.6. Using LAMBDA for Creating New Variables

The purpose of lambda is to be able to specify functions. However, we can take advantage of lambda's built-in proclivity to create new variables to simplify some common programming constructs. In particular, lambda is useful as a programming device in situations in which we want to change the value of a variable for a short duration.

Programming situations often arise in which we would like to use a variable for a short while. For example, we often want to save a partial result that may be used for more than one purpose. Most likely we would not save this partial result by assigning it to a global variable, as we would rather localize the effects of our code. Instead, we might introduce a local variable using **prog**. For example, we might write a piece of code that looks like this:

```
(prog (temp)
   (setq temp (func1 x y z))
   (func2 temp)
   (func3 temp))
```

Here we save the value produced by **(func1 x y z)** in the local **prog** variable **temp**. Then we perform the computations specified by **func2** and **func3** without having to recompute this value.

There are two problems with this piece of code, though. First, if we do not have need of other **prog** facilities, such as branching or returning, the overhead of the **prog** will be excessive for the cause. Second, the **prog** construct is somewhat misleading, as it does not in itself suggest that all we want to do is use a variable for a while.

A more elegant way to achieve the same purpose is to use lambda. Instead of the **prog** above, we could do the following:

```
((lambda (temp) (func2 temp) (func3 temp))
 (func1 x y z))
```

In the **lambda** version, we make the symbol **temp** a formal parameter of a lambda expression; the calls to **func2** and **func3** comprise the bodies of this lambda expression. When the lambda expression is applied to its argument, LISP will first create a new variable for the parameter **temp**. Then this will get assigned the value of the argument supplied, **(func1 x y z)**. The bodies of the lambda expression are then evaluated, with the new variable assigned the desired value. Of course, when we finish applying the lambda expression, new variable associated with **temp**

152

ceases to exist. So changing **temp** within the lambda expression can only have local effects.

This does the job about as efficiently as possible, although one might complain that, if this is elegance, it is an unsightly elegance at that. To provide a more convenient syntax for such expressions, Common LISP provides a special function called **let**. **let** has the following syntax:

> (**let** (($par1$ $val1$) ($par2$ $val2$) ... ($parn$ $valn$))
> $exp1$
> $exp2$
> ...
> $expm$)

A call to **let** causes the following to happen: Each of the parameters $par1$, $par2$, etc., is bound to the value of the corresponding $val1$, $val2$, etc. Then the expressions $exp1$ through $expm$ are evaluated. Finally, the parameters are restored to their old values.

let is really just a prettier way to express the same idea that we used lambda for above. For example, the lambda expression we used above involving **func1**, **func2**, and **func3** could have been written using **let** as follows:

> (**let** ((temp (func1 x y z)))
> (func2 temp)
> (func3 temp))

Most programmers find this more pleasing than allowing a lambda expression to appear explicitly.

There are several other Common LISP functions that are useful for when you need the temporary use of a symbol. For example, **let*** is similar to **let**, but assigns a value to each variable one at a time, so the expressions giving the values for subsequent **let*** variables can refer to previous **let*** variables; with **let**, all the assignments are done as if in parallel. (The situation is reminiscent of the relation between **do** and **do*** described in Chapter 5.) The special function **progv** is also like **let**, but can be used to temporarily change the values of special variables. The functions **flet** and **labels** can be used to create temporary function definitions. You might wish to examine these functions at some point in the future.

9.7. The Significance of LAMBDA

Some LISP aficionados attach a great deal of significance to the role of lambda in LISP. This may be because the lambda notation is similiar to something called the *lambda calculus,* developed by the logician Alonzo Church. Having the lambda notation seems to give LISP an air of intellectual respectability that is generally lacking in most programming languages.

Lambda is nice because it detaches the idea of a function from the idea of a name. This allows us to have "disembodied" functions, as we have seen above. In addition, it makes LISP rather elegant internally. However, the whole business is probably less of a big deal than many people would like you to believe. Lambda is useful, but most LISP programs would work just as well if lambda did not exist as a separate abstraction.

9.8. Summary

(1)　It is useful to separate the idea of a function from the need to name a function. The *lambda notation* is a way to specify a function without having to specify its name. It is useful to have such functions when they will only appear once in our code, and hence when we do not want to bother to name them and give them permanent storage space.

(2)　We create functions using lambda by building a *lambda expression.* A lambda expression is a list beginning with the symbol **lambda**. Following this should be a list of symbols, and then any number of forms. The list of symbols is interpreted as the list of formal parameters of the function, and the forms as the bodies of that function.

(3)　Lambda expressions can appear wherever LISP expects to find a function. For example, they can appear in the beginning of a list to be evaluated, or as a function argument to **apply** or to a mapping function.

(4)　Internally, LISP function definitions are kept as lambda expressions. **defun** allows the user to create function definitions without having to specify the lambda expression explicitly. **symbol–function** retrieves the function definition of a symbol.

(5)　While lambda is basically a function definition mechanism, one can also think of it as a way to control the scoping of variables. For example, the construct **((lambda (x) ...code...) arg)** is a good way to temporarily assign **x** to the value of **arg** for the duration of the evaluation of ...**code**.... The special function **let** enables us to express the same idea in a more elegant manner.

(6) The function **function** should be used to quote function arguments, including both lambda expressions and named functions. **function** is necessary for the proper handling of some functions, and is clearer programming in any case.

Exercises

(1) Evaluate the following forms:

      (a) **((lambda (x) (cons x nil)) 'y)**

      (b) **(apply '(lambda (x y) (list y x)) '(1 2))**

      (c) **(mapcar '(lambda (x) (/ 1 (sqrt x)))**
           '(1 2 3 4 5))

      (d) **((lambda (x) (setq x 5)) (setq x 4))**

      (e) **((lambda (x y) (setf (get x 'eats) y))**
          'bird 'worms)

(2) A common use of lambda is to create a new function out of an existing function by "fixing" one of the existing function's formal parameters. Use lambda to create a function that uses * to always multiply its argument by π. (Note – You can use the Common LISP symbol **pi**, a constant whose value is the implementation's best approximation to π.)

(3) The function **sum–loop** in Chapter 8 takes a function and a number, and returns the sum of that function applied to the integers up to that number. Suppose we want to use **sum–loop** just to compute the sum of the first **n** integers. What function do we have to pass to **sum–loop** to do this computation? Write this function using lambda and call **sum–loop** with it.

(4) The following is a cute puzzle among LISP hackers: What is the shortest self-reproducing non-atomic LISP form? A self-reproducing form is one that evaluates to itself. **t** would be an example, as it always evaluates to **t**. But **t** is atomic, and we seek a non-atomic solution.

It is considered cheating if your solution involves any permanent side-effects. For example, we could trivially solve the problem by first defining a function **f**, say, that returns **(f)** as its value. But we disqualify this solution because defining a function counts as a permanent side-effect.

As you might suspect, the best known solution involves the use of lambda. Use lambda to produce the shortest non-atomic self-reproducing LISP form that you can find.

Chapter 10

Reading and Writing

10.1. Introduction

So far, the LISP functions and s-expressions we have created have not done any I/O of their own. They rely on the LISP interpreter to read in their arguments and type out their results. But, as in any programming language, we may want to read and write within a procedure as well.

In this chapter we present the most basic LISP input/output constructs. Then we show some methods for dealing with the input and output of LISP symbols with unusual names. We show how to do I/O with devices other than the terminal, and how to produce neatly formatted s-expressions. In the process, we introduce several new data types, called *strings, streams,* and *pathnames.* Finally, we demonstrate how we can use I/O together with the LISP function **eval** to implement the top level of LISP in LISP.

10.2. read and print

As you might expect, I/O in LISP is done with I/O functions. Since the basic units of data in LISP are s-expressions, most of these I/O functions deal with entire s-expressions. The most basic functions are called **read** and **print**. **read** is a function of no arguments. When **read** is called, it causes LISP to wait at the terminal for you to type in one s-expression. When one is entered, this s-expression is returned as the value of **read**.

For example, suppose we evaluate an s-expression that has a call to **read** in it:

```
-> (setq x (read))
(a b c)
(A B C)
-> x
(A B C)
->
```

This interaction with the interpreter requires some explanation. The second argument supplied to **setq** here is a call to the function **read**. This is a function of no arguments, so it appears alone in a list. The function **read** causes the interpreter to go to the terminal and wait for the user to type something in. If you try this example yourself, you will notice that the LISP system pauses, waiting for you to type something; in fact, if you are not on guard, you might think the system crashed, because the interpreter has not yet responded, as it ordinarily would. In this example, we typed in the value **(a b c)**, just as we do when we ask the interpreter to evaluate expressions. However, we did not quote this expression, because LISP was not going to evaluate it. Rather, it merely read in the expression as typed. **read** returned this s-expression as its value, and the computation proceeded. Here **setq** assigned **x** this value. Since **setq** returns its second actual argument as its value, LISP printed out this value on the terminal. So the first **(a b c)** was typed by me, the second by the interpreter. Then we queried LISP about the value of **x** just to make sure that everything was done right.

It might be nice to warn the user that the call to **read** was coming, however. We can do so by using the function **print** to display something on the screen. **print** is a function of one argument. This argument is printed on the terminal; it is also returned as the value of the call to **print**.

Standardization Note: You will occasionally find a LISP in which **print** returns something other than its argument: **nil**, for example.

Let us use **print** to display some message to the user, and then use **read** as we did above:

```
-> (prog1 (print 'enter) (setq x (read)))

ENTER (a b c)
ENTER
-> x
(A B C)
->
```

We used a **prog1** here, which evaluates its arguments in order and returns the value of the first one. The first expression is a call to **print**. The argument supplied to **print** is evaluated to produce the actual argument **enter**. This is then given to **print**, which causes the argument to appear on the terminal. **print** causes a "newline" to appear before the object it prints, and a space to follow afterwards, hence the white space in this output. **print** also returns **enter** as its value. Then LISP starts evaluating the second expression of the **prog1**. This contains a call to **read**, so, as before, LISP pauses and awaits our response. We type in the s-expression (**a b c**). **x** is assigned this value. A **prog1** returns the value of its first argument, which in this case is **enter**. The interpreter prints this value out on the terminal, as it always does the value of an s-expression it has evaluated on the top level.

These simple examples illustrate some important facts about **read** and **print:**

- **read** does not prompt for input; it merely reads from the terminal. The programmer would have to have the program type out some message if he wants it to alert the user to input something (probably a good idea most of the time).

Standardization Note: In some LISPs, **read** automatically issues the current LISP prompt.

- **print** prints out a "newline" before it prints the desired object, and a single space afterwards. If you do not want either of these in your output, you can use the function **prin1** instead. **prin1** prints out only the object you give it, with no unasked for white space. If you want more blank lines, you can execute the function (of no arguments) **terpri**.

Standardization Note: In some LISPs, **print** does just what **prin1** does here - you have to supply all the white space yourself. Also, **terpri** is sometimes called **terpr**.

- A value printed by LISP and a value returned by a function are two different things. For example, evaluating the call to **print** above caused the value **enter** to be printed. However, **print** also returned **enter** as its value. LISP then printed out this value for us, because LISP always prints out the value of an expression it evaluates on the top level. Remember, though, that internally what counts is the value returned by a function. **print** causes the side-effect of something getting scribbled out on the terminal; but once this is done, the only value that will have any subsequent effect on the interpreter is the value that **print** returns.

- **read** and **print** always deal with whole s-expressions. These may be single atoms or large lists. We cannot directly read or print something like a line of text using **read** or **print**, because a line of text is not a kind of s-expression. We would have to use some other I/O functions to do such operations.

As a further example, suppose we want to write some code that requests a number from the user, computes its square root, and prints out the result. Let us write a loop that does this repeatedly:

```
-> (loop
     (print 'number>)
     (let ((in (read)))
       (if (equal in 'end) (return nil))
       (print (sqrt in))))

NUMBER> 16

4.0
NUMBER> 9

3.0
```

```
NUMBER> 25

5.0
NUMBER> end
NIL
->
```

Recall that the **loop** construct endlessly re-evaluates a sequence of forms. In this example, the first form in the sequence **prints** the symbol **number>**. The next form **reads** an input, and assigns it to the symbol **in**. Then it checks to see if **in** has the value **end**. If so, then the loop is exited. Otherwise, we assume that the input is a number, and compute and **print** its square root. Then the loop is repeated. Thus, in the transaction above, all the **number>**s were output by **print**; the numbers immediately following them were typed in by me. The results, of course, were output by the second occurrence of **print**.

A call to **print** always produces a "newline" and a space. Since we also created a blank line when we typed a carriage return to denote the end of our input, the entire transaction has quite a bit of white space in it. In particular, the white space between our input and the result is somewhat disturbing. If you want to eliminate some of this white space, we can use **prin1** instead of **print**:

```
-> (loop
     (print 'number>)
     (let ((in (read)))
          (if (equal in 'end) (return nil))
          (prin1 (sqrt in))))

NUMBER> 16
4.0
NUMBER> 9
3.0
NUMBER> 25
5.0
NUMBER> end
NIL
->
```

We can make the dialogue even prettier by outputting a "newline" after each result:

```
-> (loop
     (print 'number>)
     (let ((in (read)))
         (if (equal in 'end) (return nil))
         (prin1 (sqrt in))
         (terpri)))

NUMBER> 16
4.0

NUMBER> 9
3.0

NUMBER> 25
5.0

NUMBER> end
NIL
->
```

Note, there is nothing special about the symbol **number>**. This is just a symbol whose name happens to end with an angle bracket. If we want to print out something fancier, for example, a symbol ending with a space, we would have to have some way of specifying a space in a symbol name. Right now, we do not know how to do this.

We could try to print out a more informative message, however, by enclosing the message in a list:

```
-> (loop
     (print '(Please enter a number>) )
     (let ((in (read)))
         (if (equal in 'end) (return nil))
         (prin1 (sqrt in))
         (terpri)))

(PLEASE ENTER A NUMBER>) 38
6.164414002968976

(PLEASE ENTER A NUMBER>) 25
5.0
```

```
(PLEASE ENTER A NUMBER>) end
NIL
->
```

However, we would prefer this message to be printed without the parentheses around it. We can try to do this by using **mapc** to apply **print** to a list, but this does not have exactly the effect we seek:

```
-> (loop
     (mapc (function print) '(Please enter a number>) )
     (let ((in (read)))
         (if (equal in 'end) (return nil))
         (prin1 (sqrt in))
         (terpri)))

PLEASE
ENTER
A
NUMBER> 64
8.0

PLEASE
ENTER
A
NUMBER> end
NIL
->
```

Since **print** prints out a "newline" before each object, we get the output on several lines. Let us see if **prin1** does any better:

```
-> (loop
     (mapc (function prin1) '(Please enter a number>) )
     (let ((in (read)))
         (if (equal in 'end) (return nil))
         (prin1 (sqrt in))
         (terpri)))
PLEASEENTERANUMBER>64
8.0
PLEASEENTERANUMBER>end
NIL
->
```

prin1 prints an s-expression with no frills, so all the output runs together. Hence we are still in need of some way to print out characters like space which are not usually part of a symbol name.

10.3. Reading and Printing Symbols with Unusual Names

As the examples in the previous section illustrate, we sometimes wish to have a symbol whose name contains an unusual character. This might be a problem if that character normally serves some special function during reading. For example, if we want to have a symbol with a parenthesis in its name, we cannot just type it in. If we typed in **ab(cd**, say, LISP would think the parenthesis marked the beginning of a list, and our intention would get hopelessly garbled.

LISP provides a number of ways to input symbol names containing characters normally reserved for other purposes. One method is to precede the reserved character with the special character \ (backslash). LISP does not include the \ in the symbol's name, but it does include the following character, regardless of what it is. Thus to input the symbol alluded to above, we can type **ab\(cd**.

\ is sometimes called an *escape character* because it allows the following character to escape from its normal Common LISP interpretation. Note that part of the normal Common LISP interpretation of a character is the transformation of lower case to upper case upon reading. Therefore, if we precede an ordinary alphabetic character with an escape character, it would denote a different character than it would otherwise. That is, **abcd** would normally be read as denoting a symbol whose name is **ABCD**, but **a\bcd** would be read as denoting a symbol named **AbCD**.

If a name requires several special characters, preceding each with an escape character is awkward. For example, suppose we want to have a symbol whose name consisted of five letters with spaces in between them. We could type this in as follows using escape characters: **a\ b\ c\ d\ e**, i. e., by preceding every space by a \. But this is unappealing. To provide a more aesthetic mode of entry, Common LISP provides an alternative to escaping. If, instead of preceding each problematic character with a \, the whole sequence is surrounded by |'s (vertical bars), LISP reads the sequence of characters without interpretation. Thus the symbol named **a b c d e** can be entered by typing **|a b c d e|**. Once again, the vertical bars are not actually part of the symbol name, but merely serve to include unusual characters within its name. Since vertical bars can enclose a number of characters, the vertical bar is called the *multiple escape character*. In contrast, \ is referred to as the *single escape character*.

As for the single escape character, case distinctions are preserved within multiple escapes. That is, the symbol |a b c d e| contains all lower case characters. If we had wanted upper case here, we would have had to type |A B C D E|. Also, multiple escapes do not necessarily delineate a symbol's boundary. For example, ab| c |de is a perfectly fine Common LISP symbol. In fact, it is equivalent to having entered AB\ \c\ DE, as the characters not within the multiple escapes are converted to upper case, while escaped characters are not.

When we create a symbol whose name contains an unusual character, we have to be careful about how we print this symbol. In particular, we might print a symbol while writing an expression to a file. Later on, we may try to read this file back in. In this situation, it is important to write the symbol out in such a fashion so that it can subsequently be read correctly again.

For example, suppose we have entered a symbol by typing ab\(cd. It would be correct to print this out as AB(CD, but then we could not correctly read this output again later on. To guard against this happening, **print** always supplies enough escape characters to produce a LISP-readable name. This is done either by surrounding problematic symbol names with multiple escape characters upon printing, or by using single escape characters before problematic characters.

Since the top level of LISP uses **print** to output the values of the expressions it interprets, we can demonstrate this behavior as follows:

```
-> 'ab\(cd
|AB(CD|
```

Here LISP interpreted the input as designating the symbol AB(CD. Since this could not be read in correctly if it were printed out as is, **print** surrounded the symbol with multiple escape characters.

Standardization Note: I will assume here that multiple escape characters are always used to print problematic symbol names. However, your version of Common LISP may use single escape characters, or may use single escape characters in some situations and multiple escape characters in others.

Here are some additional examples:

```
-> '|ab(cd|
|ab(cd|
-> 'a\ b\ c\ d\ e
|A B C D E|
-> '|a b c d e|
|a b c d e|
-> 'AB\CD
ABCD
-> '|ABCD|
ABCD
->
```

All the symbol names that need special treatment in order to be read in are printed surrounded by multiple escape characters. Note in the last two examples that the single and multiple escape characters are superfluous, as there are no special or lower case characters in the symbol names. Since this is the case, LISP interprets these names just as if they were typed in without the aid of these devices; they are printed out accordingly.

We are now a step closer to being able to print out a symbol name that has a space in it, as we needed for our example in the last section. Let us try using **print** to print out a symbol name with some spaces in it as a prompt for our **sqrt** loop:

```
-> (loop
      (print '|Please enter a number> |)
      (let ((in (read)))
           (if (equal in 'end) (return nil))
           (prin1 (sqrt in))
           (terpri)))

|Please enter a number> | 27
5.196152422706632

|Please enter a number> | end
NIL
->
```

Here we passed **print** a symbol named **Please enter a number>** . The problem is that **print** always outputs such symbols with multiple escape characters, which is not exactly what we wanted. It would not have helped to enter the symbol name using single escape characters, because **print** would print this exactly the same way. We would rather print out a symbol with an unusual print name in a more pleasing format, without the associated escape characters. Since **print** will not do this for us, we need another function that will.

In Common LISP, such a function is called **princ**. **princ** is just like **prin1**, except that it prints its argument without using any escape characters. **princ** returns its argument as its value.

Standardization Note: In some LISPs, this function also goes under the name of **patom**, or some such.

Consider the following examples:

```
-> (princ '|a b c d e|)
a b c d e|a b c d e|
-> (princ 'ab\(cd)
AB(CD|AB(CD|
-> (progn (princ 'ab\(cd) (terpri))
AB(CD
NIL
->
```

In the first example, **princ** prints the symbol name without escape characters. This symbol is returned as the value of the call to **princ**, so the top level of LISP prints it out again. Since the top level normally uses **print** to do its output, the second time it is printed the symbol name is surrounded by multiple escape characters.

The second example is similar. In the third case, the call to **princ** is inside a **prog** and followed by a **terpri**, which forces a new line. **princ** causes **ab(cd** to be printed; the **terpri** causes us to move to a new line; finally, the top level prints the value of the **progn** (in this case, **nil**, the value always returned by **terpri**).

Let us use **princ** to produce, finally, a correct version of our **sqrt** loop:

```
-> (loop
     (princ '|Please enter a number> |)
     (let ((in (read)))
       (if (equal in 'end) (return nil))
       (prin1 (sqrt in))
       (terpri)))
```

Please enter a number> 1024
32.0
Please enter a number> end
NIL
->

In general, you should use **print** when your emphasis is on producing LISP-readable output, since **print** tries to output something that, when input by **read**, will produce an s-expression equivalent to that originally passed to **print**. You should use **princ** when you are interested in producing human-readable output. Note that the output of **princ** may not only not produce an equivalent s-expression when input by **read**, but may not even be acceptable LISP. For example, the expression **(princ '|Please enter a number> |)** will cause the following to be printed: **Please enter a number>** . This would be read in by **read** as four separate LISP symbols. Similarly, the expression **(princ 'ab\(cd)** will cause **AB(CD** to be printed, and this does not constitute a valid s-expression.

10.4. Strings

Although we have been quiet about it until now, there are actually a number of data types other than s-expressions supported by most LISP systems. One such data type that is relevant here is the *string*. A string in LISP is denoted by a sequence of characters with a " (doublequote) on either side. Strings evaluate to themselves. For example, all of the following involve strings:

```
-> "foo"
"foo"
-> "hello there"
"hello there"
-> "a b c d e"
"a b c d e"
-> (setq x "ab(cd")
"ab(cd"
-> x
"ab(cd"
->
```

A string looks very much like a funny symbol name surrounded by double-quotes rather than multiple escape characters. However, symbols are actually much more complex objects than strings. Symbols can have function definitions and property lists; strings can have neither of these. Symbols can be assigned different values and be used as variables; as is evidenced above, strings always evaluate to themselves.

A string is really nothing more than a sequence of characters. In contrast, a symbol has a number of different aspects, its name being merely one of these. The symbol's name is itself an actual string data type. For this reason, the name of a symbol is sometimes referred to as its *print name*. This terminology emphasizes the fact that a name is only one of several characteristics of a symbol. Thus, we might say the symbol **foo** has the print name "**FOO**", in addition to some possible value, function definition and property list.

Strings are useful primarily because they require less storage than symbols. This is the case precisely because strings do not require storage to support values, property lists, or function definitions. Thus if we are interested in a symbol only for its name, as we were in some of the examples above, it is economical to use a string instead.

The function **print** always prints strings with accompanying doublequotes. This is in keeping with **print**'s mission always to print out something that LISP can **read** back in. Similarly, **princ** prints out strings without quotation marks, in keeping with its intention to produce human-readable output. The best way to implement the prompt for our **sqrt** loop above, then, is to **princ** the appropriate string:

```
-> (loop
      (princ "Please enter a number> ")
      (let ((in (read)))
          (if (equal in ' end) (return nil))
          (prin1 (sqrt in))
          (terpri)))
Please enter a number> 1024
32.0
Please enter a number> end
NIL
->
```

This produces the output that we want, without entailing the overhead of storing an entire symbol.

Strings, as well as other miscellaneous LISP data types, will be discussed more fully in Chapter 18.

10.5. Redirecting I/O

Reading and printing can involve files and devices, not just the terminal. I/O to something other than the standard input or output is done in Common LISP by supplying an additional argument to an input or output function. This argument should be a *stream*. A stream is a special LISP data type used just for I/O. A stream serves as a source or sink of data to a Common LISP I/O function. Typically, streams are connected to files or terminals, or some other device; they serve as an interface between LISP and the operating system. (Actually, streams are rather general, and can refer to objects other than files or devices. For example, it is possible to use a stream to "read" from a LISP string. We shall not be concerned with such non-typical uses of streams here.)

To use a stream to do I/O with a given file, the user needs to set up a stream that refers to that file. This is done using the function **open**. Then a call to an input or output function that references this stream will do I/O with respect to the file attached to the stream, rather than the standard input or output device (usually the terminal). When finished with it, the user should close the stream using the function **close**.

For example, suppose we want to write some s-expressions to the file **sesame**. First, we need to set up a stream that refers to this file. We use **open** for this purpose:

```
-> (setq our-output-stream (open "sesame" :direction :output))
#<SESAME>
->
```

The first argument to **open** is a string naming the file we wish to read from. In this case, the file is named **sesame**. Next is a peculiar syntax that tells **open** how we want to use the file. In this case, we stated that the file is for output. (Don't be too put off by this notation. Symbols preceded by **:**s (colons) are *keywords* that certain Common LISP functions recognize. In this case, the keywords indicate that the **direction** of the I/O is *output*. We will discuss keywords more fully in Chapter 12.) **open** returns a stream connected to the file **sesame**. It is not really meaningful to talk about printing a stream, so LISP output the name of the file it refers to, preceding it with the characters #< and following it with a >.

Standardization Note: The convention for printing streams is not standardized in Common LISP. Therefore, it is possible that your implementation uses some different convention to print stream objects.

Now we want to write to this file. We do this by passing this stream as an additional argument to **print**:

```
-> (print '(a b c d e) our-output-stream)
(A B C D E)
-> (print 'razzamatazz our-output-stream)
RAZZAMATAZZ
->
```

As you can see, nothing much appeared on the terminal as the result of these calls to **print**, presumably because the output got sent to the file **sesame** instead. (Although, of course, the LISP interpreter printed the values of these expressions, quite independently of anything done by our explicit calls to **print**). Let us close the file and then try to read it back in:

```
-> (close our-output-stream)
NIL
-> (setq our-input-stream (open "sesame" :direction :input))
#<SESAME>
-> (read our-input-stream)
(A B C D E)
-> (read our-input-stream)
RAZZAMATAZZ
-> (close our-input-stream)
NIL
->
```

The first **close** terminated our output stream to the file **sesame**. Then we opened the file again for input, and read from it by supplying an additional argument to **read**. When we were done reading, we closed the input stream as well.

Standardization Note: close is assumed to return **nil** here, although the value of **close** is not part of the Common LISP specification and may vary from implementation to implementation.

Most LISP input/output functions conform to this redirection convention. For example, if you supply a stream as an additional argument to **princ**, it will output to the specified file.

As we suggested above, not supplying an optional stream argument to an I/O function causes that function to default to the standard input or standard output. Actually, the I/O function will default to the value of the variable ***standard–input*** or ***standard–output***, as the case may be. These variables are referenced by free symbols by the various I/O functions, so that changing their values will change the place to which I/O is directed by these functions.

10.5.1. Handling End-of-File Conditions

Suppose in the example above, we issued a third **read** from the file **sesame**. Since we had only written out two s-expressions to this file, doing so would amount to trying to read in more s-expressions that we had written out. **read** would have run into the "end-of-file", and would have generated an error.

If you do not know what to expect in a file, you might want your program to read until it encountered the end of a file. Since calls to **read** that encounter an end-of-file will typically generate an error, we need some mechanism to prevent this from happening, and, instead, signal the program that an end-of-file has been reached.

This can be done by supplying **read** with yet another couple of arguments. If a second argument of **nil** is given, **read** will not generate an error upon encountering an end-of-file. Instead, it will return the third argument of the call to **read**.

For example, if we read from the file **sesame** with calls of the form **(read our–input–stream nil 'tzadik)**, **read** would have returned the same expression as it did above for the first two cases. But if we made a third attempt to **read** from **sesame**, this latter version of the call to **read** would have returned the symbol **tzadik**, whereas the former version would have generated an error.

10.5.2. Pathnames

In the example above, we specified a file by supplying its name as a string to **open**. In general, though, files specifications can be quite complex. In most operating systems, files exist within directories, which are located on devices, which in turn may be part of a file system. In addition, there may be different types of files with the same name, such as a source file and an object file; for each such file, there may be different versions as well, corresponding to the times the file was modified.

Of course, the exact format and structure of a file specification will vary greatly from system to system. In Common LISP, you can always specify any file by passing functions such as **open** a string corresponding to the way in which the file might be specified in the given operating system. For example, the UNIX file **/usr/lisp/fun.l** could be specified simply by using the string "**/usr/lisp/fun.l**". In TOPS-20, the comparable file specification might be "**<lisp>fun.lsp.7**".

If you are doing a great deal of manipulation of file specifications within your program, however, you might find yourself writing lots of system-dependent code. To help alleviate this difficulty, Common LISP provides a data type called *pathname* that helps to standardize file specifications. A pathname has one component for each part of a file specification mentioned above. (If your file system is more complicated, for example, if it allows directories within directories, as UNIX does, then you will have to make one or more of these components a complex structure in some system-dependent way.)

You can create a pathname from a string or stream using the function **pathname**. You can then use the pathname as an argument to **open**, say. This in itself will not create any independence from the particular operating system. However, we can now do subsequent file specification manipulations by using other functions that operate on pathnames. For example, the functions **pathname-host**, **pathname-device**, **pathname-directory**, etc., all return various components of a pathname. We can use these and other pathname manipulation functions instead of writing system-dependent code to do the same for our particular operating system conventions.

You will probably not need to explore pathnames further unless your program is doing some rather elaborate file manipulation.

10.6. Pretty-printing

The function **pprint** (for "pretty-print") prints s-expressions in a nice format, generally using lots of white space. This is particularly useful for long s-expressions, or for s-expressions intended as LISP code, in which proper indentation may make the code more readable by humans.

For example, if we retrieve the function definition of a symbol, it may be incomprehensible if it is displayed as a long list. However, if we apply **pprint** to it, the output would be easily readable. Consider the function **recursive-member**, which we defined in Chapter 6. Let us apply **pprint** to its definition:

```
-> (pprint (symbol-function 'recursive-member))

(LAMBDA (E L)
  (COND ((NULL L) NIL)
        ((EQUAL E (CAR L)) L)
        (T (RECURSIVE-MEMBER E (CDR L)))))

NIL
->
```

pprint formats the code nicely, so this is a good way to check to see if you have really entered what you thought, or if you dropped a parenthesis somewhere.

Standardization Note: The exact format of output from **pprint** will vary from implementation to implementation. In addition, most LISPs have a function specifically designed to print out function definitions. While such a function is not included in Common LISP, it is relatively easy to write one.

10.7. format

Sometimes a programmer wishes to exert very precise control over how output appears. For example, the programmer may be concerned about the number of digits that appear in a floating point number, whether some fill character other than space should be used, whether commas should be printed after every three digits, and so on.

A facility to exercise such careful control over output exists in Common LISP under the auspices of the **format** function. The **format** function very loosely resembles a FORTRAN format statement. In particular, it allows you to specify a number of items to print, and a specification of how to print them.

The format function has two required arguments, and an indefinite number of optional ones. The required arguments are a destination, and a format specification string. The destination can be any stream, but usually it is **t**, meaning the standard output, or **nil**, meaning to return the would be output as a string rather than print it.

The format specification indicates how the remaining arguments are to be printed. The format specification string may contain ordinary text, with any number of *directives* mixed in. Ordinary text is simply printed. When a directive is encountered, the next argument to **format** will be printed according to the format specified by that directive.

Each directive begins with the character ˜ (tilde). The particular directive is specified by a single character following the tilde, although there may be numbers and other arguments between the tilde and the character. A large number of extremely complicated and specialized directives are available; we will not even begin to review them all here. Rather, we will merely demonstrate the overall idea.

For example, the character **O** can be used to print out an integer in octal. Let us try a simple example:

```
-> (setq n 342391)
342391
-> (format nil "n in octal is ˜O" n)
"n in octal is 1234567"
->
```

Here we passed an initial argument of **nil**, so that **format** did not print anything, but merely returned the computed string as its result. The second argument is the format specification string. It contains the single directive ˜O. Next comes the single argument corresponding to this directive. **format** builds a string consisting of the text in the specifier, but with the directive replaced by its corresponding argument in the appropriate format. Here this string was returned as the value of the call, although in most real situations, we would rather have **format** output it.

If we specify a number before the **O**, **format** will use at least that much space to print the result. For example,

```
-> (format nil "n in octal is ˜9O" n)
"n in octal is  1234567"
->
```

As we can see, the unnecessary space was padded by spaces. If we prefer, though, we can specify any padding character we like:

```
-> (format nil "n in octal is ˜9,'0O" n)
"n in octal is 001234567"
->
```

The comma above separates the number from the specification of the padding character, this is **0** (zero) precede by the prefix '(single quote).

Alternatively, we could use the modifier **:** to indicate that we want commas between every three characters:

```
-> (format nil "n in octal is ˜:O" n)
"n in octal is 1,234,567"
->
```

The directives **D**, **B**, and **X** are similar, but use decimal, binary, and hexidecimal radices, respectively.

As another example, consider the directive **P**. This causes a lower case **s** to be printed if the corresponding argument is not **1**, and prints nothing otherwise. Adding the modifier **:** here causes the previous argument to be processed again. This is useful in cases like the following:

```
-> (format nil "˜D boy˜:P left" 5)
"5 boys left"
-> (format nil "˜D boy˜:P left" 1)
"1 boy left"
->
```

In these examples, the directive **D** is used to specify that the first item should be printed in decimal notation. The next directive states that an **s** should be printed if that same argument is not **1**. The result is that the noun is pluralized correctly.

Other format directives exist that influence the output of white space, do case conversion, effect flow of control, and specify formats for other LISP objects. It is probably best not to worry about all these options until you must output something that a basic print function cannot handle. In any case, all the options are listed in the description of format that appears in Appendix A.

10.8. Miscellaneous I/O

Options to **print** and **read**

The functions **read** and **print** contain references to a number of free symbols. The user may interrogate these symbols to obtain information, or alter their values to control a number of I/O options.

For example, the symbols ***read–base*** and ***print–base***, respectively, determine the radix that **read** and the various printing function use to interpret rational numbers. Normally, these are both set to decimal 10. However, the user can re-assign them independently to any value from 2 to 36 (decimal). For example:

```
-> 10
10
-> (setq *read-base* 8)
8
-> 10
8
->
```

Here we set ***read-base*** to decimal 8, but left ***print-base*** alone. Thereafter, **10** was interpreted as an octal number. This is equivalent to 8 decimal, and it was printed out as such.

It is useful to know about this feature. But I would like to discourage the reader from using it. Globally changing either base almost always leads to confusion. In particular, if ***read-base*** is set to a value greater than 10, items that were formally read as symbols will now be read as numbers. For example, if we set ***read-base*** to 16, the character **a** will be interpreted as the number 10 (base 10), and the sequence **face** will be interpreted as the number 64206 (base 10).

In Chapter 14 we will discuss a feature that allows the specification of individual numbers in different bases, without globally affecting the LISP reader.

There are a number of other symbols whose values are of interest to the different printing functions. The value of ***print-escape***, for example, determines whether escape characters are printed; ***print-pretty*** controls whether objects are printed using normal or pretty-print mode. In fact, the functions **princ**, **prin1** and **pprint** are essentially calls to the same printing function with these symbols set to the appropriate values.

Two other useful variables are ***print-length*** and ***print-level***. The first variable controls the number of elements of a list that are printed out. Its initial value, **nil**, means to print as many items in a list as there are. However, if it is set to some integer, it will print at most that many items of a list. Omitted items will be indicated by printing the three dots . . . in place of the actual contents. Consider the following example:

```
-> (setq foo '(level 1 (level 2 (level 3 x y z)) a b c))
(LEVEL 1 (LEVEL 2 (LEVEL 3 X Y Z)) A B C))
-> (setq *print-length* 3)
3
-> foo
(LEVEL 1 (LEVEL 2 (LEVEL 3 X ...)) ...)
->
```

All lists that were more than three items long were abbreviated.

print-level can be used to determine how deeply nested expressions are printed. As with ***print-length***, this variable is initially **nil**, meaning that all levels of an expression should be printed. Setting it to an integer prevents deeply nested lists from being shown. Instead, these will be denoted by the abbreviation #:

```
-> (setq *print-level* 2)
2
-> foo
(LEVEL 1 (# # #) ...)
->
```

These variables are useful when you want to peruse a large expression. They are also helpful during debugging. In that case, s-expressions may get hopelessly garbled, and printing out abbreviated forms of them may be the only intelligent thing to do.

Creating a Transcript of a Session with the Interpreter

Another useful I/O function is called **dribble**. **(dribble** *pathname***)** causes a record of the I/O interactions with the current LISP process to be recorded in the file *pathname*. **(dribble)** terminates the recording. Recording your session with the interpreter might be useful for preparing an assignment, showing a problem to a consultant, or composing a LISP tutorial.

In addition to the functions dicussed here, Common LISP has a number of functions for doing character I/O, for determining the number of charac- ters that will be required to print an expression, for checking to see if files exist, etc., and for doing the various internal tasks required by **read**. You can browse through Appendix A to get acquainted with these functions should you find yourself engaged in a task involving considerable I/O pro- gramming.

10.9. LISP in LISP

With the functions **read**, **print**, and **eval** at our disposal, we can make an interesting insight into LISP. The LISP interpreter itself uses these same functions to interpret expressions typed in at the top level. That is, the top level of LISP is really just a chunk of LISP code that is executing the following loop: (1) **read** in a form, (2) **eval** it, and (3) **print** out the result. In fact, with these functions at our disposal, we can write such a loop ourselves in LISP:

```
-> (loop
      (princ "-< " )
      (prin1 (eval (read)))
      (terpri))
-< (setq a 'b)
B
-< a
B
-<
```

A few extra lines of code are needed here to print out the prompt symbol before reading, and the "newline" after printing. However, the bulk of the work in this loop is done by the single line of code **(prin1 (eval (read)))**.

We intentionally used a different prompt symbol from the one LISP normally uses, otherwise it would look like nothing had happened when we evaluate this expression. In fact, we would have little reason to write this exact loop, since evaluating it causes LISP to act pretty much as it did in the first place. What the example does show is that the top level of LISP (i. e., the part of LISP that we communicate with most of the time) is really not very central to what LISP is. Rather, the heart of LISP is the set of functions provided and the ability to apply and compose them.

10.9.1. Evalquote Top Level

To put this another way, we could have a quite different top level than the one we are now familiar with, and the resulting system would still be recognizable as LISP. Let us create a new top level to illustrate this point. Suppose we mostly enter expressions that cause their arguments to be evaluated, but were tired of enclosing our top level expressions in parentheses, and having to quote our arguments. Instead, we might prefer to enter the function name followed by a list containing all the actual arguments to that function. For example, to compute **(cons 'a '(b c))**, we would like to be able to type the following instead:

```
<-> cons (a (b c))
(A B C)
<->
```

(Again, we use a different prompt symbol to indicate an atypical top level.)

To implement this loop, we need to read in two s-expressions: a function name and a list of actual arguments. Then we need to apply that function to the arguments. We can do this as follows:

```
-> (loop
      (princ "<-> ")
      (prin1 (apply (read) (read)) )
      (terpri))
<-> cons (a (b c))
(A B C)
<-> car ((x y z))
X
<->
```

This code **read**s in an s-expression, which it assumes will be a function. Then it **read**s in another s-expression, which should be a list of actual arguments to this function. Then the first input is applied to the second, performing the desired computation. The result of this computation is **prin1**ed. We loop around to do this operation repeatedly.

Thus we see that it is possible to have rather different top level interpreters for the same underlying LISP language. In fact, the funny top level we just wrote was in widespread use at one time. A LISP interpreter that has this as its normal top level is sometimes called an *evalquote* mode interpreter, because it treats arguments as if they were quoted, making them actual arguments without evaluation. The interpreter whose top level operates as we have become accustomed to is called an *eval* mode interpreter.

Evalquote mode has fallen into disuse, for a number of reasons. In particular, the syntax on the top level is not homogeneous with that for the rest of LISP, and many people find this confusing. But the important point is that either mode can be implemented in the other, making neither idea central to LISP itself.

Standardization Note: Some LISPs provide a means to switch back and forth between eval and evalquote modes. However, most modern LISPs, including Common LISP, eschew evalquote mode altogether.

10.9.2. read-eval-print Loops

Since the essence of the standard top level of LISP involves reading, evaluating, and printing, it is often referred to as a **read-eval-print** loop. As the previous examples illustrate, it is possible to have alternative **read-eval-print** loops for various purposes. One example that we have already encountered is the *break package,* i. e., the mode that LISP goes into when it encounters an error. This is just another **read-eval-print** loop in which some special conveniences are available to aid debugging.

10.10. Summary

(1) I/O in LISP is done on the s-expression level. The most basic functions for doing I/O are **read** and **print**.

(2) **read** is a function of no arguments. It causes the interpreter to read an s-expression from a terminal, and it returns that s-expression as its value.

(3) **print** is a function of one argument. The argument is printed on the terminal, preceded by a "newline" and followed by a space. **print** returns its argument as its value.

(4) The function **prin1** will print an expression without any additional white space. The function **terpri** can be used to output a "newline".

(5) We can read symbols with unusual names either by prefacing the unusual characters with *single escape characters* (backslashes) or by surrounding the entire name in *multiple escape characters* (vertical bars).

(6) **print** always prints things out so that they can be read back in by **read**, so it outputs escape characters to cope with problematic characters. The function **princ** prints out s-expressions without any escape characters.

(7) Some other useful I/O functions are **pprint**, which pretty-prints s-expressions, **format**, which provides detailed control over output, and **dribble**, which causes subsequent transactions with the interpreter to be recorded in a file.

(8) It is possible to **read** from and **print** to arbitrary files. This involves setting up *streams,* using the function **open**. If **read** or **print** contains an additional argument that is a stream, it will perform I/O with

the file connected to that stream rather than with the terminal. When we are through with a stream, we can close it with the function **close**. A *pathname* is a Common LISP data type that enables a degree of system-independence when working with file specifiers.

(9) It is possible to write the top level of LISP in LISP. This is simply a loop that calls the functions **read**, **eval**, and **print**. For this reason, the normal top level of LISP is sometimes called a **read-eval-print** loop.

(10) There are any number of alternative top levels. The mode that LISP goes into after an error is an example of a useful, alternative top level. Some previous LISP interpreters had a normal top level called *evalquote* mode, in which the user is expected to enter a function followed by a list of actual arguments. This is in contrast to the commonly used *eval* mode interpreter, in which the user enters a form to be evaluated.

Exercises

(1) What do the following forms produce as output? What values do they return?

    (a)   (cons 'a (print '(b c)))

    (b)   (princ '|abcd|)

    (c)   (cons 'a (princ '(b c)))

    (d)   (cons 'a (prin1 '(b c)))

    (e)   (princ 'ab\(cd)

(2) How can we enter a symbol whose name contains the character \?

(3) Write a function that reads in a sequence of s-expressions, terminating with the symbol **end**, and returns the list of these s-expressions.

(4) Write a function to help balance your checkbook. This function will prompt the user for an initial balance. Then it will enter a loop in which it requests a number from the user, subtracts it from the current balance, and prints out the new balance. Deposits can be entered by supplying a negative number. Entering zero should cause the procedure to terminate.

(5) Write a function that reads s-expressions from a file, designated by an argument, and prints each s-expression on the terminal, separated by blank lines. Your function should print a message indicating when it has reached an end-of-file.

(6) Write a function **set–rem** that operates like **set**, but which records all calls to it. For example, **set–rem** might use the global variable ***set*** and **cons** all actual arguments which it receives onto the value of this symbol. Then write a function **set–dump** that takes as its argument a file name. **set–dump** writes to this file an appropriate call to **set** for each previous call to **set–rem**. The idea is that when we **load** the file to which we have **set–dump**ed everything, all the assignments created by previous calls to **set–rem** will be reestablished.

(7) Write a function called **pp** that pretty-prints out function definitions just like we have been typing them in. For example, if we apply **pp** to **recursive–member**, we would get the following:

```
–> (pp 'recursive–member)

(DEFUN RECURSIVE–MEMBER (E L)
    (COND ((NULL L) NIL)
          ((EQUAL E (CAR L)) L)
          (T (RECURSIVE–MEMBER E (CDR L)))))

NIL
–>
```

This function is a particularly useful debugging aid.

(8) Write a more elaborate pretty-print function called **symbol–print** that displays all the "interesting" aspects of a symbol. This includes its function definition, value, and any user-defined properties. For example, a symbol might be displayed as follows:

```
–> (symbol–print 'foo)

FUNCTION: (LAMBDA (X) (LIST X))

VALUE: (A B C)

COLOR: RED
```

AGE: 32

NIL
–>

In this example, the function and value shown are the function definition of **foo** and **foo**'s current assignment, respectively. **color** and **age** were found on **foo**'s property list.

You might want to use the function **pprint** to print out these values nicely. Also, you will need to use the function **symbol–plist** to obtain the symbol's entire property list. The function **boundp** can be used to check if the symbol has a value.

The function **symbol–print** is similar to the Common LISP function **describe**. The details of **describe** are implementation-dependent. You might want to see what your version of **describe** does, and then improve upon its characteristics in your implementation of **symbol–print**.

Chapter 11

Debugging

11.1. Debugging in LISP

We have encountered enough of LISP to write some rather serious programs. This capability entails the need for a comparably powerful set of debugging tools. In most conventional programming languages, it is difficult to provide very powerful debugging facilities. Usually, the code being executed comes from a compiler, and has a non-obvious relationship to the original source code. The run-time environment of a program probably has little to do with the user's understanding of the language, and the user must rely on debugging aids of varying quality to tamper with his program.

Fortunately, with LISP, we are somewhat better off. When a LISP interpreter encounters a form it cannot evaluate, it usually has the original source code at its fingertips. Since the code is being interpreted, the environment in which the error occurs is the same environment in which the user created the code. Moreover, the LISP interpreter itself is present, making the full power of LISP available for debugging.

In this chapter, we examine the debugging facilities that are available in Common LISP. These include an interactive debugging facility, a method for tracing functions during execution, and means of moving through the execution of a function one step at a time.

Standardization Note: The details of how debugging works in Common LISP is highly implementation-dependent. There is even more variation across LISP dialects. While facilities analogous to the ones described here are likely to be available in other LISPs you have occasion to use, you will have to allow for quite a bit of variation when you get down to the details.

11.2. The Common LISP Debugger

When a Common LISP program encounters an error, it enters an interactive debugger. In general, this debugger is a kind of special **read-eval-print** loop. Unlike the top-level **read-eval-print** loop, which we communicate with only after the evaluation of a form has been completed, we enter this **read-eval-print** loop right in the middle of an evaluation. Therefore, the event of entering the debugging upon an error is sometimes referred to as a *break*.

To help the user keep track of where he is, most LISPs, including most implementations of Common LISP, use a prompt in the break that is different from that used at the top level. Consider the following rather contrived example:

```
-> (defun foo (y) (prog (x) (setq x (cons (car 8) y))))
foo
-> (foo '(a b c))

Error: Attempt to take the CAR of 8, which is not a list.

Debug 1>:
```

Here LISP encounters an error, prints a message, and enters the debugger. This debugger prompts by printing **Debug 1>**. We can communicate with the debugger by entering certain debugging commands. In general, the debugging commands allow the user to

(1) examine the current state of the computation,
(2) evaluate forms in different contexts,
(3) abort, continue, or restart the computation.

For example, the debugger might interpret the symbol **quit** as a command to abort the current computation and return to the previous command level:

Debug 1>: quit

–>

Standardization Note: The precise commands and associated names are highly implementation-dependent. For example, on LISP machines, many of these commands would be invoked by pressing a particular button, rather than by entering a symbol. While the details vary, facilities comparable to the ones demonstrated here are likely to be provided in your Common LISP implementation, and in fact, in many other LISPs.

There are generally many other debugger commands available. In most debuggers, typing **?** will give a brief description of the possible options. Here are the options for this particular debugger:

Debug 1> ?

```
?           – Display help text for the debugger commands.
BACKTRACE – Displays a backtrace of the control stack.
BOTTOM      – Move to the first stack frame.
CONTINUE   – Causes the debugger to return NIL.
DOWN        – Move to the previous stack frame.
ERROR       – Display the current error message.
EVALUATE    – Evaluate a specified form.
GOTO        – Move to a specified control stack frame.
HELP        – Display help text for the debugger commands.
QUIT        – Exit to the previous command level.
REDO        – Invoke the function in the current frame.
RETURN      – Return one or more specified values.
SEARCH      – Search for frame containing specified function.
SET         – Modify a component of the current frame.
SHOW        – Display information about the current frame.
STEP        – Single-step evaluation from current frame.
TOP         – Move to the last stack frame.
UP          – Move to the next stack frame.
WHERE       – Redisplay the current stack frame.
```

Debug 1>

For example, we could use the command **evaluate** to determine the values of the variables appearing in the computation:

```
Debug 1> evaluate x
NIL
Debug 1> evaluate y
(A B C)
Debug 1>
```

(Note – Most debuggers accept abbreviations for commands that are long enough to disambiguate the command.) Here we interrogated the value of the **prog** variable **x**, and find that it is set to **nil**; the formal parameter **y** can be seen to have the value (**a b c**). Had this been a bug in a real program, this information might give us some indication of where the error occurred. For example, the value of **x** would suggest that the **prog** variable had been initialized, but not yet **setq**ed.

11.2.1. Examining the Stack

In the case of a real error, however, life is not this easy. In particular, we might not have any idea where the error occurred in our code. **foo** might have been called by **baz**, which in turn might have been called by another function, and so on. An error message stating that there was a bad argument to **car** somewhere would not be of much help in locating the function in which the errant code appears.

Fortunately, LISP has to remember the sequence of function calls it is in the middle of executing. We can take advantage of this fact to help us debug. For example, if LISP is evaluating the form

(cons x (foo l))

it needs to save the fact that it is in the middle of a **cons** while it is evaluating the arguments supplied to **cons**. LISP must remember this fact so it knows how to continue when it finishes evaluating the arguments. Similarly, **foo** is sure to call some other function, and LISP must remember where to continue after this evaluation is completed.

Thus LISP stores on a stack the sequence of forms that it is currently evaluating. This stack is sometimes called a *control stack*. Each entry on the stack corresponding to a form is called a *stack frame*. We can use the debugger to inspect this stack, and help determine where we are in an evaluation.

For the sake of a demonstration, let us write a function **baz** that calls **foo**, and which uses the same variable names:

```
-> (defun baz (y)
      (prog (x)
         (setq x 1)
         (foo (cons 'a y))))
baz
->
```

Now let us call **baz** and generate an error:

```
-> (baz '(b c))
```

Error: Attempt to take the CAR of 8, which is not a list.

Debug 1>

Now issuing the **backtrace** command will show a sort of history of the current evaluation:

```
Debug 1> backtrace
Frame #8: (CAR 8)
Frame #7: (CONS (CAR 8) Y)
Frame #6: (SETQ X (CONS (CAR 8) Y))
Frame #5: (PROG (X) (SETQ X (CONS (CAR 8) Y)))
Frame #4: (FOO (CONS (QUOTE A) Y))
Frame #3: (PROG (X) (SETQ X 1) (FOO (CONS (QUOTE A) Y)))
Frame #2: (BAZ (QUOTE (B C)))
Frame #1: (EVAL (BAZ (QUOTE (B C))))

You are at Frame #8: (CAR 8)
Debug 1>
```

backtrace shows the top of the stack first. At the very top, we see the expression **(car 8)**, the form that caused the difficulty. Beneath this form is the form in which **(car 8)** occurred. The form in which this form appears is shown on the line beneath it, and so on, until we get to the form **(eval (baz (quote (b c))))**. This represents the stack frame created when the top-level LISP **read–eval–print** loop applied **eval** to the expression we supplied.

Standardization Note: Exactly what is placed on the stack, and how it is printed, is implementation-dependent. However, most debuggers abbreviate forms using the conventions described in the Chapter 10.

Using this information, we can trace the sequence of calls from the initial call we made up to the error, thus helping to locate the problem area in our code.

Usually, looking at the entire stack is a bit overwhelming. Therefore, many debuggers will allow short forms of a backtrace, usually through options available to a **backtrace** type command. Using these options, it might be possible to show only function name at the head of a form, instead of the entire form, to specify that only the first *n* elements of the stack are to be shown; or to request that variables be shown as they come into existence or when their values are changed. For example, in this debugger, typing a number after **backtrace** will cause only that many stack frames to be shown:

```
Debug 1> backtrace 4
Frame #8: (CAR 8)
Frame #7: (CONS (CAR 8) Y)
Frame #6: (SETQ X (CONS (CAR 8) Y))
Frame #5: (PROG (X) (SETQ X (CONS (CAR 8) Y)))

You are at Frame #8: (CAR 8)
Debug 1>
```

11.2.2. Other Debugger Commands

Sometimes it is not immediately obvious why an error occurred or how a program got into its current state. For example, suppose **foo** calls **baz**, and that an error occurs during the evaluation of a form in **baz**. Suppose we feel that the value of a formal parameter in **foo**, say **x**, would be useful to know. Unfortunately, **baz** may also have a formal parameter named **x**. Thus typing **x** at the break will not get at the formal parameter in which we are interested.

What we would like to do is temporarily move back to the context of the previous function. In this context, **x** refers to a formal parameter of **foo** rather than to one of **baz**. More generally, we would like to move up and down the stack of active functions, evaluating forms in different contexts.

There are debugger commands to facilitate just this sort of thing. For example, we can move up and down the stack using the debugging commands **down** and **up**:

```
Debug 1> down
Frame #7: (CONS (CAR 8) Y)
Debug 1>
```

By moving up and down the stack, we can change the context in which an expression is evaluated. For example, at the current stack location, **x** and **y** designated variables local to **foo**:

```
Debug 1> evaluate x
NIL
Debug 1> evaluate y
(A B C)
Debug 1>
```

However, we can move further down the stack and evaluate expressions within the context of **baz**. For example, we can move to the point of the stack just before **foo** was called by moving down 3 more stack frames. We can accomplish this with most debuggers as follows:

```
Debug 1> down 3
Frame #4: (FOO (CONS (QUOTE A) Y))
Debug 1>
```

Now evaluations will be done relative to the new context:

```
Debug 1> evaluate x
1
Debug 1> evaluate y
(B C)
Debug 1>
```

We can move to the bottom of the stack using the command **bottom**. At this point, none of these variables have been created yet:

```
Debug 1> bottom
Frame #1: (EVAL (BAZ (QUOTE (B C))))
Debug 1> evaluate x

Error: Attempt to take the value of an unassigned variable:
X.
Continuing Debug session.

Debug 1>
```

Most debuggers are likely to have other commands for moving around the stack. For example, this debugger has a command **top** which moves to the top of the stack, a command **goto** which moves directly to a specified form, and a command **search** which searches for a frame containing the specified function. In addition, the command **where** prints out the current stack frame, and the command **show** displays information about the current stack frame.

Being able to continue the computation after a break is another common feature of a debugger. Some debuggers may provide commands for patching the current stack frame (in this debugger, the command **set**), and for then proceeding with re-evaluation (in this case, using the command **redo**). Alternatively, the user may use **setq** within the debugger to alter the values of some variables, and then issue a command to continue with the computation. There may be a command that returns a specified value from the current position and continues with the computation (called **return** here). Another option is to enter a program called a *stepper*, which "single-steps" through the computation (accomplished using the **step** command in this debugger). Such a program is described in a section below.

11.2.3. Recursively Entering the Debugger

In the course of attempting to examine an error, it is quite possible to make another error. For example, when we evaluate a form during a break, we might specify another erroneous computation. For example, if we are confused as to why the error occurred, we might want to evaluate a piece of a form again. Using our example above, if we do not think **(car 8)** should have caused an error, we might test this out by evaluating it again:

    Debug 1> evaluate (car 8)

    Error: Attempt to take the CAR of 8, which is not a list.

    Debug 2>

In this example, we made another error while already inside the debugger. LISP simply called the debugger again, keeping track of fact that we are already inside the debugger. Since we may end up entering the debugger repeatedly without leaving it, most LISPs will increment the number within the prompt symbol to indicate the number of current breaks. In the example above, our second error caused the new prompt **Debug 2>** to be used, indicating that we have now entered the debugger twice without having left in between.

We can exit this incarnation of the debugger by typing **quit**:

Debug 2> quit

Debug 1>

We are now back to the state we were in before we tried evaluating the last expression. If we issue another **quit**, we would find ourselves back at the top level:

Debug 1> quit

->

11.3. The Common LISP Trace Package

Useful as they are, the debugging tools we just described are sometimes inadequate. For example, it is often the case that a piece of code does something that is conceptually incorrect but that is not in itself a LISP error. This mistake may have repercussions that cause the interpreter to choke some time in the future. Unfortunately, examining the state-of-the-world at the time of the actual error will not be particularly revealing about how the problem came about in the first place. Rather, what we would like to do is to run our program again, this time monitoring its behavior so that unexpected events will become apparent.

A *trace package* is a debugging facility that lets the user examine the flow of control of a program as it is being executed. In Common LISP, the trace package is invoked by a call to the special function **trace**. The arguments to **trace**, which are not evaluated, are the names of functions that you wish to trace. For example, watch what happens when we define and then trace the function **xcons:**

```
-> (defun xcons (x y) (cons y x))
xcons
-> (trace xcons)
(xcons)
-> (xcons '(b c) 'a)
1 <Enter> xcons ((b c) a)
1 <EXIT> xcons (a b c)
(a b c)
->
```

193

Now each time **xcons** is called, LISP will print out the fact that it is being entered, along with its actual arguments; upon exit, the value returned by **xcons** is evidenced.

If a function is called within another traced function, most implementations of **trace** try to make this apparent. Suppose **foo** calls **xcons**, as in the following example:

```
-> (defun foo (x y) (xcons x y))
foo
-> (trace foo)
(foo)
-> (foo '(b c) 'a)
1 <Enter> foo ((b c) a)
|1 <Enter> xcons ((b c) a)
|1 <EXIT> xcons  (a b c)
1 <EXIT>  foo  (a b c)
(a b c)
->
```

From the output of **trace**, we can see that **xcons** was called in the midst of a call to **foo**.

If a function is invoked recursively, most implementations of **trace** also try to make this easier to follow. For example, let us define and trace a recursive version of the function **factorial**:

```
-> (defun factorial (n)
        (cond ((zerop n) 1) (t (* n (factorial (1- n)))))))
factorial
-> (factorial 4)
24
-> (trace factorial)
(factorial)
-> (factorial 4)
1 <Enter> factorial (4)
|2 <Enter> factorial (3)
| 3 <Enter> factorial (2)
| |4 <Enter> factorial (1)
| | 5 <Enter> factorial (0)
| | 5 <EXIT>  factorial  1
| |4 <EXIT>  factorial  1
```

```
 | 3 <EXIT>  factorial  2
 |2 <EXIT>  factorial  6
 1 <EXIT>  factorial  24
 24
 ->
```

In this trace package, the numbers at the beginning of each line represent the depth of the recursion; the indentation helps match up each function invocation with its associated termination.

We can turn off tracing by calling the function **untrace**:

```
-> (untrace factorial)
(factorial)
-> (factorial 4)
24
->
```

A call to **untrace** with no arguments will untrace all traced functions.

Sometimes such calls to **trace** result in too much information. Some Common LISP implementations therefore gives you a means to exercise selective control over when the trace information should be printed. For example, some implementations support a call to **trace** of the form

(trace (foo if *expression***))**

meaning that the trace information should only be printed if *expression* evaluates to non-**nil**. Alternatively, a call to **trace** of the form

(trace (foo in baz))

might mean that only those calls to **foo** that occur within the function **baz** should be traced; a call of the form

(trace (foo break))

might mean to enter the debugger whenever **foo** is encountered.

Standardization Note: The possible variations on the call to **trace**, and the exact format of the output, are highly implementation-dependent.

A call to **trace** with no arguments is guaranteed to return all currently traced functions.

11.4. The Common LISP Stepper

When all else fails, it is sometimes useful to move through a computation a bit at a time, observing the results of intermediate stages of the computation. This can be accomplished using a program called a *stepper*. In Common LISP, the stepper is invoked using the special function **step**. **step** takes as an argument a form, evaluates it, and returns whatever that form returns. However, **step** allows the user to interactively move through the evaluation a step at a time.

Standardization Note: The particular nature of the interaction is highly implementation-dependent.

For example, suppose we were mystified as to why calling the function **baz** resulted in an error in **foo**. We could single-step through the computation and watch what happens:

```
-> (step (baz '(b c)))
(BAZ (QUOTE (B C)))
Step 1>
```

Here the stepper has been invoked. It prints out the form it is about to evaluate, and then enters a stepper **read–eval–print** loop. This resembles the debugger **read–eval–print** loop, in that subsequent inputs will be interpreted as commands. As before, we should be able to scan the possible options by typing **?**:

```
Step 1> ?

?               - Display help text for the stepper commands.
BACKTRACE - Displays a backtrace of the current form.
DEBUG        - Invoke the debugger.
EVALUATE    - Evaluate a specified form.
FINISH         - Complete evaluation without the stepper.
HELP           - Display help text for the stepper commands.
OVER           - Evaluate current form with stepping disabled.
QUIT            - Exits the stepper.
RETURN       - Return the specified values.
```

SHOW — Display current form without abbreviation.
STEP — Single step the current form.
UP — Return to the containing form.

As you can see, some of these commands resemble those of the debugger. For example, typing **backtrace** will produce a backtrace showing the current state of the computation, and we can leave the stepper by typing **quit**. However, the interesting aspect of the stepper is that we can proceed incrementally with the computation by typing **step**:

```
Step 1> step
: (PROG (X) (SETQ X 1) (FOO (CONS (QUOTE A) Y)))
Step 2> step
: : (SETQ X 1)
Step 4> step
: : : => 1
: : : (FOO (CONS (QUOTE A) Y))
Step 4>
```

Here we completed the evaluation of the form **(setq x 1)**. (This implementation did not require a separate step to evaluate **1**, since this is a constant.) We might stop at this point and examine the value of a variable, just to make sure all is well:

```
Step 4> evaluate x
1
```

We can refresh our memory about our location using **show**:

```
Step 4> show
(FOO (CONS (QUOTE A) Y))
```

or ask for a backtrace:

```
Step 4> backtrace
(BAZ (QUOTE (B C)))
: (PROG (X) (SETQ X 1) (FOO (CONS (QUOTE A) Y)))
: : (FOO (CONS (QUOTE A) Y))
```

or continue stepping:

```
Step 4> step
: : : (CONS (QUOTE A) Y)
```

We can evaluate the next form without stepping, if we feel we understand how it will evaluate. This might be appropriate for the current form:

Step 5> over
: : : => (A B C)

Let us now continue stepping until we encounter an error:

Step 5> step
: : : : (PROG (X) (SETQ X (CONS (CAR 8) Y)))
Step 6> step
: : : : : (SETQ X (CONS (CAR 8) Y))
Step 7> step
: : : : : : (CONS (CAR 8) Y)
Step 8> step
: : : : : : : (CAR 8)
Step 9> step

Error: Attempt to take the CAR of 8, which is not a list.

Debug 10>

We have now entered the debugger. In principle we might want to use it to poke around, but in this case, let us just leave it:

Debug 10> quit

Step 9>

We are back in the stepper. If we like, we can use the stepper command **return** to return a value from the current point in the computation. The only form left to evaluate is **y**; this stepper does not step through variable evaluations, so we will continue computing now until we have completed the computation:

Step 9> return 11
: : : : : : : : => 11
: : : : : : : : Y => (A B C)
: : : : : : : => (11 A B C)
: : : : : => (11 A B C)
: : : : => NIL
: : : => NIL
: : => NIL

```
: => NIL
NIL
->
```

Here we returned the value **11** from the current step of the computation, i. e., **(car 8)**, instead of re-evaluating this erroneous form. Each of the remaining steps of the computation are then completed, and their resulting values indicated. The final value **nil**, is the actual value returned by **step**.

11.5. Summary

(1)   Upon encountering an error, Common LISP normally enters a *debugger*. This is an interactive mode in which some convention exists for issuing debugging commands. Usually there are commands for examining the stack, evaluating forms in different contexts, and restarting the computation.

(2)   A *trace package* can be used to examine flow of control at runtime. This is done by applying the special function **trace** to a function argument. Then LISP will print something on the terminal each time that function is entered or exited.

(3)   A *stepper* can be used to single-step through a computation. The function **step** can be used to invoke the Common LISP stepper.

(4)   While the existence of these debugging facilities is standard, their exact nature is highly implementation-dependent.

Exercises

(1)   Try using the various debugging facilities described in this chapter to help debug some of the functions you have written.

(2)   It may be possible in your implementation of Common LISP to handle errors by program control. For example, in some LISPs, there exists a function called **errset**. Usually, this function takes a form as its argument, and evaluates that form. If an error occurs during the evaluation of that form, rather than entering the debugger, control returns immediately to the call to **errset**. In this case, **errset** returns something indicating that an error has occurred. If the form evaluates without error, then **errset** returns something to indicate success, along with the value computed. In this way, the user's program can test for an error, and handle it its own way.

Find out if **errset** or the equivalent exists in your implementation. Use it to try to handle certain errors under program control.

(3) If you have your own ideas on how to debug programs, and they differ from those provided by your Common LISP implementation, it may be possible to install your own debugger. To do this you may have to find out the details of how errors are handled in your implementation. You might consider this as a long-term project to do when you become more familiar with the inner workings of your implementation.

Chapter 12

Writing More Flexible Functions

12.1. Introduction

We have seen that LISP has functions that treat their supplied arguments in different ways. "Ordinary" functions, like + and **cons**, evaluate all their arguments, while special functions, like **defun**, do not cause any argument evaluation. A few special functions, like **setq**, only evaluate one argument, and some, like **cond** and **prog**, evaluate their arguments based on certain conditions. In addition, some functions, like +, can tolerate any number of arguments, while others expect a fixed number.

However, the functions that we have learned to define are all ordinary functions. That is, our use of **defun** or lambda expressions to create functions has always produced functions that cause their arguments to be evaluated. In addition, these functions tolerate only a specific number of arguments. We have no way of defining a function of our own that does not cause its arguments to be evaluated or that accepts a variable number of arguments. Sometimes it is useful to define functions that behave this way. Therefore, LISP provides a means to do so.

In this chapter, we explore ordinary LISP functions more carefully. We find that we can define ordinary functions that take a variable number of arguments. In addition, we can define functions that accept *keyword* arguments in addition to ordinary arguments. We also present a built-in feature of ordinary functions that allow the user to obtain local variables for a function call. We then examine the notion of a *closure,* which is a way of defining a more specific version of an existing function. Finally, we discuss the role of compiled functions and foreign functions in LISP.

The facilities discussed in this chapter will not allow us to define functions that do not evaluate their arguments, however. We will have to wait until we examine *macros* in the next chapter to see how this might be done.

12.2. Optional Arguments

Suppose we want to write a function that took a variable number of arguments. For example, some of our ordinary numeric functions like + take an arbitrary number of arguments. Other functions, such as I/O functions like **read** and **print**, take a limited number of arguments, but some of these are optional.

We can write such functions in Common LISP by taking advantage of some special features of function definitions. One of these features allows the user to specify that certain parameters of a function are optional. This is done simply by placing the symbol **&optional** in the formal parameter list of a function definition. This symbol should appear after all the required parameters. Those symbols following the appearance of **&optional** will be assigned a value if a corresponding argument is supplied when the function is called. But if such an argument is not supplied, no error would be generated. Instead, the parameter will simply be given the value **nil**. Since the parameters following **&optional** do not require arguments to be supplied, these are often called *optional parameters.*

For example, suppose we want to write a function **power** that, if given one argument, squares that argument, but, if given a second argument, raises the first argument to the power of the second. Thus **(power 3 4)** will return **81**, while **(power 3)** should return **9**.

We can write such a function by preceding the second formal parameter of **power** with the symbol **&optional**:

```
-> (defun power (base &optional exp)
      (expt base (if exp exp 2)) )
POWER
-> (power 3)
9
```

```
-> (power 3 4)
81
->
```

power allows two arguments: The first is required, (i. e., not supplying it causes an error) and is assigned to the parameter **base**. The second argument is optional. If it is supplied, it is assigned to the parameter **exp**; otherwise, **exp** is assigned the value **nil**.

power uses LISP's exponentiation function, **expt**, always passing it its own first argument. If a second argument has been supplied by the caller, then **exp** will be non-**nil**, and its value will be returned by the call to **if**. If there is no second argument, **exp** will be **nil**, and **if** will return the value **2**.

This version of **power** has one problem with it, however. It is impossible for the function to tell whether the caller supplied no second argument, and hence **exp** was set to **nil** by default, or if the user actually supplied a second argument of value **nil**. This latter possibility almost certainly means that we made an error – perhaps we meant to use a variable whose name is similar to **nil**. However, our code does not distinguish this case from the case in which no second argument is supplied; in both cases, our code will simply use the default value **2**. Thus the case in which we made a programming error will be difficult to detect.

Since the need to supply a default value other than **nil** for an optional parameter is rather typical, Common LISP provides a special syntax for it. Rather than follow the symbol **&optional** with the lone parameter, we can follow it by the parameter inside a list. The next element of this list is the default value to be assigned the parameter should no argument be supplied.

Using this feature, we can now write the following definition of **power**

```
-> (defun power (base &optional (exp 2))
     (expt base exp))
POWER
->
```

The notation **(exp 2)** following **&optional** indicates that **exp** is an optional parameter whose default value is **2** if an argument is not supplied.

This feature solves the previous problem, as a call of the form **(power 3 nil)** will now cause an arithmetic error within the **expt** routine. (Remember, this most likely *is* a programmer error, so we wanted LISP to catch it.) However, the function **power** still has no way of knowing if the value of its optional parameter got there by default, or because the caller supplied it. For example, there is no way to tell whether the calling form was **(power 3)** or **(power 3 2)**. Of course, this no longer makes a difference in this example, but in principle, it might. For example, we might want **power** to print out a message informing the user about the fact that a default was being assumed for some computation. Obviously, it would be appropriate to do this only in those situations in which the user did not supply an optional argument.

Common LISP allows you to distinguish these situations by supplying yet another element in the list containing the optional parameter and its default value. This third element must be a symbol. It is set to **nil** if the optional argument is not supplied, and to **t** if it is. Since this symbol is used as a parameter to tell whether another parameter has actually been supplied, it is sometimes refered to as a *supplied-p* parameter.

For example, we can use a supplied-p parameter in the definition of **power** to determine whether the second parameter has been supplied. We can then know when to inform the user that we were using a default (although I can't imagine that we would really want to do this):

```
-> (defun power (base &optional (exp 2 expflag))
      (if (null expflag)
          (princ "power: second argument defaulting to 2"))
      (expt base exp))
POWER
->
```

You can have as many optional arguments as you like following the occurrence of **&optional**. The symbol **&optional** only appears once. Thus, the formal parameter list of a function might look like this:

(a b c &optional x (y yinit) (z zinit zflag))

Here **a**, **b**, and **c** are all required parameters; **x**, **y**, and **z** are all optional. **x** has no specified default value (and hence will default to **nil**), while **y**'s default value is the value of **yinit** and **z**'s the value of **zinit**. Furthermore, **z** is associated with the supplied-p parameter **zflag**.

Note that the **&optional** feature in these examples, as well as the other features described in this chapter, are features of lambda expressions in general. They have nothing to do with **defun** in particular. That is, we can use features like **&optional** in any lambda expression, whether it appears explicitly in our code, or implicitly, via function defining functions like **defun**. We will call symbols like **&optional** *parameter designators.*

Standardization Note: Other versions of LISP may have these features, but they are generally not as basic as they are in Common LISP. For example, in other LISPs, it might be possible to use these features in functions defined by **defun**, but not in lambda expressions themselves. In such LISPs, the occurrence of **&optional**, say, is typically translated by **defun** into some more primitive operations of that LISP. In Common LISP, these features are "wired" into lambda itself.

12.3. The Rest Parameter

The use of **&optional** allows us to write functions that have a number of optional arguments. But we still have no way to write a function that allows us to have *any* number of arguments. For example, functions like + are capable of adding together any number of arguments. Using the **&optional** feature, we could at best allow only as many optional arguments as there were optional parameters in the function definition.

To address the need for functions that allow an indefinite number of arguments, Common LISP provides another parameter designator. This designator is called **&rest**. **&rest** is always followed by a single parameter, called the *rest parameter.* When the function is applied, all the actual arguments that are not otherwise consumed by required or optional parameters will be put in a list and assigned to the rest parameter. So the rest parameter may end up being assigned a list containing any number of actual arguments.

For example, in Chapter 3 we introduced the function **load**, that reads in and evaluates a file of s-expressions. However, **load** only accepts a single argument. But we often want to load in a number of files at once. Using the **&rest** feature, we can define a function **dskin** that accepts any number of file names as arguments. We do this by making **dskin** a function of only a rest parameter. Then we can apply the function **load** to each file found in the list assigned to the rest parameter. We can use **mapc** to do the function application for us:

```
-> (defun dskin (&rest l) (mapc 'load l))
DSKIN
->
```

dskin has no required parameters, but only the single rest parameter **l**. When **dskin** is applied, all the actual arguments are put in a list and assigned to **l**. For example, in a call of the form (**dskin** "lamed" "vuv" "nik"), **l** would be assigned the value ("lamed" "vuv" "nik"). The body of **dskin** causes **load** to be applied to each element of this list, which is just what we want.

Of course, it is possible to have required and optional parameters in a function, along with a rest parameter. The **&rest** designator and parameter must always follow the required and optional parameters, if any are specified. Thus a parameter list with all three kinds of parameters might look like this:

(a b ... &optional x (y yinit) ... &rest restparam)

12.4. Keyword Parameters

While the introduction of optional and rest parameters provides quite a bit of flexibility, there are still some kinds of situations that they cannot handle elegantly. For example, suppose we want to have a function that has two optional arguments. Its definition might look like the following:

(defun func (... &optional x y) ...)

But suppose that each of these parameters is conceptually independent of the other, that is, that the presence of an argument for one parameter has nothing to do with the presence of an argument for the other. Now, with optional parameters, half the time we would have to supply one optional parameter just to supply the other. In this example, we could supply a value for **x** without supplying one for **y**, but we could not do the opposite. To supply a value for **y**, we would have to say (**func** ... **xarg yarg**). We had to supply a value for **x** here because we can only refer to optional parameters by the *position* of the supplied arguments.

An actual case where this problem arises in Common LISP is in the function **read**. We noted in Chapter 10 that **read** is normally called with no arguments, but accepts several optional arguments. In particular, the first optional argument specifies the stream to be read from, the next whether an error should be produced upon encountering an end-of-file condition, and the third the value to be returned upon encountering an end-of-file condition should producing an error not be required. One problem with this setup, though, is that to say something about the end-of-file condition, we have to first supply a stream argument. That is, to say that we want **flag** to be returned upon encountering an end-of-file, we need to type

(read nil nil 'flag). The first **nil** is just a placeholder – **read** interprets a **nil** stream as referring to the standard input. The second and third arguments are the ones we wanted to supply. Having to supply the first argument is bothersome, since specifying the stream and specifying what to do about the end-of-file condition are conceptually unrelated.

To make matter worse, **read** accepts yet another optional argument. This argument should be supplied when **read** is called recursively, as will be explained in Chapter 14. Suffice it to say here that this argument is unrelated to any of the previous arguments. Thus one often finds calls to **read** of the form **(read nil t nil t)** , where the only function of the first three arguments is to provide a way to enter the fourth.

In these examples, we would like some mechanism other than positional notation to be able to specify which optional parameter we wish to associate an actual argument with. In Common LISP, this is accomplished using *keyword parameters.* To indicate that a function has a keyword parameter, we put the symbol **&key** in its parameter list. Following this symbol comes the keyword parameters. To refer to a keyword parameter when calling the function, the user supplies as an argument *the name of the keyword parameter preceded by the character* : (colon). Following this signal, the user supplies *another* argument. The value of this argument becomes the actual argument assigned to the indicated keyword parameter.

For example, suppose we defined the following function:

> **(defun foo (&key switchx switchy) ...)**

This is a function of no required or optional parameters, but which has two keyword parameters, **switchx** and **switchy**. Now, to specify a value only for the keyword parameter **switchx**, we could type the following:

> **(foo :switchx 7)**

Note, we did not have to quote **:switchx**; LISP will recognize it as a keyword. The value of the argument following it will be assigned to the keyword parameter **switchx**. This parameter can be referenced in the body of **foo** just like any other parameter. Of course, had we typed **(foo :switchy 9)**, the keyword parameter **switchy** would have been assigned the value **9**. To specify values for both keyword parameters we could type either

> **(foo :switchx 7 :switchy 9)**

or

(foo :switchy 9 :switch 7)

since keyword parameters are interpreted without regard to position.

Like optional parameters, keyword parameters default to **nil** if no actual argument refers to them. Also like optional parameters, it is possible to specify defaults for keyword parameters, as well as supplied-p parameters. For example, consider the following version of **foo**:

(defun foo (&key (switchx xinit) (switchy yinit yflag) ...)

Here the keyword parameter **switchx** will default to the value of **xinit** and **switchy** to the value of **yinit**, if no reference is made to these keywords in a call to **foo**. In addition, **yflag** will be set to **t** when the keyword **:switchy** appears in a call to this function, and to **nil** otherwise.

Let us write an aesthetically pleasing interface to the function **read** using keywords:

```
(defun our-read (&key stream
                      recursivep
                      (eof nil suppliedp))
  (read stream (not suppliedp) eof recursivep))
```

Here we use keywords to handle a non-default stream, the end-of-file specifier, and the recursive flag (i. e., the fourth argument to **read**). Specifically, whenever the keyword argument **:eof** is supplied, we tell **read** not to generate end-of-file errors (this requires an argument of **nil** to **read**, hence the call to **not**). Moreover, we assume that the supplied argument is the value to return on an end-of-file condition. Thus, instead of typing **(read nil nil 'flag)**, we can type **(our-read :eof 'flag)** and get the same effect. Similarly, the keyword argument **:recursivep** is used to indicate the fourth argument to **read**. So instead of having to type **(read nil t nil t)**, we can enter **(our-read :recursivep t)**. The keyword **:stream** may be used analogously. Of course, we can enter any combination of these keyword arguments, such as

(our-read :recursivep t :eof 'flag)

or

(our-read :eof 'flag :recursivep t)

Both of these calls have exactly the same effect.

To familiarize ourselves further with keyword parameters, let us write a version of the function **power**, using keyword parameters rather than optional ones:

```
-> (defun power (base &key (exp 2))
     (expt base exp))
POWER
-> (power 3)
9
-> (power 3 :exp 4)
81
```

Note that the keyword parameters must be specified after required parameters (and after optional and rest parameters, for that matter). In addition, the keywords and associated arguments must appear after all the required arguments. For example, typing **(power :exp 4 3)** would cause an error: LISP would think the argument **:exp** was meant for the required parameter **base**; then LISP would not know what to do with the remaining arguments.

In the examples above, we required that the keyword appearing in the function call be the name of the keyword parameter preceded by a colon. For example, in our definition of **power**, the keyword **:exp** indicated that the next argument is to be assigned to the keyword parameter **exp**. However, this identity in the name of a keyword and its associated parameter is not strictly necessary. To specify a keyword whose name is different from the name of the keyword parameter, we put the keyword and parameter name in a list inside the specification. For example, in **power**, if we want to use the keyword **:e**, but still wish to call the keyword parameter **exp**, we can write the following:

```
-> (defun power (base &key ((:e exp) 2))
     (expt base exp))
POWER
-> (power 3)
9
-> (power 3 :e 4)
81
```

Everything here is identical to the previous version of **power**, except that now we can use the keyword **:e** to supply the argument, while still using **exp** as the keyword parameter.

12.4.1. More On Keywords

At this point, it is useful to clarify exactly how keywords are treated by the LISP interpreter. As was mentioned above, the LISP interpreter treats any symbol beginning with : (colon) as a keyword. Moreover, LISP assigns all keywords to have themselves as their value. This way, the LISP interpreter never has to worry about inadvertently evaluating a keyword. It is still true to say that LISP evaluates all the arguments supplied to an ordinary function: If an argument happens to be a keyword, it simply evaluates to itself.

In fact, Common LISP only checks to see if an actual argument is a keyword. That is, when checking for keywords, Common LISP examines the value of the argument supplied, not the supplied argument itself. This means that it is perfectly possible to supply an argument whose value is a keyword. In such a case, LISP will indeed interpret the argument as a keyword, and interpret the next actual argument as the value to be assigned the corresponding keyword parameter.

In general, it is an error to supply to a function a keyword that does not correspond to a keyword parameter of that function. However, there are times when you would want to write a function that accepts as an argument a keyword that is not one of its own. For example, your function might want to pass such an argument to another function that did anticipate this keyword. Common LISP allows you to accomodate this need by letting you specify the special parameter designator **&allow−other−keywords** in the function's parameter list, after the other keyword parameter specifications. Then it will not be an error to supply this function with keywords other than ones that correspond to its own keyword parameters.

Alternatively, you can supply any function with the keyword **:allow−other−keywords**, followed by a non-**nil** argument in a call to the function. This will prevent that particular call to the function from generating an error if unanticipated keywords are supplied.

12.4.2. Interaction Between Keyword and Rest Parameters

If keyword and rest parameters occur together in a function definition, the keywords and associated arguments are picked up and included in the list assigned to the rest parameter. They will still be processed as keywords, though, even if this occurs. For example, consider the following function:

```
-> (defun example (&rest x &key y)
      (list x y))
EXAMPLE
-> (example :y 3)
(( :Y 3) 3)
->
```

Here the keyword parameter **y** got assigned the value **3** because the keyword **:y** is followed by the value **3** in the function call. In addition, all the actual arguments, including the keyword **:y** and the argument **3** following it, got put into the list assigned to **x**.

12.4.3. Terminology

In a sense, the terms "optional" and "keyword" parameters are something of a misnomer. They are both really different kinds of optional parameters. The former are really "positionally-indicated optional parameters", while the later are "keyword-indicated optional parameters".

12.5. Auxiliary Variables

There is one more flourish associated with function parameters. Actually, this feature has nothing to do with parameters per se. It merely allows you to use the parameter list of a function to specify *auxiliary variables*. These are variables local to a function definition, but whose values are never supplied by arguments. Auxiliary variables can be supplied with default values, like optional parameters and keywords, and will be assigned the value **nil** if no default is specified.

Auxiliary variables are indicated by the designator **&aux** in the function's parameter list. This symbol must follow all other parameter designators. All symbols after **&aux** are treated as auxiliary variables.

Standardization Note: In many other versions of LISP, the functionality of the various parameter designators of Common LISP is achieved by having several different types of functions. For example, the function type *lexpr* allowed the programmer to create functions that accept arbitrary number of arguments; the function type *fexpr* allowed for the creation of functions that accept an arbitrary number of arguments that were never evaluated (something we have not yet seen how to do in Common LISP). Often there were several variants of lambda expressions used to implement these different function types.

Common LISP has simplied much of this by the use of parameter designators in function definitions. The functionality of fexprs can be achieved by macros, which are discussed in the next chapter.

12.6. Closures

Suppose we want to write a function that saves some value it can examine the next time it runs. For example, functions that generate random numbers often use the previous random number generated to help generate the next. To do so, we need some place to squirrel away a value so that a function can get at it next time.

We can use a global variable or a property list to store such a value. But this solution is not without risk. We might get careless, and write another function that happens to use the same global variable or property. Then the two functions may interact adversely. It is even more problematic if we want to have several incarnations of the same function around, each remembering what it computed previously, but not interfering with one another. Using a single, global object does not accommodate this.

For example, suppose we want a function that will give us the next even number each time it is called. We could write this as a function that uses the global variable ***evenseed*** to remember the last value it computed:

```
-> (defun even-generator ( )
       (setq *evenseed* (+ *evenseed* 2)))
EVEN-GENERATOR
-> (setq *evenseed* 0)
0
-> (even-generator)
2
-> (even-generator)
4
-> (even-generator)
6
->
```

This works fine, but some other function could come along and clobber **evenseed** in between calls. And we could not use **even-generator** to generate two sequences of even numbers simultaneously, each independent of the other.

A solution to this problem is to make a version of a function that has variables only it can access. This is done by taking a function that contains some free symbols, and producing a new function in which all those free symbols are given their own, unique variables. (Recall that *free symbols* are symbols used to designate variables within a function, but which are not formal parameters of that function). This is as if we replaced each free symbol with a new symbol, one we were certain no other function could ever use. When this new function is run, then, its free symbols will reference variables that no other function can reference. If the values of some of these variables are changed, their new values will be retained until the next time the function is run. However, changes to these variables will not have any effect outside of this function; moreover, the values of these variables cannot be accessed or altered outside of this function.

In the case of our example above, we would like to produce a version of **even–generator** that has its own private copy of the free variable ***evenseed***. When we create this version of **even–generator**, we would like its version of ***evenseed*** to be initialized at whatever value ***evenseed*** currently has. No matter what happens subsequently to the original version, this will not affect the new version. When we run this new version, it would update its private copy of ***evenseed***. This would not affect the version of ***evenseed*** known to the original function. But the new, updated copy of ***evenseed*** would be available to the new function the next time it is run.

In other words, we take a sort of snapshot of a function with respect to the current status of its free symbols. We now manipulate this picture rather than the function itself. The picture has about the same logical structure as the original, but if we change something in the picture, the original does not change. In fact, we should be able to take any number of such snapshots, and manipulate each one a bit differently. The alterations to each snapshot would serve to record its current state of affairs. But each snapshot could be looked at and altered quite independently of the others.

When we take such a snapshot of a function, it is called a *closure* of that function. The name is motivated by the idea that variables denoted by the free symbols of that function, normally "open" to the world outside that function, are now closed to the outside world.

In Common LISP, closures of functions are created by supplying the function **function** with a lambda expression as argument. (We discussed **function** briefly in Chapter 9.) If the free symbols of that lambda expression happen to be parameters of the function within which the lambda expression is embedded, **function** will return a snapshot of the function denoted by the lambda expression. This snapshot will contain its own variables corresponding to each of the lambda expression's free symbols.

For example, we can use **function** to write a version of the function **even–generator** that will produce a closure that includes the free symbol ∗evenseed∗ in the picture:

```
-> (defun even-generator (*evenseed*)
      (function
        (lambda ( )
          (setq *evenseed* (+ *evenseed* 2)))))
EVEN-GENERATOR
-> (setq even-gen-1 (even-generator 0))
#<CLOSURE>
-> (funcall even-gen-1)
2
-> (funcall even-gen-1)
4
-> (funcall even-gen-1)
6
->
```

When **even–generator** is called, LISP creates a new variable corresponding to ∗evenseed∗, as LISP always produces new variables corresponding to the formal parameters of a function. Then the function **function** returns a closure of the specified lambda expression. Since a new variable corresponding to ∗**evenseed**∗ exists at this time, the closure gets this version of ∗**evenseed**∗ as its own. When we exit this call to **even–generator**, no code can reference this variable except the code that comprises the closure. In effect, this closure has a variable that is closed off to the outside world. We save this closure by assigning it to the variable **even–gen–1**.

Next, we use **funcall** to invoke this function. (Remember, **funcall** is like **apply**, but expects the arguments right after the function name. In this case, there are none, as the lambda expression of **even–generator**, and hence, the closure produced from it, is a function of no arguments.) LISP prints out the closure as #<**closure**>. We run this closure a couple of times, and each time it produces a new value.

Standardization Note: The notation used here to print closures is recommended but is not part of the Common LISP standard. This is because it is not really meaningful to talk about printing a closure. Therefore, other implementations of Common LISP may use a different notation.

We can create as many independent closures of the same function as we like. For example, suppose we make another closure of **even-generator** right now:

```
-> (setq even-gen-2 (even-generator 0))
#<CLOSURE>
-> (funcall even-gen-2)
2
-> (funcall even-gen-2)
4
-> (funcall even-gen-1)
8
-> (funcall even-gen-1)
10
-> (funcall even-gen-2)
6
->
```

This closure starts off with its version of *evenseed* at the value **0**. Each closure has its own independent variable corresponding to the symbol *evenseed*. Therefore, a call to one function has no effect on the value of *evenseed* in the other.

12.6.1. Closing a Set of Functions

When we close off the free symbols of a function, a new problem presents itself. The closed variables are inaccessible outside of the closure. So it would be difficult to write a set of functions that shared the same closed variable.

For example, suppose we want to write a pair of functions. One returns the next even number, and the other the next odd number. However, we want them to work in tandem, so that a call to one advances the other. For example, if we call the even number generator three times in a row, it should return **2**, **4**, and **6**. Then a call to the odd number generator should return **7**. If we call it again, it should return **9**. The next time we call the even number generator, it should return **10**.

It is easy to write a single pair of such functions. For example, we could do the following:

```
-> (defun even-gen ( )
      (setq *seed* (cond ((evenp *seed*) (+ *seed* 2))
                         (t (1+ *seed*)))))
EVEN-GEN
-> (defun odd-gen ( )
      (setq *seed* (cond ((oddp *seed*) (+ *seed* 2))
                         (t (1+ *seed*)))))
ODD-GEN
-> (setq *seed* 0)
0
-> (even-gen)
2
-> (even-gen)
4
-> (even-gen)
6
-> (odd-gen)
7
-> (odd-gen)
9
-> (even-gen)
10
->
```

However, if we want to make closures of these functions, we are in trouble. If we use **closure** to produce a closure of each function, each closure would get its own version of *seed*. The closure of **even-gen** could not influence the closure of **odd-gen**, and conversely. But this is not what we want.

The solution to this problem is to create closures of a bunch of functions in the same context. The functions closed together would share their variables with one another, but not with anyone else. For example, here is function that creates a list of two closures, one of which generates even numbers and the other, odd:

```
-> (defun even-odd-gen (*seed*)
     (list
       (function
         (lambda ( )
           (setq *seed* (cond ((evenp *seed*) (+ *seed* 2))
                              (t (1+ *seed*))))))
       (function
         (lambda ( )
           (setq *seed* (cond ((oddp *seed*) (+ *seed* 2))
                              (t (1+ *seed*))))))))
EVEN-ODD-GEN
-> (setq fns (even-odd-gen 0))
(#<CLOSURE> #<CLOSURE>)
-> (funcall (car fns))
2
-> (funcall (car fns))
4
-> (funcall (cadr fns))
5
-> (funcall (cadr fns))
7
-> (funcall (car fns))
8
->
```

The call to **even-odd-gen** produces a pair of closures, one for each call to
function. This pair shares access to an otherwise private copy of the variable *seed*. Subsequent calls to **even-odd-gen** would create additional
pairs of such closures, each pair sharing a variable all its own.

12.7. Compiled and Foreign Functions

If you try to look at the function definitions of most LISP built-in functions, you will find that they look rather mysterious. For example, if you
use **symbol-function** to examine a built-in function like **car**, you will not
get a nice s-expression as a result. Try this on your LISP to see what happens.

The reason we do not get a nice s-expression here is that the function **car**
is not coded in LISP. This is not too surprising. **car** is a rather basic function, and so it is written in machine language. There is no really convenient LISP-way to deal with this code.

In addition to the most basic LISP functions, which must be written in machine language, more complex functions are often written in machine language as well. This is done for efficiency's sake. To facilitate this process, there exists a LISP *compiler,* that takes as input functions written in LISP, and produces as output machine language versions of those functions. The resulting functions can then be used in place of the original LISP functions, and will generally run much faster. Of course, you give up some readability and ease of debugging to get this increase in performance.

So it is possible to take all the functions you have written yourself and, when you are finished debugging them, compile them into machine language to speed up your program. The process of doing this is dealt with in Chapter 20. However, in the meantime, if you peek at a function whose definition is opaque to you, you will know where it came from.

Another possibility is that the function definition was written in another language altogether, and then interfaced with LISP. Of course, these so called "foreign functions" had better obey various conventions of the LISP nationality, or they will wreak havoc. Clearly, this is not the stuff for beginning LISP programmers to be concerned with.

12.8. Summary

(1)   Ordinary LISP functions allow a number of different types of parameters besides the normal *required parameters.* These include *optional parameters,* for which the caller need not supply arguments, *a rest parameter,* which is assigned a list of all arguments not assigned to required or optional parameters, and *keyword parameters,* which are assigned an argument indicated by the presence of keyword.

(2)   Each type of non-required parameter can be specified by the appearance of a *parameter designator* in the functions formal parameter list. The parameter designators are **&optional**, **&rest**, and **&key**. If more than one parameter designator appears, they must appear in the order given above.

(3)   In addition to special kinds of parameters, the parameter list can be used to specify *auxiliary variables* for a function. This is done by the appearence of the designator **&aux** in the formal parameter list, after all other designators.

(4)   Optional parameters, keyword parameters, and auxiliary variables all are assigned the value **nil** if no other value is specified for them. Default values for all three objects by enclosing the symbol in a list and

following it with a default. Optional and keyword parameters can also have an associated **supplied-p** variable: This variable is assigned the value **t** if an argument is supplied for its associated variable, and **nil** otherwise.

(5)   A *closure* is a version of a function with its own private copy of the variables referenced by some of its free symbols. A call to a closure may access or change its own copy of a variable. But it cannot access or influence those of other functions, including other closures of the same function. Nor may other functions access or change its private copies.

(6)   A closure can be produced by passing the function **function** a lambda expression whose free symbols are also local variables in some enclosing code. If several closures are created in the context of the same set of local variables, they will be able to share the same private versions of these variables.

(7)   Functions can be machine-coded for efficiency. We can translate LISP functions into machine-coded functions using a LISP compiler. In addition, we can interface "foreign" functions into LISP. All functions in a LISP system that are not written in LISP cannot be displayed gracefully.

Exercises

(1)   What values do the following expressions return?

    (a) ((lambda (a &optional (x 2) (y 3 yflag) &rest z)
        (list a x y yflag z))
        1)

    (b) ((lambda (a &optional (x 2) (y 3 yflag) &rest z)
        (list a x y yflag z))
        1 2 3 4 5 6)

    (c) ((lambda (a b &key x (y 4))
        (list a b x y))
        1 2 :x 9)

(d) ((lambda (a b &key x (y 4))
   (list a b x y))
 :y 7 :x 9)

(e) ((lambda (a &optional (b 7) &rest z &key x (y 4))
   (list a b x y z))
 1 6 :x 8)

(2)   Modify the function-printing functions you defined for the exercises in Chapter 10 to allow you to specify as an optional argument a stream to which the output can be directed.

(3)   Write a modified version of the function **member** that accepts the keyword **:everywhere**. If the argument given is non-**nil**, then your function will check for membership anywhere in the specified list (i. e., not just on the top level). The default for this parameter should be **nil**.

(4)   Write a function that takes any number of arguments, and computes the square root of the sum of their squares.

(5)   Write a version of **cons** called **mcons** that takes any number of argument. The next-to-last argument should be **cons**ed onto the last; the one before that should be **cons**ed onto the resulting value, and so on. For example, **(mcons 'a 'b 'c '(d e))** should return **(a b c d e)**.

(6)   Write a function **close-enough-producer** that produces functions whcih determine if two numerical values are within a certain tolerance of one another, where the tolerance is given as an argument to **close-enough-producer**.

Chapter 13

Macros

13.1. Introduction

We have now encountered all the major LISP function types save one, the macro. Macros are sufficiently different from other types of LISP functions to merit special attention. Learning to use macros is a bit harder than learning to use more prosaic LISP functions. However, once they are mastered, they provide the user with enormous flexibility at a low cost.

In this chapter we motivate the use of macros, and then present some ways of defining them. We also discuss some techniques to make macro writing easier. Some particular macros are presented, some of which are useful enough to add to one's standard repertoire of LISP programming techniques. Some of these sample macros suggest a certain programming style which many programmers find aesthetically pleasing. This style is presented for your consideration.

13.2. Using Macros to Write More Readable Code

One reason that symbolic LISP functions seem a little strange at first is that they have no "real world" semantics. By this I mean that they do not really have much meaning outside of LISP. This is not the case for more banal programming language functions, such as numerical operations. For example, the operation + is meaningful outside of LISP (or FORTRAN or PASCAL, for that matter). But **car** and **cdr** only seem to make sense within the LISP world.

Of course, the idea is to use **car** and **cdr** to implement other functions that have some a priori meaning to us. For example, suppose we represent locations by lists of the form **(city state zip)**. Then taking the **cadr** of a datum of this form would be conceptually equivalent to stating "give us the 'state' part of a location".

There is a problem with a program that accesses data fields this way, however. The inherent meaninglessness of symbolic operators makes the code rather opaque. For example, if we look at a piece of code that contains the expression

>   (cadr loc1)

it is difficult to determine that this is a reference to the "state" part of a data structure.

One way to write more transparent code would be to define a function called **get–state–field**. The body of this function definition would simply be a call to **cadr**. But now our code looks more meaningful:

>   (get–state–field loc1)

Not only is the code more meaningful, but we have obeyed an important general rule of programming. We have insulated the rest of our program from low-level implementation decisions. Now if we decide to change our location representation, we need only change **get–state–field** and a few other access functions. We do not have to run through our code in search of all references to "location" data.

But we have paid a price for this convenience. Applying **cadr** is an extremely simple LISP operation. But applying **get–state–field** entails the additional overhead of a new function call – fetching the function body, creating new variables for the function's parameters, etc. This is probably several times as costly as the original call to **cadr**. If such data accesses represent a significant portion of the time spent by our program, we may have greatly decreased its efficiency.

What we would really like to do is provide a convenient way of expressing what we want to say, but avoid any additional overhead this might entail.

Macros are a kind of LISP function that can be used to fulfill this goal.

222

Macros provide an extremely flexible mode of expression. In addition, in most systems, macros can be made to result in efficient code, combining the best of two worlds.

How do macros achieve such wonders? The basic idea is the following. Whereas other functions in LISP produce a result that is passed on as their value, LISP macros first *produce a result that is itself another piece of code.* This fabricated piece of code is then evaluated to produce the value that the code returns. In other words, the LISP interpreter evaluates a call to a macro twice. The first evaluation should return an executable form. This form is evaluated again. The result of this second evaluation is returned as the value of the call to the macro.

For example, suppose we define **get-state-field** as a macro. We would do so in such a way so that calling **(get-state-field loc1)** would first produce the piece of code **(cadr loc1)**. LISP would then evaluate this piece of code, which accesses the "state" part of **loc1**. This is just as if the actual code turned into **(cadr loc1)** before execution.

In general, macros may turn into arbitrarily complicated pieces of code. Thus, macros are a convenient way to express something whose appearance would otherwise be more cumbersome or less meaningful.

But macros sound like they would require more work than other LISP function calls, not less. After all, macros have to produce code as well as evaluate it. So how can macros be efficient? The trick is that most LISPs have some way of saving the code produced by the first phase of macro execution. Remember, macros first produce code that they subsequently evaluate. The code that the macro produces will be the same each time the macro is called. That is, each time we evaluate the expression **(get-state-field loc1)**, LISP will produce the code **(cadr loc1)** for subsequent evaluation. (Of course, each time this code is evaluated, it may return a different value, depending on the value of **loc1**.) Since the code produced by the first phase of a call to a macro will always be the same for a given macro call, our interpreter can be made to remember the code produced by such a call. Subsequently, when the interpreter comes around to evaluating that same line of code, it can find the code produced from the previous first phase of the macro call. Then it merely executes this code. For example, having saved the code produced from **(get-state-field loc1)**, the interpreter need only evaluate the expression **(cadr loc1)** when it encounters this code again. That is, it only has to execute a **cadr**.

Thus, with the exception of the initial expense of executing the macro for the first time, code written using a macro will run as fast as if we had written the code produced by the macro. But the code we actually wrote containing the macro will be much nicer to look at.

Standardization Note: Implementations of Common LISP may vary greatly in deciding exactly how and when to save the code from a call to a macro. For example, it is considered fair for **defun** to replace all the calls to macros in a function definition with the code they produce at the time that function is defined. In such an implementation, the first, code-producing phase of macro execution would actually be done at function definition time; the second, code-execution phase would be done as usual, when that code is evaluated. Alternatively, the implementation might wait until a macro call is actually evaluated to compute the code it produces, and then do the replacement. Some implementations may do the replacement conditionally, based on the value of some global flag. Of course, you should attempt to write macro definitions that are independent of these implementation details. However, knowing the details of how macros are treated in your implementation can help you understand how to make your program run more efficiently.

13.3. Defining Macros

We can define a macro in Common LISP using the special function **defmacro**. A call to **defmacro** looks just like a call to **defun**. However, a call to the macro defined by **defmacro** is evaluated differently than a call to an ordinary function. As is the case for ordinary functions, LISP creates new variables for the formal parameters of the macro. However, the arguments supplied in the call to the macro are not evaluated. Instead, each argument is directly assigned to the corresponding formal parameter. Then the body of the macro is evaluated. This evaluation presumably results in a new body of code, which LISP then evaluates again.

As an example, let us write a version of **get–state–field** as a macro. Remember, we want a call of the form **(get–state–field loc1)** to turn into **(cadr loc1)**. To do this, we can define **get–state–field** as follows:

```
-> (defmacro get-state-field (location)
       (list 'cadr location))
GET-STATE-FIELD
->
```

When we evaluate an expression like **(get–state–field loc1)**, the argument **loc1** will not be evaluated. Rather the parameter **location** will be assigned this value. The body of the macro then **cons**s the symbol **cadr** onto the beginning of this value to yield the desired expression, in this case, **(cadr loc1)**. Let us try this macro and see how it works:

> -> **(get–state–field '(berkeley california 94720))**
> **CALIFORNIA**
> ->

In evaluating this macro call, the interpreter assigned **location** the value **'(berkeley california 94720)**. Then the body of the macro got evaluated. This **cons**ed the atom **cadr** onto the value of **location** to produced the value **(cadr '(berkeley california 94720))**. Then LISP evaluated this expression. This returned the value **california**, which was returned as the value of this macro call.

13.4. Macro Expansion

If you define the **get–state–field** macro, and then test it as we did above, you will notice a small difficulty. LISP evaluates the code produced by the macro immediately after producing it. Therefore, when you use a macro, you get to see only the result of the entire evaluation of the macro. But you do not get to see the code produced by the macro along the way. Since it is sometimes useful in debugging to view this intermediate code, LISP provides us with a way of doing so. The function **macroexpand** takes as input an s-expression that may be a call to a macro. If it is, **macroexpand** will apply the macro to its arguments to produce the object code. It will not evaluate this code, but merely return it. **macroexpand** is what the LISP interpreter uses to expand a call to a macro that it is trying to evaluate. So using this function will give us an accurate picture of what the LISP interpreter itself will see.

Let us run **macroexpand** on a call to **get–state–field** and see what happens:

> -> **(macroexpand '(get–state–field loc1))**
> **(CADR LOC1) ;**
> **T**
> ->

As you probably have noticed, the output of **macroexpand** looks a bit unusual. This is because **macroexpand** is one of a number of Common LISP functions that return more than one value. The values are separated, in this implementation, by semicolons. The first value here is the code produced by the call to the macro **get–state–field**. Note that the code produced by the macro call is itself not evaluated, but just returned for our perusal. We can now examine this code to decide if it is what we want.

The second value returned by the call to **macroexpand** is **t**. This means that the argument passed **macroexpand** actually required some macro expansion. Had we passed **macroexpand** a form that did not begin with a macro, it would have returned that form as its first value, and **nil** as its second. We will discuss multiple-value functions further in Chapter 16.

The code produced by macros is generally longer than the call to the macro itself (although this is not the case for our example above). Hence the phase of interpreting the macro to produce code is called *macro expansion.* For example, we would say that the expression **(cadr loc1)** is the macro expansion of the expression **(get–state–field loc1)**.

Note that if the macro expansion produced by **macroexpand** is itself a macro call, **macroexpand** will expand that form as well. That is, **macroexpand** keeps on expanding macros until it produces a form that is not a macro call. If you want to expand a macro form only once, the function **macroexpand–1** is what you want.

13.5. Some Sample Macros

flambda

Let us take a look at a few convenient macros. We noted previously that it is generally appropriate to enclose function arguments inside a call to the special function **function**. In particular, the expression **(function (lambda ...))** occurs frequently. While we can always abbreviate **function** using the # 'shorthand, we can write a special macro to help abbreviate this particular combination. We can define a macro **flambda** that expands into **(function (lambda ...))**:

```
-> (defmacro flambda (&rest l)
       (list 'function (cons 'lambda l)))
FLAMBDA
-> (macroexpand '(flambda (x y) (cons y x)))
(FUNCTION (LAMBDA (X Y) (CONS Y X))) ;
T
->
```

Since a lambda expression may contain any number of forms, we used the **&rest** parameter designator to define a rest parameter. This parameter will get assigned the list of all the arguments supplied to **flambda**. For example, in the call to **flambda** above, the rest parameter **l** gets assigned the value **((x y) (cons y x))**. **flambda** then just sticks the atom **lambda** on the front of this list, and then puts the resulting lambda expression in a list that begins with the symbol **function**. Thus the sample "flambda expression" given above as an argument to **macroexpand** can be seen to be a shorthand for writing the full **(function (lambda ...))** business.

pop

A more interesting function is the macro **pop**. **pop** takes as its argument a symbol whose value is a list. It reduces this list to its **cdr**, and returns the first element of the list as its value. In effect, **pop** treats the list like a stack, and pops off its top element.

A call to **pop** is equivalent to executing the following piece of code:

```
(prog1 (car stack) (setq stack (cdr stack)))
```

Recall that **prog1** evaluates all its arguments in sequence, returning the value of the first one. Thus, for any particular list, we can execute a line of code like the one shown above, which carries out the desired function. What we would like to do is to define a macro that expands into code of this form. Thus we want **(pop stack)** to expand into the **prog1** shown above.

pop is actually defined in Common LISP. So we will write our own definition of it for the purpose of an example. We could use the following definition:

```
-> (defmacro our-pop (stack)
     (list 'prog1
       (list 'car stack)
       (list 'setq stack (list 'cdr stack))))
OUR-POP
-> (macroexpand '(our-pop stksym))
(PROG1 (CAR STKSYM) (SETQ STKSYM (CDR STKSYM))) ;
T
->
```

Now let us try this macro to see how it works:

```
-> (setq stack '(a b c))
(A B C)
-> (our-pop stack)
A
-> stack
(B C)
->
```

our-pop returned the first element of **stack** as its value. In addition, it reduced **stack** to its **cdr**.

Note that it would be difficult to write this function as an ordinary function, since it needs to get at the actual stack name to change its value. We would have always had to quote the name of the stack we were passing, because arguments supplied to ordinary functions always get evaluated. However, with macros, this was not a problem.

13.6. Macro Writing Techniques

As we can see from the example above, even simple macros are difficult to write. A macro is code that produces code, and this code manipulates data which are of the same form as code. Sometimes all these levels get confusing. You can avoid some of this confusion by following the following procedure whenever you write a macro:

(1) First, write down an example of the call to the macro you would like to be able to make. In the case of **our-pop**, for example, this might be the call **(our-pop stksym)**.

(2) Then write down the code that you would like the macro to produce. In our example, this would be

(prog1 (car stksym) (setq stksym (cdr stksym)))

(3) Now write a macro that transforms the likes of the first into the second.

Let us apply this procedure to define the macro **push**. This macro will expect two arguments, and will produce code that pushes the first onto the stack named by the second. The code will return the entire new stack as its value. Like **pop**, **push** is already defined in Common LISP, so we will write our own version as an illustration.

(1)   A typical call to **our-push** might be this:

      (our-push a stksym)

So our macro should have two parameters: one will get assigned **a** and the other **stksym**.

(2)   Now let us write the corresponding target code:

      (setq stksym (cons a stksym))

(3)   All that remains is to write the code that builds this expression using the assignments of the formal parameters of the macro:

```
-> (defmacro our-push (e stack)
      (list 'setq stack (list 'cons e stack)))
OUR-PUSH
```

Let us test it to check that it is correct:

```
-> (macroexpand '(our-push 'x stack))
(SETQ STACK (CONS X STACK)) ;
T
-> stack
(B C)
-> (our-push 'x stack)
(X B C)
-> stack
(X B C)
->
```

13.7. Advanced **defmacro** Features

The definition of **flambda** above used the parameter designator **&rest** to specify a parameter in which to amass all the arguments that appear in a call to this macro. In fact, all the parameter designators that are allowed in the definition of ordinary functions are allowed in a macro definition created by **defmacro**. In addition, **defmacro** allows two additional parameter designators. These are called **&body** and **&whole**.

&body is identical in function to **&rest**. The only reason to use **&body** instead of **&rest** (only one can appear in a single definition) is stylistic: Our code might appear clearer if we indicate that some part of a calling expression is intended as a body of code.

For example, our definition for **flambda** above was the following:

```
(defmacro flambda (&rest l)
  (list 'function (cons 'lambda l)))
```

However, the form that a call to the macro must take is not illuminated by the unstructured parameter list in this definition. Instead, we could use the following definition:

```
(defmacro flambda (paramlist &body l)
  (list 'function (cons 'lambda (cons paramlist l))))
```

This code is slightly less efficient than the original (it does more **cons**ing), but its intention is somewhat clearer.

The designator **&whole** must be followed by two parameters. The first is assigned the *entire* call to the macro. For example, suppose we used the **&whole** designator in the definition of **flambda**. Then a call of the form **(flambda (x) (cons x nil))** will result in this entire expression being assigned to the whole parameter.

The second parameter following the occurrence of **&whole** is not a real parameter at all. Actually, it is a variable that Common LISP will set to include certain information about the environment in which the call to the macro is made. Typical LISP programming does not require use of this variable, and we will not discuss it further. In fact, the need to use **&whole** is itself extremely rare. If you do use it, however, note that **&whole** and its two parameters must go right in the beginning of a parameter list, before any designators or parameters, even required ones.

13.7.1. Destructuring

The various parameter designators make programming easier because they provide a built-in mechanism that makes it easy to deal with arguments. However, sometimes we would like even more functionality in this regard. This is especially true when a call to a macro is known to have a lot of structure to it within individual arguments. With what we know so far, our code would have to dig out items that were buried within arguments. Since such digging around is often most of the work that a macro function must do, automating this process can greatly simplify macro writing.

For example, suppose we wanted to write our own version of the Common LISP macro **dolist**. Recall that a call to **dolist** is of the form

    (dolist (*var list-val return-val*) *exp1 exp2 ...*)

where the expression *return-val* is optional. **dolist** assigns *var* successive elements of *list-val*, and evaluates the *expi* for each assignment.

We could write a macro definition for a function like **dolist** that expanded into a call to **do**∗. For example, a call to **dolist** like the one above could turn into the following piece of code:

```
(do∗ ((ltemp list-val (cdr ltemp))
      (var (car ltemp) (car ltemp)))
    ((null ltemp) return-val)
    exp1
    exp2
    ...                                )
```

With this product in mind, we can now design a macro definition for a function **our–dolist** (you might try to do this yourself before looking at my code):

```
(defmacro our–dolist (paramarg &body l)
   (append
      (list 'do∗
         (list
            (list 'ltemp (cadr paramarg) '(cdr ltemp))
            (cons (car paramarg)
                  '((car ltemp) (car ltemp))))
         (list '(null ltemp) (caddr paramarg)))
      l))
```

Note that this code employs a number of typical macro writing techniques. For example, the code is arranged so as to contain as large constants as possible, so that as little **cons**ing as necessary will be done. Also, the code **append**s the first expression it builds onto **l**, as this will be assigned the *list* of *expi*.

One of the reasons this code is as complex as it is is that we must dig out the various elements of **paramarg** using **car**, **cadr** and the like. We need to do this because this argument is a list which has some internal structure to it. The various parameter designators could not help us here, because all the action occurs within the structure of an argument, not on the top level of the function call.

A solution to this problem is simply to allow lists that have the structure of a parameter list to appear *anywhere* that a single parameter is normally expected in a call to **defmacro**. For example, instead of the single parameter **paramarg** in the parameter list of **our–dolist**, we can allow a list of the form (**var listform &optional resultform**) to appear. **defmacro** will take care to assign these parameters to the elements that appear inside the argument that corresponds to this entire expression. Using this feature, we can write a somewhat simpler version of **our–dolist**:

```
(defmacro our–dolist ((var listform &optional resultform)
                      &body l)
   (append
     (list 'do*
       (list
         (list 'ltemp listform '(cdr ltemp))
         (cons var '((car ltemp) (car ltemp))))
       (list '(null ltemp) resultform))
     l))
```

The overall structure of this code is the same as the previous version. However, in this version, the single parameter **paramarg** has been replaced by the list (**var listform &optional resultform**). In addition, the code here can refer to the various elements within the first argument of a call to this macro using the parameters **var**, **listform** and **resultform**. The intention of the code is clearer and the code itself is simpler.

Since this feature of **defmacro** allows you to dig into a complex structure automatically, it is known as *destructuring*. In general, you can write as complicated a parameter list as you like, using an arbitrary amount of nesting of parameter lists within parameter lists. The only constraint is that you must place an embedded parameter list only in places in which LISP would not otherwise allow a list, so that your parameter list will not be ambiguous.

13.8. Special Functions and Macros

Many of the so-called special functions we have introduced are actually macros. Most notably the functions **defun**, **prog**, **cond**, **setf**, and **defmacro** itself are all Common LISP macros.

For example, a call to **setf** turns into a call to a more basic assigment function. A call to **setf** whose first argument is a symbol turns into a **setq**, e. g.:

```
-> (macroexpand '(setf a 'b))
(SETQ A 'B) ;
T
->
```

However, if the left-hand side of the call to **setf** is a call to the function **get**, the **setf** turns into a call to some internal Common LISP property list changing function.

We have been somewhat lax in distinguishing macros from other special functions. For example, in Common LISP, **setq**, **quote**, **if** and **let** are special functions that are not macros. Instead, these symbols are known to the interpreter, which is responsible for correctly interpreting forms that begin with them. To speak more properly, we should refer to functions like **setq** as a special function, and functions like **defun** as a macro. Many of their properties are the same, so we shall sometimes be sloppy and refer to any non-ordinary function as a special function. We will use the term *wired-in* special function if we need to distinguish non-macro special functions from the rest.

Standardization Note: The line between macros and wired-in special functions is actually rather thin. For example, a Common LISP implementation may implement some wired-in special functions as macros, and some macros as wired-in special forms (although it must still provide a macro definition in the latter case).

13.9. Modes of Macro Usage

The use of macros is limited only by your own creativity. For example, if you are appalled by the lack of mneumonic value for the names of LISP's mapping functions, you can define a macro to remedy this. Let us call this macro **for**. Depending on how it is called, **for** will turn into a call to the appropriate mapping function. The basic call to **for** could have the following form:

(for (x in l) (do (foo x)))

Here the literals **in** and **do** are keywords that denote which form of mapping is desired. The clause containing the keyword **in** means that we want the function to apply to successive **cars** of a list. The list is specified next. In other words, **in** means that we want to produce either a **mapc** or a **mapcar**. The clause beginning with **do** allows us to specify the body of the function to be applied to the formal parameter; in particular **do** means that this body should simply be executed, and the results thrown away. Thus, **do** would be used if we want to specify either a **map** or a **mapc**. The combination of **in** and **do** is therefore equivalent to **mapc**. Hence the following would be the macro expansion of the call to **for** given above:

> (mapc 'foo l)

Similarly, using the keyword **on** instead of **in** might denote a mapping function which applies to successive **cdr**s of a list. And in addition to **do**, we might have a number of options. For example, the keyword **save** would mean to collect the result of each function application in a list, and return this as the value. Thus we would have the following calls and associated expansions:

> (for (x on l) (do (foo x))) =>
> (map 'foo l)
>
> (for (x in l) (save (foo x))) =>
> (mapcar 'foo l)

We can add additional flourishes. For example, we can have an optional **when** clause that allows the specification of a condition which must be met before the action clause is executed, e. g.:

> (for (x in l) (when (test x)) (do (foo x))) =>
> (mapc '(lambda (x) (cond ((test x) (foo x)))) l)

for is a relatively smart macro. It performs a complicated translation operation. For example, sometimes it will actually produce a lambda expression with a formal parameter in it. Sometimes it will throw away the user-specified formal parameter because it can use a map function directly. We will not show a definition for **for** here, but a definition for a nearly identical macro is given in Charniak et al. (1979).

Another interesting way of using macros can be observed by looking at **setf** once again. As we mentioned, **setf** accepts as its first argument a form that, if evaluated, would reference some value. **setf** makes whatever change is needed to assure that subsequent evaluation of the particular form given will produce the value specified by the second argument to the call. It does this by expanding into the correct code to make the desired change.

setf allow us to change many kinds of "value holders" (most of which we have not even seen yet). In addition, **setf** allows us to extend the repertoire of items for which it can generate code. This is done by making calls to the macro **defsetf**. For example, suppose the function that replaced the entire property list of a symbol were called **putplist**. Then we would like a call of the form.

> **(setf (symbol–plist 'foo) '(prop1 val1 prop2 val2 ...))**

to turn into a call to **putplist**:

> **(putplist 'foo '(prop1 val1 prop2 val2 ...))**

Standardization Note: A function like **putplist** probably exists in every implementation, but it has no standard Common LISP name.

We can accomplish this by the following call to **defsetf**:

> **(defsetf symbol–plist putplist)**

After evaluating this form, calls to **setf** that refer to the access function **symbol–plist** will turn into calls to the updating function **putplist**.

The advantage of this kind of macro is that we need use only the one updating function **setf** whenever we want to change a value. We need only inform LISP of how that value should be changed. **defsetf** also permits a more complicated syntax in which a more elaborate type of transformation can be specified. Even more elaborate transformations can be handled by the related function **define–setf–method**.

There are a number of Common LISP macros related to **setf**. For example, the need to increment or decrement an integer-valued variable is quite common in programming. We could do this with a line of code of the following form:

> **(setq n (+ n 2))**

However, it is convenient to have a macro that expands into this. In Common LISP, this macro is called **incf**. The above line of code could be written using **incf** as:

> **(incf n 2)**

The macro **incf** happens to be part of Common LISP, although we could write it ourselves with no great difficulty. However, the need to create such *read-modify-write* macros comes up frequently enough that Common LISP provides us with a special function to help write them. This function is called **define–modify–macro** (actually, it is itself a macro). It is called with a symbol, a parameter list, and an update function. It makes the symbol into a macro that uses the update function to change its argument. It is assumed that the macro created will always require at least one argument, namely, the object to update. Therefore, the parameter list is used only to specify additional arguments.

For example, if **incf** were not defined in Common LISP, we could define it using **define–modify–macro** as follows:

```
(define–modify–macro our–incf (&optional (delta 1))
   +)
```

This call to **define–modify–macro** defines **our–incf** as a read-modify-write macro. As all such macros, **our–incf** anticipates one argument. In addition, because of the particular parameter list supplied, **our–incf** is capable of accepting an optional argument. It will update the value of its first argument by applying the function + to it and to the optional argument. Since the optional argument defaults to 1, supplying the optional argument has the effect of increasing the value of the first argument by the optional argument; if it is omitted, the first argument is increased by 1.

As another example, we previously mentioned the function **adjoin** as one which **cons**ed a value onto a list only if it were not already a member of that list. If we wanted to create a read-modify-write function that went along with this idea, we could do the following:

```
(define–modify–macro adjoinf (e)
   (lambda (l e) (adjoin e l)))
```

This defines **adjoinf** as a read-modify-write macro that expects exactly two arguments. The first is updated by applying **adjoin** to it and the second argument. Thus, a call of the form **(adjoinf foo 'a)** will reset **foo** to its old value with **a adjoin**ed into it. (The lambda expression is necessary here because **adjoin** expects its arguments in the order opposite that in which **adjoinf** will supply them.)

13.10. Macros and Programming Style

Some programmers object to the liberal use of macros of the sort suggested above. Their complaint is directed mostly at macros like **for**, **setf** and

defmacro, which have their own internal syntax. The problem here is that each of these macros has its own complicated internal structure. Hence one needs to learn what is essentially a new language in order to manipulate programs containing such macros. The macro definitions collectively constitute the compiler for this language. Thus, one is no longer programming in LISP, but in some other language in which some of the elegance and simplicity of LISP are lost.

I find this argument to be valid, but not too damaging. One does indeed often use LISP as a way to implement the language one really wishes one had in the first place. But this is probably an important reason why researchers in artificial intelligence like LISP. Problems in AI are generally less well understood than those in other areas, so the basic primitives that one would want in a language are less clear. Instead, AI needs a language where it is easy to define what you want as you go along.

So it is true that many AI programs are in effect written in their own language. But it is probably the case that the need to develop these languages is intrinsic to the problem. It is a strength of LISP that one can develop such languages so easily. And of course, all the aspects of LISP still are operative in these languages. So the full power of LISP is available in each case.

13.11. Macro Implementation

We mentioned above that **defmacro** is itself a macro. But what does it expand into? That is, what is the form of the code that actually implements a macro?

In most LISPs, including Common LISP, a macro function is implemented internally as a function of one parameter. When a macro call is evaluated, the *entire* form comprising the call is assigned to this parameter. The macro function body is then evaluated. It is up to the macro function body to find the actual arguments in this form and produce the correct code from them.

We have not had to write macro definitions that did this because the **defmacro** macro did most of the dirty work for us. Internally, though, **defmacro** produces a macro function definition that is a function of one argument, and associates this definition with the macro name. We can get at this actual definition by using the primitive Common LISP function **macro-function**. Let us use **macro-function** to retrieve the actual macro function definition produced by **defmacro** for our macro **our-push**, defined above:

```
-> (pprint (macro-function 'our-push))

(LAMBDA (DEFMACROARG)
  (LET ((E (CADR DEFMACROARG))
        (STACK (CADDR DEFMACROARG)))
    (LIST 'SETQ STACK (LIST 'CONS E STACK))))

NIL
->
```

We pretty-printed out this definition so we can get a better look at it. The code we wrote is found inside a call to **let**. The rest of this code was produce by **defmacro**. As we can see, **defmacro** produced a function of the single parameter **defmacroarg**. This parameter will get assigned the entire calling expression when this macro is used. Therefore, this code uses **let** to extract the second and third elements of the calling expression, which correspond to the arguments for the **e** and **stack** parameters of the code we wrote. Then it is safe to evaluate the code we wrote just as we wrote it.

As you can see, this definition is rather more complex than we would like to deal with. Fortunately, with **defmacro** at our disposal, we never have to write an actual macro function definition ourselves.

Standardization Note: The exact code produced by **defmacro** is implementation-dependent. In particular, most implementations produce more complex code, which might include error checking, for example. Also, other LISPs store macro function definitions in different ways, and hence require different ways of retrieving them.

13.12. Summary

(1) A *macro* is a LISP function that is evaluated in two phases. The first phase produces a piece of code, called the *macro expansion*. In the second phase, the macro expansion produced in the first phase is evaluated.

(2) A macro is a good way to write aesthetically pleasing but efficient code. Macros are efficient if the LISP implementation allows for calls to macros to be replaced by their macro expansions after they are initially evaluated.

(3) A macro can be defined using the special function **defmacro**. A call to **defmacro** looks just like a call to **defun**. In addition to the ordinary parameter designators, **defmacro** also accepts the designators **&body** and **&whole**.

(4) When a call to a macro occurs, none of the arguments supplied to the macro is evaluated. Instead, each of the parameters that appears in the call to **defmacro** is assigned the corresponding unevaluated argument. Then the body of the macro is evaluated to produce an executable form. This form is then evaluated and its value returned as the value of the macro call.

(5) The function **macroexpand** is useful to debug macro definitions. **macroexpand** expands the macro calls in its argument, and returns the resulting code as its value.

(6) A good way to write macros is to first write down a sample macro call and the code it should produce. Then write a macro definition that translates one into the other.

(7) A feature known as *destructuring* is useful in macro writing. This feature allows the placement of a parameter list within a parameter list of **defmacro** at any point at which a single parameter is otherwise expected. **defmacro** takes care of assigning the parts of the argument supplied to the various parameters within these lists.

(8) Internally, all macro definitions are really functions of one parameter. This parameter is assigned the entire calling expression of the macro. Normally, we are protected from this complexity by defining our macros using **defmacro**.

(9) Many built-in special functions are macros. These include **pop**, **push**, **defun**, **defmacro** and **setf**.

Exercises

(1) Write macros **head** and **tail** which expand into calls to **car** and **cdr**, respectively.

(2) Write a macro function **our–if** that translates calls of the form **(our–if a then b)** into **cond**s of the form **(cond (a b))**, and calls of the form **(our–if a then b else c)** into **cond**s of the form **(cond (a b) (t c))**.

(3) Write a version of the **for** macro described above that provides a uniform way of expressing calls to mapping functions.

(4) Write your own version of the Common LISP built-in macro **when** in terms of **cond**.

Chapter 14

Macro Characters

14.1. Introduction

So far in this book, we have been largely concerned with how forms are evaluated by the LISP interpreter once they have been read in. This is not remarkable, since the process of evaluation is central to LISP. However, we have also made an effort to consider LISP as a real programming language and not an abstract formalism. As such, issues such as the user interface, implementation details, error handling, debugging, compiling, and interacting with the operating system become equally important. The rest of this book is primarily concerned with such issues.

In this chapter we examine a technique that gives the LISP programmer the ability to modify the way expressions are read in by the interpreter. This involves the use of a device called a *macro character*. Through the use of macro characters, the user can designate special characters which act in unusual ways. This gives the user the ability to establish some useful shorthands that simplify some programming tasks. We discuss how to define macro characters, and suggest some uses for them. Some particularly useful macro characters, called the *backquote* macro character and the *dispatching* macro character, are discussed in some detail.

14.2. Executing Functions During read

Suppose Common LISP had no special character to abbreviate **quote**. With the machinery we have seen so far, we would have no way to extend Common LISP to accept the special notation we have been using. Of course, this is not a real problem. Virtually all LISPs come equipped with a built-in special abbreviation for **quote**. But we may need to define other abbreviations that behave similarly to **quote**. And right now, we have no way to do so.

To provide such a facility, some LISP interpreters allow the programmer to attach arbitrary functions to individual characters. When LISP reads in a character that has a function attached to it, LISP fetches the function associated with that character, and evaluates it. LISP throws away the original character, and instead, returns the value computed by the attached function.

For example, if we want to set up a special character for **quote**, assuming that none existed, we could do so by attaching the following function to the **quote** character ':

```
(lambda (stream char)
  (list (quote quote) (read stream)))
```

First, note that this is a function of two arguments, a stream and a character. This is because such functions are always applied to the current stream and current character (i. e., the character to which the function was itself attached). As is the case here, typically, the character is simply ignored, and the stream is just passed to **read**.

When we evaluate the body of this function, it will produce a list whose first element is the symbol **quote**, and the second the s-expression read in by the explicit call to **read**. If we attach this function to the character ', and type **'a**, this would turn into the list **(quote a)**.

Thus the special character for **quote** works by expanding into a normal LISP s-expression. For this reason, characters that have functions so attached to them are called *macro characters*. Macro characters have nothing to do with ordinary LISP macros. These characters are called macro characters because, like ordinary macros, they usually produce more LISP as their result. However, unlike ordinary macros, which are expanded during evaluation, macro characters are expanded during a call to **read**.

The example above illustrates an important point about macro characters. Note that for our macro character for **quote** to work, it had to read in the next s-expression explicitly. That is, **read** does not anticipate what a macro character will do or try to help out in any special way. If the macro character wants to get at something in the input stream, it must call **read** again recursively. (This is recursive because we must already be inside a call to **read** in order to be evaluating a macro character to begin with. Most of the time, this call to **read** will be implicit within LISP's top level **read-eval-print** loop.) This recursive call to **read** will swallow up a bit of input. When control is returned to the outer level, the outer **read** just continues by reading in the characters following those swallowed up by the recursive call. So if our **quote** character occurs in the middle of an expression, as in **(a 'b c)**, the macro character will cause **b** to be read in explicitly, and will return **(quote b)**. The **read** in which all this is going on will see **c** as the next expression to be read, and will therefore return the list **(a (quote b) c)**. This is just the result we want.

Let us look at another simple example. Suppose we want a shorthand for saying **(pp 'foo)** (recall that **pp** is a function we hypothesized that pretty-prints function definitions). One way to do this is to attach a function to a character, say **!**, so that **!foo** will turn into **(pp 'foo)**. To do so, we need only attach the following macro character definition to the chosen character:

```
(lambda (stream char)
  (list 'pp (list 'quote (read stream))))
```

If we attach this function to **!**, then **!foo** will expand to the list **(pp 'foo)**. LISP will then evaluate this expression, resulting in the function definition of **foo** being pretty-printed.

14.3. Defining Macro Characters

A number of familiar aspects of Common LISP syntax are actually implemented by pre-defined macro characters. For example, the symbol **(**, used to begin a list, is a macro character, as is the comment character **;** and the quote character **'**.

We have not yet seen how to attach a function to a character to create our own macro characters. In Common LISP, this can be done using the function **set–macro–character**. To implement the previous macro character, for example, we would have to type the following:

```
-> (set-macro-character #\!
      #'(lambda (stream char)
           (list 'pp (list 'quote (read stream))))))
T
->
```

The characters #\ are a special Common LISP syntax to designate character objects. We have not had to deal with characters until now, because
none of the LISP operations we have dealt with so far have been operations on characters (as opposed to strings, symbols or numbers, say). But
here, we want to specify the character !, not the symbol !, so we had to
use this special syntax. Characters always evaluate to themselves in Common LISP, so we need not worry about quoting them.

Standardization Note: The method of defining macro characters will vary
across those versions of LISP that support them. Indeed, very existence of
macro characters is not guaranteed in all LISPs.

Using **set-macro-character** to define a macro character for **!**, we could
then do the following (provided we had defined **pp**):

```
-> (defun foo (x y) (cons y x))
FOO
-> ! foo

(DEFUN FOO
    (LAMBDA (X Y)
       (CONS Y X)))

T
->
```

Note that if you define a character as a macro character, it becomes unus-
able as an ordinary character. For example, if we want to have a variable
named **a!b**, we would have to say **a\!b**, where the \ instructs LISP to
take the next character literally. The first example would be interpreted as
two separate s-expressions, namely, **a** and **(pp 'b)**, as the macro character
is treated as a token terminator and causes **read** to think it has finished
reading an atom.

Macro characters that signal the end of a token are called *terminating macro characters.* It is possible in Common LISP to define macro characters
that do not interrupt reading quite so much. In particular, if an optional

third argument to **set–macro–character** is non-**nil**, then the appearance of that macro character inside what would otherwise be a symbol name will not cause its macro function to be invoked. Instead, it will be read as an ordinary character in that context. Naturally enough, such macro characters are called *non-terminating macro characters.*

Actually, our definitions of macro characters above are slightly flawed. As we indicated previously, the calls to **read** within our macro characters will occur recursively as the result of some other initial call to **read**. However, **read** needs to know that it is being called recursively in some special cases. Exactly why this is so will not concern us for the moment. But for this reason, you may or may not have experienced some difficulty with the above definitions, depending on your implementation. However, in general, it is good form for calls to **read** to indicate that they are recursive if it is known that this is the case.

To accommodate this need, **read** is designed to accept a fourth optional argument. Recall that the first (also optional) argument to **read** indicates the stream to read from; the second tells whether an end-of-file causes an error, and the third a value to return in case **read** is told that end-of-file should not cause an error. The fourth argument is a flag that indicates, if it is non-**nil**, that the call to **read** occurred within another call to **read**. For an obvious reason, such an argument is called a *recursive-p* argument. If we supply the recursive-p argument in our definitions above, then they will be technically correct. For example, here is our version of **quote** using the proper call to **read**:

```
-> (set-macro-character #\'
        #'(lambda (stream char)
            (list 'pp
                (list 'quote (read stream t nil t)))))
T
->
```

As before, the first argument to **read** specifies a stream. The second argument simply tells **read** the end-of-file is supposed to cause an error. This of course is the default – we need to specify it here only to be able to supply the rest of the arguments. Similarly, the third argument is not interesting when the second is **t**, so it too is a dummy. Finally, we come to the recursive-p argument. As you can see, this is **t**, indicating that the call to **read** will always occur within another call to **read**.

Your calls to **read** within any macro characters you define should invariably have this format.

14.4. Macro Characters that Return No Value

Suppose we want to use a macro character to define a comment character.
A reasonable way to do this would be to have the macro character read individual characters, discarding them until it came to the end of the line.
To do so, we will need to use some Common LISP character manipulation
devices. For example, we could do the following:

```
-> (set-macro-character #\[
      #'(lambda (stream char)
          (do( )
            ((char= (read-char stream nil #\Newline t)
                    #\Newline))))
T
->
```

In this example, we attached a macro character definition to the character
[. We used the character functions **read-char** and **char=** to read in and
compare individual characters, respectively. We used these functions
within a call to **do** to read characters until we spot a newline character. To
specify the newline character, we used the expression #**Newline**. This is
a Common LISP convention that allows you to denote a number of special
non-printing characters by name. Finally, note that the arguments to
read-char have the same meaning as arguments to **read**. In particular,
here we state that we do not want an end-of-file to cause an error, but instead, to return the newline character as the value of the call to
read-char. (That is, it is all right if the last thing in a file is a comment.)
Finally, we supply a recursive-p argument of **t**, as we always do in a call to
read within a macro character.

While it meets our informal specification above, this definition of **[** would
not work very well. The problem is that this macro character returns a
value to the call to **read** in which it occurs. Specifically, our macro character function always returns **t**, the value returned by **char=** at the time the
do is exited. Thus if a comment using **!** appeared within an s-expression
that ran on for a few lines, we would end up with an extra **t** in the expression. For example,

```
(or (foo x) [here is a comment
    (baz x))
```

would turn into

```
(or (foo x) t
    (baz x))
```

where the **t** came from the comment macro character. And this can hardly be what we want!

We can solve this problem by using a very general feature of Common LISP. This is the ability of a function to return no value as its value. We can do this in Common LISP by a call to the function **values,** supplying it with no arguments. Thus, evaluating the expression **(values)** returns nothing at all. (We will discuss functions like **values** further in Chapter 16.)

To accept no value as the result of an evaluation, another LISP function must be prepared for it to happen. That is, if some LISP function unexpectedly returned no value to a function expecting a normal value, that function will actually receive the value **nil**. However, **read** is prepared for macro characters to return nothing. Therefore, we can write a correct version of a comment macro character as follows:

```
-> (set-macro-character #\[
     #'(lambda (stream char)
         (do ( )
             ((char= (read-char stream nil #\Newline t)
                     #\Newline)))
             (values)))
T
->
```

This version of the comment macro character function returns no value as its result. This results in it contributing nothing to the expression the comment may have occurred within. Of course, this is precisely what we want.

Standardization Note: Other LISPs have a special kind of macro character called a *splicing* macro. A splicing macro splices its result into whatever list is being read in. Usually, splicing macros return **nil**, and therefore, are used to the same effect as a Common LISP macro character that returns no value. However, there is no direct analog to splicing macros in Common LISP.

14.5. The Backquote Macro Character

Common LISP contains some useful built-in macro characters. One of these is called the *backquote* macro character. It is particularly useful when writing macro function definitions (i. e., real LISP macros).

The idea of the backquote macro character is the following. Usually, in LISP, we evaluate expressions, and prevent evaluation by preceding an expression by **quote**. However, an expression that is "backquoted" works just the opposite way: All its elements are not evaluated *unless* they are preceded by something that explicitly indicates evaluation.

In Common LISP, the character '(backquote) indicates the backquote macro character; the character , (comma) within a backquoted expression indicates evaluation.

For example, if we backquote an entire expression, all the elements in it are not evaluated. This is just as if we used **quote**:

```
-> '(a b c)
(A B C)
->
```

However, if any of these elements are preceded by a comma, then its *value* will be used instead. For example:

```
-> (setq b '(x y z))
(X Y Z)
-> '(a ,b c)
(A (X Y Z) C)
->
```

The interpretation of backquote, then, is "do not evaluate any of elements in a backquoted s-expression, unless the s-expression is preceded by a comma".

In addition, if an expression within a backquoted s-expression is preceded by the characters ,@ (comma followed by at-sign), the value of the expression is "spliced" into the backquoted list, rather than inserted into it. So we have the following:

```
-> '(a ,@b c)
(A X Y Z C)
->
```

We sometimes refer to the comma as *unquote* and the comma-at-sign as *splice-unquote.*

Note that the unquote and splice-unquote designators can appear anyway within a backquote s-expression. For example, the following is perfectly legal:

```
-> '(a (b (c (d ,b e) f) g) h)
(A (B (C (D (X Y Z) E) F) G) H)
->
```

Let us consider for a moment how the backquote macro character might work. When a backquote appears, the backquote macro character function is applied. It would explicitly call **read** to read in the next s-expression. The next s-expression is likely to contain occurrences of the unquote and splice-unquote designators. These may be dealt with by making , a macro character. The function attached to , may check to see if it is followed by @; then it will read in the next s-expression. It simply returns a list of that expression prefaced by a special symbol. For example, **,a** might expand into something like (∗**unquote**∗ **a**), and **,@a** into (∗**splice−unquote**∗ **a**). Thus the s-expression backquote reads in will arrive with all occurrences of unquoted and splice-unquoted expressions expanded to contain forms like the above. For example, if we type in '(a ,b c), the backquote macro character function will get to see the s-expression (a (∗**unquote**∗ b) c).

So the backquote macro character function will call **read** on an input like (a ,b c), and **read** will return an s-expression like (a (∗**unquote**∗ b) c). The backquote macro character function can then look for the appearance of special forms beginning with ∗**unquote**∗ or ∗**splice−unquote**∗ in the list it reads in. If it sees them, it composes whatever sequence of function calls is necessary to build up the appropriate list. In our example above, it would need to build an s-expression that **cons**s the value of **b** onto the list (c), and then **cons**s the value of **a** onto the result. That is, backquote would have to return an expression like (**cons** 'a (**cons** b '(c))).

In general, backquote will return a LISP form that evaluates to produce a desired expression. In examples above, the form returned by backquote is evaluated by LISP's **read-eval-print** loop. Thus we saw not the form that backquote creates, but only the result of evaluating this form. We can see the form that backquote actually creates before it is evaluated simply by quoting the expression that is read in. For example,

```
-> "(a ,b c)
(CONS 'A (CONS B '(C)))
->
```

Standardization Note: The precise s-expression produced is implementation-dependent. Each implementation must produce a form whose evaluation produces the same effect. But some implementations may retain additional information, for example, to indicate that code came from a backquote. This might be useful to help prettyprint the expression.

Remember, macro characters get expanded at **read** time, not during evaluation. Therefore, they are expanded as soon as they are read in, even if they appear in an expression that is not evaluated. This would not be true of ordinary macros. If we quoted an expression that began with an ordinary macro, it would not be evaluated and the macro would not be expanded. But an expression that begins with a macro character, like '(a ,b c), will always get expanded, in this case, to (cons 'a (cons b '(c))) .

Be warned that an expression containing a backquote may generate code that will cause a considerable amount of transparent **cons**ing when that code is evaluated. In order to produce expressions like the one above, backquote must generate whatever calls to **cons** are necessary to do the job. For example, suppose we backquote a relatively long expression:

```
-> ''(b (c (d ,b e) f) g)
(CONS 'B (CONS (CONS 'C (CONS (CONS 'D (CONS B '(E)))
'(F))) '(G)))
->
```

As we can see, the expression whose value we want occurs deeply within this list. So we must do quite a bit of list building to compute the desired list.

You should think of the backquote macro character as a shorthand for writing code that builds up s-expressions. This is quite a contrast to **quote**, for example, which just prevents evaluation of an existing expression.

14.5.1. Using Backquote in Macro Definitions

The primary purpose of backquote is to help write macro definitions.
Remember, macros always return code that is then evaluated. The body of
a macro spends all its energy building up an s-expression which is mostly
the same from occurrence to occurrence. The only thing that changes is
the part of the code that depends on the arguments. Backquote is a great
help here. It allows us to specify our macro function definition as a kind
of template of the code we would like to have it produce.

For example, consider the definition of the macro **our-push** in the last
chapter. Recall that a call to **our-push** of the form (**our-push e stack**)
should turn into code of the form (**setq stack (cons e stack)**).

Our previous definition of this macro looked rather opaque:

```
-> (defmacro our-push (e stack)
       (list 'setq stack (list 'cons e stack)))
OUR-PUSH
->
```

However, using backquote, we can write this as follows. We can backquote
a template of the code we would like to produce. Within this template, the
parts of the code that come from the arguments will be prefaced by unquote designators. Thus we would have the following alternative
definition:

```
-> (defmacro our-push (e stack)
       '(setq ,stack (cons ,e ,stack)))
OUR-PUSH
->
```

This definition is almost identical to the code we want it to produce.

Remember, one should think of backquote as a shorthand for writing code
that builds up an s-expression. Backquote just saves us the trouble of writing out a lot of **cons**es, etc., by hand. The body of the functions so produced will still contain all these list construction functions in it. For example, the definition produced by the call to **defmacro** above is exactly the
same as the definition of **our-push** given in the previous chapter. Both do
just as much work. The definition using backquote is merely easier to
write and to understand.

14.6. The Dispatching Macro Character

There are a large number of rather standard situations in which a special reader syntax may be helpful. For example, we may want to make it easy to read in expressions other than symbols and lists; we might want to be able to enter numbers in different bases; or we may want to read in forms differently depending upon some condition. A special syntax for each case might be very convenient.

We could realize each such syntactic feature by defining lots of different macro characters. For example, we could have one macro character that meant that what follows should be interpreted as an octal number, another to designate hexidecimal number, and yet another that allowed you to specify the base. The problem with this approach is that it would use up all the unspoken-for LISP characters rather rapidly.

To prevent this from happening, many special syntactic forms are recognized by a single macro character, the character #. This works by having the macro character definition of # examine the next few characters to decide which function was indicated. We can think of # as dispatching to a different routine depending upon the value of the next characters. Because of this, # is referred to as the *dispatching* macro character.

There are many different functions that # can be used to perform. We have already encountered a few. For example, the sequence #'*fn* is an abbreviation for (**function** *fn*). #*c* designates the character *c*, and #*name* designates the character named *name*. *name* can be **space** and **newline**, and possibly others. (Case is not significant in names, but it is in the actual characters. That is, #**a** and #**A** represent two different characters, while #**newline** and #**Newline** both represent the newline character.)

Also, we mentioned previously that some LISP objects, such as closures and streams, cannot really be printed out meaningfully. Instead, these are generally printed out using a notation that begins with the sequence #<. If read back in, this sequence will of course be interpreted as invoking the dispatching macro function of #. However, the routine dispatched to causes an error. This is intentional, so that forms that are cannot really be printed will not accidentally be read back in as something else.

Among the other dispatch macro character features, **#B**, **#O**, and **#X** can be followed by binary, octal and hexadecimal numbers, respectively. For example, **#B1101** denotes the equivalent to decimal 13, as does **#O15** and **#XD**. If # is followed by a number followed by the character **R**, then the next number will be read in that base. E. g., **#3R111** also denotes 13 decimal.

There are a number of other characters recognized by #, and we will encounter them by and by. (They are all described in Appendix B). However, there is really nothing special about # – it is just a macro character with a complex function attached to it. We could have written this function ourselves if it had not conveniently come with Common LISP. But to make things even more convenient for us, Common LISP has a facility to make it easy to define your own dispatching macro character, or to add more features to an existing one, including #.

The function **make–dispatch–macro–character** takes one argument, a character, and makes it into a dispatching macro character. Initially, no characters will be recognized as valid characters to dispatch on. To make a given character dispatch to a function, we use the function **set–dispatch–macro–character**. This is a function of three arguments: the dispatching macro character, the "subcharacter" to dispatch on, and the function to apply when this character sequence is seen. The subcharacter cannot be a digit, because these are reserved for expressions of the form **#3R121**. The function must be a function of three arguments. When called, it will get passed the current stream, the subcharacter that was dispatched on, and an integer created from whatever digits intervened between the dispatch character and the subcharacter, as in the example just given (or **nil** if there were none).

For example, the character **!** is unused by the # dispatching macro character. Suppose we want an expression of the form **#!foo** to turn into **(bang foo)**. We could do this by extending # to know about **!**:

```
-> (set-dispatch-macro-character #\# #\!
      #'(lambda (stream subchar arg)
          (list 'bang (read stream t nil t))))
T
```

Here we passed as arguments the dispatching macro character #, the subcharacter **!** and a function of three arguments. Now we should be able to use **#!** as we suggested:

```
-> '#!foo
(BANG FOO)
->
```

14.7. Some Additional Facts about Characters

In any version of LISP, there are a number characters that have a special meaning to the reader. For example, **(** always signals the beginning of a list, and is never assumed to be part of a name. Similarly, some character (usually ') is interpreted as an abbreviation for the function **quote**.

In Common LISP, such characters are made to behave specially by defining them to be macro characters. In particular, the characters (,), ", ', ,, ;, are all defined to be terminating macros. For example, the macro character definition of (causes it to read in the subsequent sequence of expressions and produce a list.

In fact, there are exactly six syntactically distinct types of characters in Common LISP: (1) *constituent* characters are the ones that are normally interpreted as part of a token; (2) *whitespace* characters generally act to delimit tokens; (3) the *single escape* and (4) *multiple escape* characters are as described in Chapter 10; (5) *macro characters* are described in this chapter; and (6) *illegal* characters are those whose mere presence causes an error. !, ?, [,], {, and } do not appear in any standard Common LISP construction.

A description of the standard Common LISP character set is contained in Appendix B. Note that it is possible to change the syntactic property of a character using the function **set–syntax–from–char**, although you should have little occasion to do so.

14.8. Summary

(1)   A *macro character* is a function that is attached to an individual character and used when that character is seen by **read**. The result produced by a macro character is inserted into the s-expression currently under construction by **read**. The character to which the macro character is attached is discarded.

(2)   Macro characters are defined using the function **set–macro–character**. This takes two arguments: the character to which the macro character should be attached, and a function of two arguments to attach to the character. When the function is invoked, it is passed the current a stream and the macro character itself.

(3)   In dealing with macro characters, it is often necessary to deal with character objects. We can specify individual characters in LISP by preceding them with the characters #\. We can specify some non-printing characters by name. For exmple, #**Newline** designates the newline character.

(4)   A particularly useful macro character is called *backquote*. It is designated by the character ' (backquote). The elements in a backquoted

s-expression are not evaluated, unless they are preceded by the character **,** (comma) or **, @** (comma followed by at-sign). In the former case, the value of the element is inserted into the backquoted expression; in the latter, it is spliced into it. Backquote is particularly useful for writing macro function definitions.

(5)   Another important built-in macro character is the dispatch macro character **#**. This dispatches to different functions depending on the next several characters. It is possible to define new dispatch macro characters using **make–dispatch–macro–character**, and to extend existing ones using **set–dispatch–macro–character**.

Exercises

(1)   Implement the macro character **!** that pretty-prints out all the "interesting" aspects of the next symbol. Use the function that you wrote as an exercise in Chapter 10 on I/O to do the actual printing.

(2)   Rewrite the macro definitions of the previous chapter using the backquote macro character. For example, write a macro definition of **pop**, and of the macros **when** and **if**.

(3)   Create a new comment character called **[**. Unlike the standard LISP comment character, the new character will ignore everything up to and including the next occurrence of **]**.

(4)   Many artificial intelligence programs use a technique called *pattern matching.* (We will discuss pattern matching in detail in Chapter 21.) A basic application of pattern matching is to have a data base of facts of the form **(human John)**, **(human Bill)**, **(dog Fido)**. Then, to find out which elements are known to be human, the program can query the data base with a *pattern* like **(human ?x)**. The item **?x** is meant to denote a sort of variable that matches actual items. The result of the query should be a list of all elements in the data base that match the entire pattern.

However, we need to let our pattern matcher know that items like **?x** are meant to be treated specially. One way to do this is to make **?** a macro character so that **?x** turns into a form like **(∗var∗ x)**. Then the pattern matcher can be on the lookout for forms of this kind.

Define **?** as a macro character having the behavior just described.

Chapter 15

List Representation

15.1. Introduction

All the s-expressions we have seen have been either lists or atoms. S-expressions are actually somewhat more general than this, due largely to the way LISP is implemented. I have avoided discussing general s-expressions thus far because it is better to have an understanding of LISP in terms of lists first. But there are some aspects of the language for which an understanding of the implementation is necessary.

In this chapter we present the data structures that underlie lists, which are *binary trees*. We show how lists are implemented in terms of binary trees, and how the components of binary trees, called *cons cells,* can be referred to by a notation called *dotted pairs*. We look at some of the consequences of this implementation. In particular, we examine the problems that arise from having multiple pointers to the same data object. We discuss some LISP operations that make sense in terms of this implementation, namely, the modification of existing lists. The possible horrors that may result from such manipulation are graphically depicted. Finally, we discuss when such implementation details should be considered to gain advantages in efficiency.

15.2. Internal Representation of Lists

Lists are represented in LISP using binary trees. As we all know, binary trees have nodes with exactly two pointers in them, one pointing to the left subtree and one pointing to the right subtree. In addition, binary trees can also have terminal nodes; in the case of LISP, terminal nodes are always atoms. LISP uses binary trees to represent lists as follows: The left subtree of a node points to the first element of a list, and the right subtree points to the rest of the list. For example, the list (**a b c**) is represented as the following binary tree:

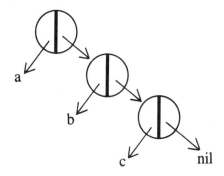

Note that the last node of the tree contains a right pointer to the atom **nil**. This is a convention indicating that there are no more elements in the list.

A list may have an element that is itself a list. Such a list will have a somewhat more complicated appearence, but will still conform to the structure described above. For example, here is the LISP representation of the list (**a (b c) d**):

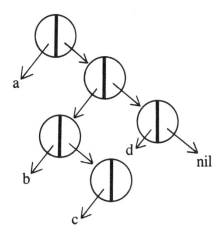

Here the left pointer of the second node of the top level list points to an object which itself represents a list.

Since lists are implemented in terms of binary trees, the various list manipulation functions we have seen carry out their function in terms of binary tree manipulation. For example, when we assign a symbol some value, LISP implements this by associating with that symbol a pointer to the desired value. If the value is a list, the pointer points to the root node of the tree representing that list. Thus if **x** were assigned the list **(a b c)**, the value pointer of **x** would point to the root of the tree representing **(a b c)**.

When we perform a **car** or a **cdr**, we are actually passing around LISP pointers. For example, when we ask LISP to evaluate **(cdr '(a b c))**, LISP starts at the root node of the tree representing **(a b c)**. It merely returns the right pointer of this node. This pointer points to a tree that represents the list **(b c)**, which is what we want. Similarly, **car** just returns the left pointer, which by convention points to the first element of the list. **cons** works by fetching an unused node from memory, and making its left pointer point to the first argument and its right pointer to the second. Then **cons** returns a pointer to this new node. You should make sure you understand why this implements **cons**.

15.3. Dotted Pair Notation

A node of a LISP binary tree is often called a *cons* cell. Cons cells, or *cons* es for short, constitute a valid Common LISP data type. In fact, each cons can be specified explicitly by the LISP user. This is done much in the same way in which LISP allows you to specify lists. To specify a single cons, the user enters the values for the left and right parts of the cell, separated by the character . (period), and encloses the whole business in parentheses. For example, if we want to designate a cons with left pointer pointing to **a** and with right pointer pointing to **nil**, we could type **(a . nil)**.

This notation for a node of a binary tree is called a *dotted pair*. The function **read** recognizes dotted pair notation. However, LISP is usually used to manipulate lists. Thus wherever possible, the function **print** tries to print out binary trees using the sort of list notation with which we have become familiar. The top level of LISP, which uses **read** and **print**, will therefore accept dotted pair notation. But it will usually print things out using list notation. For example, look what happens when we type the following dotted pair into LISP:

```
-> '(a . nil)
(A)
->
```

read recognizes the input as a representation for the list **(a)**. Had we actually typed in **(a)**, **read** would have built exactly the same internal representation. In either case, the structure can be interpreted as a list. Therefore, **print** outputs the structure using list notation (i. e., without dots) as opposed to the dotted pair notation we used to enter the object.

Since every list is represented by a binary tree, we can enter any list using dotted pair notation. For example, consider the list **(a b c)**. As we can see from its binary tree representation given above, this list consists of three conses, one corresponding to each internal node of the binary tree in the diagram. The first node comprises **a** dotted with the list **(b c)**. This list, in turn, consists of **b** dotted with the list **(c)**, which in turn consists of **c** dotted with **nil**. Or using dotted pair notation, we could express the whole list as **(a . (b . (c . nil)))**.

To make sure we got this right, let us type it into LISP:

```
-> '(a . (b . (c . nil)))
(A B C)
->
```

We typed in a complicated dotted pair. LISP cleverly recognized this representation as denoting a list, and, upon output, printed it out using list notation.

List notation is just a user convenience. It is easier to type and read **(a b c)** than **(a . (b . (c . nil)))**, so LISP was designed to accept the former notation on input and use it on output whenever it can. Internally, remember, both notations turn into exactly the same binary tree structure. This structure is more transparently reflected by the dotted pair notation, but the list notation tends to be more convenient for the user.

You can freely mix these notations if you like. For example, we could also have entered the list **(a b c)** as follows:

```
-> '(a . (b c))
(A B C)
->
```

Well, it seems as if the dotted pair notation is just a cumbersome way of typing in lists. It is true that this notation is inferior to the list notation for typing in lists. But the notation is necessary because *there are conses that are not lists.* Note that in all the examples we have seen, the last node of the tree representing the list always had a right pointer of **nil**. As we stated, this is a convention used to indicate the end of the list. But given the dotted pair notation, what is to prevent us from entering a cons that has a right pointer to something other than **nil**? Nothing:

```
-> '(a . b)
(A . B)
->
```

Here is a cons whose right pointer points to the atom **b**. As this does not correspond to any "true" list, **print** is forced to print it out using the more cumbersome dotted pair notation.

As we mentioned above, the functions that we learned for symbolic manipulation on lists really operate on conses. Thus even though conses are a more general data type than lists, we need not learn a new set of functions to operate on them. For example, we can apply **car** and **cdr** to conses that are not lists:

```
-> (car '(a . b))
A
-> (cdr '(a . b))
B
->
```

and we can use the function **cons** to create a new cons that is not a list:

```
-> (cons 'a 'b)
(A . B)
-> (cons 'a nil)
(A)
->
```

As we can see, the case where the underlying objects happen to be lists is really a special case. In general, if you want to determine if it is reasonable to take a **car** or **cdr** of some LISP object, the correct thing to do is to ask if that object is a cons. LISP supplies a predicate just for this purpose, called **consp**. Thus we have the following:

```
-> (consp '(a b c))
T
```

```
-> (consp '(a . b))
T
-> (consp 'a)
NIL
-> (consp nil)
NIL
->
```

As these transactions indicate, **consp** of **nil** is false, even though **listp** of **nil** is true. That is, **nil** represents a list, but not one composed of conses. Thus **nil** is an object that is a list, but not a cons.

So the term "list" encompasses those objects made of conses and the object **nil**. But does it exclude conses that are not lists? It might be reasonable to think that it would, but, unfortunately, this happens not to be the case. Watch what happens when we apply **listp** to a cons that is not a true list:

```
-> (listp '(a . b))
T
```

The predicate **listp** returns true on any cons, even ones that are not really lists at all. How then do we distinguish "true" lists from just any old cons? Common LISP provides no convenient predicate or data type that does so. Probably the best justification of this practice is that most functions that operate on lists actually operate on conses in general. Of course, should you find yourself in need of distinguishing between true lists and conses, you could create your own predicate to do so.

15.4. Multiple Pointers to the Same Object

The underlying representation used by LISP gives us some important insights into the way the basic LISP functions operate. For example, as mentioned above, the function **cdr** works by following the right pointer of a binary tree node. This means that, if the value returned by **cdr** is remembered by one's program, we may end up with more than one pointer to the same data object. For example, suppose we did the following:

```
-> (setq x '(a b c))
(A B C)
-> (setq y (cdr x))
(B C)
->
```

cdr returns a pointer to the second node of the tree representing **(a b c)**.
setq just associates this pointer with **y**. Hence **y** and the right pointer of
the root node of **(a b c)** point to exactly the same internal LISP structure.
We can diagram this situation as follows:

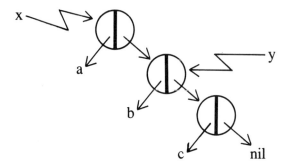

Note that if we assigned a value to **y** by typing **(setq y '(b c))**, LISP would
allocate new storage to represent **(b c)**. Then the values of **x** and **y** would
not share anything in common. This situation would have the following
internal representation:

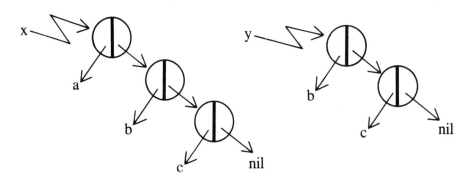

But we now have a somewhat tricky situation on our hands. Quite
different LISP internal configurations can look exactly alike as far as their
LISP value is concerned. For example, in the two cases just cited, the
value of **x** is **(a b c)** and the value of **y** is **(b c)**. However, in the first case,
x and **y** share the representation for **(b c)**. In the second case they do not.
The values are the same, but the internal representations are different.

15.4.1. eq and eql

As yet we have no reason to care about this, because all the functions we have seen operate solely on values. They do not care whether a structure is really the same as another or just has the same value as another structure. But sometimes it is important to make this distinction. LISP provides us with a simple means to do so. This is via the function **eq** (pronounced "eek"). **eq** is a function of two arguments. It returns true if the arguments are the same internal LISP object. It returns false otherwise.

Note that **eq** is fussier than **equal**. The latter function returns true whenever its two arguments are equivalent LISP values. In the case of **eq**, they must also point to the same exact internal representation. Thus in the two cases above, the value of **y** will always be **equal** to the value of **(cdr x)**, because they are both **(b c)**. But only in the first case are these **eq**, because only then do they point to the same internal representation.

Let us do an example to see that this works:

```
-> (setq x '(a b c))
(A B C)
-> (setq y (cdr x))
(B C)
-> (equal (cdr x) y)
T
-> (eq (cdr x) y)
T
-> (setq z '(b c))
(B C)
-> (equal y z)
T
-> (eq y z)
NIL
->
```

Here we first assign **x** a value, and then assign **y** the **cdr** of this value. In this case, both **y** and the **cdr** of **x** point to the same internal representation. Thus these values are both **equal** and **eq** to each other. Next, we assign **z** a new list of the same form as that assigned **y**. Since it is of the same form, this new list is **equal** to the value of the **y**. But they are different lists, and hence are not **eq** to one another.

In Common LISP, there is no guarantee that two instances of the very same number will be **eq** to each other. For example, **(eq 5 5)** might be true or false, depending on the implementation. However, it would be

263

rather painful not to have some predicate that returned true when comparing two conceptually identical objects. So Common LISP provides an additional predicate called **eql**. This is just like **eq**, except that it is always true of numbers of the same type and the same value.

Standardization Note: This is a departure from many other LISPs, in which the different occurrences of the same number are **eq**.

Since symbols are unique, each symbol will always be **eql** to itself (as well as **eq**). That is, **(eq 'a 'a)** and **(eql 'a 'a)** are always true. We can use this fact to define **equal** in terms of **eql**. Two s-expressions have equivalent values if either they are the same symbol, the same number, or if they are dotted pairs and their **car**s are equivalent and their **cdr**s are equivalent. Thus we have the following recursive definition:

```
(defun equal (x y)
   (cond ((or (atom x) (atom y)) (eql x y))
         ((equal (car x) (car y))
          (equal (cdr x) (cdr y))))))
```

In fact, the actual definition of **equal** that LISP uses looks very much like this one. The actual definition is a bit more complicated because it must take into account strings and other data types with which we have only been mildly concerned thus far.

As can be inferred from the preceding discussion, **eq** is not only more primitive than **equal**, but much more efficient. **equal** must run a recursive test to determine if two things are equivalent. But **eq** need only check if two things are the same object. In most implementations, this requires only a single machine instruction. **eql** is somewhat more complex than **eq**, but is also much simpler than **equal**. Thus most LISP programmers try to use **eq** in preference to **eql**, and **eql** in preference to **equal**, whenever they can get away with it. For example, **eq** is used if the values one is to compare are known to be symbols, since these are guaranteed to be unique. But **equal** must be used if we want to test for equivalence of value among arbitrary lists.

Most LISPs generally let you specify which function to use in other functions that make comparisons. For example, we mentioned that **member** tests if its first argument is a member of its second. In Common LISP, **member** uses **eql** to make this test. It can be made to use another equality function by supplying that function after the keyword argument **:test**. For example, **(member x y :test #'equal)** would use **equal** to make the comparison; **(member x y :test #'eq)** would use **eq**.

Standardization Note: In some LISPs, **member** uses **equal**. Often, another function is provided, called **memq**, that uses **eq**.

15.5. The Evil of **rplaca** and **rplacd**

Most of the functions we have seen so far do not change existing objects. For example, although we said informally that **car** and **cdr** tear apart lists, we noted several times that they are actually non-destructive. These functions work by merely passing around pointers to parts of an s-expression. Similarly, **cons** creates a new cons that points to old ones. But it leaves the old ones unchanged.

It is possible in LISP to alter an existing LISP object. But before I tell you how to do this, let me warn you. *There is nothing more dangerous or irksome in LISP than modifying an existing object.* Here is why. As we mentioned above, after doing some **car**s and **cdr**s on an existing LISP value, we often end up with several pointers to the same internal structure. Normally, if we only compare this structure with others or make new structures point at it, this would not cause any problems. However, suppose we *altered* the list we found at the end of one of these pointers. Since other LISP objects may point to this same list, we may have unknowingly altered the value of any number of other objects. When your program crashes because of this, it will no doubt crash when you are manipulating one of these unintentionally changed objects. You will not know where to look for the problem, because it really occurred when your program was doing some conceptually unrelated task.

Even worse, the program is likely to work just fine the first time through, but leave behind a data structure that resembles a plate of spaghetti. The second time through, everything will not look as it should, and the program will flounder.

It is hard even to look at some of the structures that can be created this way. For example, it is possible to construct circular lists that point to themselves. When LISP tries to print these out, it blindly follows pointers and so prints something like

```
-> circular-list
(A B C A B C A B C ....
```

until you stop it.

So. Whenever you find yourself writing a piece of code that involves actually changing a list, stop. Ask yourself why you are doing it and if it is really necessary. Are you sure? Are you sure it will work? Better have answers to these questions then, or you may never know what hit you.

And do not say that you were not warned that the following material is for mature audiences only.

The basic LISP functions for altering lists are called **rplaca** and **rplacd**, for "replace car" and "replace cdr", respectively. Each is a function of two arguments. The first argument should be a cons; the second may be any LISP object. **rplaca** replaces the left pointer (i. e., the **car** side) of its first argument with its second. The altered cons is returned as the value of the call to **rplaca**. **rplacd** does the equivalent to the right (i. e., **cdr**) pointer of the first value.

For example, suppose **x** were assigned **(a b c)**. If we **rplaca** the value of **x** with **d**, say, the value assigned **x** would now be **(d b c)**. Thus:

```
-> (setq x '(a b c))
(A B C)
-> (rplaca x 'd)
(D B C)
-> x
(D B C)
->
```

Note that this is quite different from taking the **cdr** of **(a b c)**, **cons**ing **d** on the front of it, and **setq**ing **x** to this value. Both processes result in lists of the same value, but in very different internal structures. Most significantly, in the case where **rplaca** is used, if another LISP object contains a pointer to the list we are changing, that value will change as well. In the **setq** case, such unnerving side-effects will never occur. Consider the following example:

```
-> (setq x '(a b c))
(A B C)
-> (setq y x)
(A B C)
```

```
-> (eq x y)
T
-> (rplaca x 'd)
(D B C)
-> x
(D B C)
-> y
(D B C)
-> (eq x y)
T
->
```

Here we see how using **rplaca** changes the value assigned **y**, a variable that does not occur in the call to **rplaca**. Using **setq**, on the other hand, would not cause changes in an unmentioned value:

```
-> (setq y (cons 'e (cdr x)))
(E B C)
-> y
(E B C)
-> x
(D B C)
```

In spite of the danger involved, these list-altering functions are useful in a number of circumstances. The most compelling reason for their use is efficiency. For example, suppose we had two lists we wanted to connect together into a one big list. We could use **append**, as follows:

```
-> (setq x '(a b c))
(A B C)
-> (setq y '(d e f))
(D E F)
-> (setq z (append x y))
(A B C D E F)
-> x
(A B C)
-> y
(D E F)
-> z
(A B C D E F)
->
```

This did what we want, but was rather costly. **append** had to build a new list, for which some additional cons cells were required. (Actually, **append** did not have to build an entirely new list. It just had to build a copy of its first argument. Then it could point the right pointer of the last cons of this new list at the second argument. It needs to copy the first argument, of course, because if it diddled with a cons of the actual argument, it would destructively change that value. In general, if we call **append** with several arguments, it would have to make copies of all but the last one.)

consing is expensive. So if we are not too concerned about preserving the integrity of the values passed to **append**, we might be tempted to alter the last cons of the first value to point to the second. This would avoid the cost of **cons**ing up a fresh copy of the value. To do this, we would have to follow the first value to its last cons. Then we could do a **rplacd** to make this cons point to the second argument.

Fortunately, LISP supplies us with a built-in function that does most of this work for us. It is called **nconc**. **nconc** takes any number of arguments, all of which should be lists. It follows each value to its end, and destructively changes its last right pointer to point to the next value.

Let us use **nconc** on the lists appended together in the previous example:

```
-> (setq x '(a b c))
(A B C)
-> (setq y '(d e f))
(D E F)
-> (nconc x y)
(A B C D E F)
-> x
(A B C D E F)
-> y
(D E F)
->
```

nconc changed a pointer in the final cons of the value of **x** to point at the beginning of **(d e f)**. While the value produced is the same as that produced by **append**, **nconc** altered the value of **x**. In contrast, a call to **append** would never change one of its arguments.

nconc is often useful in conjunction with function mapping. In Chapter 8, we described a situation in which a function returns a list of items that fit some description. We might like to apply this function to each element in a list of arguments, and then do something with all the resulting items. The problem is that if we use **mapcar** to apply this function we will get back a list that looks something like this:

((a b c) nil (d e) nil (f g h))

That is, each application of our function returns a (possibly empty) list. But we would rather get back one big list with all the interesting elements in it, and without any additional structure:

(a b c d e f g h)

We previously mentioned one way to get the list we seek from the result of a **mapcar**. This is to apply **append** to the result of the **mapcar**. For example, if our function is called **foo**, and the list of objects we wish to apply it to is **l**, then we can do the following:

```
-> (apply 'append (mapcar 'foo l))
(A B C D E F G H)
->
```

As we mentioned above, **append** may be rather costly. However, if we are sure it is safe to alter the lists **foo** returns, we can apply **nconc** to this structure instead. This will also produce the desired result, but much more efficiently. Again, we better be sure that **foo** creates its lists from scratch. Otherwise the use of **nconc** is likely to be catastrophic.

LISP provides us with a mapping function that does all this for us. It is called **mapcan**. **mapcan** is just like **mapcar**, except that it **nconc**s together all the values that result from each function application. For example, if we had used **mapcan** in the example above, we would have gotten exactly the result we wanted:

```
-> (mapcan 'foo l)
(A B C D E F G H)
->
```

There is also a **cdr** version of **mapcan**, called **mapcon**. In both cases, the function being applied must always return a list. And since both **mapcan** and **mapcon** use **nconc**, the lists that the function returns should not be referred to by any other structure.

Incidentally, LISP must use destructive functions for certain internal purposes. This is generally harmless, because the behavior is well understood in these cases. For example, **setf** applied to a call to **get** or **getf** sets a given property on a property list. To do so, **setf** must actually change the property list associated with an atom, because it would be much too expensive to build a new list every time. Since LISP users do not normally maintain their own pointers to property lists, this does not cause a problem. But should you decide to do so, be forewarned that the value at the end of your pointer may magically change after you update the property list of some symbol.

15.6. Summary

(1)   Lists are represented internally as binary trees. The individual nodes of the binary trees are called *cons cells,* or *conses* for short. The left-hand pointer of a cons points to the next element of a list; the right-hand pointer points to the rest of a list. The terminal nodes of these trees are always atoms. To represent the end of a list, a pointer to the symbol **nil** is used.

(2)   We can refer to individual conses using *dotted pair* notation. The notation consists of two s-expressions separated by a dot, and surrounded by parentheses. The LISP function **print** always tries to avoid using the dotted pair notation whenever it can. It uses the list notation instead.

(3)   There are conses that are not true lists. These are the conses whose right-hand pointer points to an atom other than **nil**.

(4)   Internally, LISP functions are implemented in terms of cons manipulation. List processing is just a special case of cons processing.

(5)   It is possible to have many pointers to the same internal LISP object. To differentiate between two pointers to the same object and two pointers to identically configured but different objects, the function **eq** can be used. **eq** returns true only if its two arguments evaluate to the identical LISP object.

(6)   Existing conses can be altered using the functions **rplaca**, **rplacd**, and **nconc**. Altering an object is extremely risky and should not be attempted casually.

(7)   The functions **mapcan** and **mapcon** are equivalent to **(apply 'nconc (mapcar ...))** and **(apply 'nconc (maplist ...))**, respectively.

Exercises

(1) Write a function that prints out an s-expression in dotted pair notation. (Hint – This is extremely simply if you write a recursive function.)

(2) Represent the following s-expressions in terms of cons cells and
pointers (i. e., as binary trees):

      (a) **((a))**

      (b) **(x (y) z)**

      (c) **(x y . z)**

      (d) **((nil . c) . b) . a)**

(3) Suppose we evaluate the following s-expressions:

```
-> (setq x '(c d))
(C D)
-> (setq y (append '(a b) x))
(A B C D)
-> (eq (cddr y) x)
???
```

What value does the last s-expression evaluate to? Why?

(4) Write the following representations as LISP would print them out:

      (a)

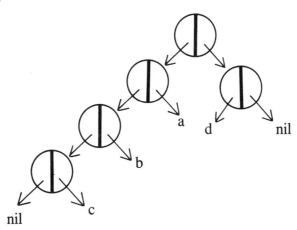

(b)

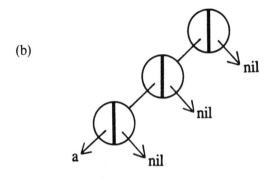

(c)

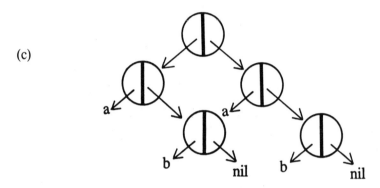

(5) Suppose we evaluated the following s-expressions:

```
-> (setq x '(a b c))
(A B C)
-> (setq y x)
(A B C)
-> (rplaca (rplacd y nil) 'd)
(D)
-> x
????
```

What is the value of **x**? What happened to the list **(a b c)**?

(6) What is the value of the following expression:

```
-> (mapcan'(lambda (x) (list x (1+ x)))'(1 2 3 4 5))
```

(7) It is easy to add something to the beginning of a list in LISP. But it is harder to add something to the end. One way to ameliorate this situation is to carry around a pointer to the end of a list. Then it is easy to find the end of the list and update it.

A *tconc structure* is a special list whose **car** is a list, and whose **cdr** points to the end of the list pointed to by the **car**. The function **tconc** takes two arguments, the first of which should be a tconc structure. It updates the tconc structure to include the second argument as its last element.

For example, we can start out with an empty tconc structure, and add an element to it:

```
-> (setq foo (tconc nil 'x))
((X) X)
->
```

The tconc structure prints out in this unusual manner because its **cdr** always points to the last part of its **car**. Now let us stick some elements onto the end of the list within this structure:

```
-> (tconc foo 'y)
((X Y) Y)
-> (tconc foo 'z)
((X Y Z) Z)
-> foo
((X Y Z) Z)
->
```

Unfortunately, **tconc** is not part of Common LISP. However, it can be implemented with the machinery described above.

Implement the function **tconc**. Then use **tconc** to implement *queues*. Recall that a queue is a data structure in which we add elements to one end, and take them off the other. Write functions **in−queue** and **de−queue**, which add objects to and remove objects from existing queues, respectively.

(8) Write a predicate **truelist** that is true only of true lists, i. e., of lists that terminate with a right-hand pointer to **nil**.

Chapter 16

Non-standard Flow of Control

16.1. Introduction

It is sometimes desirable to exit from the middle of a sequence of forms without having to evaluate all of them. For example, the **prog** feature described in Chapter 6 allows us to use the function **return** to exit the **prog** body without having to evaluate all the remaining forms.

There are several generalizations of this idea that are useful. One is the ability to exit from the middle of other fixed pieces of codes besides **prog** bodies. This is accomplished using the functions **block** and **return–from**. A more powerful idea is the ability to return to an arbitrary location that will only be known at runtime. This form of dynamic exiting is achieved via the functions **catch** and **throw**.

In addition, we sometimes want to write LISP code in which a function returns more than a single value. Common LISP provides a means to effect such *multiple value returns,* as well as to catch the multiple values that might be generated by a function. We explore these mechanisms, and examine their motivation.

16.2. Blocks

We have seen that it is possible to exit a **prog** from anywhere inside using the function **return**. However, there are other times in which an immediate exit from a sequence might be desirable. For example, suppose we had a function that contained several bodies of code:

```
(defun foo (...)
    body1
    body2
    body3
    ...              )
```

Suppose further that if a certain condition held, then after evaluating *body2*, say, we would want to exit the function without evaluating the rest of the bodies. With what we know so far, we would have to re-write our code using a **cond** or a **prog** to produce the sequence of correct evaluation. But there is another way.

Common LISP has a feature called a *block* construct. A block is established by invoking the special function **block**. A call to **block** has the form **(block** *name form1 form2 ...***)** To evaluate such a form, the *formi* are simply evaluated. However, if a call of the form **(return–from** *name form***)** appears within the call to **block**, then the block will be exited immediately. The value of *form* will be returned as the value of the call to **block**.

You can exit from anywhere within a block, even from a block within a block, as long as the call to **return–from** occurs lexically within the block it is trying to return from. Consider the following example:

```
-> (block one
       (block two
          (return-from one 3) 2)
       1)
3
->
```

The call to **return–from** causes an immediate exit from the block named **one**; the expressions **2** and **1** are never examined.

It is not possible to use **return–from** to exit from a block that cannot be lexically "seen". For example, consider the following ill-conceived attempt to exit a block that is dynamically present, but not lexically available:

```
-> (defun fntwo ( )
       (return-from one 3))
fntwo
-> (block one
       (fntwo) 1)
```

Error: No block to return to RETURN-FORM

Debug 1>:

This did not work because **return-from** can only exit from blocks that are lexically present in the definition of the code, not from blocks that come into existence dynamically.

Note that it is possible to **return-from** another function, just as long as its definition is lexically present. We can accomplish this with a lambda expression:

```
-> (block one
       ((lambda ( )
        (return-from one 3) 2))
        1)
3
->
```

This works fine because the **return-from** can "see" the block it is to return to.

A block named **nil** is established by calls to the functions **prog** and **do**. This makes it possible to return abruptly from within such constructs. In fact, the function **return** is simply a macro that expands into **(return-from nil ...)**. This is why **return** works within a **prog**.

In addition, Common LISP implicitly puts a block around the body of functions defined by **defun**; this block is given the same name as the function itself. Therefore, it is possible to use **return-from** to exit hastily from anywhere in a function. For example, if our definition of the function **foo** looked like this:

```
(defun foo (...)
    body1
    (...(return-from foo 'baz)...)
    body3
    ...      )
```

then, when the **return–from** form is evaluated, the function **foo** would exit immediately, returning the value **baz**. The expressions after this form will not get evaluated.

The block feature makes it possible to use constructs like mapping functions in situations for which they would otherwise be poorly suited. For example, suppose we want to write a function **any** that took as arguments a function and a list, and applied the function to the elements of that list until the function returned true. At that point, we would like **any** to stop execution and return the element that met the condition. Normally, we would not be able to use a mapping function here, because a mapping function keeps applying its function argument to every element of a list. But we can use blocks to prevent this from happening:

```
-> (defun any (fn l)
       (mapc #'(lambda (x)
                  (if (funcall fn x)
                      (return-from any x)))
             l))
any
-> (any #'(lambda (x)
              (if (numberp x) (setq *var* x)))
          '(a b 2 c d))
2
-> *var*
2
->
```

Here we use the free symbol *var* to illustrate where **any** terminated execution. As we can see, it stopped right in the middle of the **mapc**, so **return–from** performed as advertised.

Standardization Note: The functions **block** and **return–from** are not found in many other LISPs.

16.3. catch and throw

As was duly noted above, a call to **return–from** must be statically present in the block to which it is to return. Sometimes it is necessary to have a mechanism that allows *dynamic* returns. That is, we would like to be able to return to a point in our code, without knowing until runtime where we will be returning from.

Such a mechanism would be useful if only because it is generally desirable to organize our code into separate functions. With **return–from**, we can only escape from a lexically available location, so our exits all had to be within the same function. But we would hate to write a large program this way.

For example, suppose **fn1** is called from a function **fn**, and that **fn1** calls **fn2**, which calls **fn3**, etc. Suppose also that each function is searching for a certain value, which, if it is found, it will want to pass back to the calling function **fn**. If **fn3** finds this value, for example, it will have to return it to **fn2**; **fn2** will have to be set up to recognize this value as one it should return to its calling function; **fn1** will have to be set up the same way. This makes our code rather awkward and redundant, since each intermediate function must recognize and plan for the cases recognized by the functions that it calls.

However, if we had a facility to return from a deeply nested function upon demand, we could avoid these unfortunate complications. If we could allow some deeply nested function to return directly to some higher level function, the intermediate functions would not have to know anything about the values that the lower level functions return. We would like to use **return–from** for this. But we cannot, because **return–from** could not return to a block that is set up by a non-lexically present function.

To allow dynamic dramatic escapes, we introduce two functions, **catch** and **throw**. **catch** is somewhat like **block**, in that it provides a point to which control can be transferred later on. We will use the term *catch* to refer such a point. **throw** is similar to **return–from** – it causes control to leap to a previous **catch**.

A call to **catch** is of the form (**catch** *tag form1 form2* ...). The value of *tag* serves as a name of the catch. The forms are then evaluated. If they evaluate normally, **catch** simply returns the value of the last one as its value. However, if a call of the form (**throw** *tag form*) occurs during this evaluation, flow of control will be abruptly returned to the catch. The value of *form* will be returned as the value of the call to **catch**. In effect, the **throw** throws its argument through any number of levels of intermediate function calls directly to the **catch**.

For example, using **catch** and **throw**, the code to implement the functions **fn**, **fn1**, **fn2**, etc., alluded to above might look something like the following:

```
(defun fn (...)
   (catch 'fn (fn1 ...) ))

(defun fn1 (...)
   (cond ((user-test1 ...) 'answer1)
         ((and (user-test2 ...) (fn2 ...)) 'answer2)
         ( ... )))

(defun fn2 (...)
   (cond ((user-test3 ...) (throw 'fn 'answer3))
         ((user-test4 ...)
          'useful-value-but-not-an-answer)
         ((user-test5 ...) (fn3 ...))
         (t (fn4 ...) (fn5 ...)))))
```

Here **fn** simply establishes a catch to handle subsequent **throw**s. The functions **fn1**, **fn2**,... do all the work. **fn1** makes a test, and if it pans out, returns the answer. It uses the ordinary LISP flow-of-control mechanism since there are no intermediate functions between it and **fn**. If the test fails, **fn1** tries another test that includes a call to **fn2**. **fn2** may simply return a value that helps **fn1** continue its computation. However, in the course of computing this value, it may itself come upon the answer. In this case, it **throw**s the answer directly back to the **catch**, ignoring what **fn1** was trying to do.

As this example illustrates, **catch** and **throw** are needed mostly when some code is trying to serve two functions. If the functions **fn1**, **fn2**,... were only to search for a value, we could just have used the ordinary LISP flow-of-control regime. However, in this instance it was desirable to have a function such as **fn2** which has two functions: It might return a value to be used by some other function, but it might also find the big answer along the way. We use **catch** and **throw** here to write the code so that, from the point of view of **fn1**, **fn2** appears just as a utility. However, should **fn2** decide it found something more important, it can return to **fn** without **fn1** having to worry about what **fn2** was doing.

We can have any number of catches around at a given time. If more than one catch with the same name exists, the most recently established catch will be the target of a throw to that name.

Standardization Note: The syntax of **catch** and **throw** is different in Common LISP than in most other LISPs that have these functions.

16.4. Multiple Values

We have referred occasionally to the fact that some Common LISP functions can return more than one value. It is now time to example this feature of Common LISP more closely. First, the motivation. Just as we often need to pass a function more than one value, there are many times when there is more than one piece of information that might be passed back from a function call. Hence we need some mechanism to allow for more than one value to be returned.

Consider as an example the function **macroexpand**, which we examined in Chapter 13. Recall that the purpose of this function is to expand the macros in its argument, and return the resulting expansion as its value. However, it is also useful to inform the user whenever any macro expansion has actually been done. So there are two pieces of information we would like to communicate.

Another example is the function **round**. This is an arithmetic function that, given a floating-point number, returns the nearest integer. However, it is occasionally useful to know how much **round** had to alter its value in order to round it. **round** almost certainly had to compute this value to do its job, so it would be a shame to have to compute it again. Once again, we have two pieces of information we might like a function to return.

Note that in these two examples, one of the values is used much more often than the other. For example, we use **macroexpand** mostly for its first value, but hardly ever for its second. Similarly, we use **round** almost exclusively for its first value, availing ourselves of the second only in rare situations. Thus, we would like some way to handle multiple values that will not be too obtrusive. We want them to be available, but not to obscure the normal use of the functions that return them.

There are many possible ways to deal with this situation. For example, in some programming languages, such as FORTRAN, the arguments supplied to a function can be used to pass back additional values. This is because the argument-passing conventions of these languages are such that changing the value of a formal parameter in a function will change the value of the argument supplied. For example, in such languages, a call of the form **(func var1 var2 var3)** will change the values assigned the variables **var1**, **var2** and **var3** if the corresponding formal parameters of **func** are changed. We can use this technique to pass back as many values as there are arguments.

Of course, this technique is not an option in LISP. There is no way in LISP to change an argument supplied to a function from within that function. In addition, many programmers consider this to be a particularly gruesome way to design a language. This is because this feature allows changes in a subroutine to have unexpected changes in the calling program. Thus, this feature wreaks havoc with most people's notion of modularity.

A more LISP-like way to pass back more that one piece of information is simply to put all the values in a list. For example, we could have **macroexpand** return a list consisting of the (possibly) expanded form, and a truth value. Similarly, we could have **round** return a list of the rounded result and the difference between this result and the original value.

But there are two problems with this solution. First, the user must now dig out the desired results by using **car**, etc. This is annoying, especially because the second value is likely to be used only a small percentage of the time. Hence we have inconvenienced ourselves most of the time for a feature that we will only use rarely. The second drawback is that creating the list to return the values costs something. Namely, we have to pay the price of **cons**ing up the list to contain the values. Once again, this is an expensive price to pay for a rarely used convenience.

Another way to transmit additional values is to use free symbols. For example, we could have **macroexpand** set the value of the symbol *macroexpandflag*, in addition to returning the expanded form as its value. This overcomes the cost and inconvenience objections raised above: No **cons**ing is required, and programs not concerned with this second value may simply ignore it.

However, there are other difficulties with this approach. In particular, the programmer has to know the name of the symbol used in order to access the second value. This not only inconveniences the programmer, but makes the resulting code singularly obscure. Imagine what the code would look like if not two, but many different values had to be returned! Secondly, all the problems of dealing with free symbols arise. We now have to worry about one call to our function interacting with another call to it. Our program may have to go through some acrobatics in these cases to save one second value before calling the function a second time. And if our function happens to be recursive, the whole idea of using free symbols usually is not viable.

Using lists or free symbols are the only options available in many LISPs. However, the need to provide good communication between caller and callee was deemed important enough to institute a special mechanism in Common LISP precisely for this purpose. We refer to this as a mechanism for handling *multiple value returns*.

281

Note that when we say that a function returns more than one value, we do not mean that it returns a list of these values; any given list is always a single value. Rather, we mean that the function literally returns several values, rather than the single value most LISP functions return.

But how can this be? Virtually the entire structure of LISP seems predicated on the fact that functions return *a* value. For example, suppose our program contained the form **(setq foo (macroexpand '(setf a b)))**. **setq** would appear to expect **macroexpand** to return only one value. What is it to do when **macroexpand** unexpectedly returned three values? Furthermore, suppose we used a call to **macroexpand** as an argument to one of our own functions? For example, suppose we wrote the code **(baz (macroexpand '(setf a b)))**. How is our poor function going to cope with the two values **macroexpand** will pass it? In general, how can LISP possibly deal with more than one value, without some massive restructuring of the language?

The answer to this question, indeed, a primary advantage of the whole multiple-value-return idea, is that LISP code that is not explicitly set up to handle multiple values merely ignores the extra ones. Thus, when the calls to **macroexpand** above each return two values, **setq** and **baz** see only the first one. If we wanted to make use of the additional values, we would have to take explicit action to catch them.

This means that we can write LISP code in total ignorance of the multiple-value-return feature. Indeed, we have been doing so through this book. In fact, the only time we have seen additional values returned by a function is on the top level. This is because the top level of Common LISP is set up explicitly to catch and print every value returned by the forms it evaluates. As an illustration, watch what happens when we call **round** on the top level, and within a call to **setq**:

```
-> (round 7.6)
8 ;
-0.4
-> (setq foo (round 7.6))
8
-> foo
8
```

The top level caught both values, and obligingly printed them for us. However, **setq** is unprepared for multiple values. Therefore, it ignores the additional one made available by **round**, and assigns **foo** only the first value.

So, as we can see, this scheme does indeed solve the problem of inconveniencing the user: The user can just ignore the whole business unless he or she cares about the additional values. What about efficiency? Well, returning values is generally rather cheap – they can just be left in registers or placed on a stack in most implementations. Thus there is little or no cost associated with providing this feature.

But how can we use multiple values ourselves? How can we catch the additional values produced by those LISP functions that produce multiple values? And how can we define functions that produce multiple values?

In Common LISP, there are functions for both needs. That is, there are functions designed explicitly to catch multiple values that may be produced from evaluating a form. Similarly, there are functions for returning a set of values as multiple values.

16.4.1. Functions for Receiving Multiple Values

Let us look first at catching multiple values. For example, suppose we did indeed wish our code to capture both of the values returned by a call to **round**. Probably the simplest way to do this is to use the macro **multiple–value–list**. This macro takes one argument, a form, and returns as a list *all* the values that the form returns. Let us try this on a call to **round** and see what happens:

```
-> (multiple-value-list (round 7.6))
(8 -0.4)
->
```

As we can see, LISP captured both values produced by **round** and returned them in a list.

multiple–value–list is useful if we do indeed want a list of values. Such a list may be exactly what our program needs. Alternatively, we may not know in advance how many values a function is going to return. So putting them in a list is a sure way to deal with them.

However, in this particular case, we know in advance exactly what is to be returned, and we probably have no use for the list that is created. Rather, we would like to assign both values to individual variables and not waste resources on a useless list. We can do so using the macro **multiple–value–setq**. This function takes two arguments, a list of symbols and a form. The symbols are assigned the various values returned by evaluating the form. (Extra values are discarded; extra variables are assigned the value **nil**.) In addition **multiple–value–setq** returns the first value returned from the evaluation. Let us use **multiple–value–setq** to capture both values produced by **round**:

```
-> (multiple-value-setq (val dif) (round 7.6))
8
-> val
8
-> dif
-0.4
->
```

Here the two values returned by **round** were assigned to **val** and **dif**, respectively. In practice, these variables are likely to be parameters of a function in which the call to **multiple–value–setq** is embedded.

Frequently, we wish to create new variables to capture the values returned by some function. We could do this using **let**, but only awkwardly:

```
(let ((val nil) (dif nil))
      (multiple-value-setq (val dif) (round 7.6))
         ...
```

Here we use **let** to create new variables for us. But we must initialize the variables to **nil** and then reassign them to the multiple values before proceeding. It would be much smoother to have some function that combines **let** with **multiple–value–setq**. **multiple–value–bind** is just such a function. Like **multiple–value–setq**, it accepts a list of symbols, and a form which may return multiple values. As before, the symbols are assigned the values produced by this form. However, with **multiple–value–bind**, new variables are created for each of the symbols. In addition, **multiple–value–bind** allows any number of forms to follow the form generating the values. These forms are evaluated, and the result of evaluating the last form returned.

For example, we can use **multiple–value–bind** to return some value computed from the two values returned by **round**:

```
-> (multiple-value-bind (val dif) (round 7.6)
       (+ val (abs dif)))
8.4
->
```

Another special situation involving multiple values involves passing them as arguments to a function. For example, suppose we had a function that took two arguments, and computed a value from them:

```
-> (defun addabs (val absval)
      (+ val (abs absval)))
ADDABS
->
```

Now suppose we want to pass both values returned by **round** to this function. Note that the ordinary Common LISP argument handling mechanism *never, ever* passes more than a single value from a form to a function. Thus evaluating **(addabs (round 7.6))** will cause an error, as only the first value computed by **round** will be passed to **addabs**.

Again, we can get around this problem, but only awkwardly. It is better to have a function to do just what we want. In this case, Common LISP provides a special function called **multiple-value-call**. All the arguments supplied to **multiple-value-call** are evaluated. **multiple-value-call** takes as its actual arguments the first value produced from the first supplied argument, plus *all* the values produced from the other supplied arguments. The first actual argument, which should be a function, is applied to all the other actual arguments. For example:

```
-> (multiple-value-call #'addabs (round 7.6))
8.4
->
```

Here the form **(round 7.6)** produced two values, both of which were passed as arguments to the function **addabs**.

16.4.2. Functions For Generating Multiple Values

Now that we know how to catch multiple values when they are produced, we can look at how to return multiple values ourselves. The primary Common LISP function for producing multiple values is called **values**. **values** takes any number of arguments, all of which are simply returned as values. Let us first use **values** just on the top level:

```
-> (values 1 2 3)
1 ;
2 ;
3
->
```

values merely returned all its arguments as multiple values. They were then displayed by the top level of LISP.

values is more likely to be used in defining our own function which is to return multiple values. For example, we can use **values** to define a function **uncons** that returns as values both the **car** and the **cdr** of a list:

```
-> (defun uncons (l)
        (values (car l) (cdr l)))
UNCONS
-> (uncons '(a b c))
A ;
(B C)
->
```

Of course, we could use some of the multiple-value-receiving functions we described above to catch the values returned by a function like **uncons**.

The functions **values–list** and **multiple–value–prog1** are also useful for generating multiple values. However, they are used infrequently enough to relegate their description to Appendix A.

Note that we can use functions like **values** to build a LISP function that returns no values at all. This is done simply by calling **values** with no arguments:

```
-> (values)
->
```

Nothing at all is returned. This is particularly useful if a function is used entirely for its side effects, and you do not wish a call to it on the top level to cause any printing of results.

As a special case, if a function returns no values in a case where a multiple value return is not anticipated, LISP supplies a gratuitous value of **nil**.

16.4.3. Passing Around Multiple Values

You may have realized that the introduction of multiple values has some important consequences for the design of a LISP system. For example, we said that code that does not anticipate multiple values ignores all but the first. Now suppose a reference to a function that returns multiple values occurs within a built-in LISP function, say **cond** or **if**. That is, suppose we evaluated a form like this one:

```
(cond ((testfn ...) (multiple-value-fn ...))
      (t ...))
```

Supposing the first cond clause were chosen, would all the values returned by **multiple-value-fn** be returned by the **cond**, or would only the first one be passed along?

A moment's reflection should convince you that, if functions like **cond** do not return multiple values when they are generated, we will eventually have to write some multiple-value-returning version of **cond**. Furthermore, the same would be true of most of the basic built-in LISP functions. This is particularly true of those special functions and macros that return as their value the value of some form passed to them. For example, **cond** returns the value of some form in one of its clauses. So the need arises to return what this form returns. And that may be more than one value.

Rather than duplicate many basic LISP functions, the built-in functions that tend to return the values of other forms are set up to handle multiple values. These include the functions **return**, **let**, **do**, **block**, **progn**, **catch**, **if** and **cond**, among others. **and** and **or** return multiple values from the last subforms, but not from subforms other than the last. In addition, **eval**, **apply**, **funcall** and **multiple-value-call** all return multiple values. In general, the application of a lambda-like expression will pass on multiple values. This is true of functions created by **defun** as well macros created by **defmacro**.

Note that some functions intentionally never return more than one value. For example, **setq**, **multiple-value-setq**, **prog1** and **prog2** always return exactly one value.

As an example, let us write a version of the function **remove**. Our function with return a list that consists of its second argument with any occurrences of the first argument removed. In addition, our function will return a second value, a flag specifying whether any removal actually occurred.

First, let us write a version of the function that returns only a single value:

```
(defun our-remove (e l)
    (cond ((atom l) l)
             ((equal (car l) e) (our-remove e (cdr l)))
             (t (cons (car l) (our-remove e (cdr l)))))))
```

If you like, we can write a version using **let** that is somewhat less redundant:

```
(defun our-remove (e l)
    (if (atom l)
    l
    (let ((val (our-remove e (cdr l))))
        (if (equal (car l) e)
           val
           (cons (car l) val)))))
```

Now, to make this into a function that handles a second value, we will have to be prepared for the recursive call to return multiple values. This is done by more or less substituting the call to **let** with a call to **multiple-value-bind**. Also, we have to return two values. So we need to add some calls to **values**. If we do so, we get the following actual function definition:

```
-> (defun our-remove (e l)
       (if (atom l)
          l
          (multiple-value-bind
              (val flag) (our-remove e (cdr l))
              (if (equal e (car l))
                 (values val t)
                 (values (cons (car l) val) flag)))))
-> (our-remove 'b '(a b c))
(A C) ;
T
-> (our-remove 'b '(1 2 3))
(1 2 3) ;
NIL
```

16.5. Summary

(1)   The function **block** establishes a point to which a call to the function **return-from** can return. The call to **return-from** must occur lexical-

ly within the block it is to return to. Blocks are implicitly established by functions defined by **defun**, and by calls to **prog** and **do**.

(2)   A dynamic transfer of control can be accomplished through the use of the functions **catch** and **throw**. **catch** sets up a reference point to which a subsequent **throw** can transfer control and transmit a value. Unlike blocks, catches can be used to transfer control dynamically, i. e., to a point not determined simply by the lexical placement of these functions but by their runtime behavior.

(3)   Functions in Common LISP can return any number of values. Multiple values can be generated by using the function **values**. They can be received using the functions **multiple–value–list**, **multiple–value–bind** and **multiple–value–setq**. Multiple values returned by a function can be passed as arguments to a function using **multiple–value–call**.

(4)   Functions not prepared to accept multiple values will receive only the first value, or **nil** if there are no values returned.

(5)   Most built-in LISP functions that pass around values will pass on multiple values. A few, like **setq** and **prog1**, specifically do not pass on multiple values.

Exercises

(1)   Above we used **mapc** in conjunction with **return–from** to write the function **any**. Use this scheme to write a function that works the same way, except that it returned the list of elements starting with the first element to meet the condition.

(2)   Write a perfect number generator similar to the one you wrote for Exercise 6 of Chapter 5, but with two modifications. First, the perfect number generating routine should return the perfect numbers it finds one at a time to a printing routine, which prints them out and calls the generating routine again. Second, if a multiple of 17 is encountered as a divisor at any time, the computation prints the list of that number and the number it divides, and then continues.

(3)   Write a function that takes as input four values, the first two denoting the x and y coordinates of a point, and the third and fourth denoting the x and y coordinates of a different point. Have your function return two values, denoting the x and y coordinates of the midpoint of the line segment bounded by these two points.

(4) Write a version of the function **subst** that returns two values: the (possibly) substituted list, and a truth value specifying whether any substitution was actually done.

Chapter 17

Packages

17.1. read Reconsidered

In a previous chapter, we discussed the fact that LISP represents s-expressions internally in the form of binary trees. However, input to LISP consists of strings of characters, that is, of text typed in by the user. LISP must convert these strings of characters into binary trees in order to perform LISP operations on them.

The burden of this translation is borne by the function **read**. **read** acts as LISP's general purpose interface between the world of character strings and the world of LISP's internal representations. In our discussion of input/output, we showed how the LISP programmer can use **read** to input s-expressions to his own program; we also mentioned that LISP's **read-eval-print** loop uses this same function to input the s-expressions typed in by the user for LISP to evaluate. In both cases, **read** must recognize the s-expression being described by the string input, and build the corresponding internal representation. Once **read** has done this job, all other LISP functions can operate on the internal representation **read** produces. These other functions can then be completely oblivious to the details of the textual denotation of s-expressions.

read has a considerable job to do. For example, **read** must recognize the boundaries of atoms, detect the occurrence of imbedded s-expressions, as well as be sensitive to macro characters and other syntactic quirks. In sum, **read** must embody a full-fledged scanner and parser to detect LISP tokens and syntactic structures.

Thus **read** does much of the work that is done by a compiler in more conventional programming languages. All programming languages allow one to specify programs as strings of characters. Some translation system then converts these strings to an internal form. In the case of a compiler, the internal form is usually a parse tree that serves as the basis for code generation. In the case of LISP, the internal representation is a binary tree, which serves as the basis for evaluation.

Hence the LISP **read** function does a great deal more than the input procedures of most languages. These generally do nothing more sophisticated than converting a string of digits into a number. In contrast, **read** performs the entire scanning and parsing phases of language translation. Fortunately, LISP's syntax is very simple and closely parallels its internal representation, so these tasks can be done rather efficiently.

LISP is somewhat unusual in that it performs scanning and parsing functions intermittently. That is, because it is interpreted, some scanning and parsing are performed each time an s-expression is typed in for evaluation. Also, LISP's data structures are identical to its programming language constructs and are denoted by the same textual conventions. Thus, scanning and parsing must also occur when data are input by a program. This identity of data structures and program constructs allows for the same mechanisms to be used in either case. Namely, these are the mechanisms employed by the single LISP function **read**.

This chapter is concerned with one aspect of the LISP input phase, namely, the equivalent of a LISP symbol table. Common LISP allows the user to maintain a number of symbol-table-like objects, called *packages.* The routine use of packages by **read** is discussed. Then direct user manipulation of LISP packages is examined. This includes ways for users to create new symbols and remove existing ones. The possible dangers of such manipulation are discussed, along with some useful applications.

17.2. Tracking Symbol Names

One aspect of the processing performed by **read** involves the treatment of symbols. Most programming language translation systems keep track of the appearance of names of variables and functions during scanning and parsing. This is done to be sure that names are used consistently. A symbol table is used for this purpose. The LISP function **read** must also maintain a sort of symbol table for LISP symbols, since LISP guarantees that all symbols having the same name are the same symbol. For example, if we assign a value to a symbol named **foo**, and then ask LISP to evaluate a symbol named **foo**, LISP must make sure that both names reference the same symbol so that the latter operation will produce the previously stored value.

Since we have become accustomed to LISP operating in this manner, enforcing this constraint might seem like a trivial consideration. But LISP must do some work in order to maintain the uniqueness of symbol names. In particular, LISP must distinguish between new symbols and previously encountered ones. In the case where a name refers to a previously encountered symbol, LISP must find the representation of the old symbol and use it in building the representation of the new s-expression being read in. If the symbol is a new one, then a new representation for it must be created.

17.3. The Representation of Symbols

To make this process a bit clearer, consider all the information about each individual symbol that LISP has to store: A symbol may have a value assigned to it; it may also have a property list and it may have a function definition; and of course, it has a print name. Although we always refer to a symbol by its print name, LISP must store some internal representation of a symbol that has room for all this information.

Of course, the exact form of this internal representation may vary from one implementation to another. However, all internal references to a symbol will be references to this internal form. For example, in the internal LISP representation of the list **(a b c)**, the **car** half of the first **cons** cell designating the list points to the internal representation of the symbol named **a**. All other references to this LISP symbol also point to this same internal representation.

Thus when **read** scans the character string **(a b c)**, and recognizes a reference to the symbol named **a**, it must check to see if a representation for **a** has already been built. If so, then **read** must build a representation for this list that includes a pointer to the existing representation of **a**. It is to maintain this unique association of symbol names with their internal representations that a symbol table is useful.

17.4. Packages

In Common LISP, the role of a symbol table is played by a data structure called a *package*. A package is an interface between the print names typed by the user and the internal representations of symbols stored by LISP. Every symbol that the user can refer to by name must be accessible via a package. This includes standard LISP symbols like **car** and **cdr**, as well as symbols introduced by the user.

At any given time, there is one and only one package that is used as an interface between LISP and the world. This is called the *current package*. Every time the function **read** encounters a symbol's print name, **read** looks for a symbol with that name in the current package. If a symbol with the print name just read in is already accessible in the current package, **read** will use the existing representation for that symbol; otherwise it will create a new symbol representation, and enter the new symbol in the current package. This way, subsequent references to the same symbol name will end up referring to the same internal representation of that symbol.

All this is generally transparent to the user, and rightly so. The initial current package that comes with Common LISP is set up so that all the standard LISP functions and variables are immediately accessible. Therefore, we do not have to think about looking up symbols in packages at all, much less alter the current package or replace it with some other package.

However, there are some occasions when it is reasonable to be concerned with package manipulation. Two such situations predominate. First, there are times when a programmer wants his or her code to make up its own symbols. In this case, the programmer must make sure that the symbols are dealt with appropriately with respect to packages. Secondly, a programmer with a large program may want to organize it into semi-independent chunks. Doing package manipulation may be a useful way to easily combine programs that are created along these lines.

A word of warning, though. Woody Allen, in a treatise on mythical beasts, describes a creature called the Great Roe. The Great Roe has the head of a lion, and the body of a lion,... but not the same lion.

A similar situation can result if you manipulate packages yourself. While some package manipulations are entirely appropriate, others may have quite bizarre manifestations. For example, using package manipulation functions, it is possible to arrive at a situation in which there are several distinct symbols, all having the same name. Such symbols are as confusing as the Great Roe, as it is almost impossible to tell them apart. Programs in which this is the case are only occasionally correct, and may be extremely difficult to understand and debug.

Standardization Note: Many other LISPs have only a single symbol table, called the **oblist** (for "object list"). In such LISPs, there is nothing analogous to the Common LISP notion of packages. However, most of the functions described here that involve only the current package have direct analogues among oblist manipulation functions in other LISPs.

17.5. Symbol Creation and Package Updating Functions

First, let us look at those manipulations that involve at most the current package. In particular, we might want to create new symbols, or add or remove a symbol from the current package under program control.

17.5.1. Making New symbols

We can create a brand new symbol using the function **make-symbol**. The argument to **make-symbol** should be a string. **make-symbol** returns as its value a new symbol whose print name is that string. For example, to create a symbol with the name **abc**, we can do the following:

```
-> (make-symbol "ABC")
#:ABC
->
```

Here the result of our call to **make-symbol** was printed prefaced by the characters #:. This is Common LISP's way of indicating that symbol *has not been put in any package.* That is, **make-symbol** produced a new symbol, but has not done anything to make it accessible to **read**. As a result, we cannot reference such a symbol by its name. In fact, if there already exists a symbol named **abc** in the current package, or if we make one later on, this will be a different symbol than the one created by **make-symbol**. To demonstrate this point, let us save the symbol created by **make-symbol**, and compare it to a symbol of the same name created by **read**:

```
-> (setq x (make-symbol "ABC"))
#:ABC
```

```
-> (eq x 'abc)
NIL
-> x
#:ABC
->
```

Even though two symbols here have identical names, they are otherwise unrelated, as evidenced by applying **eq** to them.

We say that a symbol that is not entered in any package is *uninterned*. Similarly, we can talk about a symbol being *interned* in a given package. **read** interns all the new symbols it sees in the current package, so that we can reference them by name later on.

We can also specify an uninterned symbol using the # dispatching macro character. The sequence **#:sym** produces an uninterned symbol named **sym**. That is, each time this sequence is read, a new uninterned symbol will be produced.

If we want to be sure a symbol of a given name is interned in a package, then we can use the function **intern**. **intern** is passed a string as an argument. If a symbol of that name is in the package, **intern** will return it. Otherwise, it creates a symbol with that name and interns it in the package. For example, if we use **intern** to create a symbol, references to that name will behave more conventionally:

```
-> (setq x (intern "UVW"))
UVW
-> (eq x 'uvw)
T
->
```

Here **intern** put the symbol it produced into the current package. Thereafter, the appearance of the same name will refer to the same symbol.

17.5.2. Automatic Name Generation

Sometimes the need arises to create many new symbols automatically, each with a distinct name. The function **gensym** serves this purpose. **gensym** makes up a new name for a symbol each time it is called. It does this by keeping count of the number of times it has been called, and appending this number as a string to a prefix. The default for this prefix is the single character **G**. **gensym** returns the uninterned symbol it creates. For example:

```
-> (gensym)
#:G4
-> (gensym)
#:G5
-> (gensym)
#:G6
->
```

Usually, the symbols created by **gensym** will not be seen by the user, but are only used internally by the program. Therefore, it is not strictly necessary to give such symbols print names at all. However, a print name is produced so that the user can tell the symbols apart should the need arise.

It is possible to change the prefix used by **gensym** by passing a string as an optional argument. Consider the following example:

```
-> (gensym "FOO")
#:FOO7
-> (gensym)
#:FOO8
->
```

Note that the change is persistent and that the sequencing is uninterrupted. It is also possible to reset the counter:

```
-> (gensym 180)
#:FOO180
-> (gensym)
#:FOO181
```

Each call to **gensym** is guaranteed to produce a new symbol. There are many applications for this. For example, some programmers like to give names to each datum of a certain type their program encounters. If the program is going to store facts about an indefinite number of people, say, it could generate one symbol for each new person. Facts about this person can be represented by attaching properties to the corresponding symbol, or by similar techniques.

17.5.3. Removing a Symbol from a Package

We can remove a symbol already in a package using the function **unintern**. However, if we do so, and type in a symbol of the same name, a new symbol will be created. We may have s-expressions pointing to the representation of the old symbol, so we could end up with several symbols with the same name this way. Here is an example:

```
-> (setq x 'foo)
FOO
-> (unintern 'foo)
T
-> (eq x 'foo)
NIL
-> x
#:FOO
->
```

In this example, we first remove **foo** from the current package. When **foo** appears in the next s-expression, **read** no longer finds **foo** in the current package. Thus it creates a representation for a new symbol named **foo**. The symbol **x** is still assigned the old **foo**, however. **eq** demonstrates these to be distinct symbols, even though they bear the same name.

In Common LISP, once we remove a symbol from a package, there is no way to put that very same symbol back in. For example, if we remove a symbol from a package, and then try to intern it, we will get a new symbol of the same name:

```
-> (setq x 'foo)
FOO
-> (unintern x)
T
-> (setq y (intern "FOO"))
FOO
-> (eq x y)
NIL
->
```

After we remove **foo** from the current package, **x** still has this symbol as its value. However, trying to intern a symbol named **foo** merely causes a new symbol named **foo** to be created. The old **foo** is pointed to by **x** and the new one by **y**. The new symbol **foo** has nothing in common with the old symbol **foo** other than its print name.

Standardization Note: In many other LISPs, **unintern** is called **remob**. Also, in some of those LISPs, it is possible to reintern a symbol by passing it to **intern**.

17.6. Package Manipulation

So far we have assumed that we were dealing with a single package. This is most typically the case. However, having more than one package is a useful way to organize a large program. For example, suppose we are writing a compiler that comprises a scanner, a parser, and a code generator. Each of these components might require a large number of functions, and each of these functions may call the other functions in its component rather often. However, the functions in one component would call only a few of the functions appearing in another component. We could think of each component as having a set of internal functions, that no one outside that component ought to be concerned with, and a set of external functions that are advertized to the rest of the world.

Such a subsystem of a large program is called a *module.* We can use packages to implement modules as follows: We could associate with each module its own package. When we loaded that module (i. e., when we **read** in the code), we could be sure that all symbols in that module were placed in that module's package. This way, all references to the symbol **localfn**, say, within the module would refer to the same symbol. But all references to **localfn** that appeared outside that module would use some other package, and therefore, would refer to some entirely different symbol.

In this manner, we could use packages to create local versions of symbols. However, we still need some mechanism to allow the external functions of a module to be accessible outside that module. To see how to do this, we will have to explore package structure some more, and examine a few more features of the function **read**.

17.6.1. Package Structure

A package is said to *own* a number of symbols, namely, those symbols that are interned in it. We refer to that package as the *home* package of those symbols. When a package is the current package, all the symbols in it are referenced simply by typing their names to **read**.

In addition, it is possible to reference symbols that are owned by some other package. This can be done by declaring a symbol to be an *external* symbol of a package. Once a symbol is declared to be an external symbol, it may be referred to anytime by preceding it with the name of its package separated from it by a colon. For example, if the package **scan** has an external symbol named **analyze**, then the reference **scan:analyze** will refer to this symbol no matter what the current package is. We call this notation a *qualified symbol reference,* as the symbol name is qualified by a package to look it up in. Symbols that are not declared to be external are called, naturally enough, *internal* symbols.

We can declare a symbol to be external using the function **export**. For example, a call of the form **(export 'analyze)** would declare the symbol **analyze** to be an external symbol of the current package. Once this is done, we can refer to this symbol when the current package is changed to something other than **scan**, by using the notation **scan:analyze**. (Actually, **export**, like most of the functions discussed in this chapter, take an optional package argument. For example, **(export 'analyze 'scan)** will declare the symbol **analyze** to be an external symbol of the package **scan**, regardless of what the current package is.)

Typically, calls to **export** appear toward the beginning of a file containing some portion of a program. This is a convenient way of indicating which symbols in the file are meant to be used by other programs.

Using qualified symbol references, a program not associated with the **scan** package could nevertheless reference the function **analyze**. For example, a number of functions in the **parse** package might need to call the function **analyze**. They could do so by using the reference **scan:analyze**. However, it would be rather inconvenient to use this notation if many references to **scan:analyze** appeared in this code. Instead, we might like to make it more convenient to reference this symbol within another package.

We can do this by *importing* a symbol into one package from another. For example, if **analyze** is a symbol interned in the **scan** package, we can import **analyze** into the current package by a call of the form **(import 'scan:analyze)**. (Alternatively, we can import the symbol into another package by specifying that package name as an optional argument.) After importing a symbol, we can reference that symbol by name without any qualifier. Having imported **analyze** into the current package, we can reference it simply by typing its name, without the **scan:** qualifier.

It is not necessary that a symbol be external to a package in order to import it. However, right now we do not know how to reference a symbol not in the current package without having previously declared that symbol to be external. It is possible to do so using a special notation. For example, if **analyze** were not declared to be an external symbol of **scan**, we could still reference it using the following qualification: **scan::analyze**. This notation is intentionally awkward, as references to an internal symbol of another package should be rare occurrences indeed.

A more typical occurrence is that the programmer would want all the external symbols of one package to be imported in another. For example, **scan** might have a number of other functions and variables that the parser module might need to reference. We could accomplish this by explicitly importing each of them. It may be that a number of other modules also want to reference exactly the same set of symbols. This would not be at all surprising, since the external symbols of a package are meant to be that package's interface to the outside world. So we would like a way of making all these symbols readily accessible by other modules.

This can be accomplished by the function **use-package**. This function is given a package (or list of packages) as an argument. It makes all the external symbols of that package accessible as internal symbols of the current package. That is, we will subsequently be able to reference these symbols without qualification. If we make the external symbols of one package accessible in another, we say that the later package *uses* the former one.

For example, we could put the expression **(use-package 'scan)** near the beginning of the file, after some code that specifies that **parse** should be made the current package, and before the definitions of the various parser functions, etc. When the file is **load**ed, the call to **use-package** will make the various external symbols of **scan** accessible to the **parse** package. Thus the code of the **parse** functions can be written using unqualified references to the external symbols of **scan**, instead of having to use qualified symbol references.

17.6.2. Standard Common LISP Packages

As another example, consider the packages that Common LISP comes with. All the standard symbols of Common LISP are owned by the package named **lisp**. This includes all functions and variables that are visible to the user: **car**, **cdr**, **read**, **∗standard-output∗**, etc. Almost all other packages use this package, so that the normal LISP symbols will be accessible without qualification no matter what the current package is.

Initially, the current package in a Common LISP process is a package named **user**. This package will be home for all the user's symbols, unless an explicit effort is taken to do otherwise. Of course, **user** uses **lisp**, so that the user can readily access standard LISP symbols, even though these symbols are owned by a different package.

Another standard Common LISP package is called **system**. This package contains functions used internally by Common LISP, but which are not mean to be used directly by the user. For example, we said in Chapter 13 that the function **setf** is a macro, and expands into a call to whatever code is necessary to do the actual setting. But now consider a call of the form **(setf (get obj prop) val)**. Since **setf** is a macro, this should expand into some code that does the actual work. However, there is no standard Common LISP function that changes the property of a symbol. So what can this expand into? Let us use **macroexpand** to find out:

```
-> (macroexpand '(setf (get obj prop) val))
(LET* ((#:G10 OBJ) (#:G9 PROP) (#:G8 VAL)) (SYSTEM::%PUT
#:G10 #:G9 #:G8)) ;
T
->
```

The call to **setf** was expanded into a call **let***. (The call to **let*** is generated primarily to assure the order of evaluation of the arguments. The call to **let*** merely evaluates in order the arguments supplied, and assigns them to new variables, which are then used to pass these values to the function that changes the property list. The new variables are designated by the symbols **g8**, **g9** and **g10**. These are produced by **gensym**. Hence they are not interned, and are printed out with the **#:** notation.) The real work is done by a system function called **%put**. This function is owned by the package **system**. The symbol **%put** happens not to be an external symbol of this package, so it must be referred to using a **::** qualified symbol reference. In general, the user should have little need to refer directly to these internal system functions, so no attempt is made to make them easy to reference.

Standardization Note: The names of the functions in the **system** package are implementation-dependent.

There is one more standard package in Common LISP, called **keyword**. Recall that Common LISP treats symbols preceded with **:** in a special way, namely, as keywords that always evaluate to themselves. This is accomplished by having **read** always intern symbols preceded by **:** in the special **keyword** package, regardless of what the current package is. Thus, a keyword is really any symbol owned by the **keyword** package.

17.6.3. Modules

We now have almost enough machinery to implement true modules. All we need to be able to do is create a new package, make it the current package, and then specify its functions and variables. Of course, we might also want to specify which other packages this package uses, which symbols to declare external, or import a few miscellaneous symbols of another package.

We can create a package using the function **make–package**. This will create an empty package of the name given as an argument. The keyword argument **:use** can be followed by a list of packages that package uses. (This defaults to the package **lisp**, since almost all packages will want the standard LISP functions to be accessible without qualification.) Once we have created a package, we can make it the standard package simply by reassigning the value of the variable ***package***. This variable is assumed by **read** and other functions to specify the current package. Initially, ***package*** has the value **user**.

If we change ***package*** to a package created by **make–package**, then all the subsequent expressions read in will have their symbols interned in the new package. Thus, all the symbols contained in the expressions read in while the new package is in force will have nothing to do with previous symbols bearing the same names. When we restore ***package*** to its previous value, these new symbols can no longer be easily referenced. This is just what we want for those symbols that we wish to be internal to the module. We can make some symbols external, though, to provide an interface to the module.

As an example, suppose we want to have a module named **utilities** that contains a number of useful functions, including a recursive version of a function that reverses a list. Here is the definition from Chapter 6:

```
(defun recursive–reverse (l) (reverse–2 l nil))

(defun reverse–2 (original revdlist)
    (cond ((null original) revdlist)
          (t (reverse–2 (cdr original)
                        (cons (car original) revdlist)))))
```

Since no one using **recursive–reverse** need ever call **reverse–2** directly, we can make **reverse–2** an internal function of **utilities**. We should make **recursive–reverse** external, though, so that we can use it easily from other packages.

First, let us create the package **utilities**, and make it the current package:

```
-> (setq *package* (make-package "utilities"))
#<utilities package>
->
```

As we can see, Common LISP tends to use the #< notation to print packages.

Standardization Note: The exact format for printing packages is implementation-dependent.

Next, let us include the code we wish this package to contain:

```
-> (defun recursive-reverse (l) (reverse-2 l nil))
RECURSIVE-REVERSE
-> (defun reverse-2 (original revdlist)
        (cond ((null original) revdlist)
              (t (reverse-2 (cdr original)
                            (cons (car original) revdlist)))))
REVERSE-2
-> (recursive-reverse '(a b c))
(C B A)
->
```

Now let us make **recursive-reverse** an external symbol of **utilities**, and then restore the package **user**:

```
-> (export 'recursive-reverse)
T
-> (setq *package* (find-package "user"))
#<user package>
->
```

The function **find-package** is used here to return the package whose name is **user**. Now we can reference the function **recursive-reverse** using a single colon qualified symbol reference:

```
-> (utilities:recursive-reverse '(a b c))
(C B A)
->
```

To make using this function more convenient, we can import it into the current package:

```
-> (import 'utilities:recursive-reverse)
T
-> (recursive-reverse '(a b c))
(C B A)
->
```

Note that the symbol **reverse-2** of **utilities** cannot be referenced easily:

```
-> (reverse-2 '(a b c) nil)
```

Error: Symbol has no function definition: RECURSIVE-2

Debug 1>: quit

```
-> (utilities::reverse-2 '(a b c) nil)
(C B A)
->
```

Rather than manipulate ***package*** ourselves, we can use the function **in-package**. **in-package** is given a package name as an argument. ***package*** is set to this package; if no such package exists, one is created. This assignment will remain in place until it is explicitly changed.

Normally, this function is placed at the beginning of a file that is to contain a module of code. The function **load** always restores ***package*** to whatever value it had before the **load** began. So a call to **in-package** in the beginning of a file will place a new package into effect for only as long as we are loading that file.

For example, to achieve the same effect as the code we entered above, we might create a file with the following entries in it:

```
(in-package "utilities")

(export 'recursive-reverse)

(defun recursive-reverse (l) (reverse-2 l nil))

(defun reverse-2 (original revdlist)
    (cond ((null original) revdlist)
          (t (reverse-2 (cdr original)
                        (cons (car original) revdlist)))))
```

Finally, there are two functions that support modules directly. These are called **provide** and **require**. Both functions require a single argument, which is used as the name of a module. The purpose of **provide** is just to declare that the associated code constitutes a module. When a call to **provide** is evaluated, it simply adds the module name to the variable ***modules***. This indicates that the module in question has been loaded.

The function **require** is used to specify that a given module is needed in conjunction with some other code. **require** does this by examining the value of ***modules*** to see if it includes its argument. If it does, **require** does nothing. However, if the specified module is not loaded, **require** will load it in. This may involve loading a number of files that are associated with the module in some system-dependent way.

As an example, suppose we are writing a program composed of the modules **scan**, **parse**, and **code-gen**. Furthermore, **parse** might intimately use another module named **grammar**.

In this example, we will assume that each module is kept in exactly one file. We would start our **parse** module with the following code:

```
(provide 'parse)
(in-package 'parse)
```

The first line declares that this is the module named **parse**. The second creates a package by the same name (an arbitrary but eminently reasonable terminology), and also makes this package the current package.

Next, we may want to declare which functions in this module may serve as its external interface:

```
(export '(parse-statement parse-program parse-expression))
```

Now we need to mention that the parser functions require the scanner functions to be present:

```
(require 'scan)
```

This will insure that the functions of the **scan** module are loaded when we load the **parse** module.

Perhaps the only function of the **scan** module that the parser needs to use frequently is the function **analyze**. Rather than do a **use-package**, then, we can just import the desired symbol:

```
(import 'scan:analyze)
```

Now, we also need the functions of **grammar** to help with the parsing:

```
(require 'grammar)
```

Since many of these functions may be used frequently in the parser, we will make it convenient to refer to them:

```
(use-package 'grammar)
```

Now the code for the parser can appear:

```
(defun parse-statement (statement)
   (let ((token (analyze)) ...)
      ...
      (match 'statement-rule statement)
      ...                                          ))
```

We can refer to **analyze** without qualification here because we previously imported it. Similarly, the symbol **statement-rule** is owned by the **grammar** package, but since we use that package within the **parse** module, we can refer to its symbols without qualification.

The code for the code generator module might look like this:

```
(provide 'code-gen)
(in-package 'code-gen)

(export '(process-tree optimize assemble))

(require 'parse)
(use-package 'parse)

(defun make-code ( )
   (let ((code (process-tree (parse-program)))...)...)
```

Once again, here we name the module, and set up a package for it. Then we declare external symbols, state that the module requires the **parse** module, and make all the parser external symbols accessible to this module. Because this package uses the **parse** package, we can refer to **parse-program** here without qualification. Moreover, all three modules may contain any number of functions or variables with exactly the same names as those appearing in the other modules. This causes no problem at all, provided these names are internal to those modules.

In general, the order of function calls that appears in these examples is necessary for building a module correctly.

17.7. Summary

(1)   The function **read** acts as the general purpose interface between the world of character strings and the world of LISP's internal representations. Therefore, **read** performs the equivalent of scanning and parsing each time it is called.

(2)   In particular, **read** is concerned with "uniquifying" symbols – making references to the same names refer to the same symbols. **read** accomplishes this through the use of a kind of symbol table called a *package*. Every symbol seen by **read** is looked up in and perhaps entered into the current package.

(3)   A package is the *home* of a set of symbols, which it is said to *own*. A symbol that is owned by a package is said to be *interned* in that package.

(4)   We can remove a symbol from a package using the function **unintern**. We can add a symbol to a package using the function **intern**.

(5)   The function **make–symbol** creates a new symbol with its argument as print name. The function **gensym** is used to create a sequence of new symbol names.

(6)   A package has two kinds of symbols, internal and external. An external symbol can be referenced using the notation *package:symbol*; an internal symbol can only be referenced using the notation *package::symbol*. These are called *qualified symbol references*. A symbol is made external using the function **export**.

(7)   A symbol from one package can be made accessible in other (i. e., it can be referenced without qualification) by using the function **import**. The function **use–package** makes all the external symbols of one package accessible from another.

(8)   The functions **provide** and **require** are used to manipulate modules. **provide** declares that a module is being specified; **require** specifies that a certain module is needed in conjunction with the current body of code.

(9)   In general, functions that manipulate a package should be used with great caution. They can result in multiple symbols with the same name. This can make debugging the code in which they appear exceedingly difficult.

Exercises

(1)   In the chapter on property lists, we showed how we can represent a data base on a library of books. However, to create a representation of a book in this example, the user had to supply a name like **book3**. Write a version of the function **add–book** defined in that chapter which generates its own names for books.

(2)   In an exercise in Chapter 7, we discussed the technique of *marking*. In that exercise, we supposed we had two lists of symbols, and wanted to compute the intersection of these lists as sets (that is, the list that contains exactly one instance of all the elements on both lists). We noted that a fast way to accomplish this computation is to go through one list and put a property on each symbol. For example, we can set the value of the **marker** property to **t**. Then we can go through the second list, and collect only those elements whose **marker** property have this value. The resulting list will be the intersection we require. This version requires only about 2n operations, as it only involves a single sequencing through each list.

However, there is an annoying problem with this technique. If we use it several times, some of the symbols we encounter are likely to have marks on them from previous calls to this function, and we will get a spurious result.

One way around this problem is to clean up after each use. But this requires doing more work. A better solution is to use a unique marker each time. For example, we can have our intersection function first create a **gensym**ed symbol and use this to mark the symbols in one of the lists. That is, we can still mark the symbols with the property **marker**, but use a property value created by **gensym** instead of the property value **t**. (Alternatively, rather than mark the symbols with a property named **marker**, we can mark them with a property name created by **gensym**.) Then we can check for this particular mark on the symbols of the other list. Since each call to our intersection function would create a brand new marker symbol, we would not have to worry at all about the effects of previous calls.

Write a version of such an intersection function that uses **gensym**ed symbol names to avoid having to clean up after itself.

(3)   Some programmers prefer to have several independent program-generated sequences of symbols. We can use **gensym** to create symbols with different prefixes. But **gensym** uses a single counter for all the symbols it creates.

Define a function **newsym** that requires a single argument. It will generate a symbol beginning with that prefix. Unlike **gensym**, though, **newsym** will maintain separate counters for each prefix. Thus calls to **newsym** involving different prefixes will have no effect on one another.

It is useful to have several other functions that operation in conjunction with **newsym**. The symbol **oldsym** returns the last symbol generated for a specified prefix. The function **symstat** returns the value of the counter associated with a given prefix. Write these functions as well.

You may find the functions **concatenate** and **princ-to-string** useful in defining **newsym**.

(4)   Use the module and package manipulation functions described in this chapter to arrange one of your programs into separate modules with well-defined interfaces between them.

(5)   Note that when we changed the current package to one we created ourselves, we were able to restore the old current package by reassigning ***package***. But ***package*** is just a symbol, and must live in some package. What package is this symbol's home? (You might want to avail yourself of some of the package functions described in Appendix A to help with this task.) Why is it still readily accessible when we changed the current package? How might it become unaccessible? If it were no longer readily accessible, how might we then change the current package?

(6)   There are a number of circumstances under which a package manipulation might cause a reference to become ambiguous. For example, if we import a symbol whose name is the same as a symbol already directly accessible in a package, then there would be no way to determine which symbol the user intended when that symbol's name was read in.

Common LISP allows you to resolve these conflicts by specifying a set of symbols in a package that will *shadow* any other symbol of the same name that would otherwise be accessible in that package. The function **shadow** will create a new internal symbol of the specified name, provided that one by that name does not alreay exist, and then add the new symbol to that package's "shadowing-symbols list." **shadowing–import** will both import a symbol and place it on the shadowing-symbols list. All other package manipulation functions will detect conflicts that may arise from the manipulations the user specifies, and ask for user intervention to determine how the conflict should be resolved.

Use this information to deal with a situation in which you wish to import the symbol **recursive–reverse** of the package **utilities** into the current package, assuming that a different symbol named **recursive–reverse** is already present in the current package.

Chapter 18

Data Types

18.1. Introduction

We have noted that LISP programs comprise lists and symbols, and that the data they manipulate consist primarily of lists and symbols. The homogeneous nature of LISP programs and data has some interesting benefits. It is often possible and desirable in LISP to execute data, for example, through the use of functions like **eval** and **apply**; we both read in our programs and read in our data through the same mechanism, the function **read**.

However, there is nothing about LISP that restricts it to the manipulation of lists and symbols. For example, in the beginning of this book, we first applied LISP to numeric quantities. We used the machinery of LISP to write programs that do mathematical computation. The resulting programs are not substantially different from those that might be written in FORTRAN or PASCAL, except that they conform to LISP's syntax.

LISP might not be the best programming language to write such algorithms (it is probably not the worst, either). But sometimes it is useful in LISP to use data types and data structures other than symbols and lists. For this reason, almost all LISPs augment these main data types with other types.

312

We have already seen quite a few data types in Common LISP. In addition to lists and atoms, we have made at least a passing acquaintance with characters, strings, functions, packages, pathnames, and streams. In this chapter, we examine some of the other Common LISP data types. In doing so, we present a more thorough picture of what is available in Common LISP. We present methods for creating and accessing these various data types. We also make suggestions about their respective uses. However, we do not show much in the way of specific applications of them; nor will we exhaust the full complexity of Common LISP's ability to manipulate data structures. This is because the set of available data structures encompasses just about all the well known types. Also, most of these are not especially specific to LISP. Thus this chapter tends to highlight the LISP peculiarities involving these structures, rather than describe their general features.

Standardization Note: Support of the data types mentioned in this chapter varies considerably from one dialect of LISP to the next. The user should be aware that some of the data types described in this section are apt not even to exist in other LISPs. Where they do exist, the details of their structure and function may differ in important ways from those of Common LISP.

18.2. Data Types in Common LISP

Most of us have some intuitions that cause us to divide data naturally into different types. For example, numbers seem to be one sort of data, and lists another. The intuition seems based on the fact that you can do one sort of thing with numbers, but quite a different sort of thing with lists. Moreover, this distinction seems to be supported by LISP: Trying to add two lists or take the **cdr** of a number causes an error.

The notion of *data types* is a computer science attempt to codify such intuitions. That is, when we say that something is a data type of a given language, we mean that there is a set of operations in that language which are conveniently described in terms of that type. For example, the set of operations may be applicable to the class of data objects of given type, and meaningless when applied to other data.

In addition, some languages may make the intuition behind data types more explicit. For example, the language may support explicit predicates that verify that some datum is of a given type. Or it may employ some sort of mechanism that allows us to specify that objects in a program are of a certain type. Such a "type specifier" may be used in a number of different ways. For example, it may be used to detect an error (at compile time or run time), or to optimize the execution of the program.

In Common LISP, all three aspects of data types can be found. We can describe most Common LISP functions as being defined on objects of a given type. Also, as we have seen, there are many specific predicates that determine whether their argument is a particular type of data. And, although we have not discussed it, there are also type specifiers in Common LISP that let us express a particular kind of type, for a number of different purposes.

For example, numbers constitute a data type in Common LISP according to these criteria. There are quite a few functions that are easy to describe as operations on numbers (e. g., + and *), and there is a predicate (i. e., **numberp**) that distinguishes numbers from non-numbers. In addition, the symbol **number** is a valid type specifier that specifies this type. For example, passing **number** as a second argument to **typep** will cause that function to return true if and only if its first argument is indeed a number.

Standardization Note: The notion of explicit type specifiers does not appear in most LISPs other than Common LISP.

One consequence of this notion of type is that the different data types of Common LISP do not constitute entirely distinct classes. For example, the object **foo** appears to be both a symbol and an atom. Applying the three criteria of type listed above, we note that some functions can be described conveniently in terms of atoms, and some in terms of symbols. In addition, both the predicates **symbolp** and **atom** will return true when applied to **foo**, and both **(typep 'foo 'atom)** and **(typep 'foo 'symbol)** also return true. Similarly, **2.3** is a number. But it is also a floating-point number.

The upshot of all this is that it is convenient to think of the data types of Common LISP as constituting a *hierarchy*. By this we mean that some of the data types of Common LISP are more specific versions of other data types. Thus numbers constitute a legitimate data type, and so do floating-point numbers. The first type is just more general than the second. Floating-point numbers themselves comprise data of different types. Namely, there are short, single, double and long floating-point numbers, these differing from one another by their precision. Another, more abstract way of saying the same thing is that one data type *contains* another, meaning that all the data objects of the latter type are also data objects of the former type. E. g., all floating-point numbers are numbers, so the data type **number** contains the data type **float** (the official Common LISP name for floating-point numbers); all short floating-point numbers are floating-point numbers, so that data type **float** contains the data type **short–float**.

We refer to a data type contained by another data type as a *subtype* of that data type. For example, short floating-point numbers are a subtype of floating-point numbers; they are also a subtype of numbers. They are even a subtype of atoms, since all numbers are atoms as well. Symbols are also a subtype of atoms. "Atom" might seem like a more artificial category than "number", because it seems to make sense only within LISP. However, all these types are just as valid as far as LISP is concerned.

One consequence of the hierarchical nature of data is that it is meaningless to ask what *the* data type of an object is. For example, what is the data type of **3.2**? Is it **number**? or perhaps **float**? **atom** and **single–float** (assuming that the datum is in this format) are also applicable. So instead, we have to ask what data types an object *belongs* to. **3.2** belongs to each of the categories just listed. The function **typep** can be used to make this determination in a program, by supplying it with a data object and a type.

There is also a function in Common LISP called **type–of**. The idea behind this function is to query a particular data object and return its type. But, as the previous discussion points out, there is no single correct answer for **type–of** to return. Instead **type–of** returns some type that is correct. In fact, it is supposed to return the most specific type of the object that is useful to the programmer, but the exact result of **type–of** will depend on the implementation.

The function **subtypep** may also be useful in answering questions about the relation between two types. **subtypep** takes two arguments, each representing type specifiers. It tries to determine if the type specified by the first argument is a subtype of that specified by the second, and will return **t** if this is the case. However, **subtype** cannot always determine the answer to its query. Thus a result of **nil** can mean either that the answer is no, or that it cannot ascertain the answer. To provide additional information, **subtype** returns a second value. This value is true if the answer is known to **subtype**, but will be **nil** if **subtype** cannot determine the answer.

18.3. The Standard Common LISP Data Types

As we have seen above, the types we have become familiar with have official Common LISP names. **number**, **atom**, **float** and **symbol** are examples of such data type names. These names are recognized or used by certain Common LISP functions which deal directly with data type concepts. For example, one of these names may constitute a type specifier for a call to **typep**; alternatively, it may be returned as the value of a call to **type-of**.

There are a number of other data types whose names are recognized by Common LISP. It is possible to create more data types than these, as we will see below. But first let us briefly examine the types Common LISP comes with. These are listed below, with some of the subtypes listed within more major categories. The significance of being on this list is that there are likely to be a number of Common LISP functions for dealing with objects of that type. That is, Common LISP is essentially a set of functions that manipulate objects of these data types. We have become familiar with many of these types in our progress through this book, and will not elaborate on those here. Some description of the types we have not yet discussed adequately or at all appear in the subsequent sections of this chapter.

In addition, the symbols below denoting each type will be recognized by functions dealing with types, such as **typep**. There are also apt to be specific predicates for each type; when there are, these will appear in parentheses next to the name of the type:

First, we have the rather standard data types pertaining to ordinary symbolic expressions:

cons (**consp**)
> All objects produced by **cons**ing are considered to be of type **cons**. This includes all lists, except **nil**.

list (**listp**)
> This type includes all **cons**es and **nil**. It is something of a misnomer, as non-lists, i. e., **cons**es whose right pointer is non-**nil**, are considered to be of the **list** data type.

null (**null**)
> This type includes only the single data object **nil**.

symbol (**symbolp**)
> This is the basic LISP symbolic object. Common LISP recognizes one subtype of **symbol**, called **keyword**. This represents that class of keywords, namely, all symbols **intern**ed in the **keyword** package. These are the symbols that are normally entered preceded by the character **:**.

number (**numberp**)

There are several different subtypes of numbers in Common LISP: **integer**, **ratio**, **rational** (which includes integers and ratios), **float** (floating-point numbers) and **complex** (complex numbers). Several of these also have subtypes. **fixnum** denotes the "small" integers, and **bignum** the "large" ones (the dividing line being implementation-dependent). In addition, the type **bit** contains just the two elements **0** and **1**. The types **short–float**, **single–float**, **double–float** and **long–float** denote the corresponding floating-point representations, and are all subtypes of **float**. The predicates **integerp**, **floatp**, and **complexp** determine whether their argument is of the corresponding type; **rationalp** returns true if its argument is a ratio or an integer.

Then there are data types pertaining to arrays:

array (**arrayp**)

Arrays are objects with components that can be referenced by a coordinate system. They are created and manipulated by functions especially designed for these purposes. The subtype **simple–array** refers to those arrays that are of a fixed size and shape.

vector (**vectorp**)

Vectors are one dimensional arrays. The subtype **simple–vector** applies to one dimensional simple arrays. In addition, **bit–vector** refers to those vectors whose elements are constrained to be bits, and **simple–bit–vector** to those vectors that are both simple and constrained to contain only bits.

string (**stringp**)

Strings are vectors of characters. The subtype **simple–string** refers to those strings that are also simple vectors.

There are data types pertinent to I/O, several of which were discussed in Chapter 10:

readtable (**readtablep**)

A readtable is used to map characters to their syntactic interpretations by **read**. The user may change the way expressions are interpreted by manipulating readtables. We shall not pursue readtables further because of their specialized nature.

package (**packagep**)

A package is a symbol table used by **read** to map strings to symbols.

pathname (**pathnamep**)
> Pathnames are used to interface to the external file system.

stream (**streamp**)
> Streams are sources or sinks of data.

Then there are data types that can be thought of as the logical combination of other data types:

atom (**atom**)
> An atom is anything that is not of type **cons**.

Standardization Note: In many LISP dialects, only symbols and numbers are considered to be atoms.

---

sequence
> A sequence is either a vector or a list. This exists in Common LISP because there are many operations one wants to perform on data that has a sequential character to it, regardless of the underlying implementation.

common (**commonp**)
> This represents all the required data objects of Common LISP. That is, all the standard types are subtypes of **common**. A particular implemention may contain additional types that are not included in **common**.

t

> This represents all possible data objects in the particular implementation. These include the standard Common LISP data types, plus any additional types that may have been added to the particular implementation.

nil

> This is the "empty" data type, that is, a data type consisting of no objects at all. It is included primarily for completeness.

The following are miscellaneous data types:

character (**characterp**)
> Characters correspond to the ordinary notion of a character object. **standard–char** is a subtype consisting of the ordinary ASCII characters plus the newline character. **string–char** is a subtype consisting of

all the characters that may appear in strings; these are basically all the characters that are not control characters and have no font characteristics.

function (functionp)

A function is anything that can properly be supplied to **funcall** or **apply**. These include symbols that denote ordinary definitions, as well as lambda expressions, including compiled versions of either of these. Special functions and macros are *not* considered to be of type **function**. The subtype **compiled-function** refers to those functions whose definitions have been compiled into machine code.

hash-table (hash-table-p)

Hash tables provide an efficient, transportable means of mapping from one LISP object to another object associated with it.

random-state (random-state-p)

A random state is an object used *only* by the function **random**, the Common LISP random number generating function. It is used to encode the internal state of this function so that a subsequent call will cause a new random number to be produced. Its exact nature will vary from implementation to implementation.

Finally, there are user-defined data types called *structures.* These are similar to the records of PASCAL. As we will see below, defining a new type of structure generally causes a new data type to come into existence.

18.3.1. Combining and Specializing Data Types

It is possible to define additional data types by combining and specializing the type specifiers just mentioned. For example, it is possible to have a type comprising all the integers between 0 and 100, or one comprising all vectors of 50 elements, each of whose elements must be a long floating-point number. The type specifiers denoting such types are valid arguments to **typep**, and to other type-oriented functions.

But what would we ever use such type specifiers for? After all, specifying a new type does not create any functions to manipulate these new data types. In fact, type specifiers are generally used to allow an implementation to do error-checking, or to make code run more efficiently. This may be accomplished by informing the LISP system that a particular variable will only take on values of a certain sort, or that a particular function will only return values of a certain sort, etc. We can inform LISP of such a fact issuing what is known as a *declaration* .

However, this use of type specifiers is completely advisory in nature in Common LISP. That is, an implementation may ignore all declarations pertaining to type (and most other declarations as well). In fact, most LISP interpreters ignore type declarations completely. The one place in an implementation where such declarations are actually heeded is in the compiler. For this reason, we will hold off from discussing type specifiers and their use in making declarations until we discuss compiling in Chapter 20.

Instead, we will now look at each of the standard Common LISP data types that have not received adequate treatment thus far.

18.4. Arrays

Arrays in LISP serve pretty much the same function as arrays do in other programming languages. They allow the LISP user to create and access data via a coordinate system.

Common LISP arrays can have any number of dimensions.

Standardization Note: Some implementations may impose a limit, but it is not supposed to be less than 7.

An array can be a *general array,* meaning that its elements may be any LISP object, or a *specialized array,* i. e., one whose elements are of a certain type. In addition, one-dimensional arrays are called *vectors.* A specialized vector that can contain only characters as elements is called a *string.* So the strings we have become familiar with are really a special case of array. A vector allowing only the integers 0 or 1 as elements is called a *bit-vector.*

We can create an array in Common LISP using the function **make–array**. We supply **make–array** with a list of the dimensions of the array (if it is to be an array of only one dimension, a single integer rather than a list will do). **make–array** creates an array of this shape and returns it as its value. For example, to create an array of dimensions 4 by 2, we can type the following:

```
-> (setq foo (make-array '(4 2)))
#2A((NIL NIL)(NIL NIL)(NIL NIL)(NIL NIL))
->
```

Note that **print** outputs arrays using the following notation: First it prints the character #. Then it prints the rank of the array (i. e., the number of its dimensions), followed by the character **A**. Then the contents of the array is printed in a kind of list format. The list format parallels the structure of the array. In this case, the array is two-dimensional, so it is printed as a list of four lists, each of which are in turn lists of 2 elements each. Each of elements here is **nil**, the default value for unspecified array elements.

Standardization Note: Actually, the value of an unspecified array element is supposed to be undefined. However, most implementations of Common LISP seem to initialize array elements to **nil**.

This notation is recognized by the # dispatching macro character during **read**. That is, had you typed in the form printed above, LISP would have built an array identical in nature to the array created by **make–array** in our example.

This syntax for printing arrays will be used only if the value of **∗print–array∗** is non-**nil**. Otherwise, a more concise format beginning with #< will be used. Of course, this format cannot be read back in by **read**.

Standardization Note: The initial value of **∗print–array∗** is implementation-dependent.

We can reference an element of an array using the function **aref**. **aref** is passed an array and as many arguments as the array has dimensions. These are interpreted as subscripts of the element to reference. The subscripts are zero-based, so the first element of the array defined above is referenced by the expression **(aref foo 0 0)**. The next element is **(aref foo 0 1)**, and so on.

To change the value of an array element, we use the function **setf** in conjunction with **aref**. For example, to store the value **baz** as the last element of the array assigned to **foo**, we would type

```
-> (setf (aref foo 3 1) 'baz)
BAZ
->
```

We could now reference this element using **aref**:

```
-> (aref foo 3 1)
BAZ
->
```

make-array allows a large number of keyword arguments. These allow the programmer to specify a type for the elements of the array, a default value to which array elements can be initialized, and a number of other options. For example, all the elements of the array can be initialized to a given value by using the keyword argument **:initial-element**:

```
-> (make-array '(2 3 4) :initial-element 'e)
#3A(((E E E E)(E E E E)(E E E E))((E E E E)(E E E E)(E E E E)))
->
```

Here we created a three dimensional array of dimensions 2x3x4. We also specified that each element of the array should have the value **e**.

The keyword argument **:initial-contents** can be used to initialize the elements of an array to different values. This argument should be followed by the desired values in the sort of list notation we have just seen. For example, to create a 2x3x4 array filled with the integers 1 to 24, we can do the following:

```
-> (setq al (make-array '(2 3 4)
                    :initial-contents
                    '(((1 2 3 4)
                       (5 6 7 8)
                       (9 10 11 12))
                      ((13 14 15 16)
                       (17 18 19 20)
                       (21 22 23 24)))))
#3A(((1 2 3 4) (5 6 7 8) (9 10 11 12)) ((13 14 15 16)
(17 18 19 20) (21 22 23 24)))
-> (aref al 0 0 0)
1
-> (aref al 1 2 3)
24
->
```

The array references above select the first and last elements of the array, respectively, because arrays use zero-based indexing.

Standardization Note: Different dialects of LISP support very different array conventions. One of the more common is the "MacLISP" style array. These arrays are created by a call to the function **array** of the form (**array** *name type d1 d2 ...*), where *type* determines the type of the array elements, and the *di* its dimensions. The array is given the name *name*. Its elements are referenced using function call syntax. For example, to reference the (2,3) element of a two-dimensional MacLISP array **arr**, we would type (**arr 2 3**). To assign an element a value, the function **store** is used. For example, to assign the (2,3) element of **arr** the value **baruch**, we would type (**store (arr 2 3) 'baruch**).

18.5. Vectors

Vectors in Common LISP are simply arrays of one dimension. There are a few functions, however, that are applicable only in this case.

We can create a vector using the function **vector**. Consider the following example:

```
-> (setq v1 (vector 'a 'b 'c 'd))
#(A B C D)
->
```

An identical object would have been created by a call of the form

```
(make-array '(4) :initial-contents '(a b c d))
```

No matter how they are defined, LISP will print vectors by preceding their elements with the characters #(and following them with a). Naturally, this notation is recognized by the # dispatching macro character as specifying a vector.

Since vectors are simply arrays, we can reference their elements using **aref**:

```
-> (aref v1 2)
C
->
```

One set of functions that can be performed only on vectors involves a notion called a *fill-pointer*. A fill-pointer can be used if you wish to fill in the elements of a vector incrementally. For example, you may want to use the vector as a stack; then you need to keep track of where in the vector the last element was placed. A fill-pointer is the index of such an element.

We can create a vector with a fill-pointer by supplying an option to **make–array:**

```
-> (setq fillv (make-array '(10) :fill-pointer 0))
#( )
->
```

Here we specified a fill-pointer of **0**, meaning that we have put no interesting elements into the vector. Note that only the "interesting" elements of a vector with a fill-pointer are displayed. In this case, there are none yet, so it looks deceivingly as if the vector has no length at all.

We can put an element into the vector and keep track of how much of the vector we have filled using the function **vector–push:**

```
-> (vector-push 'first fillv)
0
-> (vector-push 'second fillv)
1
-> (vector-push 'third fillv)
2
-> fillv
#(FIRST SECOND THIRD)
->
```

vector–push returns the index of the element it just added. Of course, we can always retrieve any element randomly using **aref**. In addition, we can use **vector–pop** to retrieve and "remove" the last element put in:

```
-> (vector-pop fillv)
THIRD
-> (vector-pop fillv)
SECOND
->
```

vector–pop does not really remove an element; it merely decreases the fill-pointer.

An array without a fill pointer, and which is not defined as sharing storage with another array (an option we can specifiy to **make–array**), and whose size cannot be adjusted dynamically (the default, which can be overridden with an option to **make–array**) is called a *simple array*.

18.6. Strings

Strings are actually vectors of characters. Just as Common LISP has a special syntax for reading and printing arrays that are vectors, it has a special syntax for reading and printing vectors that are strings. Namely, strings are denoted by surrounding a sequence of characters with double quotes. For example, "abc", "**string**", and "**string with spaces**" are all strings. In Common LISP, strings always evaluate to themselves.

Most LISP functions that apply to symbols also apply to strings, and conversely. For example, most functions that take package arguments expect those arguments to be strings, but if they are passed a symbol, they will use its print name instead.

The function **char** returns the nth character of a string or symbol name:

```
-> (char "abcde" 3)
#\d
->
```

char always returns a character as its value.

The functions **string**=, **string/**=, **string**<, **string**>, **string**<= and **string**>= are used for string comparisons. **string**= returns true if two strings have the same characters in the same sequence; **string/**= is the logical negation of **string**=. The other functions judge lexicographic ordering. All these functions take the keyword arguments **:start1** and **:end1**, and **:start2** and **:end2**. These are indices into the respective strings specifying substrings that are to be considered for the comparison.

The functions **string–equal**, **string–not–equal**, **string–lessp**, **string–greaterp**, **string–not–greaterp** and **string–not–lessp** are similar to those above, except that they do not distinguish between upper and lower case.

Other string functions exist to do case manipulate and string trimming. It is also possible to convert an s-expression into a string using the functions **prin1–to–string** and **print–to–string**. These functions simply return as a string what their associated print function would have output. Also, the function **format**, discussed in Chapter 10, has an option that serves the same function.

We can get the print name of a symbol using the function **symbol–name:**

```
-> (symbol–name 'foo)
"FOO"
->
```

The function **string** is useful if we want to be sure we are dealing with a string, but are not sure of the nature of our data. If passed a string, **string** returns it; if passed a symbol, it returns its print name; if passed a character, it returns a string of that one character.

18.7. Sequences

A sequence is either a list or a vector. Although these are quite different data structures, they both share the common property of having ordered elements. Since there are quite a few LISP functions that require only ordered elements to be meaningful, it is worth having a data type **sequence** that includes precisely such structures, and therefore have the same functions operate on either subtype.

Standardization Note: In many other LISPs, separate functions might be needed to do essentially the same operation on a list as on a vector.

Some typical sequence operations include reversing, concatenating, and selecting an element or a subsequence of a sequence, merging and sorting sequences, removing items from sequences, substituting one item for another in a sequence, and iterating over a sequence. For example, the function **remove** is defined over sequences. It takes two arguments, an item and a sequence, and returns a new sequence which is like its second argument, but with all occurrences of the first argument removed from it. For example:

```
-> (remove 'b '(a b c b d e))
(A C D E)
-> (remove 'b '#(a b c b d e))
#(A C D E)
```

Here we used **remove** to eliminate occurrences of **b** from the list **(a b c b d e)**, and then vector #**(a b c b d e)**.

Like **remove**, many sequence functions need to determine if an element of a sequence matches an item. Normally, the function used to make the comparison is **eql**; it is applied to an element of the sequence and the item it is to be compared with. However, sometimes it is desirable to alter the details of the match. For example, we might want to use the function **equal** rather than **eql**. We can do this by using the **:test** keyword argument. The argument passed is a function to be used in the match. For example, **(remove '(b) '(a (b) c (b) d e))** will not remove anything from the list because the various **(b)**s are not **eql** to one another:

> ```
> -> (remove '(b) '(a (b) c (b) d e))
> (A (B) C (B) D E)
> ->
> ```

But we can accomplish this as follows:

> ```
> -> (remove '(b) '(a (b) c (b) d e) :test 'equal)
> (A C D E)
> ->
> ```

Similarly, the **:test–not** keyword argument can be used to specify a function, in which case the comparison will be considered true if the function specified returns false.

In addition, we often want to specify a portion of a sequence upon which to operate. The keywords **:start** and **:end** can be used for this purpose. **:start** and **:end** specify the subsequence beginning with the element indexed by the **:start** argument but ending before the element indexed by the **:end** argument. The indexing is zero-based. Consider the following example:

> ```
> -> (remove 'b '(a b c b d e b) :start 2 :end 6)
> (A B C D E B)
> ->
> ```

Here only the subsequence **c b d e** was examined for removal of the item. Note that entire sequence is used to compute the sequence to return, even though portions of it were not examined for the comparison.

In sequence functions in which two sequences are involved, the keyword arguments **:start1**, **:end1**, **:start2**, and **:end2** are typically allowed, and have the obvious interpretation.

Other useful sequence keywords are **:count, :from–end** and **:key**. **:count** is used to specify a limit on the number of items processed. For example:

```
-> (remove 'b '(a b c b d e b) :count 2)
(A C D E B)
->
```

:from-end can be used to specify the direction of the search: A non-**nil** argument means to search from right to left; normally, the search is conducted from left to right. For instance:

```
-> (remove 'b '(a b c b d e b) :count 2 :from-end t)
(A B C D E)
->
```

If the **:key** argument is given, it is applied to the element of the sequence and the value it returns is used in the comparison; it is supposed to return a component of the element. For example, consider the following

```
-> (remove 'b '((a) (b) (c) (b) (d) (e) (b)) :key 'car)
((A) (C) (D) (E))
->
```

Often, sequence functions have **-if** and **-if-not** variants. These do not take an item as an argument, but instead, a predicate of one argument. These examine the sequence argument for an element satisfying the predicate. For example, consider the functions **remove-if** and **remove-if-not**:

```
-> (remove-if #'oddp '(1 2 3 4 5 6 7))
(2 4 6)
-> (remove-if-not #'oddp '(1 2 3 4 5 6 7))
(1 3 5 7)
->
```

You can peruse the section of sequences in Appendix A to acquaint yourself with the complete set of functions that operate on sequences in Common LISP.

18.8. Hash Tables

A hash table is a Common LISP data type that is used to associate one LISP object with another LISP object. A hash table comprises a set of *entries,* which map a *key* to a *value.* Only one value can be associated with given key at any one time. Thus, hash tables are similar in function to property lists or association lists. The basic difference is that accessing an entry in a hash table should be very fast.

We can create a hash table using the function **make–hash–table**. Afterwards, we can look up an item in the hash table using the fuction **gethash**; this function returns two values, the object asociated with the key, if one is found, and a flag indicating whether the fetch was successful. We can update the hashtable by using **gethash** in conjunction **setf**. For example:

```
-> (setq mealtable (make–hash–table))
#<hashtable>
-> (setf (gethash 'lunch mealtable) 'sandwich)
SANDWICH
-> (setf (gethash 'breakfast mealtable) '(bacon and eggs))
(BACON AND EGGS)
-> (setf (gethash 'high–tea mealtable) 'scones)
SCONES
-> (gethash 'lunch mealtable)
SANDWICH ;
T
-> (gethash 'breakfast mealtable)
(BACON AND EGGS) ;
T
-> (gethash 'high–tea mealtable)
SCONES ;
T
-> (gethash 'snack mealtable)
NIL ;
NIL
```

Both the keys and values can be any LISP object, although the default comparison function is **eql**.

Some other useful hash table functions are **remhash**, which removes an entry from a table, and **maphash**, which applies a function to each entry in a hash table.

18.9. Structures

Structures are user-defined data types similar to "records" in PASCAL or "structures" in PL/1. In general, user-defined records provide the user with a convenient, modular way of structuring data that also provides type-checking. Structures are LISP's way of providing such a facility.

As an example, supposed we were working with data items of the form (*state city zip*). As suggested in Chapter 13, to write clear code, we would like to access such structures by calling functions like **get–state**, even though **car** would do just as well. Besides being clearer, having such "access functions" would insulate the rest of our code from changes to these data structures. For example, suppose we were using **car** to access the "state" field of a location, and then decided to add a "country" field to the beginning of our "location" data structure. Then we would have to march through our code for all references to locations, and change all the **car**s to **cadr**s. However, if we had used the **get–state** access function instead, we would only have to change the definition of this function in order to update all references to the "state" field of the new "location" format.

One problem with using such functions is that they are a bit tedious to define. In the example above, we would have to define **get–state**, **get–city** and **get–zip** access functions. We would also like to define a function to create individual "location" data objects, and perhaps one to test if some object were a "location" object. These are relatively easy to define, but constitute a considerable amount of "grunt" programming.

Structures are a way of automating this "grunt" programming task. This is accomplished through the use of the macro **defstruct**. Using **defstruct**, a programmer merely specifies the fields a particular data structure is to have. **defstruct** creates a function that creates data structures of this sort; it also creates functions that access the fields of these data structures, and a predicate function that will return true when applied to data structures of this type.

For example, consider the following call to **defstruct**:

```
-> (defstruct location state city zip)
LOCATION
->
```

This call to **defstruct** causes the following events to occur:

(1)   A new data type called **location** is created. Among other things, this data type would be returned by a call to **type–of** if that function were passed a **location** data structure.

(2)   A function named **make–location** is created. This is a function of three keyword arguments, representing the components of a **location** data structure. When called, **make–structure** will create a structure of type **location** whose components are the arguments specified in the call. Functions like **make–location** produced by **defstruct** are called *constructor functions*.

(3) Functions named **location–state, location–city** and **location–zip** are created. These so-called *access functions* will return the contents of their respective field when applied to a **location** datum.

(4) A function called **location–p** is created. This is predicate function that will return true when applied to items of type **location**.

(5) A function called **copy–location** is created. This function, when applied to a **location** object, will produce another **location** object with the same components as its argument. This is called a *copier function*.

For example, consider the following use of these functions, now that we have used **defstruct** to define the **location** data type:

```
-> (setq loc1 (make-location :state 'california
                             :city 'berkeley
                             :zip '94709))
#S(LOCATION :STATE CALIFORNIA :CITY BERKELEY :ZIP 94709)
```

Here we used **make–location**, the constructor function created by **defstruct**, to create a **location** data object. First note that all the arguments to this function are keyword arguments; therefore, none are mandatory, nor is order significant. Second, LISP printed out this structure using a form of the # dispatching macro character. This form is also acceptable to **read**.

Now we can access the fields of this item using the access functions created by **defstruct**:

```
-> (location-city loc1)
BERKELEY
```

We can verify that the value of **loc1** is indeed a **location**:

```
-> (location-p loc1)
T
```

Finally, we can destructively change the structure by using **setf** in conjunction with an access function:

```
-> (setf (location-city loc1) 'berserkeley)
BERSERKELEY
-> loc1
#S(LOCATION :STATE CALIFORNIA :CITY BERSERKELEY :ZIP 94709)
->
```

There are quite a few variations to the call to **defstruct**. However, just the simple format described above will be all that is needed in most cases. Probably the most important option has to do with setting default values for the constructor function. For example, to make "Brooklyn, New York 11235" the default value for call to **make-location**, we should have done the following:

```
-> (defstruct location
        (state 'newyork) (city 'brooklyn) (zip '11235))
LOCATION
-> (make-location)
#S(LOCATION :STATE NEWYORK :CITY BROOKLYN :ZIP 11235)
->
```

Of course, if a keyword argument were given to **make-location**, it will override the default initial value.

Note that the default initial value will be reevaluated each time a call to the constructor function uses it. If the default initial value were some function call, it would be evaluated each time the constructor supplied a default, possibly returning a different initial value each time.

18.10. Summary

(1)   Most LISPs support several different types of data. Some of the more important data types known to Common LISP are **cons**, **list** (**cons** plus **nil**), **symbol**, **atom** (anything that is not a **cons**), **number** (these come in several varieties), **character**, **array**, **vector** (arrays of one dimension), **string** (vectors of characters), **stream** (I/O interfaces), **hash-table** (fast key-value mappings) **readtable** (character-syntactic interpretation mappings), **package** (symbol tables), **pathname** (system-independent file naming objects), **function** and **structure** (user-defined records).

(2)   The function **type-of** will return a type of a datum. Individual predicates exist which determine if a datum is of a particular data type, or combination of data types. The function **typep** determines if its first argument is of the type specified by the second, and the

function **subtypep** determines if the type specified by its first argument is a subtype of the type specified by the second argument.

(3)   *Arrays* are blocks of data that can be addressed using a coordinate system. Arrays can be created with the function **make–array**. Using this function, it is possible to initialize the contents of an array at creation time. Elements of arrays are accessed using the function **aref**.

(4)   *Vectors* are arrays of one dimension. One special feature of vectors is that they may have *fill-pointers.* These are counters that keep track of how much of the vector contents useful information.

(5)   *Strings* are vectors of characters. Special string functions exist for creating, comparing, and accessing the characters of strings.

(6)   *Sequences* include both vectors and lists. Most Common LISP functions that require only that they operate on sequential data are defined to work on sequences.

(7)   *Hash tables* are used to provide a property list-like mechanism that will be fast for large collections of LISP objects.

(8)   *Structures* are user-defined data types. These are created by the macro **defstruct**. A call to **defstruct** creates a new data type, along with a function to create objects of that type (a *constructor function*), a function to copy objects of that type (a *copier function*), functions to access the components of the structure (*access functions*), and a predicate that determines whether a given object is of the data type created. There are many options to **defstruct**, including the ability to specify default initial values for the components not specified in a call to a constructor function.

Exercises

(1)   Use vectors or arrays to implement your own favorite hashing scheme. Note — LISP is particularly well-suited to implement a hash table with buckets.

(2)   Write a LISP function **matrix–multiply** that takes two arrays as input. **matrix–multiply** interprets these arrays as two-dimensional matrices and returns their matrix product.

(3)   Write a LISP function that interprets a vector as a point in n-dimensional space, and computes the distance between two of them.

(4)   Specify as structures some of the data that your LISP programs manipulate. Rewrite your programs to make use of the functions generated by **defstruct**.

Chapter 19

System Functions

19.1. Introduction

LISP has a number of functions that reflect aspects of LISP as a system. This chapter describes such system functions. These functions pertain to characteristics of a LISP process or of the particular environment in which it is running.

19.2. Internal LISP System Functions

These functions are useful for finding information about the current LISP process.

19.2.1. Time and Space Functions

The macro **time** evaluates its argument and returns it as its value. As a side effect, **time** outputs various timing data to the stream assigned to the variable ***trace—output***. Usually, this is the same stream that is used for terminal I/O.

To demonstrate **time**, let us write a function that we know can do a significant amount of computing:

```
-> (defun factorial (n)
      (cond ((zerop n) 1)
            (t (* n (factorial (1- n)))))))
FACTORIAL
->
```

Now let us use **time** to see just how costly it is to use this function:

```
-> (time (factorial 6))
CPU Time: 0.04 sec., Real Time: 0.09 sec.
720
-> (time (factorial 10))
CPU Time: 0.08 sec., Real Time: 0.13 sec.
3628800
-> (time (factorial 20))
CPU Time: 0.18 sec., Real Time: 0.64 sec.
2432902008176640000
->
```

Here **time** first output the amount of CPU time and the amount of real time that the evaluation required. Then the value computed by the computation being timed was returned.

Standardization Note: The exact output of **time** is implementation-dependent.

There is also a function **get–internal–run–time** that returns the amount of time the LISP process has consumed so far. The difference between two calls to **get–internal–run–time** should say something about the amount of effort expended on the computation in between. For example:

```
-> (let ((init (get–internal–run–time)))
      (factorial 10)
      (- (get–internal–run–time) init))
80000
->
```

Here we used **get–internal–run–time** to compute our own measure of the cost of running **factorial**. The value returned by **get–internal–run–time** is in *internal time units*, which are some implementation-dependent fraction of a second. We can find out what these are by examining the value of the variable **internal–time–units–per–second**:

```
-> internal-time-units-per-second
1000000
->
```

So in this implementation, an internal time unit is a millionth of a second. Thus, the result computed by **get-internal-run-time** above is in remarkable agreement with the output of **time**.

We can find out information about space as well as time. The function **room** prints information about internal storage management. Specifying an argument of **t** to **room** causes it to provide as much information as it has available; an argument of **nil** produces a minimal amount.

Standardization Note: The details of the output of **room** will make sense only with respect to a particular implementation.

19.2.2. Object Description Functions

A number of functions exist that provide information about LISP objects. The function **describe** prints information about the object passed to it as an argument. For example, applied to a symbol, **describe** will print out that symbol's value, function definition and properties, if it has any of these. Consider the following examples:

```
-> (defun foo (x) (car x))
FOO
-> (setq foo 'baz)
BAZ
-> (setf (get 'foo 'color) 'red)
RED
-> (describe 'foo)
It is the symbol FOO
Package: USER
Value:    the symbol BAZ
Function: interpreted
   FOO x
   Properties:
      COLOR - the symbol RED
```

```
-> (describe 1.0)
It is the single-float 1.0
Sign:       +
Exponent:   1 (radix 2)
Significand: 0.5

-> (describe '(a b))
It is a cons
Car: the symbol A
Cdr: a cons

-> (describe nil)
It is the symbol NIL
Package:  SYSTEM
Constant: the symbol NIL
    This constant represents the logical false value
    and also the empty list.  It evaluates to itself.
Function: undefined

Type:
   Specifier: NIL

    The type nil is a subtype of every type whatsoever.
    No objects belong to type nil.
->
```

Standardization Note: As is the case for most of the functions in this chapter, the exact format of the output is implementation-dependent.

There is also a function **inspect**, which is an interactive version of **describe**.

The function **apropos** is useful for finding symbols related to a certain theme. A call of the form (**apropos** *string*) will print out all symbols whose print names contain the substring *string*, along with some information about each symbol. For example, applying **apropos** to **setf** will print all the symbols in which the substring **SETF** occurs:

```
-> (apropos 'setf)

Symbols in package USER containing the string "SETF":
 PSETF, has a definition
 GET-SETF-METHOD-MULTIPLE-VALUE, has a definition
 SETF, has a definition
 DEFSETF, has a definition
 DEFINE-SETF-METHOD, has a definition
 GET-SETF-METHOD, has a definition
->
```

The function **apropos-list** is just like **apropos**, except that it returns a list of the symbols that match, rather than printing out that information.

19.3. External LISP System Functions

19.3.1. File System Functions

A number of functions concern the file system in the environment of the current process is running. For example, the function **user-homedir-pathname** returns a pathname for the user's home directory. Let us use it to determine my home directory:

```
-> (user-homedir-pathname)
#S(PATHNAME :HOST "kim:" :DEVICE NIL :DIRECTORY
"/na/bair/wilensky" :NAME NIL :TYPE NIL :VERSION NIL)
->
```

This represents my home directory as a pathname.

Standardization Note: There is no Common LISP standard for the printed representation of pathnames. This particular implementation happens to implement pathnames as structures, and hence uses that notation for I/O.

The function **directory** can be applied to a pathname that specifies a directory, and returns a list of pathnames representing the contents of that directory. My home directory has quite a few files in it, so let us examine the contents of a smaller one. Also, since pathnames are generally quite long, let us use **pprint** to make the result more readable:

```
-> (pprint
     (directory
       (make-pathname :directory
                        "/na/bair/wilensky/letters")))

(#S(PATHNAME
       :HOST "kim:"
       :DEVICE NIL
       :DIRECTORY "/na/bair/wilensky/letters"
       :NAME "."
       :TYPE ""
       :VERSION NIL)
 #S(PATHNAME
       :HOST "kim:"
       :DEVICE NIL
       :DIRECTORY "/na/bair/wilensky/letters"
       :NAME "mc"
       :TYPE NIL
       :VERSION NIL)
 #S(PATHNAME
       :HOST "kim:"
       :DEVICE NIL
       :DIRECTORY "/na/bair/wilensky/letters"
       :NAME "a-w"
       :TYPE NIL
       :VERSION NIL)
 #S(PATHNAME
       :HOST "kim:"
       :DEVICE NIL
       :DIRECTORY "/na/bair/wilensky/letters"
       :NAME "norton"
       :TYPE NIL
       :VERSION NIL))
->
```

The function **probe-file** can be used to check to see if a particular file exists. (**probe-file** *file*) will return **nil** if *file* does not exist, and a pathname for that file if it does:

```
-> (probe-file "/na/bair/wilensky/letters")
#S(PATHNAME :HOST "kim:" :DEVICE NIL :DIRECTORY
"/na/bair/wilensky" :NAME "letters" :TYPE NIL
:VERSION NIL)
-> (probe-file "foo")
NIL
->
```

Standardization Note: Your particular Common LISP implementation is likely to allow additional options to some of these functions, or provide some more powerful directory-searching functions.

We can find out some facts about a particular file using the functions **file-write-date**, **file-author** and **file-length**. These all return about what you would expect. And we can act upon files using the functions **rename-file** and **delete-file**. **rename-file** renames its first argument to its second argument; **delete-file** removes the file specified by its argument.

Finally, the function **ed** invokes the resident editor, if there is one. **(ed)** or **(ed nil)** simply enters the editor, placing the user in the same state the user was in the last time the editor was entered. **(edit** *filename*) edits the specified file, and **(edit** *symbol*) edits the textual definition of the function attached to *symbol*.

19.3.2. Static Environment Functions

Functions exist that return user- or process-independent information. The function **machine-type** is typical of these. It returns the generic name of the computer hardware on which the current LISP process is running:

```
-> (machine-type)
"DEC VAX-11/780/785"
->
```

Other functions of this sort exist that return information about the Common LISP implementation, the supporting software environment, and the physical location of the machine. See Appendix A for details.

19.3.3. Other System Functions

The functions **get–universal–time** returns the number corresponding to the number of seconds since midnight, January 1, 1900 GMT. Alternatively, the function **get–decoded–time** returns nine values representing the second, minute, hour, date, month, year, day-of-week, whether daylight saving time is in effect, and time zone.

There are no other system functions that are standard in Common LISP. But that does not prevent your particular implementation from having some useful functions to spawn new processes or communicate with the environment. You will have to examine the documentation for your implementation should you wish to avail yourself of such features.

19.4. Summary

(1) There are Common LISP functions for finding out information about the current process, and for finding out about and affecting the external environment.

(2) Some functions that find out information about the current process are **time**, **get–internal–run–time** and **room**, and the functions **describe**, **inspect**, **apropos** and **apropos–list**.

(3) Functions that operate on items external to the LISP process include **user–homedir–pathname**, **directory**, **probe–file**, **file–write–date**, **file–author**, **file–length**, **rename–file**, **delete–file**, **ed** and **get–universal–time**. In addition, a number of functions exist that return static characteristics of the environment in which the LISP process resides.

Chapter 20

Compilation

20.1. Introduction to LISP Compilation

As we discussed throughout this book, LISP code is usually interpreted. There are many advantages to interpretation. In particular, interpreted programs are easier to debug because the actual code is readily accessible. However, there is a price to pay for this convenience. Most LISP programs execute more slowly than they might if they were not interpreted. If the added flexibility of interpretation is outweighed by its cost, the user may wish to sacrifice the former for the latter.

This trade-off can be accommodated by *compiling* LISP code. Compiling in LISP can be similar to compiling in other languages. A file of LISP code is passed through a program called a *compiler*. The output of the compiler is an *object* file. This file contains machine language versions of the original LISP code. When loaded into LISP, the compiled functions can be called just like ordinary LISP functions. The only differences are (1) the code will run much faster and (2) the original LISP code is no longer there to inspect.

Compiling LISP code can differ from compiling code written in other languages in two minor ways. First, it is possible to compile individual functions as well as entire programs. Individual compiled functions can be used together with interpreted code without any difficulties – the

343

individual compiled functions will simply run faster and be difficult to inspect. Second, the LISP compiler is itself a LISP program, and is invoked just like any other LISP function. In this way, all the capabilities of LISP are available during compiling as well as during execution.

Compiled code is much faster than interpreted code because it is possible to eliminate all sorts of overhead built into the interpretation process. For example, to interpret a call to a function, LISP must first **cdr** down a list to reach the next s-expression. Then it must test to see if this form is an atom or a list. If it is a list, it must take its **car** to get its first element. This might be a symbol representing an ordinary function, a built-in special function, or a macro; it might also be a lambda expression. The interpreter must determine which of these it is in order to decide how to deal with it. For example, if it is an ordinary function, the interpreter will evaluate all the remaining elements of a list; if it is a macro, it will not. The subsequent evaluation will also depend on the nature of the function being applied.

If the function were **car**, for example, the actual code might be a single machine instruction (all **car** has to do is follow a pointer). However, the LISP interpreter spent most of its time just getting to this instruction. If we translate this call into machine code, we could replace it by code that evaluates the argument and then executes the one machine instruction that is equivalent to **car**. The resulting code should therefore be enormously faster. And it is.

In this chapter we introduce the Common LISP compiler. The Common LISP compiler performs the transformation of LISP code into more efficient machine code. While the details of this compiler are specific to Common LISP, most of the considerations applicable to compiling Common LISP programs are the same as those for compiling programs written for other LISPs. We describe these special considerations that one may take into account to allow compilation to produce effective code.

20.2. Using the Common LISP Compiler

In Common LISP, we can compile individual functions or entire files. The function **compile** compiles the individual function passed to it as an argument; **compile–file** compiles the file passed to it. For example, to compile the single function **foo**, we would type **(compile 'foo)**. Afterwards, **foo** would run faster. Alternatively, we can compile the file **foo.l** by typing **(compile–file "foo.l")**; Each function in the file will get compiled. A new file would be created, its name determined by each implementation's file systems' conventions.

Standardization Note: In some LISP systems, the compiler is a separate program. It would be applied to the file at the operating system-level. For example, we might say

% lisp-compiler foo.l

to the operating system to compile the file **foo.l**.

Once the object file has been produced by the compiler, the user may load it into a LISP process using the command **load**. This function should be smart enough to distinguish compiled files from source files, and load the one appropriate to the current circumstances.

As an example let us compile an individual function. Suppose the code for **factorial** were the following:

```
(defun factorial (n)
    (cond ((zerop n) 1)
          (t (* n (factorial (1 - n))))))
```

First, let us use **time** to determine the cost of using this function:

```
-> (time (factorial 10))
CPU Time: 0.08 sec., Real Time: 0.13 sec.
3628800
-> (time (factorial 20))
CPU Time: 0.18 sec., Real Time: 0.64 sec.
2432902008176640000
->
```

Now let us run this source code through the compiler to produce a compiled function definition:

```
-> (compile 'factorial)
FACTORIAL compiled.
FACTORIAL
%->
```

We are now ready to use the compiled version of this function:

```
-> (factorial 8)
40320
->
```

The compiled version appears to work. Let us measure the speed-up we anticipated:

```
-> (time (factorial 10))
CPU Time: 0.00 sec., Real Time: 0.01 sec.
3628800
-> (time (factorial 20))
CPU Time: 0.01 sec., Real Time: 0.02 sec.
2432902008176640000
->
```

The compiled version of the function seems much more efficient. We could use **get–internal–run–time** if a more precise determination of the speed-up were desired.

20.3. eval–when

Having a compiling phase in LISP introduces some more distinctions than we have had to deal with previously. If we do not compile our code, forms in a file are simply **load**ed, causing them to be read and evaluated. Then the user is likely to use the resulting function definitions, etc., to perform some computation. However, if the file is to be compiled, the code is in effect read twice: once when the compiler reads it, and again when the compiled code is **load**ed.

There are some very specific situations in which the introduction of this extra reading phase causes some complications. It is quite possible that you will not encounter these situations in the code you write. But you should know about them, just in case.

For example, consider the following situation. Suppose our code contains a call to a macro. Most Common LISP compilers expand macros when they are encountered and then compile the expanded code. This requires that the macro definition be encountered by the compiler before a call to the macro is seen. So we might arrange our file so that our macro definition procedes a call to the macro in the file, just to be sure that the definition is available to the compiler when it needs it.

But even if this is done, there is another potential problem. Suppose our macro definition makes use of some utility function, say the function

macro–utility. Clearly, this function must also be defined before a call to the macro is encountered, since it is needed to do the macro expansion. However, just putting the definition of **macro–utility** in the file will not help. The compiler will treat this like any other function and simply compile its definition. This is not what we want. Rather, we want the compiler to *evaluate* this definition, not compile it. But so far, we have no way of instructing the compiler to evaluate a function in a file rather than compile it.

To exercise some control over when a form is evaluated and when it is compiled, the special function **eval–when** may be used. A call to **eval–when** takes the form (**eval–when** *(-keywords-) -exps-*). The keywords may be any of **eval**, **compile**, or **load**. If the keyword **compile** is present, then the compiler will evaluate each of the subsequent expressions when it is compiling the file. If **load** is specified, then the compiler will arrange its output so that each of the expressions will be evaluated when the file containing the compiled code is loaded. The keyword **eval** is ignored by the compiler; its presence will cause the interpreter to evaluate the expressions, however.

Thus if we include the expression

(eval–when (compile) (defun macro–utility ...))

in a file we are compiling, then the function **macro–utility** will be defined during the compilation. If we include the expression

(eval–when (compile load) (defun macro–utility ...))

in the file, **macro–utility** will both be defined during the compilation and be included in the object file.

20.3.1. #, and #.

Another related complication occurs if we use an expression that causes an evaluation at **read** time. This might be desirable if the object we would like to read does not have a convenient textual representation, but can be computed. For example, there is no convenient way to read in a hashtable. So we might like to create one when our code is read in, and then refer to it in our code.

Of course, we could always do this by using a free symbol. That is, our file of code could look something like this:

```
(setq *fnhashtable* (make-hash-table))

(defun fn (...)
    ...
    (setf (gethash ... *fnhashtable*) ...)
    ... (gethash ... *fnhashtable*) ...
    ...                                          )
```

However, as usual, using free symbols is undesirable. In particular, we have no guarantee that some other function with not change the value of ***fnhashtable*** at run time. To circumvent this problem, a special feature of the # dispatching macro character has been devised. When an expression of the form #.*form* is read, *form* is evaluated and its value returned as if it were read in. Thus, instead of writing the code above, we can write the following:

```
(defun fn (...)
    (let ((hashtab '#.(make-hash-table))...)
        ...
        (setf (gethash ... hashtab) ...)
        ... (gethash ... hashtab) ...
        ...                                      )
```

A new hashtable will be created when the code is read, and we are guaranteed that the code will do what we desire.

What does all this have to do with compiling? Well, suppose we tried to compile the file containing **fn**. #.*form* evaluates *form* when it is *read*. So a hashtable will be created at compile time. Of course, this is not what we want at all. We want the hash table to be created when the program is **load**ed, not when our code is compiled.

To address this problem, yet another # dispatching macro character feature is supplied with Common LISP. An expression of the form #,*form,* when read by the interpreter, will behave exactly like #.*form* would. However, if the expression is read by the compiler (i. e., when compiling a file), the compiler will arrange its output so that *form* will be evaluated when the compiled code is loaded. Hence the code above will compile correctly if we substitute #, for #.

20.4. Declarations

Sometimes we know a fact about our program that we would like to communicate to the compiler. For example, we might know that some variable will always be assigned objects of a certain type. If the compiler knew this fact, then it might be able to produce more efficient code where references to this variable are compiled. Of course, there are some occasions when a smart compiler might deduce such facts on its own. But sometimes, this may be very difficult. For example, the value that gets assigned a variable may be returned by some other function. That other function may not be available to the compiler when it compiles the first function. So there is no way the compiler could determine that the value assigned the variable will be special in any way.

In fact, the statement we would like to make to the compiler might express a desire. For example, we may want the compiler to optimize for speed, or, alternatively, for space. Of course, there is no way the compiler could guess our intention. Therefore, we need a mechanism to assert facts or intentions about our program, so that the compiler may behave accordingly.

We can communicate facts to the compiler by including *declarations* in our program. A declaration is simply an assertion of a statement about a characteristic of a LISP object, or of a desire of the programmer. We will call a particular statement about a program a *declaration specification*. We make a declaration by supplying a declaration specification to one of a number of special functions designed just for this purpose.

It should be pointed out that communicating declarations to the compiler is strictly voluntary. The compiler might find a declaration helpful. But if it is not supplied, the compiler should produce correct code nevertheless.

20.4.1. declare

The primary function for making declarations is called **declare**. The call to **declare** would appear at the beginning of a chunk of code within which the declaration is to have an affect.

As an example, consider the case in which we would like to instruct the compiler to *open-code* a function call. Open-coding is compiler jargon for replacing calls to a function with the entire code of that function. Generally, this is done for efficiency. For example, suppose **location–state** is an access function to a data structure whose form is (*state city zip*). **location–state** simply returns that **car** of its argument, and exists primarily to help structure the program (see the section on *structures* in Chapter 19 for further discussion of this topic). While having functions like **location–state** makes our code very clear, it would be a lot more efficient to replace calls to this function with calls to **car**. If we did this when we compiled the program, we would still have our original, pretty code to look at, but the compiled version would run as quickly as if we had written the code for efficiency ourselves.

There are some disadvantages to open-coding, by the way. In particular, we cannot trace calls to a function that has been open-coded. This is because no reference to the function call will be present in the object code. So we gain some efficiency here at the price of debuggability – a price we would probably be willing to pay after we had tested the code to our satisfaction.

We can instruct the compiler to open-code calls to the function **location–state** by making a declaration using the **inline** declaration specifier. This declaration would look like this:

```
(declare (inline location–state))
```

We would place this declaration at the beginning of the body of code within which we wanted calls to **location–state** to be open-coded. For example, if we want to open-code these calls within the function **caller**, we would modify the definition of **caller** to look like the following:

```
(defun caller (param1 param2)
   (declare (inline location–state))

   ... (location–state ...) ...                )
```

As this example indicates, declarations have a scope, in the same way that variables do. In this case, the scope of the declaration is the definition of the function **caller**. In general, the scope of a declaration is the body of code in which the call to **declare** appears. You can use **declare** in most forms that should require it, including **defmacro**, **defun**, **do** (and related iteration functions), **let** and **prog**, as well as a few other less popular functions. You can also place declarations directly in lambda expressions. In general, the call to **declare** appears right after some expression that specifies variables, and right before the forms of the function that might be evaluated.

You can include as many declarations as you like within a single call to **declare**. For example, the following usage of **declare** is valid:

```
(declare
    (notinline fun1)
    (inline func2 func3)
    (integer x y)
    (float z)
    (special var1 var2 var3))
```

This call to **declare** contains a number of different declaration specifications. We will explain the meaning of each of them later on in this section.

20.4.2. Local Declarations

declare special forms can only appear toward the beginning of a number of other forms, such as calls to **let** and **defun**. In these instances, the scope of the calls to **declare** is the scope of the forms in which they are embedded. However, it is possible to have the scope of a declaration apply only to a smaller body of code through the use of the **locally** macro. A call to this macro specifies a sequences of declarations, followed by some forms; the scope of the declarations is just those forms. Thus a call of the form

```
(locally (declare (inline fn)) (fn x y))
```

will allow only this particular call to **fn** to be compiled in-line.

20.4.3. Global Declarations

Suppose we want a declaration to apply to all of our code. For example, suppose we want all references to the function **location–state** to be open-coded. We cannot do this using **declare**, since it only affects the form in which it occurs. So we need another mechanism.

The other mechanism is the function **proclaim**. **proclaim** is an ordinary function whose supplied argument should evaluate to a declaration specification. **proclaim** puts the declaration into effect globally. For example, the expression **(proclaim '(inline location–state))**, once executed, states that **location–state** should always be open-coded. If we want to, we can override a proclamation within a particular body of code by using the function **declare**.

20.4.4. Types of Declarations

In addition to the **inline** declaration specifier, there are several other specifiers that can be used to make declarations in Common LISP. We cover these in the next several sections. We begin with type declarations, as these are the most pervasive and the most complex.

20.4.5. Type Declarations

Probably the most common declarations are those that specify the type of the value that a variable will be assigned. This is done by using the declaration specifier **type**, in the following format:

> (**type** *type var1 var2 ...*)

Here *type* is any valid Common LISP type specifier. For example, the declaration

> **(declare (type integer x y))**

states that, in the scope of this declaration, **x** and **y** will be assigned only integer values.

Type declaration specifications are so common that Common LISP provides the following shorthand for them:

> (*type var1 var2 ...*)

That is, instead of the declaration given above, we could have typed the following:

> **(declare (integer x y))**

As we mentioned in Chapter 18, Common LISP supplies us with a set of standard type specifiers, e. g., **integer**, **array**, **list**, **hashtable**, etc. All of these are valid inside of a declaration.

20.4.5.1. More Elaborate Type Specifiers

It is possible to create more complex type specifiers in Common LISP. These new specifiers are also valid in type declarations. We can create more elaborate type specifiers in one of four ways:

(1)   We can form logical combinations of existing type specifiers.

(2)   We can list explicitly the set of objects that the type comprises.

(3)   We can specify a particular predicate that a datum must satisfy in order for it to be considered of a given type.

(4)   We can restrict an existing type specifier.

Let us examine each alternative in turn.

Logical Combinations of Type Specifiers

We can form logical combinations of existing type specifiers using the terms **and, or** and **not**. For example, **(or null cons)** is a type specifier that specifies exactly the same type as does the specifier **list**; **(and number (not integer))** specifies all numbers that are not integers.

Explicitly Defined Data Types

We can specify a type consisting of a particular set of data objects using the term **member**. The expression **(member** *obj1 obj2* ...**)** denotes a type consisting of precisely the objects named. Thus **(member 17 foo "banana")** specifies a type consisting of exactly three objects, the number **17**, the symbol **foo**, and the string **"banana"**. (This specification looks superficially like a call to the function **member**. But, as a type specification, this expression is not evaluated. It has an altogether different interpretation as a description of a data type.)

Data Types That Satify Predicates

We can specify a type in terms of a predicate that it must satisfy using the specifier **(satisfies** *predicate***)**. This defines a type that includes all objects for which *predicate* returns true. For example, the specifier **(and integer (satisfies evenp))** specifies the even integers.

Restricting Existing Data Types

It is possible to restrict certain Common LISP data types to specify a smaller class of data. This is done by placing one of these specifiers in the beginning of a list. The rest of the list restricts that type in a way that depends on the type.

For example, we can restrict the data type **array** by specifying its dimensions and the type of its elements. This specifier has the form (**array** *element-type dimensions*), where *element-type* is a type specifier, and *dimensions* is either an integer, meaning the number of dimensions of the array, or a list of integers, each one denoting the length of a dimension of the array. For example, (**array integer 3**) specifies a three dimensional array of integers; (**array character (2 3)**) specifies a two dimensional 2x3 array of characters.

We can indicate that we wish not to restrict some aspect of a specifier by using the symbol *. For example, (**array integer ***) specifies the set of all integer arrays; (**array character (2 ***)) specifies the set of two dimensional arrays of characters whose first dimension is of length 2; (**array * 3**) describes all three dimensional arrays. Also, we can simply omit unrestricted fields if they occur at the end of a specifier. For example, (**array integer**) is identical to (**array integer ***); (**array * ***) is equivalent to (**array**), which in turn is the same as **array**.

As a type specifier, **t** comprises all data objects, so it might seem that (**array * 3**) and (**array t 3**) were identical. But there is a subtle difference between them. The first specifier denotes all three dimensional arrays, whereas the second denotes only those three dimensional arrays whose elements can be of any data type. For example, a three dimensional array that was restricted only to contain integers would be of data type (**array * 3**), but not of type (**array t 3**).

In place of **array**, the specifier **simple–array** may be used, and has exactly the same interpretation (except, of course, the arrays are also restricted to be special arrays). The form (**vector** *element-type size*) is exactly equivalent to (**array** *element-type (size)*), so that (**vector integer 5**) specifies those vectors of length 5 whose elements are integers. In fact, the data type **string** is nothing more than (**vector string–char**). (**string** *size*) is also recognized, and is equivalent to (**vector string–char** *size*). (**simple–vector** *size*) is identical to (**vector t** *size*), except that it also specifies that the vectors are simple; **simple–string**, **bit–vector** and **simple–bit–vector** can be used analogously. Also, the form (**complex** *type*) specifies those complex numbers whose real and imaginary parts are of type *type*.

We can restrict the function data type using the following format:

(**function** (*arg1-type arg2-type ...*) *value-type*)

This means that the function accepts at least those actual arguments that are of the specified types, and that its value is of the specified type. For example, **cons** is of the type **(function (t t) cons)** because it can accept two arguments that are of any type and always returns something of type **cons**. If a function returns more than one value, the type of each value can be specified inside a list that begins with the symbol **values**. For example, the function **floor** is of type

> **(function (number &optional number)**
> **(values integer integer))**

since it takes as input two numbers (one optional) and returns two integer values.

(We can use this particular type specifier only in declarations. That is, passing such a specifier as an argument to **typep** or the like will cause an error.)

We can restrict the data type **integer** to include only those integers lying within a certain range. **(integer** *low high***)** denotes the integers that lies between *low* and *high*. If these are just integers, then they are interpreted as *inclusive* limits; if they are lists of integers, they are interpreted as *exclusive* limits. We can restrict **rational**, **float** and the various subtypes of **float** similarly.

Finally, the form **(mod** *n***)** is recognized as an abbreviation for **(integer 0** (*n***))**; **(signed–byte** *s***)** represents those integers that can be represented in two's-complement form in a byte of *s* bits; and **(unsigned–byte** *s***)** represents those non-negative integers that can be represented in a byte of *s* bits.

These more complex specifiers can go wherever a declaration specifier is expected. For example, the following declaration states that **x** will take on only values that are integers between 10 and 100:

> **(declare ((integer 10 100) x))**

20.4.5.2. Defining New Type Specifier Symbols

All the type specifiers for the standard Common LISP data types are symbols, while all the more elaborate type specifiers are lists. Therefore, there is no possibility of confusion between the two. However, writing an elaborate type specifier may be tedious, especially if the same type specification is used repeatedly. It would be more convenient to define a symbol to stand for one of these more elaborate specifications. So Common LISP allows us to do so.

We can specify a symbol to stand for a new type using the function **deftype**. **deftype** is very similar to **defmacro** in that it allows the user to provide a name, a list of parameters and then some code; the name then becomes a new type whose appearance will be replaced by the value of this code. For example, consider the following call to **deftype:**

(deftype old–atom ( ) '(or number symbol))

This causes the symbol **old–atom** to represent the type consisting of both symbols and numbers. That is, if we supply **old–atom** to something expecting a type, this would have an identical effect to supplying **(or number symbol)**. Similarly, the following call will produce a type specifier that admits a single field:

(deftype mod (n) '(integer 0 (,n)))

After this call, a specifier of the form **(mod** n**)** is valid, and specifies a type consisting of the integers from 0 to $n-1$.

20.4.5.3. Declaring Function Types

We have used type specifiers so far only to specify the value that a variable may be assigned. However, there are other instances in which it may be useful to specify a type. In particular, it might be useful to tell the compiler about the types of the arguments of some function, and about the type of the values computed by that function.

We can give the compiler type information about a function using the declaration specifier **ftype**. For example, to declare that the functions **numfn1** and **numfn2** take one argument that is any number, but always return a floating point number, we can say the following:

(declare (ftype (function (number) float) numfn1 numfn2))

This can also be specified in the following format:

(declare (function numfn1 (number) float)
(function numfn2 (number) float))

This format may be more convenient in some instances.

20.4.5.4. Declaring the Type of the Value of a Form

Above we saw how to specify the value returned by a given function. But in some cases, we might have more specific information about the type of the value of a given form. For example, suppose the form (+ **x** **4**) appeared in our code. If we knew that **x** was always an integer, then this form will always return an integer. Of course, this is not true of + in general, but only of this particular call to +. If we want the compiler to be able to take advantage of such a fact, we will need a way to make a declaration about this particular form.

Note that surrounding the form with a call to **locally** (described above) does not help. We could use such a declaration to specify other characteristics of the form, but as yet have no way of talking about the *value* that a form returns.

It is possible to declare the type computed by an individual form using the special function **the**. We surround the form by a call to **the**, inserting a type in the beginning. Thus, the expression

    (the integer (+ x 4))

will compute and return the value of (+ **x** **4**). However, it also specifies that the computation will always return an integer.

20.4.6. Other Declaration Specifiers

The remaining declaration specifiers are much less complex than type specifiers. So we will present them all together in this section.

20.4.6.1. Open-coding

As mentioned previously, we can declare that a function is to be compiled in line (i. e., open-coded) using the specifier **inline**. In addition, we can specify that it should not be compiled this way, using the specifier **notinline**. **inline** is somewhat peculiar in that it merely advises that compiler that open-coding is acceptable; it does not compel the compiler to produce code of this sort. In contrast, **notinline** forbids the compiler to open-code a function call; the compiler is not free to ignore this declaration.

20.4.6.2. Ignoring Variables

The specifier **ignore** tells the compiler that the variables following it are not used by the code within the scope of the declaration. This is useful when you are forced to write code that has a certain number of parameters because of the convention of the calling routine. For example, in our discussion of macro characters in Chapter 14, we stated that a macro character function was always passed the character and the input stream. However, most macro character functions simply ignore the character argument. This is true of our version of the macro character function for **quote** given in that chapter:

```
(lambda (stream char)
  (list (quote quote) (read stream)))
```

The compiler might be able to make this code more efficient if it were told that we had no use for **char**. We can do this by defining a function containing an **ignore** declaration:

```
(defun quote-fn
  (declare (ignore char))
  (list (quote quote) (read stream)))
```

Now we can compile **quote-fn**, and use it as the macro character function for a macro character that will behave just like '. Because of our declaration, the compiler might be able to save a little overhead when this function is applied.

20.4.6.3. Tailoring Optimization

The specifier **optimize** allows the user to tell the compiler which qualities it should compile for. For example

```
(declare (optimize (speed 3)))
```

says that speed is of the utmost important (the scale is 0-3). Other qualities are **space**, **safety** and **compilation-speed**.

20.4.6.4. Special Variables

Most declarations have no effect at all on interpreted code. The sole exception to this rule is declaring something to be a special variable. As previously discussed, a special variable is scoped dynamically rather than statically. We can use either **declare** or **proclaim** in conjunction with the specifier **special** to declare a variable to be special. For example, the following code asserts that **x** is special within the function **fn**:

```
(defun fn (x y)
    (declare (special x))
    ...                              )
```

Declaring **x** to be special here means that, if **fn** calls some other function in which **x** appears as a free symbol, that appearence of **x** might reference this **x**; of course, if we did not declare **x** to be special, there would be no way any function besides **fn** could reference its parameter **x**.

Since special declarations are heeded by the interpreter as well as the compiler, special declarations really have nothing to do with compiling per se. They are merely make use of the same functions used for declarations that only affect the compiler.

Standardization Note: In other LISPs, with dynamic scoping being the rule, this is not the case. In those LISPs, there are some situations in which it is necessary to declare a variable to be special to the compiler, while the interpreter would function properly without this declaration. In fact, the major motivation in having lexical scoping be the default in Common LISP is that, this way, compiled and interpreted code behave the same way. In most other LISPs, should you forget a special declaration, interpreted and compiled code may behave differently.

20.5. Summary

(1)   A LISP compiler translates LISP code into machine code. The resulting code is more efficient but harder to debug.

(2)   The Common LISP compiler is applied to a function using the function **compile**. It is applied to the contents of a file by using the function **compile–file**.

(3)   Declarations are useful for communicating information the compiler. Declarations applying to a specific construct are made with the special function **declare**, and global declarations with the function **proclaim**. Declarations that apply only to a specific form can be made using the functions **locally** and **the**. Declarations can be used to specify the type of the data to be assigned a variable, the type of a

function, that a variable is special, whether function calls are to be open-coded, that a variable is ignored by a section of code, and the user's preferences for optimization.

(4)   **eval–when** allows for conditional evaluation of an s-expression, depending upon whether the code is being loaded or compiled.

Exercise

(1)   Compile the various functions you have written. Use the function **time** or **get–internal–run–time** to compare the performance of compiled and interpreted code. You might want to compile your code using some of the declarations described in this chapter, and see how different declarations affect performance.

Chapter 21

LISP Applications:
Pattern Matching

21.1. Introduction

Novice LISP programmers often know some other programming language. As a result, their code has more of the appearance of PASCAL or FORTRAN than would code written by more experienced LISP hands. To rectify this situation, the next two chapters present some complete LISP programs. The intent of these sample programs is to convey the flavor of writing in LISP.

We also take this opportunity to discuss two important applications of LISP. These are *pattern matching* and *associative, deductive data base management*. We first present a description of each task. Then we provide and discuss actual LISP programs that perform these tasks. Possible extensions and modifications of each program are discussed in the exercises.

21.2. Pattern Matching

We begin with a LISP pattern matching program. Pattern matching is the process of comparing two expressions to see if one is similar to the other.

Pattern matching has a number of important uses. For example, many programs need to determine if a certain datum has one of a given set of properties. Often, these properties can be expressed as patterns. If so, we can use our pattern matcher to classify the data by matching the data against various patterns.

Another use of pattern matching is in artificial intelligence programs. Many artificial intelligence programs need to perform some kind of reasoning about the information they encounter. This reasoning typically requires access to knowledge about the world. For example, a program trying to understand a natural language text may encounter the sentence "John hit Mary." To really understand this sentence, the program would need to realize that Mary may be hurt as a result of John's action. To deal with this sentence appropriately, a program must have recourse to information about the possible consequences of hitting someone.

Thus artificial intelligence programs need to have some sort of representation of facts about the world. They must then be able to access these facts when they are applicable to the task at hand. And they must be able to apply these facts to produce valid results.

Many artificial intelligence programs use pattern-like elements to represent facts about the world. For example, we might use a pattern to denote the general fact that hitting someone may hurt that person. Then if our program learned the particular fact that John hit Mary, it could use a form of pattern matching to determine if it had any knowledge applicable to this situation. If our program successfully matched the particular fact that John hit Mary against a piece of the general pattern about the consequences of hitting, our program could then conclude that Mary is apt to be hurt.

Of course, this description of the application of pattern matching to reasoning is necessarily vague at this stage. By the end of the next chapter, however, we will see how to write code that performs such operations.

21.3. A Notion of Similarity

To build a pattern matcher, we first need to have some notion of when two items are similar. Of course, there are many ways in which we might judge similarity. The simplest way two expressions could be similar is if they are identical. In addition, we might want to classify as similar those expressions that are identical except in certain parts. For example, we might decide that expressions are similar if they begin with the same three elements, or if they are the same except for the second item, and so on.

Since we would like to build a general pattern matcher, we cannot decide in advance exactly what criteria we will use to judge similarity. Instead, we would like to provide a fairly general scheme. Then we could implement different criteria of similarity for different applications. One way to implement such a flexible pattern matching scheme is to allow patterns to contain *pattern matching variables*. When a pattern matching variable occurs in an item, the pattern matcher matches it against anything that appears in the corresponding position of the item being matched. Everything that is not a pattern matching variable is allowed to match only itself. We call items that are not variables *literals*.

For example, suppose we follow the standard practice and designate all our pattern matching variables by beginning their names with the character **?** (question mark). Then the following is a pattern:

    (a b ?x d e)

This pattern should match any list beginning with the literals **a** and **b**, followed by any expression, which is in turn followed by the literals **d** and **e**. For example, this pattern should match the expressions

    (a b c d e)

    (a b (x y z) d e)

but not the expressions

    (a b c d e f)

    (a b c c d e)

    (a b (c d e))

In a real program, patterns are more likely to reflect some content, in contrast to the patterns in the examples above. For example, we might represent a fact about the world with the following pattern:

    (causes (hit ?x ?y) (hurt ?y))

This is supposed to mean that **?x** (i. e., someone) hitting **?y** (i. e., someone) causes **?y** (the person hit) to become hurt. Of course, our pattern matcher does not know this interpretation of the pattern, nor does it care about it. Rather, it will blindly match this pattern against any item that has the literals **causes**, **hit**, and **hurt** in the right place, and has anything where this pattern has variables. However, the matcher will make sure that whatever matches **?y** in one place matches it in the other. Other than that, it is up to us humans to use this pattern in some fashion so that it ends up acting like the fact it is supposed to represent.

Allowing variables in patterns does not give us complete flexibility in how we can represent similarity. For example, it does not provide us with a convenient way of talking about the length of a pattern. Nevertheless, it does provide a great deal of expressive power.

21.4. Pattern Matching Variable Bindings

When we match two expressions, we may want the result of a match to tell us more than just whether or not the expressions matched. For example, if we match **(a b ?x d e)** against **(a b c d e)**, we might like to know not only that they matched, but also that the variable **?x** matched the literal **c**. Similarly, if we have a pattern with more than one variable in it, we would like to know all the correspondences that need to be made for there to be a match. For example, if we match **(a ?x c ?y e)** against **(a b c d e)**, we would like to know that **?x** matches **b** and that **?y** matches **d**.

One way to do this is to have the result of the match return a list of *bindings*. A binding, in the context of pattern matching, is a correspondence of a pattern matching variable to an item made in the course of a match. We can represent a binding as a list of the variable and the item. Thus we can represent the fact that **?x** matches **b** in the above example by specifying the binding **(?x b)**.

We can represent the set of bindings that result from a match as a list. For example, the two bindings produced as a result of the previous example would be represented as the list **((?x b) (?y d))**.

Determining the bindings required for two items to match imposes some important constraints on the matcher. For example, suppose we want to know if the pattern **(a ?x ?x d)** matches **(a b c d)**. We would like the result to be negative, because there is no consistent binding of **?x** that makes this a valid match. This means that, during the course of a match, we need to check to see if the binding for a variable has already been assumed. If so, we need to make sure that subsequent bindings conform to this assumption.

Also, in the examples we have seen so far, we have assumed that we would be matching a pattern, which may contain variables, against a literal item, which does not. However, it may be desirable to match two patterns against each other. For example, we may want to ask if the following two items can be considered equivalent:

(a ?x c ?y e)

(a b ?z d e)

We would like the answer to be yes, if **?x** were bound to **b**, **?y** to **d**, and **?z** to **c**.

The meaning of a successful match between two patterns can be thought of this way: It yields a set of substitutions, which, if they are made in both patterns, will yield the same thing. Thus if **b**, **c**, and **d** were substituted for **?x**, **?z**, and **?y**, respectively, in both patterns, the result of both substitutions would be **(a b c d e)**.

Note that for this to work properly, we need to assume that the variables in different patterns are distinct from one another. We will make this assumption for the time being.

It should also be possible to match two items that have variables in the same place. For example, suppose we try to match the following together:

(a b ?x d e)

(a b ?y d e)

We would like the answer to be affirmative, with the proviso that **?x** is bound to **?y**. Intuitively, this would mean that the two items are the same whenever **?x** is the same as **?y**, or that the resulting expressions would be the same if we substituted **?y** for **?x** in the two patterns.

Similarly, we could allow variables to get bound to items that have variables in them. For example, suppose we match the following together:

(a b ?x d e)

(a b (1 ?y 3) d e)

We would like to know that these two can be the same if **?x** is bound to **(1 ?y 3)**.

This sort of match is actually very useful. For example, recall the representation shown above for the fact that hitting someone can hurt that person:

(causes (hit ?x ?y) (hurt ?y))

Suppose now that some program had just learned that John hit Mary. That is, suppose the program was given the input **(hit john mary)**. Suppose further that this program wants to infer the consequences of this action. To do so, it might try to find some applicable knowledge about what might happen next. Since patterns that begin with **causes** encode such knowledge, our program might want to find those facts beginning with **causes** that are relevant to this input. This can be done by first building the following pattern:

(causes (hit john mary) ?r)

This pattern can be interpreted as meaning "What is caused by John hitting Mary?" Now we can match this pattern against facts we know until we come to the fact about hitting. When we match these two items together, the match succeeds, and returns the following bindings:

((?x john) (?y mary) (?r (hurt ?y)))

If we ask for the binding of **?r** in this result, and then substitute variables in the answer with their bindings, we get the item **(hurt mary)**. Thus our program could conclude that Mary is likely to be hurt as a result of John hitting her.

Matching variables against items that contain variables has some important consequences for our matcher. For example, suppose we match together the following expressions:

(a ?x ?x)

(a ?y c)

If we bind **?x** to **?y**, we cannot also bind **?x** to **c**, because the same pattern matching variable cannot be bound to two different items. If we added no additional binding, the result would be erroneous: Just substituting **?y** for **?x** will not produce identical expressions. It also would be incorrect to call the match a failure, as the two expressions can be made identical. This happens whenever we substitute **c** for both variables.

To represent this condition of the match, **?y** must be bound to **c**. This binding is different from any we have seen so far. It binds a variable against an item that occurs in the same pattern as that variable. To come up with this binding, we need to be a bit cleverer than before. Whenever we match a variable against an item, we should first check to see if it already has a binding. If it does, we continue the match using the *binding* of the variable instead of the variable itself. In our example here, we would first bind **?x** to **?y**. Next, when we try to match **?x** against **c**, we check to see if **?x** has a binding. Since **?x** is bound to **?y**, we continue the match with **?y** instead of **?x**. This results in matching **?y** against **c**, which is exactly what we want.

Note that, in general, if we go about matching in different orders, we could come up with different sets of bindings. For example, in the case above, the matcher could just as well have bound **?y** to **?x** rather than the other way around. Then when it got around to matching **?x** to **c**, **?x** would have no binding and **c** could be assigned to it. We would then have the binding list **((?x c) (?y ?x))** rather than **((?y c) (?x ?y))**.

There is no real problem here. You just should be aware of the fact that there may be several different sets of bindings that constitute a valid result of a match.

21.5. Unification

If our matcher has the capability to match together two patterns in the manner just described, it is called a *unification pattern matcher*. This is a term from theorem proving. The intuition is that we "unify" two expressions by finding some appropriate bindings for their variables.

Matching two items with variables can lead to some rather nasty problems. For example, suppose we try to match the following expressions against one another:

(a ?x ?x ?x)

(a ?y ?y ?y)

As above, we begin by binding **?x** to **?y**. Then when we try to match **?x** against **?y** the second time, we recall the current binding of **?x** and match it against **?y**. Since the current binding of **?x** is **?y**, we end up matching **?y** against itself. Since **?y** has no previous binding, we might simply bind **?y** to **?y**, and add this to the current bindings.

But now look what happens. When we match **?x** against **?y** for the third time, we again get the current binding of **?x**, namely **?y**. And, as before, we match this against **?y**. But **?y** has just been given the binding **?y**. Now when we check to see if **?y** has a current binding, we find that it has the value **?y**. We continue the match with this value, first checking to see if it has a binding. Thus we keep on endlessly asking for the binding of **?y**.

The solution to this problem is to check to see if we are trying to match a variable against itself. If so, this is all right (after all, we want this match to succeed). But we had better not put the binding on the binding list in such an instance.

But an even worse problem can occur. Suppose we try to match the following:

(a ?x ?x)

(a ?y (b ?y))

As before, we end up matching **?y** against **(b ?y)**. Since **?y** has no previous binding, we might be tempted to bind **?y** to **(b ?y)** and say that the match succeeds. However, this cannot be right. If two patterns match, this means that we could substitute variables for their bindings and get identical expressions. But there is in fact no consistent binding of these variables that allows this to happen. If we try substituting **?y** for its value in **(b ?y)**, we would get the expression **(b (b ?y))**. We could now substitute the **?y** in this expression for its value, and so on ad infinitum.

Situations like this one are called *circularities*. To deal with circularities, a pattern matcher must explicitly check each variable against the item it is attempting to bind to it. If the item contains an instance of that same variable, we declare the match a failure. We have to be a bit careful while doing this, though. For example, in the course of some match, **?x** may get **?y** bound to it. Later on, if we try to match **?y** against **(b ?x)**, the match should fail, because the latter form implicitly contains **?y**.

21.6. The Matcher

The nasty situations described in the previous section occur infrequently in practice. We check for them in the algorithm given here for completeness and to demonstrate the LISP programming they require. Should you decide to implement your own version of a pattern matcher, you may decide to build one that is less complete, but perhaps a bit simpler.

First, we need to decide exactly what the input and output of our matcher will be. In our examples above, we expressed patterns as lists in which a symbol beginning with a question mark denotes a variable. However, if the question mark is actually part of the symbol's name, it is difficult to determine if something is a pattern matching variable as opposed to an ordinary symbol. A better solution is to represent pattern matching variables as something like (*var* x), where *var* is some predetermined special symbol. Then we can check if something is a pattern matching variable simply by checking if it is a list beginning with the symbol *var*.

We would still like to enjoy the convenience of the question mark notation, however. We can do so by making question mark a macro character. Question mark will read in the next s-expression, which should always be a symbol, and return a list beginning with *var*, followed by the symbol it has read. We can implement such a macro as follows:

```
(set-macro-character #\?
  #'(lambda (stream char)
      (list '*var* (read stream t nil t))))
```

This defines **?** to be a macro character such that **?x** turns into (*var* x).

Now for the result of the match. Above we saw that we could represent the result of a match as a list of bindings. However, if we return a binding list as the result of a match, we would have an ambiguous situation. Presumably, if a match fails, we would like the matcher to return **nil**. But consider the case where we match an item against an identical item. We would not need any bindings to show that the two are equivalent. So if we return the binding list as the result, we could not tell whether the match failed, or whether it succeeded but without any bindings.

To represent the result of a match, we need to deal with three cases: (1) The match may fail altogether; (2) the match may succeed, and produce an associated list of bindings; or (3) the match may succeed, but not require any bindings. There are a number of ways to accommodate these three possibilities. One way is to return, when the match succeeds, a cons whose first element is **t**, and whose second element is a (possibly empty) list denoting the bindings required for the match to succeed. We could have **nil** represent that the match failed, (**t**) represent the fact that it succeeded but with no bindings, and (**t** . (... *bindings* ...)) represent the fact that it succeeded with the specified bindings.

In fact, we could return a slightly less elaborate structure by noting that whenever we return a non-**nil** list, that fact itself indicates that match succeeded. That means the presence of the symbol **t** is redundant. We could be somewhat more frugal by having our matcher return a *list of a binding list* should it succeed, and **nil** if it fails. In this way we distinguish between the match failing, which should return **nil**, and the match succeeding with no bindings required, which should return **(nil)**. If the match succeeds with the bindings **((?x b) (?y d))**, say, the matcher will return the list **(((?x b) (?y d)))**.

Some individuals may find this notation less clear than the one proposed previously. Therefore, it is debatable whether it is worth the gain in efficiency. However, Common LISP provides a solution that offers the best of both worlds. This is to use multiple value returns. That is, we can have our matcher return two values, using the facilities described in Chapter 16. One value would be **t** or **nil**, representing the success of the match. The other would be the binding list, should the match succeed. This is more efficient than either solution proposed above, because returning two values does not require the extra **cons** that we must provide when we return a *list* of the binding list or a list consisting of the binding list preceded by **t** or **nil**.

Standardization Note: While using multiple value returns is the best solution, multiple value returns are not yet common to most LISPs. Thus the code we will write below may not be transportable to another LISP. You will have to use one of the other representations suggested above if you are operating in some LISP without multiple value returns.

Our matcher will work by recursively matching one part of a pattern against another. The matcher will maintain a list of the bindings it has accumulated thus far. Each subsequent match will be done in the context of the previous bindings to make sure that we continue to bind variables consistently.

Thus the main burden of our matcher will be a routine called **match–with–bindings**. This will take as input two items to be matched, and a list of current bindings. **match–with–bindings** will conclude that the two items match if they do so in a way that is consistent with the list of current bindings. It will return two values, the first being **t** or **nil**, representing the result of the match, and the second being the binding list, as described above.

We will interface to this routine through a routine called **match**. **match** simply calls **match–with–bindings**, passing it the two items to be matched and an empty list of current bindings.

As our matcher recursively descends both items, it checks to see if it has reached an atom or a pattern matching variable in either one. If it reaches an atom, it just needs to check if the atom is being matched against an

eq atom. If it reaches a pattern matching variable, it will call the special routine **variable–match**. This routine checks to see if the variable can be bound to its corresponding item in the current context. This involves looking at the current binding of the variable, checking to see if the variable is being bound to itself or to an item that contains it. This latter check is done by the routine **contained–in**. If necessary, **variable–match** will add a new binding to the binding list. **variable–match** also returns two values, a flag indicating success, and a (possibly extended) binding list.

Without further ado, here is the top-level matcher function:

```
(defun match (pattern1 pattern2)
    (match-with-bindings pattern1 pattern2 nil))
```

match–with–bindings does all the work:

```
(defun match-with-bindings (pattern1 pattern2 bindings)
    (cond ((pattern-var-p pattern1)
           (variable-match pattern1 pattern2 bindings))
          ((pattern-var-p pattern2)
           (variable-match pattern2 pattern1 bindings))
          ((atom pattern1)
           (if (eq pattern1 pattern2) (values t bindings)))
          ((atom pattern2) nil)
          (t (multiple-value-bind
                 (flag carbindings)
                 (match-with-bindings
                     (car pattern1) (car pattern2) bindings)
               (and flag
                    (match-with-bindings (cdr pattern1)
                                         (cdr pattern2)
                                         carbindings)))))))
```

This routine uses the parameter **bindings** to carry along the bindings that have been computed thus far in the match. First, the routine checks to see if either pattern is a pattern matching variable. To do so, it uses **pattern–var–p**, a predicate we define below that returns true when its argument is a pattern matching variable. When **match–with–bindings** runs into a pattern matching variable, it calls the routine **variable–match** to handle the matching. Otherwise, it checks if it has bottomed out on an atom. Note that if it succeeds, **match–with–bindings** uses the function **values** to return two items: the symbol **t**, indicating that the match succeeded, and the binding list required to unify the patterns.

In the recursive step, we would like to match the **car** and the **cdr** of the patterns, and agree that the two patterns match if both of these submatches work. The difficulty here is that either submatch might return bindings that are inconsistent with those of the other. To prevent this from happening, we first match the **car**s of the two patterns. This returns two values, which are "caught" by the function **multiple-value-bind**. This function assigns the variables in its first argument to the (supposedly multiple) values returned by the second; then it evaluates the rest of the forms in its call. In this case, it assigns **flag** and **carbindings** the values returned from matching the two **car**s. **flag** will be **nil** if the match failed, and **t** if it succeeded. If it succeeded, **carbinding** will be assigned the (possibly longer) binding list. We will proceed to match the **cdr**s only if matching the **car**s is successful. If we do so, we will use the bindings produced from matching the **car**s. This assures us that the second half of the match will be consistent with the first half.

Note that if the match fails, we only return the single value **nil**. This is okay, because routines using the matcher should not expect a binding list if the match fails; moreover routines expecting multiple values will supply the value **nil** if not enough values are returned.

The major part left is dealing with the pattern variables. This is done by **variable-match**:

```
(defun variable-match (pattern-var item bindings)
   (if (equal pattern-var item) (values t bindings)
      (let ((var-binding (get-binding pattern-var
                                             bindings)))
          (cond
            (var-binding
             (match-with-bindings var-binding
                    item
                    bindings))
            ((not (contained-in pattern-var
                    item
                    bindings))
             (values t (add-binding pattern-var
                    item
                    bindings)))))))
```

First, we check if we are matching a variable against itself. Doing so succeeds, but does not produce a new binding. Then we check to see if there is a binding of the variable on the current binding list. If so, we continue by matching this binding against the corresponding item. If there is no current binding, we check for circularities using the function

contained-in. If the item does not contain the pattern variable, then we add a new binding to the current binding list and return this list as one of the results.

The only complicated function left is **contained-in**:

```
(defun contained-in (pattern-var item bindings)
   (cond ((atom item) nil)
         ((pattern-var-p item)
          (or (equal pattern-var item)
              (contained-in
                  pattern-var
                  (get-binding item bindings)
                  bindings)))
         (t (or (contained-in pattern-var
                     (car item)
                     bindings)
                (contained-in pattern-var
                     (cdr item)
                     bindings)))))
```

This function checks to see if the containing item is itself a variable. If so, it continues the search through that variable's binding. Otherwise it recursively descends through the item looking for an occurrence of the variable.

All that remains are a few utility functions. We add to a binding list by **cons**ing onto it a list of a variable name and the item bound to it:

```
(defun add-binding (pattern-var item bindings)
   (cons (list pattern-var item) bindings))
```

We determine if something is a pattern matching variable if it is a list beginning with **∗var∗**:

```
(defun pattern-var-p (item)
   (and (listp item) (eq '∗var∗ (car item))))
```

We get a binding by doing an **assoc**, and then taking a **cadr**. Note that the **cadr** of **nil** in Common LISP is **nil**, so this is safe to do even if there is no binding:

```
(defun get-binding (pattern-var bindings)
   (cadr (assoc pattern-var bindings :test #'equal)))
```

Having gone to all this trouble, let us see how the matcher actually works:

```
-> (match '(a b c) '(a b c))
T ;
NIL
->
```

Here we succeed in matching two identical objects. The success of the match is indicated by the first value, **t**. The binding list required for the match is **nil**, as indicated by the second result.

Let us try some expressions with variables. First we match two patterns with variables in different places:

```
-> (match '(a ?x c ?y e) '(a b ?z d e))
T ;
(((*VAR* Y) D) ((*VAR* Z) C) ((*VAR* X) B))
```

The second result is the correct list of bindings for the variables in both patterns. Note that the result is hard to read because it contains pattern matching variables in their internal representation rather than in the more convenient input form.

Now let us do an example in which the same variable occurs more than once in a pattern:

```
- (match '(a ?x ?x) '(a ?y b))
T ;
(((*VAR* Y) B) ((*VAR* X) (*VAR* Y)))
```

As we can see, a consistent set of bindings is found, including the binding of **?y** to **b**.

Here are some more complicated matches:

```
-> (match '(a ?x (c ?y)) '(a (b ?z) (?w ?z)))
T ;
((((*VAR* Y) (*VAR* Z)) ((*VAR* W) C) ((*VAR* X) (B (*VAR*
Z)))))
```

```
-> (match '(causes (hit john mary) ?r)
           '(causes (hit ?x ?y) (hurt ?y)) )
T ;
(((*VAR* R) (HURT (*VAR* Y))) ((*VAR* Y) MARY) ((*VAR* X)
JOHN))
->
```

Finally, let us test some of the pathological cases we described above:

```
-> (match '(a ?x ?x ?x) '(a ?y ?y ?y))
T ;
(((*VAR* X) (*VAR* Y)))
-> (match '(a ?x ?x) '(a (b ?y) ?y))
NIL
->
```

As the examples demonstrate, the matcher correctly handles the cases of matching variables against themselves and of matching a variable against an item that contains that variable.

21.7. Summary

(1)   Pattern matching is a way of judging the similarity of LISP objects.

(2)   A *pattern* is an s-expression that may contain *pattern matching variables.* A pattern matching variable will get bound to that part of the s-expression against which it is matched.

(3)   *Unification* is a kind of pattern matching in which variables are allowed in both objects being matched. A unification pattern matcher tries to find some consistent set of bindings for the variables in both objects. If it is successful, then the substitution of variables by their bindings in each object will result in identical expressions.

(4)   A unification pattern matcher is complicated by the need to check for a number of anomalous situations. In particular, it must detect *circularities,* i. e., circumstances in which the matcher is compelled to bind a variable against an expression containing that variable.

(5)   A unification pattern matcher can be implemented by a modest amount of LISP code. The implementation is recursive in nature.

Exercises

(1)   Modify the pattern matcher to use dotted pairs instead of lists to represent bindings.

(2)   The result of a match is rather messy. This is the case because the result contains the internal representation of pattern matching variables. The function **print** just prints these out as ordinary lists.

Write a version of **print** that prints out pattern matching variables using the question mark notation (i. e., **?x** rather than **(*var* x)**). Now install your print function in your own **read-eval-print** loop so that the result of a match is displayed more legibly.

(3)   The scheme we used to represent bindings is rather inefficient. The first element of a binding is always a pattern matching variable, so there is no reason to store the representation of the entire pattern matching variable. That is, instead of representing the binding of **?x** to **(a b c)** as **((*var* x) (a b c))**, we can simply use **(x (a b c))** without introducing any ambiguity.

Write a version of the pattern matcher which stores binding lists using this more economical representation.

(4)   We could represent pattern matching variables as "marked" symbols instead of as lists beginning with a unique symbol. That is, instead of internally representing **?x** as **(*var* x)**, we could represent this pattern matching variable by setting the **pattern–matching–variable** property of **x** to **t**. Modify the pattern matcher to use this representation of pattern matching variables.

Note that a disadvantage of this representation is that pattern matching variables are no longer obvious when we print out a pattern. Write a function **pattern–print** which causes pattern matching variables to be printed preceded by a question mark.

(5)   Suppose we want to specify a pattern that would match only those items that have *numbers* in a certain position. We currently have no way to do this, as we cannot constrain a match so that a variable will match only items of a certain type.

One way to implement this feature is to allow the user to attach an arbitrary predicate as a property of a pattern matching variable. Then when the matcher tries to match a variable against an item, it checks the attached predicate, if one exists. It allows the match only if the item satisfies the attached predicate.

Add a facility to attach arbitrary predicates to pattern matching variables. Then modify the matcher so that variables will be bound only to those items that satisfy their predicates.

(6) Rewrite the code of the matcher so that it does not require multiple value returns. Use one of the representations of matcher output discussed above to achieve this goal.

Chapter 22

LISP Applications:
Associative Data Base Management

22.1. Introduction

Having implemented a pattern matcher in the previous chapter, we are now in a position to maintain an *associative data base* of facts. An associative data base is a collection of facts that are retrievable by their content. This is in contrast to a data base in which you can only ask to see the nth element. For example, we might ask an associative data base to tell us all the objects it knows about that happen to be animals, or all the events in which John hit someone, or whether Fido is a dog.

In this chapter, we describe and implement a simple associative data base system. We then extend it to handle large data bases more efficiently. Finally, we add to our system the ability to do automatic deduction. This will enable the system to "retrieve" facts that are implied by items in the data base, but which are not literally present.

22.2. An Associative Data Base Implementation

One way to implement an associative data base is to represent all facts as patterns. Simple facts may be represented as literal items, and more complex facts as items that contain variables. For example, we can represent the simple fact that Fido is a dog by the literal item **(dog fido)**. We can represent the more complex fact that all dogs are animals by an item of the form **(implies (dog ?x) (animal ?x))**. This pattern is meant to denote the idea that being a dog implies being an animal. Now if we want to know which elements in our data base happen to be dogs, we can run through the collection of facts in the data base looking for all those that match the pattern **(dog ?x)**. Or if we want to know if it is true that Fido is a dog, we can check to see if the literal pattern **(dog fido)** matches anything in our data base. Similarly, if we want to know what is implied by being a dog, we can look for all items that match the pattern **(implies (dog ?x) ?what)**. We will call a pattern that we use to interrogate a data base a *request*.

Of course, for this scheme to work, we need to have some uniform way of representing facts as patterns. Exactly how to do this is a topic of active research in artificial intelligence. It is referred to as the problem of *knowledge representation*. We will not examine or endorse any of the prevailing theories of knowledge representation here. Instead, we shall assume that some simple scheme exists which allows us to represent an individual fact by an individual pattern. The techniques demonstrated here will apply to any such scheme. It makes no difference whether you choose to represent "John loves Mary" as **(loves john mary)** or **(john loves mary)**, or **(mumble frump gezork)**, as long as you do so consistently.

22.2.1. Some Implementation Considerations

To build an associative data base, we first need to store all facts in some fashion. In the version shown here, the data base will be a simple list. We will add to that data base by **cons**ing onto it, and look for items in the data base by marching down the list. This is rather inefficient for large data bases, but we will not be concerned with such matters for now.

When we retrieve facts from any associative data base, however, we must be careful that the variables in our request pattern do not clash with those in the patterns in the data base. For example, suppose we represent the fact that everybody loves Mary as **(loves ?x mary)**. Now suppose we want to know who John loves. We would eventually match the request **(loves john ?x)** against the previous pattern. But rather than succeeding, the match will fail. This happens only because we happened to use the same variable name in one pattern as in the other: After binding **?x** to **john**, the matcher finds that it cannot also match **?x** against **mary**, so the match fails. Had the request pattern been **(loves john ?z)**, we would have had no problem.

To guard against such difficulties, we can do one of two things. The matcher can be designed so as to remember which variables are associated with which pattern. Alternatively, it can automatically generate new names for variables in patterns. The solution we will use is a variant of the latter. We will rename all variables in a pattern when the pattern is added to the data base. This is better than renaming the variables in the request pattern, because programs making the request may make assumptions about the names of variables in requests they generate.

Our matcher will return all the items in the data base it finds that match a given request. So in general, the result of querying the data base will be a (possibly empty) list of answers. Each answer will be the form of a binding list. For example, suppose we had a data base that contained the items **(loves ?z ?z)**, **(loves john mary)**, and **(loves john sue)**. Then if we queried the data base with the pattern **(loves john ?x)**, we would get the following answer:

> ((((*var* x) mary))
>   (((*var* x) sue))
>   (((*var* z) john) ((*var* x) (*var* z))))

This answer indicates three matches. The first binding list says that the request matched an item in the data base with **?x** bound to **mary**; the second that it matched an item with **?x** bound to **sue**; and the third that it matched an item with **?z** bound to **john** and **?x** bound to **?z**. The last binding list is a somewhat convoluted way of saying that the request matches an item with **?x** bound to **john**.

Note that if we query our data base with a literal item, we will get a list of at most one answer. This answer will not have bindings. For example, if we queried our sample data base with the request **(loves john mary)**, we would get the answer **(nil)**. As in the case of pattern matching, this result indicates a successful operation with no associated bindings. Failure to match anything in the data base will be represented by returning **nil**.

22.2.2. The Manager

We will call our code for dealing with associative data bases a *data base manager*. It consists of two routines. One adds an item to a data base; the other searches through the data base matching each item against the specified request.

An Associative Data Base Implementation

First we define **add-to-data-base**, the routine that adds an item to a given data base. We will normally store a data base as the value of a symbol. It is therefore useful to pass **add-to-data-base** an unevaluated symbol, and change its value to store the updated data base. In addition, patterns usually are known in advance rather than produced on the fly. So we will want our data base updater not to evaluate the item we pass it. We can accomplish these desirata by making **add-to-data-base** a macro.

Also, we must remember to replace with new names the pattern matching variables in the item being added. We will call the routine that does this replacement **replace-variables**. Thus we have the following:

```
(defmacro add-to-data-base (item d-b-name)
    '(setq ,d-b-name
        (cons (replace-variables (quote ,item))
            ,d-b-name)))
```

We use the backquote character macro to facilitate the writing of this macro. Other than that, the code is straightforward.

Writing the routine **replace-variables** is a bit trickier. This routine can use **gensym** to create new names for variables. But it must be sure to use consistently the variables it creates. That is, if it replaces the first **?x** in **(loves ?x ?x)** with **?var3**, then it must be sure to replace the second occurrence of **?x** with **?var3**. To do this, **replace-variables** will maintain a list of bindings that associate old variables with their new replacements. Then if it encounters those variables again, it can use the same replacements it used for them last time.

replace-variables will do a normal recursive pass through an item with one twist. A name created for substitution while descending through the **car** of an item needs to be available when we descend through **cdr** of that item. Thus we need to have the bindings produced while descending through the one part of the recursion available when we descend through the other part. In our pattern matcher we were able to solve a similar problem simply by returning the bindings as the result of a recursive step. But here we will need to return as a result the new edition of the item that the function is constructing.

Since we have two values we would like each recursive call to return, we will use Common LISP's multiple value return feature here. **replace-variables** will use a function called **replace-variables-with-bindings**. This function will expect an item and a binding list, and will return two values, a rebuilt item, and a (possibly extended) binding list. **replace-variables** will simply start things off by cal-

ling **replace–variables–with–bindings** with the initial item and a binding
list of **nil**:

```
(defun replace-variables (item)
    (values (replace-variables-with-bindings item nil)))

(defun replace-variables-with-bindings (item bindings)
    (cond ((atom item) (values item bindings))
          ((pattern-var-p item)
           (let ((var-binding (get-binding item bindings)))
             (if var-binding
                 (values var-binding bindings)
                 (let ((newvar (makevar (gensym "VAR"))))
                   (values newvar
                           (add-binding item
                                        newvar
                                        bindings))))))
          (t (multiple-value-bind
               (newlhs lhsbindings)
               (replace-variables-with-bindings
                   (car item)
                   bindings)
               (multiple-value-bind
                 (newrhs finalbindings)
                 (replace-variables-with-bindings
                     (cdr item)
                     lhsbindings)
                 (values (cons newlhs newrhs)
                         finalbindings))))))

(defun makevar (sym)
    (list '*var* sym))
```

Note that **replace–variables** explicitly returns only one value, as the binding list producing by **replace–variables–with–bindings** is not of interest
to anyone after the call to **replace–variables** has been completed.

Let us exercise these functions a bit before going on. First, let us test
replace–variables on some typical patterns. It should leave literal expressions alone:

```
-> (replace-variables '(loves john mary))
(LOVES JOHN MARY)
->
```

It should replace different variables with new, different variables:

```
-> (replace-variables '(loves ?x ?y))
(LOVES (*VAR* #:VAR0) (*VAR* #:VAR1))
->
```

And it should replace the same variable consistently:

```
-> (replace-variables '(loves ?x ?x))
(LOVES (*VAR* #:VAR2) (*VAR* #:VAR2))
->
```

(Remember, **gensym** produces uninterned symbols, so they are printed out with a **#:** prefix, as discussed in Chapter 17).

Now let us add a few expressions to a test data base. We will call this data base ***d-b*** to indicate that it is a global variable. We will begin by initiating it:

```
-> (setq *d-b* nil)
NIL
->
```

We can now use **add-to-data-base** to update ***d-b***:

```
-> (add-to-data-base (loves john mary) *d-b*)
((LOVES JOHN MARY))
-> (add-to-data-base (loves ?x ?x) *d-b*)
((LOVES (*VAR* #:VAR3) (*VAR* #:VAR3)) (LOVES JOHN MARY))
-> (add-to-data-base (dog fido) *d-b*)
((DOG FIDO)
 (LOVES (*VAR* #:VAR3) (*VAR* #:VAR3))
 (LOVES JOHN MARY))
->
```

All that remains is to write a routine that retrieves all items from a data base that match a given pattern. We will call this routine **query**. **query** will simply march through the data base, matching each item against the specified pattern. Since **match** returns two values, the second being a binding list, we can get the result we want by **nconc**ing together the results of successful matches. The function **mapcan** does most of this for us, so our retriever is quite simple:

```
(defun query (request data-base)
  (mapcan #'(lambda (item)
              (multiple-value-bind
                (flag bindings)
                (match item request)
                (if flag (list bindings))))
          data-base))
```

Let us test out our retriever on the data base ***d-b*** created above. First, let us check to see whether some literal propositions are known to be true:

```
-> (query '(loves john mary) *d-b*)
(NIL)
->
```

The result is a list of one element. This means that we found one item in the data base that matched the request. The one element in our result is **nil**, which means that the item that matched did so without requiring any variable bindings. That is, the request was **equal** to something in the data base. Now let us try the retriever on something we do not know is true:

```
-> (query '(loves john sue) *d-b*)
NIL
->
```

The retriever does not find any expression in the data base that matches this one. It returns **nil** to indicate failure.

We now ask the question "Who does John love?":

```
-> (query '(loves john ?x) *d-b*)
((((*VAR* X) JOHN) ((*VAR* #:VAR3) JOHN))
 (((*VAR* X) MARY)))
->
```

(Note: I adjusted the spacing of the actual output in this and the next few examples in order to better reveal the structure of the results.) The result is a list of two elements, meaning that we found two matches. The first is a binding list that has **?x** bound to **john**, and **?var3** bound to **john**. So this is a baroque way of saying that John loves himself. The second element shows **?x** bound to **mary**, meaning that John loves Mary too.

Note that our simple retriever has a fair amount of power. In particular, we can query on any part of an item. Thus we can ask questions like "Who loves Mary?" as well as "Who does John love?":

```
-> (query '(loves ?x mary) *d-b*)
(((((*VAR* X) MARY) ((*VAR* #:VAR3) (*VAR* X)))
 (((*VAR* X) JOHN)))
->
```

We can even ask what relationships exist between John and Mary:

```
-> (query '(?r john mary) *d-b*)
(((((*VAR* R) LOVES)))
->
```

Or who loves whom:

```
-> (query '(loves ?x ?y) *d-b*)
(((((*VAR* X) (*VAR* Y)) ((*VAR* #:VAR3) (*VAR* X)))
 (((*VAR* Y) MARY) ((*VAR* X) JOHN)))
->
```

Note that we can get an affirmative answer to a literal query that is not actually in the data base. For example, suppose we asked the question, "Does John love himself?" We would like to conclude that he does, as our data base knows that everyone loves himself. In fact, our data base retriever makes exactly this conclusion:

```
-> (query '(loves john john) *d-b*)
(((((*VAR* #:VAR3) JOHN)))
->
```

The result indicates that the query is true, although the answer is a bit cryptic.

In fact, we have observed several other cases in which the results of a query contain distracting references to variables that occur in items in the data base rather than in items in the request. We could modify our retriever to examine each result of the matcher, and eliminate such references. This is left as an exercise to the reader.

22.3. Indexing

As noted above, our retriever will be rather inefficient on large data bases. We could speed it up considerably if we had some clever way to select good candidates for matching rather than looking at every item in the data base. There are a variety of techniques to do so, all of which involve some sort of *indexing*. Indexing means organizing data in some manner so as to facilitate subsequent retrieval of that data. For example, sorting a list is a form of indexing, since sorting makes subsequent look-up amenable to efficient binary search.

Indexing patterns is more difficult than indexing many other forms of data. Patterns have a great deal of structure to them, so it is not obvious exactly how to organize them. Also, patterns may contain variables. The appearance of variables tends to throw a wrench into most simple schemes. For example, it is not clear where patterns with variables should be placed if we tried sorting a data base of facts.

There are a variety of techniques that have been developed to index patterns in a data base. Most of these would take us well beyond the scope of this book. However, we shall look at one simple idea here. The idea takes advantage of LISP property lists to break up a large data base into several small ones. When we add an item to a data base in this scheme, we shall look to see if its **car** is an atom. If so, we will store the item on a list under some property name of that atom. Then, when we try to retrieve a request, we will examine its **car** for a property of this name. Then we need only look down the resulting value to find candidates with which to unify the request.

Since we may want to support several data bases at the same time, we can use the name of the data base as the name of the property to index under. For example, suppose we want to add **(loves john mary)** to the data base **∗d–b∗** using this scheme. We do so by adding this item to the list stored under the **∗d–b∗** property of the atom **loves**. When fetching a request like **(loves ?x ?y)** from this data base, we first get the list under the **∗d–b∗** property of **loves**. Then we search this list in the usual fashion.

There are two problems with this scheme, however. First, we may want to store items in the data base that begin with either variables or lists. Such cases are rare in practice. In an actual retriever, we might be willing not to allow such patterns in a data base at all. However, we allow them here for completeness. The solution is simple in any case. Anytime we are asked to add an item to the data base that begins with a list, we stick it on the property list of some special atom, say **∗list∗**. When we add an item that begins with a pattern matching variable, we will put it under a property of the atom **∗var∗**. When we retrieve an item beginning with a list, we will look under **∗list∗**. We will look under **∗var∗** for every request, however. We need to do this because an item in the data base beginning with a variable might match a request beginning with anything.

The second problem is a bit trickier. Suppose we try to retrieve a request that begins with a variable. We do not want to look solely at the list under *var*. After all, the request could match items that begin with anything. So we need to search the whole data base in such cases. Again, we could constrain our system not to handle such requests, but we will allow them here.

The reason this is a problem is that we do not have the data base in any one place. We know what is in the data base only via the property lists of a number of atoms. But we have not been keeping track of which atoms we have been using. To do so, we will place on a list each atom which we use to index an item. We will keep this list under a property of the data base name, say *keys*. Now whenever we need to search the entire data base, we can do so through this property.

We will call our new routine to build up a data base **index**. **index** will determine if the **car** of the item to be added is an atom. If so, it will store the item under a property of that atom. If the item begins with a list, it will be stored under the corresponding property of the symbol *list*; if it begins with a pattern matching variable, it will be stored under a property of the atom *var*. **index** will also add the atom name it used to index the entry to a list kept under the *keys* property of the name of the data base. To make sure that the name is not added twice, **index** uses **adjoin** to update this list (recall that **adjoin** adds an element to a list only if it is not already there):

```
(defun index (item data-base)
    (let ((place (cond ((atom (car item)) (car item))
                       ((pattern-var-p (car item)) '*var*)
                       (t '*list*))))
        (setf (get place data-base)
            (cons (replace-variables item)
                  (get place data-base)))
        (setf (get data-base '*keys*)
            (adjoin place (get data-base '*keys*)))))
```

We can use **index** to add some items to a test data base:

```
-> (index '(loves john mary) '*d-b*)
(LOVES)
-> (index '(loves ?x ?x) '*d-b*)
(LOVES)
-> (index '(person john) '*d-b*)
(PERSON LOVES)
-> (index '((a b c)) '*d-b*)
(*LIST* PERSON LOVES)
```

387

```
-> (get 'loves '*d-b*)
((LOVES (*VAR* #:VAR4) (*VAR* #:VAR4)) (LOVES JOHN MARY))
-> (get 'person '*d-b*)
((PERSON JOHN))
-> (get '*list* '*d-b*)
(((A B C)))
->
```

Note that unlike **add-to-data-base**, **index** requires its arguments to be quoted. It also returns a list of atom names used to index items rather than the entire data base. These are fairly arbitrary design decisions. In addition, **index** does not require initialization of a data base. Do you see why? It might be useful to have a routine to initialize a data base, however, if we want to start over from scratch.

Now we will define **fast-query**, our data base retrieval function that accesses an indexed data base. If the request to **fast-query** begins with a pattern matching variable, **fast-query** will search the entire data base starting from the ***keys*** property of the data base name. Of course, in this case, the retrieval is no faster than in our original scheme. If the request begins with anything else, **fast-query** will get the data base list either from the **car** of the request or from ***list***, depending upon whether the request begins with an item or a list. It will then search this list using **query**. In these cases, **fast-query** will also search the list under ***var***, as the request may also match some item in the data base that begins with a variable:

```
(defun fast-query (request data-base)
   (if (pattern-var-p (car request))
      (mapcan
         #'(lambda (key)
              (query request (get key data-base)))
         (get data-base '*keys*))
      (nconc
         (query request
               (get (if (atom (car request))
                        (car request)
                        '*list*)
                     data-base))
         (query request
               (get '*var* data-base)))))
```

Let us test **fast-retrieve** on the test data base ***d-b*** we created with **index**:

```
-> (fast-query '(loves john ?x) '*d-b*)
((((*VAR* X) JOHN) ((*VAR* #:VAR4) JOHN)) (((*VAR* X)
MARY)))
-> (fast-query '(?r john mary) '*d-b*)
((((*VAR* R) LOVES)))
->
```

Note that we cannot tell **fast-query** from **query** insofar as these examples are concerned. This is just what we want, of course, provided that **fast-query** is actually faster than **query** when the data base is large.

22.4. A Deductive Retriever

We noted above that our retriever does a simple form of deduction. Namely, it will conclude that a particular fact is true if the data base contains a more general version of that fact. In an example above, we saw our retriever conclude that John loves himself because the data base contains the fact that everyone loves himself.

It is possible to add a great deal more deductive power to a retriever. For example, suppose our data base contains the fact that dogs are mammals. That is, suppose it contains the pattern **(implies (dog ?x) (mammal ?x))**. Suppose it also contains the item **(implies (poodle ?x) (dog ?x))**, meaning that poodles are dogs. Suppose further that we know that Fido is a poodle, i. e., that our data base contains the item **(poodle fido)**. Now we would like to be able to ask our retriever the question "Is Fido a mammal?" and get an affirmative reply. That is, we would like to query the data base with the request **(mammal fido)**, and have the retriever *deduce* that this it true, even though this fact is not literally in the data base.

When a retriever has such capabilities, it is called, naturally enough, a *deductive data base retriever.* We can think of deductive retrievers as implementing a kind of "virtual" data base. A deductive retriever may tell us that an item is in the data base if the item can be inferred from other items in the data base, even though the item itself is not explicitly present.

Many artificial intelligence systems use some form of deductive retriever. In some systems, the inferential mechanism of the retriever does the main part of the system's computation. Other systems use deductive retrievers merely as a convenience. In the latter case, the deductive retriever is used to handle many details of the computation. In this way, the rest of the program, which does the interesting part of the work, need not be concerned about bookkeeping tasks.

22.4.1. Backward Chaining

We can implement a form of deduction through a technique called *backward chaining*. In backward chaining, we store implications in the data base in the form (<– *consequent antecedent*). This means that *antecedent* being true implies that *consequent* is true. Then, when we want to know if some item *request* is true, in addition to our normal querying process, we do the following. We fetch all items in the data base of the form (<– *request antecedent*). If we find any, we recursively query the data base to see if *antecedent* is true. If so, then we can conclude that *request* is true, even if it is not explicitly present in the data base.

Note that the process of querying the data base to see if *antecedent* is true might result in the consultation of another "backward" implication rule. In general, we may chain through any number of such rules to make a deduction. From this process, the name of the technique is derived.

Let us look at an example. In the case of our Fido example above, our data base will contain the backward chaining rules **(<– (mammal ?x) (dog ?x))** and **(<– (dog ?x) (poodle ?x))**, in addition to the fact **(poodle fido)**. Now when we retrieve the request **(mammal fido)**, the retriever accesses the first of these rules. This causes it to recursively retrieve on **(dog fido)**. Doing so will result in accessing the second rule, and thereby retrieving on **(poodle fido)**. This is known to be true, so the query succeeds.

22.4.2. A Deductive Retriever Implementation

Building such a deductive retriever is simple. All we need to do is supplement our normal querying operation with a component that chases down backward implications. This component will query the data base with the pattern (<– *request* **?antecedent)**. This request will match all the backward implications that can imply the original request. Then we need only get the binding of **?antecedent** in the result of each match. This binding represents a fact, which, if true, implies the original request. We determine if this fact is true simply by trying to retrieve it using the deductive retriever.

We will call our deductive retriever **retrieve**. The only complication in it is that the binding of **?antecedent** may contain variables whose bindings are known. For example, if we unify (<– **(mammal fido) ?antecedent)** with (<– **(mammal ?x) (dog ?x))**, the binding of **?antecedent** would be **(dog ?x)**. We do not want to continue the search using this pattern, though, but with **(dog fido)**. So we need to substitute all variables in the binding of **antecedent** with their values, if they have any, before doing the recursive step of the retrieval. **retrieve** relies on the routine **substitute—vars** to do this:

```
(defun retrieve (request data-base)
   (nconc
      (fast-query request data-base)
      (mapcan #'(lambda (bindings)
                   (mapcar
                      #'(lambda (rbindings)
                           (append rbindings bindings))
                      (retrieve
                         (substitute-vars
                            (get-binding '?antecedent
                                          bindings)
                            bindings)
                         data-base)))
         (fast-query '(<- ,request ?antecedent)
                     data-base)))))
```

Note that we use **fast—query** to do the explicit interrogation of the data base. Also, it is safe to **nconc** together the results of the explicit and deductive parts, because both generate fresh s-expressions as their results. Finally, we indiscriminately collect together the results of the deductive component; as a result, some of our answers will have bindings for variables that did not occur in the request. (See Exercise 1.)

Now for **substitute—vars**. This is a fairly standard recursive function that goes down an s-expression until it finds a pattern matching variable. When it finds one, it returns the binding if there is one. The only thing to be careful about is that the binding of the variable may itself contain substitutable variables. For example, suppose our binding list is

((?antecedent (loves john ?y)) (?y ?z) (?z mary))

If we substitute variables in the binding of **?antecedent**, we will get **(loves john ?z)**. However, we do not want to retrieve on this, but on **(loves john mary)**.

This difficulty is easy to overcome. We merely call **substitute—vars** recursively on the variable's binding. Here is the complete function:

```
(defun substitute-vars (item bindings)
    (cond ((atom item) item)
          ((pattern-var-p item)
           (let ((binding (get-binding item bindings)))
             (if binding
                 (substitute-vars binding bindings)
                 item)))
          (t (cons (substitute-vars (car item) bindings)
                   (substitute-vars (cdr item) bindings)))))
```

Now let us test **retrieve** on the example used to motivate it above. First, let us load up a data base:

```
-> (index '(<- (mammal ?x) (dog ?x)) '*d-b1*)
(<-)
-> (index '(<- (dog ?x) (poodle ?x)) '*d-b1*)
(<-)
-> (index '(poodle fido) '*d-b1*)
(POODLE <-)
->
```

A literal examination of the data base using **fast-query** should show that the item **(mammal fido)** is not present:

```
-> (fast-query '(mammal fido) '*d-b1*)
NIL
->
```

Now let us see if our deductive retriever can infer the answer:

```
-> (retrieve '(mammal fido) '*d-b1*)
((((*VAR* ANTECEDENT) (POODLE (*VAR* #:VAR40))) ((*VAR*
#:VAR40) FIDO) ((*VAR* ANTECEDENT) (DOG (*VAR* #:VAR31)))
((*VAR* #:VAR31) FIDO)))
->
```

The result shows that the request is true, with no bindings required. (All the variables present in the answer are not from the request.) This is equivalent to what would be returned if the fact were literally present.

While deductive data base management is an attractive technique, the programmer is advised to use it cautiously. An unbounded amount of computation may be triggered by a simple query. Thus the convenience of hiding all the details of a computation may result in hiding a lot of computation one would rather not perform.

22.5. Summary

(1) Associative data base management involves updating and accessing a collection of s-expressions in a flexible fashion.

(2) We can use pattern matching as the basis for an associative data base system. Facts are represented as patterns; patterns are also used to query the data base. Patterns used in the latter fashion are called *requests*. The retriever will return all items in the data base that can be unified with the specified request.

(3) We can make accessing an associative data base faster by using *indexing*.

(4) We can extend a data base manager to do automatic deduction. A *deductive retriever* is one which can infer items not explicitly present in the data base.

(5) A technique used to implement deduction is called *backward chaining*. With this technique, implications are stored as facts in the data base. When a request is retrieved, these implications are used to suggest items that may imply the request. These items are then recursively retrieved from the data base. If one of them turns out to be true, this confirms the original request.

Exercises

(1) Modify the retriever so that its answers do not contain references to variables that do not occur in requests.

(2) An alternative means of efficient storage for a data base is to keep the data base in a hash table. Write a version of **fast–query** that uses the Common LISP hash table feature, described in Chapter 18, in place of property lists, to speed up retrieval.

(3) While backward chaining has its uses, it may be inefficient. For example, suppose the data base contains many items of the form

(<– (mammal ?x) (dog ?x))

(<– (mammal ?x) (cat ?x))

(<– (mammal ?x) (horse ?x))

Now when we retrieve on **(mammal fido)**, a deductive retriever will look for *all* backward implications that might be useful. So our retriever will try to deduce that Fido is a cat and that he is a horse. Both efforts will fail, of course, but only after a potentially arbitrary amount of effort.

It may be more efficient in such cases to have explicitly in the data base the fact that Fido is a mammal. However, we would like to avoid the effort of explicitly adding the proposition that something is a mammal whenever we add one asserting that something is a dog.

We can accomplish this through a technique called *forward chaining.* In forward chaining, we use implication rules to add new information to the data base upon *learning* a fact; this is in contrast to backward chaining, in which we use implications to deduce something upon *retrieving* a request.

We implement forward chaining using "forward" implications. For example, we could represent the forward implication that dogs are mammals as **(–> (dog ?x) (mammal ?x))**. Now whenever we add an item to our data base, we will check to see if we can unify it with the left-hand side of any forward implication. If so, then we will add the right-hand side to the data base. Thus if the above rule were in the data base, and we add the proposition **(dog fido)**, the data base manager will automatically add the assertion **(mammal fido)**.

Modify the data base manager to allow forward chaining. Be sure that your code really *chains* forward. That is, adding an item to a data base may entail adding another item, and adding that one may entail adding yet another item, and so on.

(4)   We currently have no easy way to answer questions like "Who is a famous movie actress who is also a political activist?" We could represent this logically as an expression of the form **(and (actress ?x) (activist ?x))**. However, if we merely queried a data base with this request, it would fail even if **(actress janefonda)** and **(activist janefonda)** were both in the data base. Why?.

Requests of this form are sometimes called *conjunctive requests,* or *conjunctive subgoals.* Write a version of the retriever that handles conjunctive requests properly.

Appendix A

Summary of Common LISP Functions

For each Common LISP function, we present a typical instance of a call to that function. Generic arguments are shown in italics, where the argument name suggests the type of the corresponding actual argument. For example, (**member** *object list*) indicates that **member** takes two arguments, the first of which can be any LISP object, and the second of which must be a list. Optional arguments are surrounded by square brackets – [and]. Indefinite repetition is indicated by forms surrounded by hyphens. For example, –*integers*– means that an indefinite sequence of integer-type arguments is permitted. Permissible keyword arguments are noted in the text. Arguments to special functions and macros are normally assumed *not* to be evaluated, unless otherwise noted. The abbreviation "iff" is used to mean "if and only if".

1. Data Structure Access and Manipulation Functions

The following functions allow one to create, access, and manipulate the various types of LISP data structures.

396

1.1. General Data Structure Predicates

1.1.1. Data Type Determination Functions

(arrayp *object***)**
> Returns **t** iff *object* is an array.

(atom *object***)**
> Returns **t** iff *object* is not a cons. **(atom nil)** returns **t**.

(characterp *object***)**
> Returns **t** iff *object* is a character.

(commonp *object***)**
> Returns **t** iff *object* is any standard Common LISP data type.

(compiled–function–p *object***)**
> Returns **t** iff *object* is a compiled code object.

(complex *object***)**
> Returns **t** iff *object* is a complex number.

(consp *object***)**
> Returns **t** iff *object* is a cons. **(consp nil)** is **nil**.

(constantp *object***)**
> Returns non-**nil** if *object* always evaluates to itself, i. e., if it is a number, character, string, bit-vector, keyword, constant declared by **defconstant** (including **nil**, **t** and **pi**) or a list beginning with **quote**.

(floatp *object***)**
> Returns **t** iff *object* is a floating-point number.

(functionp *object***)**
> Returns **t** iff *object* is something potentially suitable for applying to arguments. This includes any and all symbols, lambda expressions, anything returned by the special function **function**, and anything returned by **compile** when its first argument is **nil**.

(hash–table–p *object***)**
> Returns **t** iff *object* is a hash table.

(integerp *object***)**
> Returns **t** iff *object* is an integer.

(listp *object***)**
> Returns **t** iff *object* is a cons or **nil**.

(null *object***)**
> Returns **t** iff *object* is **nil**.

(numberp *object***)**
> Returns **t** iff *object* is a number.

(packagep *object***)**
> Returns **t** iff *object* is a package.

(pathnamep *object***)**
> Returns **t** iff *object* is a pathname.

(rational *object***)**
> Returns **t** iff *object* is a rational number (i. e., a ratio or an integer).

(readtablep *object***)**
> Returns **t** iff *object* is a readtable.

(streamp *object***)**
> Returns **t** iff *object* is a stream.

(stringp *object***)**
> Returns **t** iff *object* is a string.

(symbolp *object***)**
> Returns **t** iff *object* is a symbol.

(vectorp *object***)**
> Returns **t** iff *object* is a vector.

(typep *object type***)**
> Returns true iff *object* is of the type specified by *type*. *type* can be any type specification that does not involve the specifier **function** or **values.**

(type–of *object***)**
> Returns a type of *object;* it is desirable for an implementation to return the most specific useful type that is applicable.

1.1.2. Data Structure Comparison Functions

(**eq** *object1 object2*)

Returns **t** iff *object1* and *object2* are the same LISP object. It is possible in an implementation of Common LISP that a number or character may be represented by different LISP objects at different times. Therefore, (**eq 3 3**) may be true or false, depending on the implementation.

(**eql** *object1 object2*)

Returns **t** iff *object1* and *object2* are either **eq**, or if they are the same number or the same character. Note that 3.0 and 3 are different numbers, although implementations are allowed to consider as **eql** single and double precision floating-point numbers of the same value. **eql** does not guarantee the equivalence of identical strings.

(**equal** *object1 object2*)

Return **t** iff *object1* and *object2* have the same structure. Numbers and characters are compared as for **eql**, symbols as for **eq**. Two arrays are **equal** only if they are **eq**, except for strings and bit-vectors, which are compared element by element. In general, two objects are usually **equal** if they are printed the same way.

(**equalp** *object1 object2*)

Returns **t** iff the objects are **equal**, if they are characters that are **char—equal**, if they are numbers with the same numeric value (regardless of type), or if all of their respective components are **equalp**.

(**not** *object*)

Return **t** iff *object* is **nil**.

1.2. Sequences

Sequences comprise both lists and vectors. Since these both are ordered sets of elements, many functions are applicable to both types. The functions in this section are "generic" sequence functions that can apply to both lists and vectors.

Many sequence functions need to determine if an element of a sequence matches an item. Normally, the function used to make the comparison is **eql**; it is applied to an element of the sequence and the item the elements are to be compared with. However, sometimes it is desirable to alter the details of this comparison. For example, we might want to use a function other than **eql**, or we may want to examine only a portion of the sequence, or we may want to use some component of each element rather than the element itself for the comparison. To accommodate these needs, many sequence functions accept the keyword arguments **:test**, **:test–not**, **:start**, **:end**, **:from–end** and **:key**. **:test** is used to supply a function to be used for the comparison; if the **:test–not** keyword argument is specified instead, the comparison will be considered true if the function supplied returns false. If the **:key** argument is specified, it is applied to the element of the sequence and the value it returns is used in the comparison (it is supposed to return a component of the element). **:start** and **:end** specify the portion of the sequence to be searched (i. e., the subsequence beginning with the element indexed by the **:start** argument but ending before the element indexed by the **:end** argument. **:from–end** can be used to specify the direction of the search: A non-**nil** argument means to search from right to left; normally, the search is conducted from left to right.

If two sequences are involved, the keyword arguments **:start1**, **:end1**, **:start2**, and **:end2** are typically allowed.

Often, sequence functions have **–if** and **–if–not** variants. These do not take an item as an argument, but instead, a predicate of one argument. These examine the sequence specified for an element satisfying the predicate.

We will use the term "test" below to refer either to the comparison between an item and an element of a sequence (possibly filtered through the application of some **:key** keyword argument) or to the application of a predicate argument to an element of a sequence.

1.2.1. Sequence Creation Functions

(copy–seq *sequence***)**

> Returns a new sequence **equalp** to *sequence*.

(make–sequence *type size***)**

> Returns a new sequence of type *type* of length *length*. If a **:initial–element** keyword argument is specified, it is used to initialize the elements of the sequence. It defaults to an implementation-dependent value.

(subseq *sequence start* [*end*]**)**

> Returns a new sequence equivalent to the subsequence of *sequence* beginning at *start* and ending at *end*.

1.2.2. Sequence Predicates

(every *predicate –sequences–***)**

> *predicate* is applied to successive elements of the sequences (so *predicate* must be a function of as many arguments as there are sequences supplied to **every**). **every** returns **nil** as soon as any application of *predicate* returns **nil**. If the end of a sequence is reached without this happening, **every** returns a non-**nil** value.

(notany *predicate –sequences–***)**

> Like **every**, except that it stops and returns **nil** as soon as any application of *predicate* returns a non-**nil** value; it returns a non-**nil** value if the end of a sequence is reached.

(notevery *predicate –sequences–***)**

> Like **every**, except that it stops and returns a non-**nil** value as soon as any application of *predicate* returns **nil**; it returns a **nil** if the end of a sequence is reached.

(some *predicate –sequences–***)**

> Like **every**, except that it stops as soon as any application of *predicate* returns a non-**nil** value; **some** returns that value. It returns a **nil** if the end of a sequence is reached.

1.2.3. Sequence Accessing Functions

(count *item sequence***)**
(count–if *test sequence***)**
(count–if–not *test sequence***)**

> Returns the number of elements in the sequence satisfying the test. The normal sequence keyword arguments are allowed.

(elt *sequence index***)**

> Returns the *index* element of *sequence*, the first element being 0.

(find *item sequence***)**
(find–if *test sequence***)**
(find–if–not *test sequence***)**

> *sequence* is searched for an occurrence of an element satisfying the test; the first one that matches is returned. The normal sequence keyword arguments are allowed.

(length *sequence***)**

Returns the number of elements in the sequence. If the sequence is a vector, and has a fill pointer, then only the "filled" length is computed.

(mismatch *sequence1 sequence2***)**

Returns the first position in the sequences where they fail to match, or **nil** if they do match. The normal sequence keyword arguments are allowed.

(position *item sequence***)**
(position–if *test sequence***)**
(position–if–not *test sequence***)**

The index of the first item in *sequence* satisfying the test is returned. The normal sequence keyword arguments are allowed.

(search *sequence1 sequence2***)**

sequence2 is searched for a subsequence that matches *sequence1*. The index of the first element of the first such subsequence in *sequence2* is returned. The normal sequence keyword arguments are allowed.

1.2.4. Sequence Manipulation Functions

(concatenate *result-type –sequences–***)**

Returns a new sequence of type *result-type* containing all the elements of all the sequences, in order.

(delete *item sequence***)**
(delete–if *test sequence***)**
(delete–if–not *test sequence***)**

Elements matching *item* are destructively removed from the top level of *sequence*. The resulting modified list is returned. Thus, **delete** is a destructive version of **remove**. In addition to the normal sequence keyword arguments, the keyword **:count** is allowed. If a **:count** keyword argument of *number* is specified, then only the first *number* occurrences of *item* are deleted.

(delete–duplicates *sequence***)**

Like **remove–duplicates**, except that *sequence* may be altered in the process.

402

(fill *sequence item***)**

> *sequence* is destructively modified by replacing each element by the value *item*. **fill** allows the keyword arguments **:start** and **:end**.

(map *result-type function –sequences–***)**

> *function* is applied to successive elements of the sequences, and a sequence of type *result-type* comprising the computed values is returned. If *result-type* is **nil**, then **map** will return **nil** (i. e., the computation is done only for its side effects).

(merge *result-type sequence1 sequence2 comp-pred***)**

> The sequences are destructively merged into a sequence of type *result-type* (which, of course, must be either **list** or **vector**). The elements of the two sequences are compared according to *comp-pred*. The result, which is guaranteed to be stable, is returned. The keyword **:key** is allowed.

(nreverse *sequence***)**

> Like **reverse**, but may modify its argument. The modified argument is not guaranteed to be the reversed sequence, though, so the user should always use the value returned by **nreverse**.

(nsubstitute *newitem olditem sequence***)**
(nsubstitute–if *newitem test sequence***)**
(nsubstitute–if–not *newitem test sequence***)**

> This is just like **substitute**, except that *sequence* may be altered in the process.

(reduce *function sequence***)**

> *function* is applied to the first two arguments of *sequence*. It is then applied to the resulting value and the next argument, and so on, until all the arguments have been combined by *function*. The resulting value is returned. For example, **(reduce #'– '(1 2 3 4))** computes the same thing as does **(– (– (– 1 2) 3) 4)**, i. e., –8. **reduce** allows the standard sequence keyword arguments.

(remove *item sequence***)**
(remove–if *test sequence***)**
(remove–if–not *test sequence***)**

> Returns a new sequence having the same elements as *sequence* except for those elements satisfying the test. In addition to the standard sequence keyword arguments, the keyword **:count** is allowed. If a **:count** keyword argument of *number* is specified, then only the first *number* occurrences of *item* are removed.

(remove–duplicates *sequence***)**

Returns a sequence having the same elements as *sequence* except that duplicates of elements occurring earlier in the sequence are not included. *sequence* is left unchanged. **remove–duplicates** does not necessarily produce a new sequence. For example, it may return *sequence* as its result if this already has no duplicates in it. The standard sequence keyword arguments are allowed.

(replace *sequence1 sequence2***)**

sequence1 is destructively modifying by replacing its elements with the corresponding elements of *sequence2*. **replace** allows the keyword arguments **start1**, **end1**, **start2** and **end2**. **replace** assumes that the two sequences are either **eq**, or totally unrelated objects. If they are not **eq**, but share some structure, the result is unpredictable.

(reverse *sequence***)**

Returns a sequence with the same elements as *sequence,* but in the reverse order. **reverse** never modifies its argument, and always creates a new list, while **nreverse** modifies its argument, and may return the modified list as its value.

(sort *sequence predicate***)**

sequence is destructively sorted according to the order determined by *predicate*. *predicate* should be a function of two arguments, and should return non-**nil** iff the first argument comes strictly before the other, according to some metric. **sort** accepts the keyword **:key**. The sort is not guaranteed to be stable (see **stable–sort**).

(stable–sort *sequence predicate***)**

This is just like **sort**, except that the sort is guaranteed to be stable.

(substitute *newitem olditem sequence***)**
(substitute–if *newitem test sequence***)**
(substitute–if–not *newitem test sequence***)**

Returns a sequence having the same elements as *sequence* except that those elements satisfying the test are replaced by *newitem*. *sequence* is left unaltered. In addition to the standard sequence keyword arguments, the keyword **:count** is allowed. If a **:count** keyword argument of *number* is specified, then only the first *number* elements are altered.

1.3. Lists

1.3.1. List Creation Functions

(append –*lists*–**)**
Returns the list formed by joining the elements of the lists together.

(cons *object1 object2***)**
Returns a cons whose **car** is *object1* and whose **cdr** is *object2*.

(butlast *list* [*n*]**)**
Creates and returns a list with the same elements as **list**, but missing the last *n* (which defaults to 1). If *list* has fewer than *n* elements, **nil** is returned.

(copy–list *list***)**
Returns a structure **equal** to *exp* but made of new **cons**es. Only the top level of the list is copied.

(copy–tree *list***)**
Copies a list recursively. **copy–tree** does not preserve shared structures or circularies.

(list –*objects*–**)**
Returns a list of the objects.

(list∗ –*objects*–**)**
Returns a list made by **cons**ing all but the last argument onto the last. E. g., **(list∗ 'a 'b 'c 'd)** returns **(a b c . d)**; **(list∗ 'a 'b 'c '(d e f))** returns **(a b c d e f)**; **(list∗ 'a)** returns **a**.

(make–list *size***)**
This returns a new list of *size* elements. If a **:initial–element** keyword argument is specified, it is used to fill the elements of the list. Otherwise, **nil** is used.

1.3.2. List Predicates

(endp *list***)**
This is the recommended way to test for the end of a list. **endp** is true of **nil**, but false of conses, and generates an error when applied to any other argument.

(member *object list***)**
(member–if *predicate list***)**
(member–if–not *predicate list***)**
>   Returns the sublist of *list* beginning with the first element that satisfies the test, or **nil** if none does. The "test" is the same as that described in the section on sequences. As with sequences, the default test for **member** is **eql; member** also accepts the keyword arguments **:test, :test–not** and **:key. member–if** and **member–if–not** accept **:key**. See the description of sequence functions above for further clarification.

(tailp *list1 list2***)**
>   Returns *list1* if a cons **eq** to *list1* is found by **cdr**ing down *list2* zero or more times, and **nil** otherwise.

(tree–equal *list1 list2***)**
>   Returns true if the two objects have the identical cons structure with identical elements. Unlike **equal, tree–equal** does not examine the components of any objects other than conses.

1.3.3. List Accessing Functions

(car *list***)**
>   Returns the first element of *list.*

(cdr *list***)**
>   Returns the sublist of *list* after its first element.

(c...r *list***)**
>   Here the **...** represents a sequence of up to four **a**'s and **d**'s. This is the equivalent to applying the corresponding sequence of **car**s and **cdr**s. For example, **(cadar x)** is equivalent to **(car (cdr (car x)))**.

(last *list***)**
>   Returns the last cons in *list.*

(list–length *list***)**
>   Returns the number of elements on the top level of *list.*

(nth *number list***)**
>   Returns the *number*-th element of *list,* assuming zero-based index. Thus **(nth 0 l)** is equivalent to **(car l)**.

(first *list***)**
(second *list***)**
(third *list***)**
(fourth *list***)**
(fifth *list***)**
(sixth *list***)**
(seventh *list***)**
(eighth *list***)**
(ninth *list***)**
(tenth *list***)**

These functions are a convenient way to access the elements of a list. **first** is the same as **car**, **second** is the same as **cadr**, and so on.

(nthcdr *number list***)**

Returns the result of **cdr**ing down *list number* times. If *number* is less than 0, **(cons nil** *list***)** is returned.

(rest *list***)**

This is the same as **cdr**, but is meant to complement **first**.

1.3.4. List Manipulation Functions

(ldiff *list1 list2***)**

Returns a list of all elements in *list1* that are not in *list2*. *list2* must be a "tail" of *list1*, that is, **eq** to some sublist of *list1*. The value returned is always a new list structure, unless *list2* is not a tail of *list1*, in which case *list1* is returned.

(nconc *–lists–***)**

nconc is like **append**, except that it destructively changes the last cons of each of the lists to point to the next list.

(nreconc *list object***)**

Computes the same thing as **(nconc (nreverse** *list***)** *object***)**, but may be more efficient.

(nsubst *new old list***)**
(nsubst–if *new test list***)**
(nsubst–if–not *new test list***)**

This is just like **subst** (below), except that *list* is destructively altered to produce the desired result.

(pop *place***)**   [*Macro*]

The argument should be some location acceptable to **setf** that contains a list. The list stored in *place* is reduced to its **cdr**; its **car** is returned.

(push *item place***)**   [*Macro*]

place should be some location acceptable to **setf** that contains a list. *item* is evaluated, and the resulting value is **cons**ed onto the front of this list. The new list is stored back in *place* and returned as the value of the call to **push**

(pushnew *item place***)**   [*Macro*]

This is just like **push**, except the value of *item* is **cons**ed onto the list in **place** only if it is not already there. The test is done with **eql**. This can be overridden by specifying the comparison function using the **:test** keyword argument; alternatively, supplying a **:test−not** argument will specify a comparison function that will be used to determine if the elements do not match. Furthermore, the **:key** keyword argument can be used to specify a function that will return a component of *item* to use for the comparison.

(revappend *list1 list2***)**

Computes the same thing as **(append (reverse** *list1***)** *list2***)**, but may be more efficient.

(rplaca *cons object***)**

The **car** of *cons* is actually changed to *object*, and the resulting list is returned.

(rplacd *cons object***)**

The **cdr** of *cons* is actually changed to *object*, and the resulting list is returned.

(subst *new old list***)**
(subst−if *new test list***)**
(subst−if−not *new test list***)**

list is descended recursively. Each cons or atom satisfying the test is replaced by *new*. The test is as described in the introduction to sequences above. **subst** accepts the keyword arguments **:test**, **:test−not** and **:key**; **subst−if** and **subst−if−not** also accept **:key**. These are interpreted as they are for sequences.

1.3.5. Association List Functions

An *association list* is a list of the form
        ((*key1* . *value1*) (*key2* . *value2*) ... (*keyn* . *valuen*))

(acons *key datum assoc-list*)
> Returns a new assocication list by **cons**ing *key* and *datum* together, and then **cons**ing the result onto *assoc-list*.

(assoc *object assoc-list*)
(assoc–if *predicate assoc-list*)
(assoc–if–not *predicate assoc-list*)
> Return the first top level element of *assoc-list* whose **car** satisfies the test. The test is performed as for sequences; similarly, **assoc** allows the keyword arguments **:test**, **:test–not** and **:key**; these have the same interpretation as they do for sequences.

(copy–alist *assoc-list*)
> This is used for copying association lists. It copies the top level of a list, just like **copy–list** above, but also makes copies of the association list's elements.

(pairlis *list1 list2* [*assoc-list*])
> Returns a new association list created by pairing the corresponding elements of the two lists. If the optional argument is provided, the new association list is added to the front of it.

(rassoc *exp assoc-list*)
(rassoc–if *predicate assoc-list*)
(rassoc–if–not *predicate assoc-list*)
> These are just like the **assoc** functions, except they search for a **cdr** that satisfies the test, rather than a **car**.

(sublis *assoc-list list*)
> Returns a list just like *list* with every occurrence of a key in *assoc-list* replaced by its corresponding value. *list* is descended recursively to do the substitution. **sublis** is non-destructive. It accepts the keyword arguments **:test**, **:test–not** and **:key**, which have the same interpretation as they do for sequences.

1.3.6. Set Functions

Some functions treat lists as if they represented finite sets.

(adjoin *item list*)

> *item* is **cons**ed onto *list* only if it is not already there. The test is made using **eql**, although the keyword arguments **:test** and **:test–not** allow this default to be changed. The keyword argument **:key** is also allowed. If one is used, it will be applied both to *item* and to the element of the list before a comparison is attempted.

(intersection *list1 list2*)

> Returns a new list that contains all those elements that are members of both *list1* and *list2*. If neither list has duplicates, there will be no duplicates in the result; however, if either argument contains duplicate elements, there is no telling whether the result will or will not have duplicates. The keywords **:test**, **:test–not**, and **:key** are allowed, and are interpreted as for sequences.

(nintersection *list1 list2*)

> This is just like **intersection**, except that the arguments may be altered.

(nset–exclusive–or *list1 list2*)

> This is a destructive version of **set–exclusive–or** (see below).

(nset–difference *list1 list2*)

> This is a destructive version of **set–difference** (see below).

(nunion *list1 list2*)

> This is just like **union** (see below) except that the arguments may be altered.

(set–difference *list1 list2*)

> Returns the list of those elements of *list1* that do not appear in *list2*. The keywords **:test**, **:test–not**, and **:key** are allowed, and are interpreted as for sequences.

(set–exclusive–or *list1 list2*)

> Returns a list of those elements that appear in one of the two lists, but not in both. The keywords **:test**, **:test–not**, and **:key** are allowed, and are interpreted as for sequences.

410

(subsetp *list1 list2*)
This predicate is true if every element of *list1* matches an element of *list2*. The keywords **:test**, **:test-not**, and **:key** are allowed, and are interpreted as for sequences.

(union *list1 list2*)
Returns a new list that contains all those elements that are members of either *list1* or *list2*. If neither list has duplicates, there will be no duplicates in the result; however, if either argument contains duplicate elements, there is no telling whether the result will or will not have duplicates. The keywords **:test**, **:test-not**, and **:key** are allowed, and are interpreted as for sequences.

1.4. Symbols and Packages

1.4.1. Symbol and Package Creation Functions

(copy-symbol *symbol* [*flag*])
Returns an uninterned symbol with the same print name as *symbol*. If *flag* is non-**nil**, then the value, function definition, and property list of the new symbol are made the same as those of *symbol*.

(gensym [*x*])
Returns a new uninterned symbol with a made-up print name. The print name consists of a prefix followed by a number. The prefix defaults to **G**, and the number is incremented by one each time **gensym** is called. If *x* is a string, then it is used as the new default prefix; if it is a number, the internal counter is set to that number.

(gentemp [*prefix* [*package*]])
gentemp is like **gensym** except that it interns the symbol in the specified package (or the current package, if a package not is specified). **gentemp** guarantees that the symbol will be different from any symbol already in the package by incrementing its counter as many times as needed for this to be the case. The default prefix is **T**. If the user supplies a prefix, it is not remembered from call to call.

(make-package *name*)
Returns a new package named *name*. **make-package** accepts the keyword arguments **:nicknames** and **:use**. The **:nicknames** arguments should be a list of strings (or symbols) to be used as alternative names for the package. The **:use** argument should be a list of package to be used by this package. If not supplied, the single package **lisp** is used.

411

1.4.2. Symbol and Package Predicates

(boundp *symbol***)**
> Returns **nil** if the special or global variable referred to by *symbol* has no value, and non-**nil** otherwise.

(fboundp *symbol***)**
> Returns **nil** if the *symbol* has no global function definition, and non-**nil** otherwise.

(keywordp *object***)**
> Returns true iff *object* is a keyword.

(macro–function *symbol***)**
> Returns the macro expansion function of *symbol*, or **nil** if *symbol* is not a macro.

(special–form–p *symbol***)**
> Returns a function that can be used to interpret a special form beginning with the special function *symbol*, or **nil** if *symbol* is not a special function.

1.4.3. Symbol and Package Accessing Functions

(documentation *symbol doc-type***)**
> Returns the documentation string of type *doc-type* associated with *symbol*. A documentation string may be attached to a symbol by one of a number of functions that associate important features with symbols. Such actions include giving a symbol a function definition, defining it to be a particular kind of variable, making the symbol the name of a structure or of a data type, or attaching a **setf** method to the symbol. Each of these actions can associate a different documentation string with the symbol. The possible types of documentation strings are **variable** (used by **defconstant**, **defparameter** and **defvar**), **function** (used by **defun**, **defmacro** and **define–modify–macro**), **structure** (used by **defstruct**), **type** (used by **deftype**) and **setf** (used by **define–setf–method** and **defsetf**).

(get *symbol propname* [*default*]**))**
> Returns the value associated with property **eq** to *propname* in *symbol*'s property list. If none is found, *default* is returned, which itself defaults to **nil**.

(getf *place propname* [*default*]**)**
> This is the same as **get**, except that the property list is expected to be stored in *place*, rather than be attached to a symbol.

(get–properties *place prop-list***)**
> This is like **getf**, except that the the second argument is a list of properties. **get–properties** searches the property list in *place* until it finds one that is in *prop-list*. Three values are returned: The property found, its value, and the tail of the property list from the point of the match. All three values are **nil** if there is no match.

(package–name *package***)**
> Returns the string that is the name of *package*.

(package–nicknames *package***)**
> Returns the list of nicknames of *package*.

(package–shadowing–symbols *package***)**
> Returns a list of the symbols in *package* that have been declared to be shadowed symbols by **shadow** or **shadowing–import**.

(package–use–list *package***)**
> Returns the list of the packages used by *package*.

(package–used–by–list *package***)**
> Returns a list of the packages that use *package*.

(symbol–function *symbol***)**
> Returns the (global) function definition of *symbol*.

(symbol–name *symbol***)**
> Returns the string that is the print name of *symbol*.

(symbol–package *symbol***)**
> Returns the package that owns *symbol*.

(symbol–plist *symbol***)**
> Returns the property list of *symbol*.

(symbol–value *symbol***)**
> Returns the value of *symbol*; if *symbol* has no value, an error occurs.

1.4.4. Symbol and Package Manipulation Functions

(defconstant *symbol init-val* [*string*]**)**

> *symbol* is declared to be special, and is assigned the value *init-val*. It is an error to attempt to change the value of *symbol* thereafter. *string* is stored with the symbol under the documentation type **variable** (see **documentation**).

(defparameter *symbol init-val* [*string*]**)**

> *symbol* is declared to be special, and is assigned the value *init-val*. *string* is stored with the symbol under the documentation type **variable** (see **documentation**).

(defvar *symbol* [*init-val* [*string*]]**)**

> *symbol* is declared to be special. If *init-val* is supplied, *symbol* will be assigned that value unless it already has a value. If it has a value already, *init-val* will not even be evaluated. *string* is stored with the symbol under the documentation type **variable** (see **documentation**).

(do–all–symbols (*symbol* [*result*])   [*Macro*]
     –declarations–
     –forms–   )

> This is like **do–symbols** below, except that all symbols of all packages are examined.

(do–external–symbols (*symbol* [*package* [*result*]])   [*Macro*]
     –declarations–
     –forms–   )

> This is just like **do–symbols** below, except that only the external symbols of the package are examined.

(do–symbols (*symbol* [*package* [*result*]])   [*Macro*]
     –declarations–
     –forms–   )

> A new variable is created for *symbol*, and is assigned successive symbols of *package* (which defaults to the current package); for each assignment, the forms are evaluated in order. Then the value of *result* (evaluated with *symbol* assigned the value **nil**) is returned. If *result* is not supplied, **nil** is returned. **return** can be used to exit from the computation before completion.

(export *symbols* [*package*]**)**

> *symbols* should be a list of symbols, or a single symbol. The symbol or symbols specified are made accessible in *package* (which defaults to the current package) as external symbols. Returns **t**.

(find–all–symbols *string***)**
> Returns a list of every symbol in every package with name *string*.

(find–package *name***)**
> Returns the package whose name or nickname is *name*, or **nil** if none exists.

(find–symbol *string* [*package*]**)**
> This is the same as **intern** (see below), except that it does not create a new symbol if one is not found. Instead, **find–symbol** returns **nil** in this situation.

(fmakunbound *symbol***)**
> *symbol* is made not to have a global function definition.

(import *symbols* [*package*]**)**
> *symbols* should be a list of symbols, or a single symbol. The symbol or symbols specified are made internal symbols of *package* (which defaults to the current package). If a symbol of the same name is already accessible in *package,* a correctable error is signaled. Returns **t**.

(in–package *name***)**
> *name* becomes the current package; it is created if it does not already exist. The keyword arguments **:use** and **:nicknames** have the same interpretation as for **make–package**, except that if the package already exists, the existing attributes are updated..

(intern *string* [*package*]**)**
> The package (including symbols inherited from other packages) is searched for a symbol named *string.* If one is found, it is returned. Otherwise, a new symbol with that name is created and *package* is made its home package. The symbol will be an internal symbol, unless the package is the **keyword** package, in which case the symbol is made external. If *package* is not supplied, it defaults to the current package. Two values are returned. The first is the symbol found or created. The second is a value indicating the status of that symbol, to be interpreted as follows: **nil** => no existing symbol was found (i. e., the symbol returned had to be created), **:internal** => the symbol found is directly present in *package*, **:external** => the symbol found is an external symbol of *package,* **:inherited** => the symbol found was inherited from some other package.

(list–all–packages)
Returns a list of all packages that currently exist.

(makunbound *symbol*)
The global or special variable referred to by *symbol* is made not to have a value.

(provide *name*)
A module named *name* is added to **∗modules∗**, the list of currently loaded modules.

(psetq –[*symbol form*]–) [*Macro*]
This is like **setq** (see below), except that the assignments are done "in parallel", i. e., all the forms are evaluated first, and then the assignments are made.

(remf *place indicator*)
Like **remprop** (see below) except that the property list is expected to be found stored in *place,* rather than be associated with a symbol.

(remprop *symbol prop-name*)
The property *prop-name* and its associated value are removed from the property list of *symbol.* A non-**nil** value is returned if such a property was found, and **nil** otherwise.

(rename–package *package new-name* [*new-nicknames*])
package is renamed *new-name*, and its nicknames are set to *new-nicknames*, which defaults to **nil**.

(require *name* [*pathname*])
require assures that the module named *name* is loaded. If it is not already loaded, it will load it by loading the files specified by *pathname* (which is either a single pathname or a list of pathnames). If *pathname* is not supplied, or is **nil**, the files to be loaded will be determined in some implementation-dependent way.

(set *symbol form*)
The value of the special or global variable referred to by *symbol* is set to *form,* and that value is returned.

(setq –[*symbol form*]–) [*Special function*]
symbol, which is not evaluated, is set to *form*. **setq** allows any number of *symbol-form* pairs, and sets the first to the value of the second. For example, **(setq x 'a y 'b)** sets **x** to **a** and **y** to **b**. The

value of the last form is returned as the value of the call to **setq**. If no arguments are supplied, **setq** returns **nil**.

(shadow *symbols* [*package*]**)**

symbols should be a list of symbols, or a single symbol. *package* is searched for symbols with the same names as the specified symbols. If such a symbol is not found to be directly present in the package, a new symbol of this name is created and made an internal symbol of the package. It is also placed on the shadowing-symbols list of *package*. If such a symbol is already directly present, nothing is done. The shadowing symbols take precedence over any other symbols of the same name in the package. Returns **t**.

(shadowing–import *symbols* [*package*]**)**

Just like **import**, except that an error is not signaled if there is a name conflict. Instead, the symbols are placed on the shadowing-symbols list of *package*. The shadowing symbols take precedence over any other symbols of the same name in the package; these will be uninterned if they are directly present in the package.

(unexport *symbols* [*package*]**)**

symbols should be a list of symbols, or a single symbol. The symbol or symbols specified, which should all be directly accessible in *package*, are made internal symbols of *package* (which defaults to the current package). It is an error if a symbol is not directly accessible in *package*. Returns **t**.

(unintern *symbol* [*package*]**)**

If *symbol* is found in *package* (which defaults to the current package), it is removed. In addition, if *package* is the home package of that symbol, the symbol is made to have no home package. Also, if the symbol was on *package*'s shadowing-symbols list, it is removed. **t** is returned if the symbol is found and removed, and **nil** otherwise.

(unuse–package *packages* [*package*]**)**

packages should be a list of packages or package names, or a single package or package name. These packages are removed from the use-list of *package* (which defaults to the current package). I. e., the external symbols of these packages will no longer be accessible in *package* as internal symbols. Returns **t**.

(use–package *packages* [*package*]**)**

packages should be a list of packages or package names, or a single package or package name. These packages are added to the use-list of *package* (which defaults to the current package). I. e., all the external symbols of these packages become accessible in *package* as internal symbols. Returns **t**.

1.5. Arrays

1.5.1. Array Creation Functions

(make–array *dimension-list***)**
> Returns an array with dimensions as specified by the list *dimension-list*. (If this is **nil**, a zero-dimensional array is created.) Unless specified by a keyword argument, the values of the elements of the array will be undefined. The following keyword arguments are accepted and have the specified interpretation: **:element–type** => the type of the elements the array can accommodate (default is **t**, meaning any LISP object), **:initial–element** => the initial value of every array element, **:initial–contents** => the initial contents for each element of the array, taken from a nest list structure matching the structure of the array, **:adjustable** => if non-**nil**, then it is possible to dynamically alter the size of the array (default is **nil**), **:fill–pointer** => the initial value of the array's fill pointer (for a one-dimensional array only), either **t**, meaning the length of the array, or a numeric value between 0 and the length of the array, **:displace–to** => the argument is an array, and the array created (called a *displaced array)* shares its contents (in effect, the two arrays become different schemes for describing the same chunk of memory), **:displace–index–offset** => an index into the array specified by the **:displace–to** option at which the array being created should begin, both arrays being treated as if they were converted into one-dimensional arrays in row-major order.

(vector *–objects–***)**
> Creates a simple general vector whose initial elements are the objects.

1.5.2. Array Predicates

(adjustible–array–p *array***)**
> Returns true iff *array* is an adjustible array.

(array–has–fill–pointer–p *array***)**
> Returns **t** iff *array* has a fill pointer.

418

(array–in–bounds–p *array –integers–***)**
Returns true iff the integers interpreted as subscripts refer to a legitimate element of *array*.

(bit–vector–p)
Returns true iff *object* is a bit vector.

(simple–vector–p *object***)**
Returns true iff *object* is a simple vector.

(simple–bit–vector–p *object***)**
Returns true iff *object* is a simple bit vector.

1.5.3. Array Accessing Functions

(aref *array –numbers–***)**
Returns the element of the array referred to by interpreting the numbers as subscripts.

(array–dimension *array number***)**
Returns the length of the *number*-th dimension of *array.*

(array–dimensions *array***)**
Returns a list whose elements are the dimensions of *array.*

(array–element–type *array***)**
Returns a type general enough to describe all the elements that can be stored in *array.*

(array–rank *array***)**
Returns the rank of *array.*

(array–row–major–index *array –numbers–***)**
Returns a number specifying the element of *array* referred to by interpreting the numbers as subscripts and traversing the array in row-major order, with zero indicating the first element.

(array–total–size *array***)**
Returns the total number of elements provided for the *array.*

(bit *bit-array –numbers–***)**
Just like **aref**, except that the array must be an array of 0's and 1's. This may be faster than **aref**.

(fill–pointer *vector***)**
> Returns the fill pointer of *vector*.

(sbit *simple-bit-array –numbers–***)**
> Just like **bit**, except that the array must be a simple bit-array. This may be faster than **bit**.

(svref *simple-vector index***)**
> Returns the element of *simple-vector* specified by *index*. This is just like **aref** when the array is a vector, but may be more efficient for simple vectors.

1.5.4. Array Manipulation Functions

(adjust–array *array dimension-list***)**
> *array* is modified to conform to the new specifications (either by modifying *array* itself, or by creating a new array and modifying *array* to be displaced to the new array). The resulting, modified array is returned. The same keyword arguments that are acceptable to **make–array** may be supplied. The only differences in interpretation are that **:initial–element** initializes only new elements of the array; to supply a **:fill–pointer** argument, the array must have had a fill pointer; the **:element–type** supplied must be compatible with the original specification of the array.

(bit–and *bit-array1 bit-array2* [*result-bit-array*]**)**
(bit–ior *bit-array1 bit-array2* [*result-bit-array*]**)**
(bit–xor *bit-array1 bit-array2* [*result-bit-array*]**)**
(bit–eqv *bit-array1 bit-array2* [*result-bit-array*]**)**
(bit–nand *bit-array1 bit-array2* [*result-bit-array*]**)**
(bit–nor *bit-array1 bit-array2* [*result-bit-array*]**)**
(bit–nandc1 *bit-array1 bit-array2* [*result-bit-array*]**)**
(bit–nandc2 *bit-array1 bit-array2* [*result-bit-array*]**)**
(bit–norc1 *bit-array1 bit-array2* [*result-bit-array*]**)**
(bit–norc2 *bit-array1 bit-array2* [*result-bit-array*]**)**
> Returns an array containing the result of the specified bit-wise logical operation. If the third argument is not supplied, then a new array is created; if the third argument is an array, its contents are destructively changed to contain the result; if the third argument is **t**, the result is placed back in the first argument. The only operations that may require explanation are the ones referred to by **andc1**, **andc2**, **orc1** and **orc2**. These **and** or **or** the complement of the argument designated by the digit with the other argument.

(bit–not *bit-array* [*result-bit-array*]**)**
 Similar to the above logical operations, returning the bit-wise inversion of the bits in *bit-array*.

(vector–pop *vector***)**
 The fill pointer is decremented, and the element it then designates is returned.

(vector–push *item vector***)**
 item is stored in the element designated by the fill pointer, and the fill pointer is incremented; the former value of the fill pointer is returned.

(vector–push–extend *item vector* [*integer*]**)**
 Just like **vector–push**, except that the vector is extended by at least *integer* elements if the fill pointer gets too large. The default value of *integer* is implementation-dependent. If the array is not adjustable, an error is signalled.

1.6. Strings and Characters

1.6.1. String and Character Creation Functions

(code–char *integer* [*bits*] [*font*]**)**
 Returns the character corresponding to the code *integer*, with bits attribute *bits* and font attribute *font* (both of which default to 0). If no such character is to be had, **nil** is returned.

(make–char *char* [*bits*] [*font*]**)**
 Returns a character with the same character code as *char*, but with bits attribute *bits* and font attribute *font* (both of which default to 0). If no such character can be constructed, **nil** is returned.

(make–string *size***)**
 Returns a simple string of length *size*. If an **:initial–element** keyword argument is supplied, then each character in the string is initialized to that value; otherwise, the string will be initialized in an implementation-dependent way.

1.6.2. String and Character Predicates

(alpha–char–p *char*)
> Returns **t** iff *char* is an alphabetic character.

(alphanumericp *char*)
> Returns **t** iff *char* is an alphabetic or numeric character.

(both–case–p *char*)
> Returns **t** iff *char* is an uppercase character and there exists a corresponding lowercase character, or vice versa.

(char–bit *char bitname*)
> Returns non-**nil** iff the *bitname* attribute of *char* is set.

(char= [*–chars–*])
(char/= [*–chars–*])
(char< [*–chars–*])
(char> [*–chars–*])
(char<= [*–chars–*])
(char>= [*–chars–*])
> The arguments are tested to see if they conform to the ordering specified by the function. In particular, the standard alphabetic ordering is adhered to within sets of characters having the same bits and fonts attributes. Characters whose bits and fonts attributes are different are considered to be different characters.

(char–equal [*–chars–*])
(char–not–equal [*–chars–*])
(char–lessp [*–chars–*])
(char–greaterp [*–chars–*])
(char–not–greaterp [*–chars–*])
(char–not–lessp [*–chars–*])
> Just like the above functions, except that bits attributes and case are ignored. Font is taken into account in an implementation-independent way.

(digit–case–p *char* [*radix*])
> If *char* is a digit in radix *radix* (defaulting to 10), **digit–case–p** returns the corresponding number. Otherwise, it returns **nil**.

(graphic–char–p *char*)
> Returns **t** iff *char* has standard textual representation as a single glyph, i. e., it is not a control or formatting character.

422

(lower–case–p *char*)
    Returns **t** iff *char* is a lowercase character.

(standard–char–p *char*)
    Returns **t** iff *char* is a standard character. The Common LISP standard characters include the alphanumerics, the usual punctuation marks, and the characters "space" and "newline".

(string–char–p *char*)
    Returns **t** iff *char* is a character than can be included in a string.

(string=   *string1 string2*)
(string/=   *string1 string2*)
(string<   *string1 string2*)
(string>   *string1 string2*)
(string<=   *string1 string2*)
(string>=   *string1 string2*)
    The strings are tested to see if they conform to the ordering indicated by the function. In the case of testing for equality, if the strings match, the function will return true. In the other cases, if the condition is satisfied, the index of the position of the first character at which the strings differ is returned. The ordering is lexicographic, using the character comparison function **char**<. The keywords **start1**, **start2**, **end1** and **end2** can be used to specify the portions of the strings to be considered for the comparison. If so, then in case of a mismatch, an index into *string1* is returned.

(string–equal *string1 string2*)
(string–not–equal *string1 string2*)
(string–lessp *string1 string2*)
(string–greaterp *string1 string2*)
(string–not–greaterp *string1 string2*)
(string–not–lessp *string1 string2*)
    Just like the above functions, except that the ordering is determined as if by **char–lessp**, i. e., case is ignored.

(upper–case–p *char*)
    Returns **t** iff *char* is an uppercase character.

1.6.3. String and Character Accessing Functions

(char *string integer***)**

    Returns the character at the *integer* position in *string*, beginning with a zero-origin.

(char–bits *char***)**

    Returns the bits attribute of *char*.

(char–code *char***)**

    Returns the code attribute of *char*.

(char–font *char***)**

    Returns the font attribute of *char*.

(schar *simple-string integer***)**

    Just like **char**, except that the argument must be a simple string. Where applicable, this function may be faster than **char**.

1.6.4. String and Character Manipulation Functions

(character *object***)**

    Coerces *object* to be a character, if possible, and returns that character.

(char–downcase *char***)**

    Returns a lowercase version of *char*.

(char–int *char***)**

    Returns an integer encoding *char*. This function exists to facilitate hashing characters.

(char–name *char***)**

    Returns the name (a string) of *char*, if one exists, and **nil** otherwise. For example, the newline character has the name "**Newline**"; space has the name "**Space**".

(char–upcase *char***)**

    Returns an uppercase version of *char*.

(digit–char *integer* [*radix* [*font*]]**)**

    Returns the character equivalent of the integer *integer*, considered in radix *radix* (defaulting to 10), and whose font attribute is *font* (default 0), or **nil**, if there is no such character.

(int–char *integer***)**
> Returns the character encoded by *integer*, consistent with **char–int** above.

(name–char *name***)**
> Returns the character named by *name*, or **nil** if there is none.

(nstring–downcase *string***)**
(nstring–upcase *string***)**
(nstring–capitalize *string***)**
> These are just like the functions **string–downcase**, **string–upcase** and **string–capitalize**, except that they destructively modify *string* to produce the result.

(set–char–bit *char bitname value***)**
> Returns a character just like *char*, but with the bit named *name* set if *value* is non-**nil**, or unset otherwise. The set of valid names is implementation-dependent, but might include things like **:control** and **:meta**.

(string *object***)**
> **string** attempts to return a string derived from *object*. If *object* is a string, it is returned; if it is a symbol, its print name is returned; if it is a character, a string containing that one character is returned. Passing **string** any other object results in an error.

(string–capitalize *string***)**
> Returns a string just like *string* but with the first charcter of every word in *string* in uppercase characters, and every other character in lowercase characters. Non-alphanumeric characters separate words. The keyword arguments **:start** and **:end** may be used to specify the portion of the string that is affected.

(string–downcase *string***)**
> Returns a string just like *string* but with uppercase characters substituted for lowercase characters. The keyword arguments **:start** and **:end** may be used to specify the portion of the string that is affected.

(string–left–trim *char-sequence string***)**
> Returns a substring of *string* with all the characters in *char-sequence* removed from the beginning.

(string–right–trim *char-sequence string*)
> Returns a substring of *string* with all the characters in *char-sequence* removed from the end.

(string–trim *char-sequence string*)
> Returns a substring of *string* with all the characters in *char-sequence* removed from both the beginning and end.

(string–upcase *string*)
> Returns a string just like *string* but with lowercase characters substituted for uppercase characters. The keyword arguments **:start** and **:end** may be used to specify the portion of the string that is affected.

1.7. Other Data Structure Functions

1.7.1. Hash Table Functions

(clrhash *hash-table*)
> Removes all entries from *hash-table*, and returns it.

(gethash *object hash-table* [*value*])
> *hash-table* is searched for an entry whose key is *object*. If such a key is found, the associated value is returned; otherwise *value* (defaulting to **nil**) is returned.

(hash–table–count *hash-table*)
> Returns the number of entries in *hash-table*.

(make–hash–table)
> Returns a new hash table. The keyword arguments **:test**, **:size**, **:rehash–size** and **:rehash-threshold** are accepted, and have the following interpretation: **:size** sets the initial number of entries the table can contain (which the system may choose to round up to a "nicer" value); **:rehash–size** specifies how much to increase the table by when it becomes full (an integer indicates a number of entries, a floating-point number a percentage); **:rehash-threshold** specifies how full the table can get before it should grow (again, either an integer or a floating-point number); and **:test** specifies the function to use to compare keys (defaulting to **eql**).

(maphash *function hash-table*)
> *function* is applied to each element of *hash-table*. *function* should be a function of two arguments, and is applied to the key and value of each entry. Returns **nil**.

426

(remhash *object hash-table***)**

Any entry with key *object* is removed from *hash-table.* Returns true if there was such an entry and false otherwise.

(sxhash *object***)**

Returns a hash code for *object.* This will always be a small, non-negative integer, useful for user-designed hashing schemes.

1.7.2. Miscellaneous Data Structure Functions

(check-type *place typespec* [*string*]**)**   [*Macro*]

Signals an error if the contents of *place* does not conform to *typespec.* *place* must be a location acceptable to **setf**, and *typespec,* which is not evaluated, must be a type specification. *string* must be an English description of the type, beginning with an indefinite article. The user may continue from this error, in which case he is asked for a new value. The new value is placed in *place,* and **check-type** is called on it again.

(coerce *object type***)**

object is converted to a similar object of the type specified by *type,* a type specification. An error is signalled if the coercion cannot be performed. In particular, a sequence of one type can be converted into a sequence of any other type; strings of length 1, symbols whose print names are length 1, and integers can be converted to characters; any non-complex number can be converted to a **short-float**, **single-float**, **double-float** or **long-float** number (just specifying **float** converts to **single-float**); any number can be converted to a complex number; any object can be coerced to its own type or to **t** – doing so just causes that object to be returned.

(get-setf-method *form***)**

Five values are returned, representing the **setf** method that would be used on *form.* The five values are a list of temporary variables, a list of forms, a list of one "store" variable, a storing form, and an accessing form. During the application of a **setf** method, the temporary variables will be assigned the values of the forms, and the store variable will be assigned the value resulting from the evaluation of the second argument to **setf**. Evaluating the access form (which may contain references to the temporary variables) will return the value of the location to be **setf**ed; evaluating the storing form (which may contain references to both the temporary variables and the store variables) will update the location.

(get–setf–method–multiple–value *form***)**
> Just like **get–setf–method**, except that there may be more than one store variable, corresponding to the case in which some **setf** method is defined that stores multiple values into a location.

(identity *object***)**
> Returns *object*.

(psetf –*[place form]*–**)**   *[Macro]*
> Like **setf** below, except that the assignments are done "in parallel". I. e., all the forms are evaluated first; then the assignments are made.

(rotatef –*places*–**)**   *[Macro]*
> The values in places (which can be any location acceptable to **setf**) are rotated to the left, with the value of the leftmost place going into the rightmost place.

(setf –*[place form]*–**)**   *[Macro]*
> Stores the value *form* into the location referred to by *place*. Virtually any Common LISP expression that can be thought of as referencing a location can be used for *place*.

(shiftf –*places*– *form***)**   *[Macro]*
> The values in the places are shifted to the left, with *form* being shifted in from the right, and the value of the first place begin returned.

2. Arithmetic Functions

Most arithmetic functions operate on all types of numbers, automatically coercing values when arguments are of different types.

2.1. Arithmetic Predicates

(evenp *number***)**
> Returns **t** iff *number* is even.

(logbitp *index integer***)**
> Returns true iff the *index*-th bit of *integer* is 1.

(logtest *integer1 integer2***)**
> Returns true iff any of the bits designated by the 1's in *integer1* are 1's in *integer2*.

(minusp *exp***)**
>   Returns **t** iff *exp* is a negative number.

(oddp *number***)**
>   Returns **t** iff *number* is odd.

(plusp *number***)**
>   Returns **t** iff *number* is greater than zero.

(zerop *exp***)**
>   Returns **t** iff *exp* is a number equal to 0.

(= *–numbers–***)**
(/= *–numbers–***)**
(< *–numbers–***)**
(> *–numbers–***)**
(<= *–numbers–***)**
(>= *–numbers–***)**
>   Return **t** iff all the arguments comply with the specified predicate.
>   E. g., /= is true iff all its arguments are all different; < is true iff all
>   the arguments are in strictly increasing order. Since coercion is done
>   when necessary, different kinds of numbers having the same value
>   will be judged to be the same.

2.2. Simple Arithmetic Functions

(+ *–numbers–***)**
>   Return the sum of the arguments. If no arguments are given, **0** is re-
>   turned.

(1+ *number***)**
>   Return *number* plus 1.

(– *–numbers–***)**
>   Return the result of subtracting from the first argument all subse-
>   quent arguments. If one argument is given, the result of substracting
>   that argument from **0** is returned.

(* *–numbers–***)**
>   Return the product of all of the arguments. **1** is returned if no argu-
>   ments are given.

429

(/ –numbers–)
Return the result of dividing the first argument by succeeding ones. If there is only one argument, its reciprocal is returned.

(1– number)
Return *number* minus 1.

(conjugate number)
Returns the complex conjugate of *number*.

(decf place [delta])   [*Macro*]
The value in *place* is decremented by *delta* (which defaults to 1) and the new value is stored back in *place* and returned.

(gcd –integers–)
Returns the greatest common divisor of all the integers.

(incf place [delta])   [*Macro*]
The value in *place* is incremented by *delta* (which defaults to 1) and the new value is stored back in *place* and returned.

(lcm –integers–)
Returns the least common multiple of all the integers.

2.3. Trigonometric Functions

(acos number)
Returns the arc cosine of *number* in radians.

(acosh number)
Returns the hyperbolic arc cosine of *number* in radians.

(asin number)
Returns the arc sine of *number* in radians.

(asinh number)
Returns the hyperbolic arc sine of *number* in radians.

(atan number1 [number2])
Returns the arc tangent of *number1* divided by *number2* (which defaults to 1), in radians.

430

(atanh *number***)**
> Returns the hyperbolic arc tangent of *number*.

(cis *number***)**
> Returns a complex number whose real part is **(cos** *number***)** and whose imaginary part is **(sin** *number***)**, where *number* is assumed to be in radians.

(cos *number***)**
> Returns the cosine of *number*. *number* is assumed to be in radians.

(cosh *number***)**
> Returns the hyperbolic cosine of *number*. *number* is assumed to be in radians.

(phase *complex-number***)**
> Returns the phase of *complex-number*. For a complex number **x**, the phase is defined as **(atan (imagpart x) (realpart x))**.

(signum *number***)**
> **(signum x)** is defined to be **(if (zerop x) x (/ x (abs x)))**.

(sin *number***)**
> Returns the sine of *number*. *number* is assumed to be in radians.

(sinh *number***)**
> Returns the hyperbolic sine of *number*. *number* is assumed to be in radians.

(tan *number***)**
> Returns the tangent of *number*. *number* is assumed to be in radians.

(tanh *number***)**
> Returns the hyperbolic tangent of *number*. *number* is assumed to be in radians.

2.4. Logical Operations on Numbers

(ash *integer1 integer2***)**
> Returns *integer2* arithmetically shifted left *integer1* bit positions.

(boole *op x y***)**
> Returns the result of the bitwise boolean operation indicated by the symbol *op*. The value of *op* may be one of sixteen different symbols; these symbols are all defined to be constants in Common LISP (i. e., they evaluate to themselves). They enable **boole** to compute all sixteen logical operations of two arguments. Individual Common LISP functions are also available for most of these operations (see the various **log***op* functions below). When it is known in advance what particular logical operation a procedure is to perform, then that particular function should be used. **boole** should be used when the logical operations a procedure has to perform is not known in advance, and is specified by passing that procedure an argument. The sixteen possible values of *op* and their associated operations are as described below. Here Λ represents bitwise *and,* V represents bitwise *or,* and X represents bitwise *xor.* $\neg$ represents bitwise negation and has the highest precedence: **boole–clr** => 0 (i. e., the result is always 0), **boole–set** => 1 (i. e., the result is always 1), **boole–1** => x, **boole–2** => y, **boole–c1** => $\neg x$, **boole–c2** => $\neg y$, **boole–and** => $x \Lambda y$, **boole–ior** => $x V y$, **boole–xor** => $x X y$, **boole–eqv** => $x = y$, **boole–nand** => $\neg(x \Lambda y)$, **boole–nor** => $\neg(x V y)$, **boole–andc1** => $\neg x \Lambda y$, **boole–andc2** => $x \Lambda \neg y$, **boole–orc1** => $\neg x V y$, **boole–orc2** => $x V \neg y$.

(integer–length *integer***)**
> Computes
> **(ceiling (log (if (minusp** *integer***) (–** *integer***) (1+** *integer***)) 2))**

(logcount *integer***)**
> Returns the number of bits needed for the binary representation of *integer*.

(logand *–integers–***)**
> Returns the bit-wise "and" of the integers. If no arguments are given, the result is –1.

(logeqv *–integers–***)**
> Returns the bit-wise "equivalence" of the integers. If no arguments are given, the result is –1.

(logior *–integers–***)**
> Returns the bit-wise "inclusive or" of the integers. If no arguments are given, the result is 0.

(lognot *integer***)**

> Returns the bit-wise logical "not" of *integer*.

(logxor *–integers–***)**

> Returns the bit-wise "exclusive or" of the integers. If no arguments are given, the result is 0.

(lognand *integer1 integer2***)**
(lognor *integer1 integer2***)**
(logandc1 *integer1 integer2***)**
(logandc2 *integer1 integer2***)**
(logorc1 *integer1 integer2***)**
(logorc2 *integer1 integer2***)**

> Returns the result of the specified bit-wise logical operation.

2.5. Byte Manipulation Functions

(byte *size position***)**

> Returns a byte specifier that can be used by byte manipulation functions, of size *size* and position *position*.

(byte–position *bytespec***)**

> Returns the position of the byte specifier *bytespec*.

(byte–size *bytespec***)**

> Returns the size of the byte specifier *bytespec*.

(deposit–field *integer1 bytespec integer2***)**

> Returns an integer that contains the bits of *integer1* within the byte specified by *bytespec*, and the bits of *integer2* elsewhere.

(dpb *integer1 bytespec integer2***)**

> Returns a number that is the same as *integer2*, except that the portion of *integer2* specified by *bytespec* is replaced by the lower-order bits of *integer1*.

(ldb *bytespec integer***)**

> Returns an integer equivalent to the portion of *integer* specified by *bytespec*.

(ldb–test *bytespec integer***)**

> Returns true iff any of the bits in *integer* specified by *bytespec* are 1.

(mask–field *bytespec integer***)**
> Like **ldb**, but puts the byte extracted from *integer* in the same position in the result, and makes the rest of the bits 0.

2.6. Other Arithmetic Functions

(abs *number***)**
> Returns the absolute value of *number*.

(ceiling *number1* [*number2*]**)**
> *number1* is divided by *number2* (which defaults to 1), and two values are returned: The first is the smallest integer greater than or equal to the quotient; the second value is the difference between *number1* and the first value times *number2*. See also **floor**, **truncate** and **round**.

(complex *number1* [*number2*]**)**
> A complex number is returned whose real part is *number1* and whose imaginary part is *number2* (defaulting to 0). Both parts of the complex number will be of the same type. Note that if the arguments are rational and *number2* is 0, the result will be a rational rather than complex number.

(decode–float *float***)**
> Returns three values, representing the significand, the exponent, and the sign of *float*. The first and last values are floating-point numbers of the same format as *float*; the second value is an integer.

(denominator *rational***)**
> Returns the denominator of the canonical reduced form of *rational*.

(exp *number***)**
> Returns *e* raised to the *number* power. **exp** always returns a floating-point number.

(expt *number1 number2***)**
> Returns *number1* raised to the *number2* power. If *number1* is rational and *number2* is an integer, the result will be exact; otherwise, it will be a floating-point approximation.

(fceiling *number1* [*number2*]**)**
> Just like **ceiling**, except that the first value is returned in a floating-point format.

(ffloor *number1* [*number2*]**)**
    Just like **floor** below, except that the first value is returned in a floating-point format.

(float *number1* [*number2*]**)**
    Returns a floating-point number of the same format as *number2* whose value is equivalent to *number1*. The default format is single precision floating-point (i. e., **single–float**).

(float–digits *float***)**
    Returns the number of digits used in the representation of *float*.

(float–precision *float***)**
    Returns the number of significant digits in *float*.

(float–radix *float***)**
    Returns an integer representing the radix of *float*.

(float–sign *float1* [*float2*]**)**
    Returns a floating-point number with the same sign as *float1* and the same absolute value as *float2*. *float2* defaults to the value of **(float 1** *float1***)**.

(floor *number1* [*number2*]**)**
    number1 is divided by *number2* (which defaults to 1), and two values are returned: The first is the largest integer less than or equal to the quotient; the second value is the difference between *number1* and the first value times *number2*. See also **ceiling**, **truncate** and **round**.

(fround *number1* [*number2*]**)**
    Just like **round** below, except that the first value is returned in a floating-point format.

(ftruncate *number1* [*number2*]**)**
    Just like **truncate** below, except that the first value is returned in a floating-point format.

(imagpart *number***)**
    Returns the imaginary part of *number*.

(integer–decode–float *float***)**
    Like **decode–float**, except that the first result is scaled to be an integer; the third value will be an integer also.

(isqrt *integer***)**

Returns the largest integer less than or equal to the square root of *integer*.

(log *number* [*base*]**)**

Returns the logarithm of *number* to base *base*, which defaults to *e*.

(make–random–state [*state*]**)**

Returns a new "random state" object for the random number generator. Random states are used to help compute sequences of random numbers. If *state* is omitted or is **nil**, a copy of the current random state (i. e., the value of the variable **∗random–state∗**) is used; if *state* is a random state, a copy of it is returned; if it is **t**, a new random state is created and returned. In the latter case, value of the new random state is chosen at random.

(max *–numbers–***)**

Returns the maximum of the numbers.

(min *–numbers–***)**

Returns the minimum of the numbers.

(mod *number1 number2***)**

Applies **floor** to the two arguments and returns the second result of **floor** as its result. See also **rem**.

(numerator *rational***)**

Returns the numerator of the canonical reduced form of *rational*.

(random *number* [*state*]**)**

Returns a number between 0 (inclusive) and *number* (exclusive). *state* is of type **random–state**, and is altered as a side effect to hold the state of the random number generator from invocation to invocation.

(rational *number***)**

Returns a rational number whose value is equal to *number*, which can be any non-complex number.

(rationalize *number***)**

Returns some rational number for which *number* would be approximation in its format. *number* can be any non-complex number.

(realpart *number***)**

> Returns the real part of *number*.

(rem *number1 number2***)**

> Applies **truncate** to the two arguments and returns the second result of **truncate** as its result. See also **mod**.

(round *number1* [*number2*]**)**

> *number1* is divided by *number2* (which defaults to 1), and two values are returned: The first is the integer closest in value to the quotient; the second value is the difference between *number1* and the first value times *number2*. See also **ceiling**, **floor**, and **truncate**.

(scale–float *float integer***)**

> Returns (∗ *float* (**expt** (**float** *radix float*) *integer*)), where *radix* is the radix of the floating-point representation.

(sqrt *number***)**

> Returns the square root of *number*.

(truncate *number1* [*number2*]**)**

> *number1* is divided by *number2* (which defaults to 1), and two values are returned: The first is the integer of the same sign as the quotient and with the greatest magnitude less than or equal to that of the quotient; the second value is the difference between *number1* and the first value times *number2*. See also **ceiling**, **floor** and **round**.

3. Stream, File and Input/Output Functions

The following functions are used in reading from and writing to external devices, files, and other processes.

(clear–input [*stream*]**)**

> Clears any buffer associated with *stream*. Returns **nil**.

(clear–output [*stream*]**)**

> Aborts any outstanding output operations to *stream*, and returns **nil**.

(close *stream***)**

> The specified stream is closed, and no further I/O may be performed using it. The keyword argument **:abort** is accepted: If non-**nil**, it indicates that the use of the stream is ending abnormally. The system may then try to clean up any side effects that may have resulted from the stream having been open.

(copy–readtable [*from-readtable* [*to-readtable*]]**)**
Returns a copy of *from-readtable*, which defaults to the current readtable (**nil** indicates that the standard LISP readtable should be used). If *to-readtable* is supplied, it is destructively copied into; otherwise, a new readtable is created.

(delete–file *file***)**
The file *file* is deleted. Returns non-**nil** if successful, and causes an error otherwise.

(directory *pathname***)**
Returns a list of pathnames, consisting of all the pathnames in the file system that match *pathname*. *pathname* may contain components such as **:wild** and **:newest**.

(directory–namestring *pathname***)**
Returns a string consisting of the directory component of *pathname*.

(enough–namestring *pathname1* [*pathname2*]**)**
Returns a string that is just sufficient to identify *pathname1* if it were to be considered using *pathname2* (defaulting to ***default–pathname–defaults***) to specify the defaults.

(file–author *file***)**
Returns the name of the author of *file*. *file* can be a filename or a stream open to a file.

(file–length *stream***)**
Returns the length of the file to which *stream* is attached.

(file–namestring *pathname***)**
Returns a string consisting of the name, type and version components of *pathname*.

(file–position *stream* [*position*]**)**
If *position* is given, the next byte to be read from or written to the stream will be at that position. *position* can be an integer, or one of the keywords **:start** or **:end**. If *position* is not given, the current position in the file is returned (**nil** is returned if the current position cannot be determined).

(file–write–date *file***)**
Returns the time of creation of, or last writing to, *file*, which can be a filename or a stream open to a file.

(finish—output [*stream*]**)**

Waits until any output already sent to *stream* has been outputted, and only then returns **nil**.

(force—output [*stream*]**)**

Initiates the emptying of output buffer to *stream*, and immediately returns **nil**.

(format *destination string –objects–*)

The printed representation of the objects is created, in accordance with the format specified by *string*. This representation is either printed or made into a string, as specified by *destination*. *destination* may be a stream, in which case output is sent to that stream, and **format** returns **nil**; it may be **t**, in which case output is sent to the standard output and **nil** is returned; it may be a string with a fill pointer, in which case the printed representation is added to the end of the string, and **nil** is returned; or it may be **nil**, in which case a string containing the printed representation is returned as the value of the call to **format**.

string is referred to as a *format control string.* It consists of ordinary characters, intermixed with format directives. The former simply become part of the printed representation, and the latter describe how to represent the objects supplied to the function call. All the directives begin with the character ˜, and the particular directive is identified by a single character. The character may be preceded by a number of parameters, usually integers or single characters, separated by commas, and one or both of the modifiers **:** and **@**. The parameters are generally optional. A parameter may be omitted simply by inserting a comma, in which case a default value will be chosen for it. If the parameter is a character, it may be designated by the form '*c,* that is, quote followed by the desired character. Also, the parameter **#** represents the number of objects remaining to be processed. The parameter **V** (or **v**) causes the next object to be used as the value of the parameter (if that object is **nil**, however, it is as if the parameter were omitted).

The format directives are as follows:

˜**A** – the next object is printed as if by **princ**; ˜**:A** causes the object to be printed as ( ) if it is **nil**; ˜*i,j,k,l***A** causes the output to be padded on the right (on the left if **@** is specified) with at least *k* (default 0) copies of padding character *l* (default is space); then padding characters are inserted *j* (default 1) at a time until the output is at least of length *i* (default 0).

~**B** – Like ~**D** but in base 2.

~**C** – Prints some (implementation-dependent) abbreviation for the object, which should be a character; ~**:C** prints the character's name, e. g., control-F would be printed as **Control–F**; ~**:@C** prints what ~**:C** prints, and then describes how to enter that character if an unusual shift key is required; ~**@C** prints the character using the #\ notation, which LISP can read back.

~**D** – The object is printed in decimal radix, without a decimal point. ~i,j,k**D** causes the output to be padded on the left with enough copies of padding character j (default is space) to make the output at least i columns long. The **:** modifier causes the character k (defaulting to comma) to be inserted between pairs of three numbers. **@** causes the sign always to be printed.

~**E** – ~i,j,k,l,m,n,o**E** prints the object as a floating-point number, using exponential notation, consisting of i characters. If l is zero, j digits are printed after the decimal point; if it is positive, l significant digits are printed before the decimal point; if it is negative, $-k$ zeros are printed after the decimal point, followed by $j+l$ significant digits; then the exponent character o is printed, followed by k digits used to print the exponent. The number is padded on the left with copies of the character n, if necessary. If the number cannot be printed in the specified field, i copies of the character m are printed instead. A plus sign is printed iff a **@** modifier is given.

~**F** – ~i,j,k,l,m**F** prints the object as a floating-point number consisting of i characters, with a magnitude equal to 10^k times the value of the object, rounded to j fractional digits, padded on the left with copies of the character m, if necessary. If the number cannot be printed in the specified field, and l is supplied, then i copies of the character l are printed instead; otherwise as many characters as are needed are used. A plus sign is printed iff a **@** modifier is given. If i and j are omitted, then as much space as is needed is used.

~**G** – The object is printed as a floating-point number in either fixed-format, if that can accommodate the number, or exponential notation, if the number is too large.

~**O** – Like ~**D** but in base 8.

~**P** – If the object is not the integer 1, then a lowercase **s** is printed; otherwise, nothing is printed; ~**:P** does the same thing, but applies its test to the previous object rather than the current one; ~**@P** prints **y** if the object is 1, and **ies** if it is not.

~**R** – Prints the object as an English cardinal number, e. g., **3** would be printed as **three**; ~**:R** prints the object as an English ordinal (e. g., **third**); ~**@R** prints the object as a Roman numeral (e. g., **III**); ~**:@R** prints the object as an old Roman numeral (e. g., **IIII** instead of **IV**). ~*r,i,j,k***R** prints the object in radix *r*, with the rest of the parameters having the same interpretation as in ~**D**.

~**S** – Like ~**A**, except that the object is printed as if by **prin1**.

~**T** – ~*i,j***T** spaces over to column *i*, if possible; otherwise, it moves to column *i*+*k*∗*j* for the smallest positive integer *k* for which this is possible (if *k* is zero, then, in this situation, nothing is output). ~*i,j***@T** outputs *i* spaces followed by the smallest number of spaces necessary to move to a column that is a multiple of *j*.

~**X** – Like ~**D** but in base 16.

~**$** – ~*i,j,k,l***$** prints the object as a floating point number, using at least *k* characters, with *j* (defaulting to 1) before the decimal point, and *i* (defaulting to 2) after the decimal point, padding on the left with copies of character *l*, if necessary. A + sign is output only if the @ modifier is supplied.

~**%** – Outputs a newline character; ~*i***%** outputs *i* newlines.

~**&** – Outputs a newline character only if not at the beginning of a line; ~*i***&** outputs *i*–1 newlines.

~**|** – Outputs a page separator, if possible; ~*i***|** outputs *i* page separators.

~ – Outputs a tilde; ~*ĩ* outputs *i* tildes.

~*newline* – Tilde followed by an actual newline character simply ignores the next block of whitespace. This is used to allow a long format string to occupy more than one line. ~*:newline* will skip over the newline, but not over subsequent white space; ~*@newline* does not ignore the newline, but does ignore the subsequent block of whitespace.

~∗ – Ignores the next object; ~*i*∗ ignores the next *i* objects. ~*i:*∗ backs up over the last *i* objects so that they will be processed again. ~*i***@**∗ will transfer attention to the *i*th object (with 0 indicating the first one), so that processing will continue from there.

~? – The object is processed as a format control string, with the next object interpreted as a list of objects to apply the control string to. ~@? also processes the object as a format control string, but applies the directives to the objects in the original call, just as if the object processed by ~@? had appeared as part of the original control string.

~(ctrl-str~) – ctrl-str is processed as a control string, and case conversion is performed on the result. ~(converts all the upper case characters in the result to lower case; ~:(capitalizes all the words of the result; ~@(capitalizes the first word, and converts the others into lower case; ~:@(converts lower case characters to upper case characters.

~[str0~;str1~;...~;strn~] – This construct allows the selection of one of a number of control strings to be used to process an object. The stri are all format control strings. The object, which should be an integer, is treated as an index, and selects a format control string (with 0 referring to the first one). That control string is used; the others are ignored. If the directive begins with ~i[, then the ith control string is chosen (useful in conjunction with the parameter # or **V**). If the last string is prefaced by ~:; rather than ~;, then the last string is selected iff the object specifies some index that is out of bounds. (Without ~:;, an improper references is not an error, but causes no string to be selected.) ~:[fstr~;tstr~] selects fstr if the object is **nil**, and tstr otherwise. ~@[str~] test the object to see if it is true. If it is, str is used, beginning with that object; otherwise, nothing happens.

~{str~} – This construct allows a control string to be used repeatedly. str should be a format control string, and the object it is applied to should be a list of objects. (If str is empty, the next object is taken as the format control string instead.) The control string is interpreted, using objects from the list. The string is re-used repeatedly, until all the objects have been processed, or until the directive ~^ is encountered. If a prefix parameter is supplied, the string will be processed at most that many times. Terminating the construct with ~:} instead of ~} causes str to be interpreted at least once (unless a prefix parameter of 0 is supplied). ~@{str~} is similar, except that the control string is applied to all the remaining objects, rather than interpreting the next one as a list of objects. ~:@{str~} interprets all the remaining objects as lists of objects, and applies the string to each of them repeatedly.

~i,j,k,l<str1~;str2~;...~;strn~> – The text produced by processing the strings (which may contain format directives) is justified within n equal fields, the total length of which is at least i columns. The text produced by processing str1 is left justified, and that produced by processing *strn* is right justified (if there is only one element, it is right justified). At least *k* (default 0) copies of the padding character *l* (default is space character) are output between the pieces of text produced; if more than *i* columns are needed, then *j* (default 1) more columns at a time will be added until the output can be accommodated. The modifier **:** causes spacing to be placed to the left of the first text segment, **@** to the right of the last. The directive ˜ˆ will terminate processing; only completely processed segments will be output.

If *str1* is terminated by ˜**:;** instead of ˜**;** then the system will process all the strings, and then determine if the representation produced by the rest of the strings can fit on the current line. If so, it is used, and the result of processing the first string is discarded; otherwise, the result of processing the first string is used first (which, hopefully, will advance to a new line), before the result of processing the rest is used. ˜*m***:;** will do the same, except that there must be at least *m* characters to spare for the test to be considered true. With ˜*m,n***:;**, the line will be assumed to be of length *n*, and there must be at least *m* characters to spare for the test to be considered true.

˜ˆ – Terminates the processing of the current ˜**{**, ˜**<** or ˜**?** directive, or, if there is none, of the entire formatting operation, if there are no more objects to be processed. ˜*m,n*ˆ causes termination to occur only if *m* and *n* are equal; ˜*m,n,o*ˆ causes it to occur only when the parameters are weakly monotonically increasing. (Of course, for either of these cases to be interesting, one of the arguments should be **#** or **V**.) If ˜ˆ occurs with a ˜**:{** directive, it terminates only the current iteration. Within a ˜**<** directive, the formatting is performed on the text segments already processed; if it occurs within a ˜**[** or ˜**(**, then all text processed up to the occurrence of ˜ˆ undergoes selection or case conversion, respectively, and then the current ˜**{**, ˜**<** or entire formatting operation is terminated.

(fresh–line [*stream*]**)**

A newline character is sent to *stream* (defaulting to the standard output) iff *stream* is not already at the beginning of a line. Returns non-**nil** iff a newline is output.

(get–dispatch–macro–character *char1 char2* [*readtable*]**)**

Returns the macro character function for the character *char2* of dispatching macro character *char1*, or **nil** if there is none.

(get–macro–character *char* [*readtable*]**)**
> Returns two arguments, the function associated with the macro character *char*, and a value that is non-**nil** iff *char* is a non-terminating macro character.

(get–output–stream–string *stream***)**
> Returns the string consisting of the characters output to *stream* since the last call to this function. *stream* must have been produced by **make–string–output–stream**.

(host–namestring *pathname***)**
> Returns a string consisting of the host component of *pathname*.

(input–stream–p *stream***)**
> Returns non-**nil** iff input can be requested from *stream*.

(listen [*stream*]**)**
> Returns true iff a character is currently available from *stream*.

(load *filename***)**
> **load read**s in the file *filename*, and evaluates each form in it. The file may contain compiled or interpreted code. If *filename* does not completely specify the file, defaults are taken from the value assigned the variable ***default–pathname–defaults***. If the specification still does not uniquely determine a file, **load** tries to select the more appropriate file by some implementation-dependent means. The keyword arguments **:verbose**, **:print** and **:if–does–not–exist** are accepted. **:verbose**, if non-**nil**, permits **load** to print a message in the form of a comment to the standard output indicating the name of the file being loaded, along with other interesting information. If not supplied, this argument defaults to the value of ***load–verbose***. If **:print** is non-**nil**, then the value of each form loaded is printed on the standard output. If not supplied, this argument defaults to **nil**. If **:if–does–not–exist** is supplicd and is **nll**, then, if the file specified does not exist, **load** returns **nil** rather than signalling an error (the norm). In the case where a file is loaded successfully, **load** returns some non-**nil** value.

(make–broadcast–stream *–streams–***)**
> Returns an output stream, which, if sent output, will send that output to all the named streams. In general, stream operations performed on the resulting stream return the result of performing that operation on the last stream, the other results being discarded. If no streams are supplied as arguments, a stream is created which merely throws away everything written to it.

(make–concatenated–stream *–streams–***)**
Returns an input stream, which, if read from, will take input from the first stream until there is an end-of-file; then it will take input from the next stream, and so on. If no streams are supplied as arguments, a stream is created which results in an end-of-file when read from.

(make–dispatch–macro–character *char* [*flag* [*readtable*]]**)**
Makes *char* a dispatching macro character in readtable *readtable* (which defaults to the current readtable). If *flag* is non-**nil**, then *char* may occur within tokens. The initial dispatch table for *char* is empty. Returns **t**.

(make–echo–stream *i-stream o-stream***)**
Returns a stream that gets input from *i-stream* and sends output to *o-stream*; in addition, all input from *i-stream* is echoed on *o-stream*.

(make–pathname)
Returns a pathname constructed from the components supplied as arguments using the keywords **:host, :device, :directory, :name, :type** and **:version**, merged with the default pathname supplied by the keyword argument **:defaults** (the default for which has the same host as that specified by **∗default–pathname–defaults∗**, and all other components being **nil**).

(make–string–input–stream *string* [*integer1* [*integer2*]]**)**
Returns an input stream that will supply the characters of *string* from *integer1* to *integer2*.

(make–string–output–stream)
Returns an output stream that collects characters output to it. These can be accessed using the function **get–output–stream–string**.

(make–synonym–stream *symbol***)**
Returns a "synonym stream" for the stream assigned the special variable associated with *symbol*. I. e., operations performed on the new stream will also be performed on the stream assigned to *symbol*, whatever that happens to be at the time of the operation.

(make–two–way–stream *i-stream o-stream***)**
Returns a stream that gets input from *i-stream* and sends output to *o-stream*.

(merge–pathnames *pathname1* [*pathname2* [*version*]]**)**
Returns a pathname by filling in the unspecified components of *pathname1* from *pathname2* (which defaults to ***default–pathname–defaults***) and the version from *version* (defaulting to **:newest**) if none is otherwise specified.

(namestring *pathname*)
Returns the full form of *pathname* as a string.

(open *filename*)
Returns a stream connected to the file *filename* (which may be a string, pathname, or stream). The following keywords and associated arguments specify the details: **:direction** => specifies the direction of stream, using the arguments **:input**, **:output**, **:io** (for a bidirectional stream) and **:probe** (a no-directional stream, useful for determining if a file exists); **:element–type** => specifies the type of the unit of transaction of the stream, either a finite subtype of **integer** or **character**, or **:default**, which causes the file system to choose the type based on what it knows about its files; **:if–exists** => specifies what to do if the file is being opened for output, and it already exists, using the keywords **:error** (signal an error), **:new–version** (create a new version), **:rename** (change the name of the existing file), **:rename–and–delete** (change the name of the existing file, and then delete it without expunging it), **:overwrite** (destructively modify the file), **:append** (add to end of existing file), **:supersede** (like **:new–version**, except the same version number as the existing file is used), and **nil** (return **nil** to indicate failure); **:if–does–not–exist** => specifies what to do if the file being opened does not already exists, using the keywords **:error** (the default if the direction is **:input**, or if the **:if–exists** argument is **:overwrite** or **:append**), **:create** (create an empty file – the default if opened for output, and if the **:if–exists** argument is anything other than **:overwrite** or **:append**), and **nil** (return **nil** to indicate failure).

(output–stream–p *stream*)
Returns non-**nil** iff output can be sent to *stream*.

(parse–integer *string*)
string is scanned for a number. Two values are returned: the number scanned, and an index into *string* of the first character after the number's representation. The keywords **:start** and **:end** can be used to delimit the segment of the string scanned, and **:radix** to specify the radix of the number scanned for (normally 10). If the **:junk–allowed** keyword is supplied and is **nil** (the default), then an error is signalled if the entire substring scanned cannot be interpreted as a number. Otherwise, either the first number found will be re-

turned, or **nil** will be returned if a number cannot be extracted from the string. Does not recognize the # radix-specifying prefixes.

(parse–namestring *object* [*host* [*defaults*]]]**)**

Returns a pathname parsed from *object*, which is usually a string, but which may be a pathname, symbol, or stream. For a string or symbol, the keyword arguments **:start** and **:end** can be used to delimit the portion of the string examined. Normally, an error is signalled if the string contains anything other than the pathname and whitespace, but if a non-**nil :junk–allowed** keyword argument is supplied, and the string cannot be parsed as a pathname, **nil** is returned. A second value is returned, consisting of an index into the string of the first character after the portion parsed into a pathname, if the argument is a string. In general, *host* and *defaults* may be supplied if such information is needed to help the parse.

(pathname *object***)**

Returns a pathname derived from *object*, which may be a pathname, string, symbol, or stream.

(pathname–host *pathname***)**
(pathname–device *pathname***)**
(pathname–directory *pathname***)**
(pathname–name *pathname***)**
(pathname–type *pathname***)**
(pathname–version *pathname***)**

Returns the designated component of *pathname*.

(peek–char [*flag* [*stream* [*eof-error-p* [*eof-value* [*recursive-p*]]]]]**)**

If *flag* is **nil** (the default), the next character of *stream* is returned without actually removing it from *stream*. If *flag* is **t**, then whitespace is skipped over before peeking at the character. If *flag* is some character, then input characters are skipped until that character is observed, and then that character is peeked at. The other optional arguments are interpreted as for **read** below.

(pprint *object* [*stream*]**)**

Prints *object* on *stream* (which defaults to the standard output) in a pleasing format. Returns no values.

(princ *object* [*stream*]**)**

Prints *object* on *stream* (which defaults to the standard output), and returns *object*. No escape characters or double quotes are output, so that the output is human-readable, but may not be LISP-readable.

(princ–to–string *object***)**
> Returns a string containing the printed representation of *object* that **princ** would produce.

(print *object* [*stream*]**)**
> Prints *object* on *stream* (which defaults to the standard output) preceded by a newline, and followed by a space. Returns *object*. Escape characters and double quotes are output, a la **prin1**, so that the output is generally LISP-readable.

(prin1 *object* [*stream*]**)**
> Prints *object* on *stream* (which defaults to the standard output), and returns *object*. Escape characters and double quotes are output, so that the output is generally LISP-readable.

(prin1–to–string *object***)**
> Returns a string containing the printed representation of *object* that **prin1** would produce.

(probe–file *name***)**
> Returns a pathname for that file if it does exist, and **nil**.

(read [*stream* [*eof-error-p* [*eof-value* [*recursive-p*]]]]**)**
> Returns the next LISP expression read from *stream* (which defaults to the standard input; also, **t** is interpreted as **∗terminal–io∗**). If *eof-error-p* is true (the default) reading past the end of a file causes an error, otherwise, no error is signalled, and **eof-value** is returned. If *recursive-p* is supplied and is non-**nil**, then this specifies that the call to **read** is imbedded within another call to **read** (probably from a macro character function).

(read–byte *stream* [*eof-error-p* [*eof-value*]]**)**
> Returns the first byte read from *stream*, which must be a binary input stream. The optional arguments are interpreted as for **read**.

(read–char [*stream* [*eof-error-p* [*eof-value* [*recursive-p*]]]]**)**
> Returns the next character read from the stream, and returns it as a character object. The arguments are interpreted as for **read**.

(read–char–no–hang [*stream* [*eof-error-p* [*eof-value* [*recursive-p*]]]]**)**
> Just like **read–char**, except that, if it would be necessary to wait for a character, **nil** is returned immediately.

(read–delimited–list *char* [*stream* [*recursive-p*]]]**)**

Returns a list of the object read from *stream* until the next character to be read is *char*. *char* should not be considered whitespace in the current readtable. The optional arguments are interpreted as for **read**.

(read–from–string *string* [*eof-error-p* [*eof-value*]]]**)**

The characters of *string* are given to **read**, until a LISP object can be returned. The characters thus read are subject to the normal interpretations. The keywords **:start** and **:end** can be used to delimit the segment of the string that is read from. In addition, a non-**nil** **:preserve–whitespace** keyword argument will preserve whitespace as if **read–preserving–whitespace** were used to do the reading. The optional arguments are interpreted as for **read**.

(read–line [*stream* [*eof-error-p* [*eof-value* [*recursive-p*]]]]**)**

Returns two values: a character string consisting of a line of text from *stream* up to (but not including) a newline, and a flag that is **nil** iff the line was terminated normally. The optional arguments are interpreted as for **read**.

(read–preserving–whitespace [*stream* [*eof-error-p* [*eof-value* [*recursive-p*]]]]**)**

Just like **read**, except that it will not throw away white space, even if the white space is not syntactically meaningful. This is used only in special situations in which the user does some character I/O, and does not want white space disturbed. Note that if *recursive-p* is non-**nil**, **read–preserving–whitespace** will behave exactly like **read**. Otherwise, the optional arguments are interpreted as in **read**.

(rename–file *file new-name***)**

The file *file* is renamed *new-name*, if it can be; otherwise an error is signalled. Three values are returned: the new name with any unspecified components filled in from *file*, the true name of the file before it was changed, and the true name of the file after it was renamed.

(set–dispatch–macro–character *char1 char2 function* [*readtable*]**)**

Makes *function* the function called when the dispatching macro character *char1* is followed by *char2*, in readtable *readtable*, which defaults to the current readtable. Returns **t**.

(set–macro–character *char function* [*flag* [*readtable*]]**)**
> Causes *char* to be a macro character having function *function* in the readtable *readtable* (which defaults to the current readtable). If *flag* is supplied and is non-**nil**, then the macro character may be embedded in tokens; otherwise it may not be. Returns **t**.

(set–syntax–from–char *char1 char2* [*readtable1* [*readtable2*]]**)**
> The syntax of *char1* in readtable *readtable1* (defaulting to the current readtable) is made to be the same as the syntax of *char2* in readtable *readtable2* (defaulting to the standard LISP readtable).

(stream–element–type *stream***)**
> Returns a type specifier indicating what kind of objects may be handled by *stream*.

(terpri [*stream*]**)**
> A newline character is sent to *stream* (defaulting to the standard output). Returns **nil**.

(truename *pathname***)**
> Returns the "true name" of the file associated with *stream*, taking into account any file-name translations performed by the system.

(unread–char *char* [*stream*]**)**
> Puts *char*, which must be the last character read from *stream*, back onto the front of *stream*. **unread–char** cannot be invoked twice without an intervening reading operation, i. e., only one character may be put back in a stream. Returns **nil**.

(user–homedir–pathname [*host*]**)**
> Returns the pathname for the user's home directory on *host* (the default for which is implementation-dependent).

(with–input–from–string (*var string*) –*forms*–**)**   [*Macro*]
> A new variable *var* is created, and is assigned an input stream that takes characters from *string*. Then the forms are evaluated. The stream is closed, and the value of the last form is returned. In addition, the following keyword arguments are allowed right after *string*: An **:index** keyword argument provides a place in which to store, after a normal exit, the index into *string* of the first character not yet read; **:start** and **:end** specify the segment of the string to consider.

(with–open–stream (*var stream*) *–forms–***)**   [*Macro*]
A new variable *var* is created, and is assigned the value of *stream*. Then the forms are evaluated. The stream is closed, and the value of the last form is returned.

(with–output–to–string (*var* [*string*]) *–forms–***)**   [*Macro*]
A new variable *var* is created, and is assigned an output stream that puts characters into a string. Then the forms are evaluated. If *string* is specified, it must have a fill-pointer and the output to the stream assigned to *var* is appended to *string*; the value of the last form is returned. If no string is specified, the string containing the output is returned as the value of the call.

(with–open–file (*var filename –options–*) *–forms–***)**   [*Macro*]
filename and the options are passed to **open**, and the resulting stream is assigned to *var*, a new variable; then the forms are evaluated, the value of the last one being returned. The file is closed when the function is exited.

(write *object*)
A printed representation of *object* is output. The following keywords are accepted, and the arguments they provide, have the associated interpretation: **:stream** => the stream to send the output to; **:escape** => escape characters are output iff this is non-**nil**; **:radix** => radix specifiers are output iff this is non-**nil**; **:base** => the radix to use when outputting rational numbers; **:circle** => an attempt is made to detect circular structures iff this is non-**nil**; **:pretty** => an attempt is made to pretty-print output iff this is non-**nil**; **:level** => the number of levels to print of nested s-expressions, with **nil** meaning to print all levels; **:length** => the number of elements of a list to print, with **nil** meaning to print the entire length; **:case** => upper case characters are printed in upper case, in lower case, or as capitalized words according to whether this value is **:upcase**, **:downcase** or **:capitalize**; **:gensym** => the prefix **#:** is printed before symbols that have no home package iff this value is non-**nil**; **:array** => the contents of an array (other than a string) is printed iff this is non-**nil**. These keywords have as their default values the value of the following global variables: **∗standard–output∗**, **∗print–escape∗** (initially **t**), **∗print–radix∗** (initially **nil**), **∗print–base∗** (initially **10**), **∗print–circle∗** (initially **nil**), **∗print–pretty∗** (the initial value is implementation-dependent), **∗print–level∗** (initially **nil**), **∗print–length∗** (initially **nil**), **∗print–case∗** (initially **:upcase**), **∗print–gensym∗** (initially **t**) and **∗print–array∗** (the initial value is implementation-dependent).

(write–byte *integer stream***)**
> A byte with value *integer* is output to the binary output stream *stream*, and returns *integer*.

(write–char *char* [*stream*]**)**
> Outputs *char* to *stream*, and returns *char*.

(write–line *string* [*stream*]**)**
> Outputs *string* to *stream*, followed by a newline, and returns *string*. The keywords **:start** and **:end** can be used to delimit the substring of *string* that is output.

(write–string *string* [*stream*]**)**
> Outputs *string* to *stream*, and returns *string*. The keywords **:start** and **:end** can be used to delimit the substring of *string* that is output.

(write–to–string *object***)**
> Returns a string containing the printed representation of *object*. Accepts all the keywords that **write** accepts, with the same interpretation, except for **:stream**, as there is no stream involved.

(y–or–n–p [*string –objects–*]**)**
> If *string* is supplied, a **fresh–line** is done, and the objects are printed as if *string* and the objects were passed to **format**. Otherwise, nothing is printed. In any case, a response, which should be something very short (e. g. "y" or "n") indicating "yes" or "no", is read from the terminal (i. e., from the stream ***query–io***); returns true or false if the response is "yes" or "no", respectively.

(yes–or–no–p [*string –objects–*]**)**
> Like **y–or–n–p**, except that it does something to attract the users attention, and requires something more than a single keystroke response (e. g., typing "yes" or "no"). This is meant to be used for very important questions, or questions unlikely to have been anticipated by the user.

4. Flow of Control Functions

(and *–forms–***)**   [*Macro*]
> The expressions are evaluated left to right. Evaluation ceases when the first **nil** is computed. Returns the value(s) of the last expression evaluated. **and** returns **t** if called with no arguments.

(assert *form* [**(** *–places–* **)** [*string –objects–*] **]) **   [*Macro*]
Signals an error if the value of *form* is **nil**. Upon such an error, the
objects are evaluated, and along with *string*, are passed to **format** to
produce a message to the user (a default message is used if these are
omitted). The user is then given the opportunity to specify some new
values for the places, which should be locations acceptable to **setf**
whose values will influence the value of *form*. In this process, the
various subforms of each *place* may be evaluated. Then the call to
assert is re-evaluated, causing a repetition of this entire process if
form still evaluates to **nil**.

(block *name –forms–***)**   [*Special function*]
The forms are evaluated in order. Returns the value(s) of the last
form evaluated, unless a call to **return** or a call to **return–from** specifying *name* occurs during the execution of some form. In that case,
block immediately returns the result(s) specified by that call, i. e., no
further evaluation of the forms is performed.

(case *form –(key –forms–)–***)**   [*Macro*]
The *key*s are typically lists, but may also be atoms; in either case,
they are not evaluated. *form* is evaluated, and is examined for
membership in those *key*s which are lists, and for equality with those
*key*s that are atoms. The forms of the clause that accepts the key are
evaluated, and the value(s) produced from the last form returned. It
is an error if more than one form can match the value of *form*. As a
special case, the key may be the symbol **t** or **otherwise**; in this case,
the clause that contains the key must appear last, and that clause will
be used if none of the other clauses are satisfied. If no match occurs,
nil is returned.

(catch *tag –forms–***)**   [*Special function*]
tag is evaluated to produce a name. Then the forms are evaluated in
order, and, if they are evaluated normally, **catch** returns the value(s)
produced from the last form. If, however, a call to **throw** occurs during the evaluation of the forms, and the tag of the throw matches the
name produced from evaluating *tag*, then the evaluation of the forms
is aborted. In this case, we exit from the most recent call to **catch** es-
tablishing this tag, restoring special variables to their status upon
entering the **catch**, and returning the value(s) specified by the call to
throw.

(ccase *place –(key –forms–)–***)**   [*Macro*]
This is similar to **case**, except that no **t** or **otherwise** clause is permitted, *place* must be a location acceptable to **setf**, and not matching
a clause signals an error. Continuing from this error requires the user

to supply a new value, which is stored in *place*, and the whole form is evaluated again.

(cerror *string1 string2 –objects–***)**

A continuable error is signalled. If the user continues from the error, **cerror** will return **nil**. Both strings are format control strings; each is passed to **format** along with the objects. The error handler uses *string2* to describe the error, and *string1* to describe the consequences of continuing.

(cond *–(test-form –forms–)–***)**   *[Macro]*

The test forms are evaluated in order until one returns non-**nil**. Then the forms following that test are evaluated, and the value(s) produced from the last form returned. If there are no forms following the test form, then the value of the test form is returned. If no test form returns non-**nil**, **nil** is returned.

(ctypecase *place –(type –forms–)–***)**   *[Macro]*

Just like **typecase** below, except that no **t** or **otherwise** clause is permitted, *place* must be some location acceptable to **setf**, and failure to match signals a error. Continuing from this error requires the user to supply a new value, which is stored in *place*, and the whole form is evaluated again.

(do (*–(var [initform [repform]])–*)   *[Macro]*
    (*test –resforms–*)
    –declarations–
    –forms–   )

New variables are created for each *var*. The *initform*s are evaluated, as if in parallel, and the variables are initialized to the corresponding values. Then the following loop is entered into: First, *test* is evaluated. If it returns non-**nil**, the *resform*s are evaluated in order, and **do** returns the value(s) produced from evaluating the last *resform*. (If there are no *resform*s, **nil** is returned.) Otherwise, the forms are evaluated in order; then the *repform*s are evaluated as if in parallel, and the variables assigned the corresponding values. The forms of the **do** may be interspersed with tags, a la **prog**, and the functions **go** and **return** are valid here.

(do∗ (*–(var [initform [repform]])–*)   *[Macro]*
    (*test –resforms–*)
    –declarations–
    –forms–   )

This is identical to **do**, except that, after the evaluation of each *initform* or *repform*, the resulting value is assigned to the corresponding symbol before the next form is evaluated.

(do–all–symbols (*symbol* [*result*])   [*Macro*]
              –declarations–
              –forms–   )
Just like **do–symbols** below, except that all symbols in all packages
are processed.

(do–external–symbols (*symbol* [*package* [*result*]])   [*Macro*]
              –declarations–
              –forms–   )
Just like **do–symbols** below, except that only the external symbols of
the package are processed.

(dolist (*var listform* [*resform*])   [*Macro*]
              –declarations–
              –forms–   )
A new variable is created for *var*. Then *listform* is evaluated, and
should produce a list. Next, the forms are evaluated in order, once
for each element of the resulting list assigned to the variable. Then
resform is evaluated with the variable assigned the value **nil**, and
dolist returns the resulting value(s). If *resform* is not specified, **nil** is
returned. Tags and occurrences of calls to **go** and **return** are permitted among the forms.

(do–symbols (*symbol* [*package* [*result*]])   [*Macro*]
              –declarations–
              –forms–   )
A new variable is created for *var*. Then *package* is evaluated, and
should produce a package. Next, the forms are evaluated in order,
once for each symbol in *package* assigned to the variable, in no particular order. Then *resform* is evaluated with the variable assigned
the value **nil**, and the resulting value is returned. If *resform* is not
specified, **nil** is returned. Tags and occurrences of calls to **go** and
return are permitted among the forms.

(dotimes (*var countform* [*resform*])   [*Macro*]
              –declarations–
              –forms–   )
A new variable is created for *var*. Then *countform* is evaluated, and
should produce an integer. Next, the forms are evaluated in order,
once for each integer from 0 to one less than the value of *countform*
assigned to the variable. Then *resform* is evaluated with the variable
assigned the value **nil**, and **dotimes** returns the resulting value(s). If
resform is not specified, **nil** is returned. Tags and occurrences of calls

to **go** and **return** are permitted among the forms.

(ecase *form –(key –forms–)–)*   [*Macro*]
This is similar to **case**, except that no **t** or **otherwise** clause is permitted, and not matching a clause signals an error from which it is
not possible to continue.

(error *string –objects–)*
A fatal error is signalled, from which it is not possible to return.
format is applied to *string* (which should be a format control string)
and the objects, and the resulting string is passed to the error-
handling mechanism, which displays it to the user.

(etypecase *form –(type –forms–)–)*   [*Macro*]
Just like **typecase** below, except that no **t** or **otherwise** clause is permitted, and failure to match signals a error, from which it is not possible to continue.

(go *tag*)   [*Special function*]
tag is a symbol or an integer, and is not evaluated. Control is
transferred so that the next form to be evaluated is the one just after
the most recent lexical appearence of *tag* in the body of some surrounding "tagbody". Such "tagbodies" include **prog, prog∗, do, do∗**
and **tagbody**.

(if *test-form then-form2* [*else-form*])   [*Special function*]
test-form is evaluated; if it returns non-**nil**, *then-form* is evaluated,
and the resulting values returned. Otherwise, *else-form* is evaluated,
and the resulting values returned. If *else-form* is not supplied, then **if**
will return **nil** if *test-form* evaluates to **nil**.

(loop *–forms–)*   [*Macro*]
The forms are evaluated in turn, over and over again. Normally,
loop never returns, although it can be exited by a call to **return** or
throw.

(mapl *function –lists–)*
The function *function* is applied to successive sublists of the lists, terminating when the shortest list runs out of elements. The first argument list is returned.

(mapc *function –lists–)*
function is applied to successive elements of the lists, terminating
when the shortest list runs out of elements. The first argument list is
returned.

(mapcan *function –lists–***)**

    function is applied to successive elements of the argument lists, terminating when the shortest list runs out of elements. The resulting values (one from each function application) are **nconc**ed together and returned.

(mapcar *function –lists–***)**

    function is applied to successive elements of the argument lists, terminating when the shortest list runs out of elements. The list of the resulting values (one from each function application) is returned.

(mapcon *function –lists–***)**

    function is applied to successive sublists of the argument lists, terminating when the shortest list runs out of elements. The resulting values (one from each function application) are **nconc**ed together and returned.

(maplist *function –lists–***)**

    function is applied to successive sublists of the arguments lists, terminating when the shortest list runs out of elements. The list of the resulting values (one from each function application) is returned.

(multiple–value–bind (*–vars–* **)** *values-form*   *[Macro]*
                    –declarations–
                    –forms–   **)**

    New variables are created for each of the *vars*. Then *values-form* is evaluated, and each of the variables is assigned one of the resulting values. (Extra values are discarded; extra variables are assigned the value **nil**.) Then the forms are evaluated, and the value(s) of the last one returned.

(multiple–value–call *function –forms–***)**   *[Special Function]*

    All the arguments are evaluated, and all the values resulting from evaluating the forms are passed to the function computed from *function*. Returns whatever is computed from this function application.

(multiple–value–list *form***)**   *[Macro]*

    Returns a list of the (potentially multiple) values computed by evaluating *form*.

(multiple–value–prog1 *form –forms–***)**   *[Special Function]*

    Like **prog1**, except that it returns all the values produced by *form*, whereas **prog1** would have returned only one.

(multiple–value–setq *symbol-list form***)** [*Macro*]
   symbol-list is not evaluated; it must be a list of symbols. Each of the variables named by the symbols in *symbol-list* is assigned a value returned from the evaluation of *form*. (Extra values are discarded; extra variables are assigned the value **nil**.) Returns the first value returned by *form*, or **nil** if *form* returns no values.

(or *–forms–***)** [*Macro*]
   Evaluation proceeds left to right and stops as soon as one of the forms evaluates to a non-**nil** value. **or** then returns the value(s) produced from the evaluation of this form. If no form evaluates to non-**nil**, **or** returns **nil**. **or** of no arguments returns **nil**.

(prog (*–inits–*) *–declarations– –forms–***)** [*Macro*]
   The *inits* are either individual symbols, or lists of the form (*symbol initform*). New variables are created for the symbols. The associated initialization forms, if given, are evaluated as if in parallel, and the variables are assigned the corresponding values. If just a symbol is given, it is initialized to **nil**. Then the forms of the **prog**, which may be interspersed with tags (i. e., symbols or integers), are evaluated in sequence. If the end of the forms is reached, **prog** returns **nil**. The functions **return** and **go** are allowed.

(prog∗ (*–inits–*) *–declarations– –forms–***)**
   Like **prog**, except that each variable named in the *inits* is assigned a value before the next initialization form is evaluated.

(prog1 *form –forms–***)**
   The forms are evaluated from left to right and the value of *form* is returned.

(prog2 *form1 form2 –forms–***)**
   The forms are evaluated from left to right and the value of *form2* is returned.

(progn *–forms–***)** [*Special function*]
   The forms are evaluated from left to right and the value(s) of the last form returned.

(progv *symbol-list value-list –forms–***)** [*Special function*]
   Both *symbol-list* and *value-list* are evaluated, and should evaluate to a list of symbols and a list of any type objects, respectively. A new, special variable is created for each of the symbols in *symbol-list*, and assigned the corresponding objects in *value-list*. If there are too few values, the remaining variables will be made to have no value. If

there are too many, the extra ones are ignored. Then the forms are evaluated left to right. Thus, references to the free symbols of *symbol-list* in the forms will refer to the new variables created by **progv**. So this is a way to temporarily change the values of some free symbols during the evaluation of some forms. Returns the value(s) produced from the last form evaluated.

(return [*form*]**)**   [*Macro*]

Causes the most recently created block named **nil** to return the value(s) produced from the evaluation of *form*. The call to **return** must appear textually within the form that caused the creation of the block. A block with name **nil** is set up implicitly by a call to **do**, **do***, **prog** and **prog*** (and, of course, may be set up by an explicit call to **block** using the name **nil**). If *form* is not supplied, it is assumed to be **nil**.

(return—from *name* [*result*]**)**   [*Special function*]

name is not evaluated. An immediate return is made from the most recently created block named *name*. A block with name **fn** will be created every time a function named **fn** is invoked; blocks named **nil** are implicitly created as described in the definition of **return** above; and a block is explicitly created by a call to **block**. The call to **return—from** must appear textually within the code that causes the block to be created. **return—from** returns the value(s) produced from the evaluation of *result* (which defaults to **nil**).

(tagbody *–forms–*)   [*Special function*]

The forms may be interspersed with *tags*, which are either symbols or integers. The forms are evaluated in order, and the tags are ignored, until an expression of the form **(go** *tag*) is evaluated. At this point, control is transferred to the form following the most recent lexically available tag named *tag*. If the end of the forms is reached, **tagbody** returns **nil**.

(throw *tag form*)   [*Special function*]

tag and *form* are both evaluated. Then a return is made from the first enclosing catch that has established the tag *tag*. The code that establishes the catch does *not* have to lexically contain the call to **throw**. **catch** returns as its value(s) the value(s) produced from the evaluation of *form*. Special variables are restored to their status as of the point of the catch. It is an error if there is no catch to catch a throw.

(typecase *form –(type –forms–)–)* [*Macro*]

The *types* are type specifiers; they are not evaluated. *form* is evaluated, and the first clause whose type specifier describes this value has its forms evaluated. **typecase** returns the value(s) produced from the evaluation of the last form. As a special case, the type may be the symbol **t** or **otherwise**; in this case, that clause will be used if none the other clauses are satisfied. If no match occurs, **nil** is returned.

(unless *test-form –forms–)* [*Macro*]

test-form is evaluated. If it is **nil**, then the forms are evaluated in order, and the value(s) of the last one returned. Otherwise **nil** is returned.

(unwind–protect *form –forms–)* [*Special function*]

form is evaluated and its value(s) saved; then the forms are evaluated and the saved value(s) of *form* returned. If, during the evaluation of *form* control is caused to pass through *form* and thus through the call to **unwind–protect**, the forms will still be evaluated. The forms are usually used to cleaned up something that may be untidy if *form* is not completely evaluated.

(warn *string –objects–)*

This just applies format to *string* and the objects, and directs the output to ***error–output***, perhaps taking some other implementation-dependent actions. **warn** does not normally enter the debugger (unless the variable ***break–on–warnings*** is non-**nil**, in which case **warn** behaves like **break**). Returns **nil**.

(when *test-form –forms–)* [*Macro*]

test-form is evaluated. If it is non-**nil**, then the forms are evaluated in order, and the value(s) of the last one returned. Otherwise **nil** is returned.

5. Evaluation Control Functions

(apply *function –objects– list)*

Returns the result(s) of applying function *function* to the arguments consisting of all the objects plus the elements of *list*.

(applyhook *function args evalfunction applyfunction* [*env*])

The symbol ***evalhook*** is assigned the value of *evalfunction,* and, ***applyhook*** the value of *applyfunction*. (See **eval** below for a description of how these free variables are used during evaluation). The optional argument should be an environment; if it is not supplied, then the null lexical environment is assumed. Then *function* is applied to the *args*. The check for these hook functions is omitted for the application of *function* to *args* itself, but it is considered for subsequent evaluations of the subforms and applications of functions to arguments within *form*. Typically, a user-defined debugging function will be installed as the value of ***applyhook***. This function may do something useful for debugging (output some data, for example), and then continue by calling **applyhook**, passing it the function and arguments to be processed, and itself as the *applyfunction* argument. This way, it is easy to recursively trace through function applications, doing something useful for debugging at each level.

(compiler–let (*–inits–*) *–forms–*)   [*Special form*]
During interpretation, this is just like **let** (see below), except that all the variables created are special variables. During compilation, however, the *inits* are actually processed, so that the special variables they refer to are assigned a value in the context of the compilation. Then the compiler processes the body of the **compiler–let**. This peculiar construct is useful if one needs to assign a value to special variables that are accessed by some macro during its expansion.

(eval *form*)
Returns the result(s) of evaluating *form*. Of course, since this is an ordinary function, the argument supplied has been evaluated, and the resulting actual argument is passed to **eval** for subsequent evaluation. There is assumed to be no lexical environment for the form, i. e., there cannot be valid references to lexical objects outside of the form itself. **eval** references two free symbols, ***evalhook*** and ***applyhook***, which the user may change for debugging purposes. If the value of ***evalhook*** is non-**nil**, then it should be a function of two arguments, a form and an environment. (An environment is some structure containing information about the current lexical environment, encoded in an implementation-dependent format. The user need not be concerned with the details of this structure, but merely be sure to accept it as an argument in situations like this one, and to provide it as an argument to whatever subsequent functions the user might call that might make use of an environment. For example, if the user's evalhook function calls **evalhook**, **applyhook** or **macroexpand**, each of which accepts an optional environment, the user probably wants to pass them the environment the evalhook function was passed, so that these functions perform their tasks in the correct context). In this case, instead of evaluating its argument, **eval** will simply pass its argument and the current environment to this function, set ***evalhook*** to **nil** for the duration of the call to this function, and return whatever value(s) this function computes. If the

value of ***applyhook*** is non-**nil** when **eval** is about to cause a function to be applied to some arguments, then it should be a function of three arguments: a function, a list of arguments, and an environment. In this case, instead of applying the function to its arguments, **eval** will apply the value of ***applyhook*** to the function, the arguments, and the current environment, set ***applyhook*** to **nil** for the duration of the function application, and return whatever value(s) this function computes.

(evalhook *form evalfunction applyfunction* [*env*]**)**

The symbol ***evalhook*** is assigned the value of *evalfunction,* and, ***applyhook*** the value of *applyfunction*. (See **eval** for a description of how these free symbols are used during evaluation). The optional argument should be an environment; if it is not supplied, then the null lexical environment is assumed. Then *form* is evaluated. The check for these hook functions is omitted for the evaluation of *form* itself, but it is considered for subsequent evaluations of the subforms and applications of functions to arguments within *form*. Typically, a user-defined debugging function will be installed as the value of ***evalhook***. This function may do something useful for debugging (output some data, for example), and then continue by calling **evalhook**, passing it the form to be evaluated, and itself as the second argument. This way, it is easy to recursively trace through an evaluation, doing something useful for debugging at each level.

(eval–when (–*keywords*–) –*forms*–**)**   [*Special form*]

The keywords may be the symbol **eval**, **load**, or **compile**. If the keywords include **eval**, then the forms are evaluated by the interpreter. The other keywords are meaningful only to a Common LISP compiler. **compile** means that the compiler will evaluate each of the forms in the compilation context. **load** means that the compiler will arrange things so that the *forms* are evaluated when the compiled code is subsequently loaded.

(flet (–(*symbol lambda-list* –*defforms*–)– **)**   [*Special form*]
            –*declarations*–
            –*forms*–   **)**

Each *symbol* is given a local function definition, having *lambda-list* as the formal parameter list and *defforms* as the body. Then the forms are evaluated, using these local definitions, and the value(s) from the last form returned. The scope of the local function definitions is just the forms, so the local function definitions themselves cannot refer to one another (but see **labels** below).

(funcall *function –objects–***)**
> Returns the value(s) of applying function *function*, which must be an ordinary function, to the objects.

(function *function***)**   *[Special form]*
> Returns the function associated with *function*, if *function* is some object, such as a symbol having a function definition, and returns the lexical closure of *function* if it is a lambda-expression.

(labels (*–(symbol lambda-list –defforms–)–)*   *[Special form]*
>   *–declarations–*
>   *–forms–*   **)**
> Just like **flet**, except that the local function definitions may refer to each other (so it is possible to write local recursive functions).

(let (*–inits–***)** *–declarations– –forms–***)**   *[Special form]*
> Each *init* is either a symbol, or a list of the form (*symbol initform*). A new variable is created for each symbol. Then all the initialization forms are evaluated, as if in parallel, and the associated variables are assigned these values. If just a symbol is supplied, it is assigned the value **nil**. Then the *forms* are evaluated, and the value(s) of the last form returned.

(let∗ (*–inits–***)** *–declarations– –forms–***)**   *[Special form]*
> This is just like **let** except that each variable in the *inits* is assigned its value before the next initialization form is evaluated.

(macroexpand *form* [*env*]**)**
> Expands *form* until it is not a macro call. Returns two values, the expansion, and **t**. If *form* is not a macro call, it is returned along with the value **nil**. *env* is an environment as described for **eval**, and defaults to the null environment. **macroexpand** works by passing three arguments, the macro expansion function associated with the **car** of *form*, *form* itself, and *env*, to the function that is the value of the variable ∗**macro–expand–hook**∗. This is normally assigned the value **funcall**, so that macro expansion works as expected. However, a LISP implementation or user may use this scheme to expand macros more cleverly, say, through the use of a hashing mechanism. The LISP evaluator (i. e., **eval**), expands macro calls as though it uses **macroexpand**.

(macroexpand–1 *form* [*env*]**)**
> This is just like **macroexpand**, except the macro call is only expanded once.

(macrolet (–(*symbol lambda-list –defforms–***)–)**   [*Special form*]
      –declarations–
      –forms–   **)**
      Like **flet**, but defines local macros.

(quote *object***)**   [*Special form*]
      object is not evaluated, but is simply returned.

(values *–forms–***)**
      The values computed by the forms are all returned as values. This is
      the basic mechanism to perform multiple-value returns.

(values–list *list***)**
      Returns as multiple values all of the elements of *list*.

6. Debugging Functions

(apropos *string* [*package*]**)**
      Prints out information about the function definition and current spe-
      cial variable value of those symbols whose print names contain *string*
      as a substring. All packages are examined from such symbols unless
      the *package* argument is specified, in which case only that package is
      examined.

(apropos–list *string* [*package*]**)**
      Returns a list of all symbols whose print names contain *string* as a
      substring. All packages are examined from such symbols unless the
      package argument is specified, in which case only that package is ex-
      amined.

(break [*string –objects–*]**)**
      string, which should be a format control string, and the objects are
      passed to **format**, and the resulting message is printed. Then the de-
      bugger is entered. The exact nature of the debugger is
      implementation-dependent. A provision should exist for continuing
      from the call to **break**; in this case, **break** will return **nil**.

(describe *object***)**
      Some useful information about *object* is printed on the standard out-
      put. For example, applied to a symbol, **describe** will print the
      symbol's value, its function definition, and its properties. Returns no
      values.

(dribble [*pathname*]**)**

    (dribble *pathname*) causes a record of the current session with the LISP interpreter to be printed to the file specified by *pathname*. **(dribble)** ceases recording the current session and closes the dribble file.

(ed [*x*]**)**

    Invokes the resident editor, if there is one. With no argument, the editor is entered in the same state it was in last time it was visited. **(ed** *filename*) edits the file named *filename*; **(ed** *symbol*) edits the function named *symbol*.

(inspect *object*)

    This is an interactive version of **describe**.

(room [*x*]**)**

    room prints information about memory utilization. If *x* is **nil**, a minimal amount of information is printed; if it is **t**, the maximum amount of information is printed; if it is omitted, an intermediate amount of information is printed.

(step *form*)   [*Macro*]

    The form is evaluated, but the user is allowed to interactively move through the interpretation process a step at a time. The exact nature of the interactions is implementation-dependent. Returns the value of *form*.

(time *form*)   [*Macro*]

    Returns the value of *form*, but also places some useful data on the stream that is the value of ***trace–output***. The details are implementation-dependent.

(trace *–function-names–*)   [*Macro*]

    After a call to **trace**, a call to one of the functions named will cause information about that function call to be printed on the stream that is the value of ***trace–output***. A call to **trace** with no arguments produces a list of the functions currently being traced. **trace** may also accept some additional implementation-dependent argument formats, in order to enable some more sophisticated modes of tracing.

(untrace *–function-names–*)   [*Macro*]

    The specified functions are untraced. If no argument is given, all currently traced functions are untraced.

7. Function Definition Functions

A number of Common LISP function definition functions allow both an optional documentation string and any number of declarations. For example, a valid call to **defun** is as follows:

```
(defun foo (x) "This is similar to 1+"
    (declare (integer x))
    (declare (inline 1+))
    (1+ x))
```

As in this example, in the descriptions of such functions below, the documentation string is shown coming before the declarations. Actually, the documentation string and declarations may appear in any relative order, including the documentation string appearing in the midst of a number of declarations. Thus the following is also permissible:

```
(defun foo (x)
    (declare (integer x))
    "This is similar to 1+"
    (declare (inline 1+))
    (1+ x))
```

Only one documentation string is allowed, although a given implementation may not check for this, and will act unpredictably if such a form is supplied. Also, a documentation string must be followed by some form or declaration; otherwise it will be interpreted as a form.

(define–modify–macro *symbol lambda-list function* [*string*])   [*Macro*]
     Defines a read-modify-write macro named *symbol*. *symbol* is made to have the documentation string *string* of type **function**, if *string* is supplied (see **documentation**). *function* must be a function of at least one argument; *lambda-list* describes the remaining arguments to *function*. The resulting macro *symbol*, when called, will apply *function* to the old contents of its argument, which should be some location acceptable to **setf**, (plus any additional arguments, in accordance with *lambda-list*). The old contents of this location is then replaced with the value computed by *function*.

(define–setf–method *access-fn lambda-list* [*string*]   [*Macro*]
          –*declarations*–
          –*forms*–   )
     This is similar to the more complex form of **defsetf** below, but does not require *access-fn* to be an ordinary function or a function-like macro; in addition, an arbitrary **defmacro**–like destructuring pattern

466

is permitted in *lambda-list*, and nothing is done to make the code insensitive to order of evaluation. Used only for those cases in which **defsetf** cannot be applied, such as writing a **setf** method for some location specifier, the evaluation of which will cause an error.

(defmacro *symbol lambda-list* [*string*] *–declarations– –forms–*)   [*Macro*]
Defines a macro named *symbol* having *lamda-list* for its lambda-list and the forms for its body. If *string* is supplied, it is attached to *symbol* as a documentation string of type **function** (see **documentation**). Returns *symbol*.

(defsetf *access-fn update-fn* [*string*])   [*Macro*]
(defsetf *access-fn lambda-list* (*symbol*) [*string*] *–declarations– –forms–*)
Specifies how **setf** should process a particular kind of call. A call of the form **(defsetf** *access-fn update-fn* [*string*]) states that when **setf** is called with a first argument beginning with *access-fn*, it should expand into a call to *update-fn* applied to all the arguments appearing in the call to *access-fn* plus, as its last argument, the second argument to **setf**. In addition, *access-fn* is given *string* as a documentation string of type **setf** (see **documentation**). For all this to work correctly, *access-fn* must be an ordinary function, or a macro that evaluates its arguments; *update-fn* must be a function of one more argument than *access-fn*, and it must return the value of the new value (i. e., the second argument to **setf**) as its value.

A call of the form

(defsetf *access-fn lambda-list* (*symbol*) [*string*] *–forms–*)

states that when **setf** is called with a first argument beginning with *access-fn*, it should expand into the code produced by the last form. This code can be written as if the variables in the lambda-list were assigned the arguments passed to *access-fn*, and *symbol* the second form passed to **setf**. The code is arranged so that the forms can be written without regard for order of evaluation. The code must return the value that is to be stored in the location specified in the call to **setf**. This format can handle some cases that the former format cannot, for example, a case in which a destructive function is used to change the contents of the location. However, both formats always cause all the arguments supplied to *access-fn* to be evaluated. The macro **define–setf–method** must be used if an argument to *access-fn* is to be treated specially.

(defstruct *name-exp* [*string*] *slot-desc* *–slot-descs–***)**   [*Macro*]
Defines a new data type which resembles a record structure. *name-exp* has the form (*name option1 ... optionn*), where *name* is a symbol; if there are no options, *name-exp* may be a symbol. A data type named *name* is established, and *name* is returned as the value of the call. If *string* is present, it is attached to *name* as a documentation string of type **structure** (see **documentation**). Each *slot-desc* is of the form

> (*slotname default-form option-name1 option-value1*
>
> .
>
> .
>
> .
>
> *option-namen option-valuen*)

where *slotname* is a symbol; if there are no default or options, *slot-desc* may be a symbol. The options resemble the syntax for keyword arguments, but the *option-value*s are not evaluated. The *option-name*s are either **:type**, in which case the *option-value* is a type specification declaring the type of the objects that will fill that slot, or **:read–only**, in which case non-**nil** means that the slot may not be altered.

Elements of the defined data type will have as many slots as there are *slot-desc*s when an element is created; if no value is specified for a slot, that slot will get its initial value by evaluating *default-form*. (If this is not supplied in the call to **defstruct**, the initial contents of that slot will be implementation-dependent.) **defstruct** defines an access function, named *name–slot-name*, for each slot, and arranges for **setf** to recognize calls to this function as locations whose values it can change. **defstruct** also creates a constructor function named **make–***name*; without further specification, the slots of the datum produced can be specified by using keyword arguments of the name **:***slot-name*. In addition, **defstruct** produces a predicate for that data type named *name*-**p**, and a copy function named **copy–***name*.

The options to **defstruct** are either keywords, or lists of a keyword and an argument for that keyword. In any case, none of the arguments or their components is evaluated. The following options are allowed:

:conc–name – The argument following this keyword specifies the prefix to use for names of the access functions; **nil** means that no prefix is used. (The prefix defaults to the name of the data type followed by a hyphen.)

468

:constructor – If given a single argument, that argument specifies the name of the constructor function; **nil** means not to create a constructor function at all. (The default name for the constructor function is the name of the data type prefixed with the string **MAKE–**.) If two arguments are supplied, the second argument should be a lambda-list. Instead of creating a constructor function in which slot values are specified by keywords (the default), the function that is created will accept the slot values as ordinary positional arguments, in the manner described by lambda-list. The variables appearing in the lambda-list must be the names of the slots of the data type, and will be accepted in that order. All the lambda-list specifiers are allowed. Note that specifying an optional *or* an auxiliary variable that is a slot name, and giving it a default value, will cause that slot to be given that default value. If no default value is specified for these parameters, only then will the default values specified in the slot descriptions be used. Any number of appearances of the **:constructor** keyword is allowed, each one producing a different constructor function.

:copier – The argument specifies the name of the copier function; **nil** means not to create a copier function at all. (The default name for the copier function is the name of the data type prefixed with the string **COPY–**.)

:predicate – The argument specifies the name of the predicate function; **nil** means not to create a predicate function at all. (The default name for the predicate function is the name of the data type suffixed with the string **–P**.) Predicate functions can only be created if the structure is "named" (see the **:named** option below).

:include – The argument specifies another structure; its slot names are included as slot names for the new data type. The access functions of the old data type will also work on the new data type. The **:type** options for the two structures must be compatible (see **:type** below). Default values for the individual slots can be specified as slot specifications following the name of the included structure; otherwise, the defaults of the included structure are used. At most one **:include** option can be specified for a call to **defmacro**.

:print–function – The argument should be a function of three arguments, and will be used to print data objects of this type. Upon printing, the specified function will be passed the structure to be printed, a stream to which to print it, and an integer representing the current depth within a list structure at which the printing will occur. If not specified, data of this type will be printed using the **#S** nota-

notation. This argument may not be given if a **:type** option is specified (see below).

:type – The argument specifies the internal representation to be used for the structure. This is always a sequence. The possible arguments are **vector**, (**vector** *element-type*) and **list**. Unless the **:named** option (see below) is also specified, structures in which the **:type** option appears will not be named. In an unnamed structure, each datum is stored without anything to identify it as an instance of a particular kind of structure: The first slot of the structure is stored in the very first element of the sequence; if the structure were named, it would be stored in the second element, and the first would contain the name of the structure. In this case, a predicate can be created for the data type. If a type option is specified, then the structure name itself does not become a valid type specifier, nor may a **print–function** argument be specified. If it is not specified, the structure will be named, the structure name becomes a valid type specifier, and the structure is represented in an implementation-dependent manner.

:named – No argument is specified. The structure is named, even if a type option is specified (see **:type** above).

:initial–offset – This is permitted only if a type option is also specified (see **:type** above). The argument is the number of elements of the sequence representing the structure to leave empty before using them to house the name and the slots of the structure. If used together with **:include**, then the argument will specify the number of elements to skip after the elements representing the slots of the included data type before representing elements of the new data type.

(**defun** *symbol lambda-list* [*string*] *–declarations– –forms–*)   [*Macro*]
Defines a function named *symbol* having *lamda-list* for its lambda-list and the forms for its body. If *string* is supplied, it is attached to *symbol* as a documentation string of type **function** (see **documentation**). Returns *symbol*.

8. Miscellaneous Functions

8.1. Declaration Functions

(**declare** *–declarations–*)   [*Special form*]
Calls to **declare** can only appear in the beginning of the bodies of code of certain special functions. The declaration is in force for the extent of such a body of code. Declarations are meaningful only to

470

the compiler, except for special declarations, which the interpreter heeds also. See Chapter 20 for more detail.

(**deftype** *name lambda-list –string– –declarations– –forms–*)   [*Macro*]
A new type specifier called *name* is created, and returned as the value of the call to **deftype**. If *string* is supplied, *name* is made to have *string* as a documentation string of type **type** (see **documentation**). The presence of *name* in the beginning of a type specification will cause that specification to expand into a new type specification. The expansion is done in the same manner as for macros defined by **defmacro**: The rest of the elements in the list are assigned to the variables in *lambda-list*, and the forms evaluated to produce the new specification.

(**locally** *–declarations– –forms–*)   [*Macro*]
The specified declarations are put into effect for the extent of the forms.

(**proclaim** *decl-spec*)
The declaration specified by *decl-spec* is put into effect globally.

(**the** *type-spec form*)   [*Special function*]
Returns whatever *form* evaluates to. Moreover, it is an error if the value produced by *form* does not conform to the type specified by *type-spec*. In effect, this declares the resulting value to be of type *type-spec*.

8.2. Systems Functions

(**decode–universal–time** *universal-time* [*time-zone*])
Returns nine values representing the time *time-integer*, which is interpreted as a Universal Time (i. e., the number of seconds since January 1, 1900 GMT) in the time zone *zone-integer* (which defaults to the current time zone). The nine values are as described for **get–decoded–time** below.

(**encode–universal–time** *second minute hour date month year* [*time-zone*])
The Universal Time (i. e., the number of seconds since January 1, 1900 GMT) is computed for the arguments given (interpreted as described for **get–decoded–time** below). If no time zone is specified, the current time zone adjusted for daylight saving time is used; if it is specified, no adjustment is made for daylight saving time.

(get–decoded–time)

Nine values are returned representing the following aspects of the current time: second (0-59), minute (0-59), hour (0-23), date (1-31), month (1-12), year (an integer representing the year A.D., but with the integers 0-99 representing those years within 50 years of the current year in the obvious fashion), day of week (0-6), and whether daylight saving time is in effect (non-**nil** or **nil**),

(get–internal–real–time)

Returns some implementation-dependent measurement of the amount of elapsed time relative to some arbitrary base. The measurement is in terms of *internal time units*. The number of internal time units to the second is implementation-dependent, but is the value of the symbol **internal–time–units–per–second**.

(get–internal–run–time)

Returns the number of *internal time units* that the current LISP process has consumed. The exact quantity measured is implementation-dependent. The number of internal time units to the second is implementation-dependent, but is the value of the symbol **internal–time–units–per–second**.

(get–universal–time)

Returns the current time as a Universal Time, i. e., the number of seconds since January 1, 1900 GMT.

(lisp–implementation–type)

Returns a string indicating the generic name of the particular Common LISP implementation.

(lisp–implementation–version)

Returns a string indicating the version of the particular Common LISP implementation.

(long–site–name)

Returns a long string indicating the name of the physical location the machine is located at.

(machine–instance)

Returns a string identifying the specific machine upon which the current Common LISP process is running. This may be a serial number or a local nickname.

(machine–type)

> Returns a string indicating the generic name of the machine upon which the current Common LISP process is running.

(machine–version)

> Returns a string indicating the version of the machine upon which the current Common LISP process is running.

(short–site–name)

> Returns a short string indicating the name of the physical location the machine is located at.

(sleep *number***)**

> The current LISP process ceases execution for about *number* seconds, and then execution is resumed.

(software–type)

> Returns a string indicating the generic name of the supporting software system.

(software–version)

> Returns a string indicating the version of the supporting software system.

8.3. Other Functions

(compile *symbol* [*lambda-expression*]**)**

> If *lambda-expression* is supplied, then it is compiled; if not, then the function definition of *symbol* is compiled. The result, a "compiled-function object", is made the function definition of *symbol*. If *symbol* is **nil**, however, the compiled-function object is simply returned.

(compile–file *file-spec***)**

> The contents of the LISP source file specified by *file-spec* is compiled and written out to a binary object file. The keyword argument **:output–file** can be used to specify an output file; otherwise, this defaults in some manner dependent upon the implementation's file system.

(disassemble *function***)**

> The compiled code of *function* is reverse-assembled and printed out in a symbolic format. If *function* is not compiled, then **disassemble** compiles it.

Appendix B

Special Common LISP
Symbols and Characters

A number of symbols have a special interpretation in Common LISP. Some symbols denote constants. Others are used to refer to global variables that may be inspected or assigned by various Common LISP functions. In addition, various characters are treated diferently by the Common LISP reader. Each character and special symbol, and its associated interpretation, is described below. The abbreviation "iff" is used below to mean "if and only if".

applyhook   [*variable*]
   Used by **eval** to aid debugging. If the value of ***applyhook*** is non-**nil** when **eval** is about to cause a function to be applied to some arguments, then it should be a function of three arguments: a function, a list of arguments, and an environment. In this case, instead of applying the function to its arguments, **eval** will apply the value of ***applyhook*** to the function, the arguments, and the current environment, set ***applyhook*** to **nil** for the duration of the function application, and return whatever value(s) this function computes. (See **eval** for further information.)

array–dimension–limit   *[constant]*
> Specifies the upper bound (exclusive) on each individual dimension of an array. Implementation-dependent, but guaranteed to be at least 1024.

array–rank–limit   *[constant]*
> Specifies the upper bound (exclusive) on the rank of an array. Implementation-dependent, but guaranteeed to be at least 8.

array–total–size–limit   *[constant]*
> Specifies the upper bound (exclusive) on the total number of elements in an array. Implementation-dependent, but guaranteeed to be at least 1024. The actual number of elements in an array may vary with their type – this limit is the minimum for any possible type.

boole–clr   *[constant]*
boole–set   *[constant]*
boole–1   *[constant]*
boole–2   *[constant]*
boole–c1   *[constant]*
boole–c2   *[constant]*
boole–and   *[constant]*
boole–ior   *[constant]*
boole–xor   *[constant]*
boole–eqv   *[constant]*
boole–nand   *[constant]*
boole–nor   *[constant]*
boole–andc1   *[constant]*
boole–andc2   *[constant]*
boole–orc1   *[constant]*
boole–orc2   *[constant]*
> These constants are interpreted by the function **boole** as specifying a particular logical operation to perform. (See **boole** for further information.)

break–on–warning   *[variable]*
> If non-**nil**, then the function **warn** behaves like **break**. Useful for debugging programs that issue warnings. (See **warn** for further information.)

call–arguments–limit   *[constant]*
> Specifies the upper bound (exclusive) on the number of arguments that can be passed to a function. Implementation-dependent, but guaranteed to be at least 50.

char–bits–limit [*constant*]
> Specifies the upper bound (exclusive) on the "bits" component of a character (i. e., the component that distinguishes things like "control" and "meta" characters from each other and from ordinary characters). Guaranteed to be a power of two.

char–code–limit [*constant*]
> Specifies the upper bound (exclusive) on the "code" component of a character (i. e., the component that distinguishes among the various characters proper).

char–control–bit [*constant*]
char–hyper–bit [*constant*]
char–meta–bit [*constant*]
char–super–bit [*constant*]
> These constants specify the four bits of the "bits" attribute for which Common LISP provides explicit names. The specification is in terms of numerical "weights": The weight of the control bit is 1, of the meta bit, 2, of the super bit 4, and of the hyper bit, 8.

char–font–limit [*constant*]
> Specifies the upper bound (exclusive) on the "font" component of a character (i. e., the component that specifies the style of a character).

debug–io [*variable*]
> Its value is the stream used for interactive debugging purposes.

default–pathname–defaults [*variable*]
> Its value is a pathname that is used by any pathname function that needs a set of defaults, but is not given one.

double–float–epsilon [*constant*]
> Its value is the smallest positive double floating-point number e such that **(not** (= **(float** 1 e) (+ **(float** 1 e) e))) evaluates to true.

double–float–negative–epsilon [*constant*]
> Its value is the smallest positive double floating-point number e such that **(not** (= **(float** 1 e) (– **(float** 1 e) e))) evaluates to true.

error–output [*variable*]
> Its value is the stream to which error messages are sent.

evalhook   [*variable*]

If the value of ***evalhook*** is non-**nil**, then it should be a function of two arguments, a form and an environment. In this case, instead of evaluating its argument, **eval** will pass its argument and the current environment to this function, set ***evalhook*** to **nil** for the duration of the call to this function, and return whatever value(s) this function computes. (See **eval** for further information.)

features   [*variable*]

Its value is a list of symbols that name features provided by the implementation, most of which will be implementation-dependent. (The only standard feature name is **ieee–floating–point**.) The value of ***features*** is used by the #+ and #– dispatching macro character forms.

internal–time–units–per–second   [*constant*]

Its value is the number of internal time units that comprise a second in the given implementation.

lambda–list–keywords   [*constant*]

Its value is a list of all lambda list specifiers used in the implementation, including those used by **defmacro**. The list will contain at least **&optional**, **&rest**, **&key**, **&aux**, **&allow–other–keywords**, **&body**, **&whole** and **&environment**.

lambda–parameters–limit   [*constant*]

Specifies the upper bound (exclusive) on the number of parameters that may appear in a lambda-list. Implementation-dependent, but guaranteed to be at least 50.

least–negative–double–float   [*constant*]
least–negative–long–float   [*constant*]
least–negative–short–float   [*constant*]
least–negative–single–float   [*constant*]
least–positive–double–float   [*constant*]
least–positive–long–float   [*constant*]
least–positive–short–float   [*constant*]
least–positive–single–float   [*constant*]

These constants specify the smallest (in absolute value) non-zero number of the specified type.

load–verbose   [*variable*]

Its value is the default for the **:verbose** argument to **load**. If this argument is non-**nil**, **load** will print a message in the form of a comment to the standard output indicating what file is being loaded, etc. Its initial value is implementation-dependent.

long–float–epsilon [*constant*]

Its value is the smallest positive long floating-point number *e* such that **(not (= (float 1** *e*) **(+ (float 1** *e*) *e*)))** evaluates to true.

long–float–negative–epsilon [*constant*]

Its value is the smallest positive long floating-point number *e* such that **(not (= (float 1** *e*) **(– (float 1** *e*) *e*)))** evaluates to true.

∗macroexpand–hook∗ [*variable*]

Used by **macroexpand** and **macroexpand–1** to facilitate user-modification of the manner in which macros are expanded. To compute a macro expansion, these functions apply the value of this variable to three arguments: the macro expansion function associated with the **car** of the form it is evaluating, the form itself, and the current environment. The value computed by this function application is the expansion of that macro form. The initial value of this variable is **funcall**.

∗modules∗ [*variable*]

Its value is the list of names of those modules that have been loaded into the current LISP process. Used by the functions **provide** and **require**.

most–negative–double–float [*constant*]
most–negative–fixnum [*constant*]
most–negative–long–float [*constant*]
most–negative–short–float [*constant*]
most–negative–single–float [*constant*]
most–positive–double–float [*constant*]
most–positive–fixnum [*constant*]
most–positive–long–float [*constant*]
most–positive–short–float [*constant*]
most–positive–single–float [*constant*]

These constants specify the largest (in absolute value) finite number of the specified type.

multiple–values–limit [*constant*]

Specifies the upper bound (exclusive) on the number of values that may be returned from a function. Implementation-dependent, but guaranteed to be at least 20.

nil   [*constant*]

    Represents the empty list, and the logical value "false". Always evaluated to **nil**. Can also be written as **( )**.

package   [*variable*]

    Its value is the current package. This is the default package for most package functions, since they specify as their default package the value of a special variable of this name. Its initial value is the **user** package. **load** creates a new variable named ***package***, and assigns it the same value as the previous variable of this name. This new variable persists for the duration of the call to **load**, so that if the value of the current ***package*** variable changes during this period, the previous variable of this name will remain unchanged.

pi   [*constant*]

    The best approximation to π, in long floating-point format.

print—array   [*variable*]

    The contents of an array (other than a string) is printed iff this is non-**nil**. Its initial value is implementation-dependent.

print—base   [*variable*]

    Its value is the radix used when outputting rational numbers. Its initial value is 10.

print—case   [*variable*]

    Uppercase characters are printed in upper case, in lower case, or as capitalized words according to whether this value is **:upcase**, **:downcase** or **:capitalize**. Its initial value is **:upcase**.

print—circle   [*variable*]

    An attempt is made to detect circular structures iff this is non-**nil**. Its initial value is **nil**.

print—escape   [*variable*]

    Escape characters are output iff this is non-**nil**. Its initial value is **t**.

print—gensym   [*variable*]

    The prefix #: is printed before symbols that have no home package iff this value is non-**nil**. Its initial value is **t**.

print—length   [*variable*]

    The number of elements of a list to print, with **nil** meaning to print the entire length. Its initial value is **nil**.

print–level [*variable*]

The number of levels to print of nested s-expressions, with **nil** meaning to print all levels. Its initial value is **nil**.

print–pretty [*variable*]

An attempt is made to pretty-print output iff this is non-**nil**. Its initial value is implementation-dependent.

print–radix [*variable*]

Radix specifiers are output iff this is non-**nil**. Its initial value is **nil**.

query–io [*variable*]

Its value is the stream to which questions to the user are sent, and from which answers from the user are read.

random–state [*variable*]

Holds a **random-state** data structure which encodes the internal state of the random-number generator used by the function **random**.

read–base [*variable*]

Its value is the radix in which integers and ratios are read. It may be any integer between 2 and 36, inclusive. Its initial value is 10 (decimal).

read–default–float–format [*variable*]

Its value is the default type for floating point numbers whose precise format is not specified. Its initial value is **single–float**.

read–suppress [*variable*]

This variable exists primarily to support the #– and #+ features of the # dispatching macro character. If its value is non-**nil**, most of the important reader operations are turned off. In particular, when a token is scanned, it will not be interpreted, but instead, **nil** will be returned. In addition, while the value of ***read–suppress*** is non-**nil**, most of the various # dispatching macro character options will just skip over the expressions to which they are prefixed, and return **nil**. The initial value of ***read–suppress*** is **nil**.

readtable [*variable*]

Its value is the current readtable. The reader uses this readtable to determine the syntax of each character. Its initial value is a readtable that supports the standard Common LISP syntax.

short–float–epsilon   [*constant*]
   Its value is the smallest positive short floating-point number *e* such that (**not** (= (**float 1** *e*) (+ (**float 1** *e*) *e*))) evaluates to true.

short–float–epsilon   [*constant*]
   Its value is the smallest positive short floating-point number *e* such that (**not** (= (**float 1** *e*) (– (**float 1** *e*) *e*))) evaluates to true.

single–float–epsilon   [*constant*]
   Its value is the smallest positive single-precision floating-point number *e* such that (**not** (= (**float 1** *e*) (+ (**float 1** *e*) *e*))) evaluates to true.

single–float–negative–epsilon   [*constant*]
   Its value is the smallest positive single-precision floating-point number *e* such that (**not** (= (**float 1** *e*) (– (**float 1** *e*) *e*))) evaluates to true.

∗standard–input∗   [*variable*]
   Its value is the stream from which many input functions, including **read** (and, thereby, the normal top-level of LISP), take their input.

∗standard–output∗   [*variable*]
   Its value is the stream to which many output functions, including **print**, etc. (and, thereby, the normal top-level of LISP), send their output.

t   [*constant*]
   The default generic non-**nil** LISP symbol. **t** always evaluates to **t**.

∗terminal–io∗   [*variable*]
   Its value is the stream which prints to the user's display screen, and reads from the user's keyboard.

∗trace–output∗   [*variable*]
   Its value is the stream to which trace functions send their output.

+   [*variable*]
++   [*variable*]
+++   [*variable*]
   During the evaluation of a form by the top-level loop, + is assigned the previous form read by the top-level loop; ++ is assigned the form before that one, and +++ the form before that one.

481

–   [*variable*]

During the evaluation of a form by the top-level loop, – is assigned the form being evaluated.

*   [*variable*]
**   [*variable*]
***   [*variable*]

During the evaluation of a form by the top-level loop, * is assigned the first value printed by the previous pass through the top-level loop; ** is assigned the first value printed by the pass before that one, and *** the first value printed by the pass before that one.

/   [*variable*]
//   [*variable*]
///   [*variable*]

During the evaluation of a form by the top-level loop, **/** is assigned the list of all the values printed by the previous pass through the top-level loop; **//** is assigned the list of all the values printed by the pass before that one, and **///** the list of all the values printed by the pass before that one.

A-Z, a-z, 0-9, !, $, &, *, +, –, ., /, :, <, =, >,   [*character*]
%, ?, @, [,], ˆ, _, {, }, ˜, <*backspace*>, <*rubout*>

These are the standard constituent characters, which normally become part of Common LISP tokens. The characters **!, ?, [,], {** and **}** are explicitly reserved for the user. That is, they are not used in any standard Common LISP construction, so the user may change their syntactic character with impunity.

<*space*>, <*tab*>, <*page*>,   [*character*]
<*return*>, <*newline*>, <*linefeed*>

These are the standard Common LISP whitespace characters. Reading such a character terminates the token being read. Whitespace is usually skipped over by **read**, but not by **read–preserving–whitespace**.

([*character*]

This terminating macro character indicates the beginning of list or dotted pair, and is invalid elsewhere.

)   [*character*]

This terminating macro character indicates the end of a list or dotted pair, or one of a number of # dispatching macro character constructs, and is invalid elsewhere.

'
                                     [*character*]

'*object* is an abbreviation for (**quote** *object*). Syntactically, ' is a terminating macro character.

;
                                     [*character*]

The comment character: All characters up to and including the next newline are ignored. Syntactically, ; is a terminating macro character.

"
                                     [*character*]

A pair of double quotes delimits a string. Syntactically, a double quote is a terminating macro character.

`
                                     [*character*]

"Backquotes" the next expression, so that the resulting structure will be a form, which, when evaluated, will produce the next expression, but with all occurrences of subexpressions prefixed with , (comma) replaced by their values, and all occurrences of subexpressions prefixed with ,@ (comma followed by at-sign) having their values "spliced" into the structure being built. Syntactically, backquote is a terminating macro character.

,
                                     [*character*]

Comma is used within a backquoted expression, as described above, and is invalid elsewhere. Syntactically, , is a terminating macro character.

\
                                     [*character*]

Backslash is the single escape character, used to prevent the normal syntactic interpretation of the next character read.

|
                                     [*character*]

Vertical bar is the multiple escape character. The usual syntactic interpretation of constituent, macro, or whitespace characters is ignored within a pair of multiple escapes.

#
                                     [*character*]

The standard dispatching macro character. # is a non-terminating macro character. The following subforms are recognized:

#*n***A** – Reads the next object as an *n*-dimensional array whose contents are specified as for the **:initial-contents** argument to **make-array**.

#**B** – Reads the next object as a binary number.

#O – Reads the next object as an octal number.

#nR – Reads the next object as a number in radix n.

#S – Reads the next object, which should have list syntax, as a structure. The type of the structure is specified by the first element of the list; the rest of the elements of the list are interpreted as alternating slot names and their respective values.

#X – Reads the next object as an hexadecimal number.

#** – Reads the next character as a character object. #\\$name$ reads $name$ as the character object with name $name$, e. g., #**newline reads as the newline character; #**space** reads as the space character. Other names that may be supported are **rubout**, **page**, **tab**, **backspace**, **return** and **linefeed**; characters with more attributes may be supported by hyphenated names, such as #**Control–Meta–\A** or #**Meta–<**.

#' – #'fn is an abbreviation for (**function** fn).

#(– A series of objects between #(and) is read as a simple vector whose elements are those objects. #n(indicates that the vector is n elements long – it is an error if too many objects are specified; if too few appear, the last object specified is used to fill the remaining elements.

#* – A series of binary digits following this form is read as a simple bit-vector containing those bits, the leftmost bit designating bit 0 of the bit vector. #n* indicates that the vector is n elements long – it is an error if too many bits are specified; if too few appear, the last bit specified is used to fill the remaining elements.

#: – Reads the next token, which should have no embedded colons, as a new uninterned symbol.

#. – Reads the next object as the value resulting from the evaluation of that object.

#, – Reads the next object as the value resulting from the evaluation of that object, except during compilation, in which case the code that is produced will cause the evaluation to be done when the object is read at load time.

#n= – Reads the next object normally, except that the object is labelled by the integer n. This object may be referred to by the expression #n# within the scope of the outermost call to **read**.

#n# – Refers to the same object labelled by the form #n+, within the scope of the outermost call to **read**. For example, the expression (#1 =(a b) #1#) produces a list **equal** to the list ((a b) (a b)), but in which the first and second elements are the exact same LISP object.

#+ – This is a "conditional read" form. #+*feature form* reads *form* iff *feature* is a member of the list that is the value of the variable ∗**features**∗, or if *feature* is a Boolean expression composed of the operators **and**, **or** and **not** applied to operands that are *feature*s. The *form* is read safely by assigning the variable ∗**read–suppress**∗ a non-**nil** value, and then calling the function **read**.

#– – This is a "conditional read" form such that #–*feature form* is equivalent to #+(**not** *feature*) *form*.

#| – Text between a #| and a |# is treated as a comment by the reader. Embedded occurrences of these delimiters is permitted, and must also be balanced, so that "commenting out" a block of text that has this kind of comment in it will have the desired effect.

#< – This causes an error. Most probably, the reader is trying to read in some Common LISP output that was printed so that it could not be read back in.

#*whitespace* – # followed by whitespace causes an error.

#) – Causes an error.

All other combinations are undefined. The combinations #!, #?, #[, #], #{ and #} are explicitly reserved for the user.

Bibliography

Allen, John. (1978). *Anatomy of LISP.* McGraw-Hill, New York.

Charniak, E., and McDermott, D. (1984). *Introduction to Artificial Intelligence.* Addison-Wesley, Reading, Massachusetts.

Charniak, E., Riesbeck, C., and McDermott, D. (1979). *Artificial Intelligence Programming Techniques.* Lawrence Erlbaum Associates, Hillsdale, New Jersey.

Church, Alonzo. (1941). "The Calculi of Lambda-Conversion." In *Annals of Mathematical Studies,* Vol. 6. Princeton University Press, New Jersey.

Foderaro, John. (1985). "The Franz LISP Manual." Franz, Inc., Alameda, California.

McCarthy, John. (1960). "Recursive Functions of Symbolic Expressions and their Computation by Machine, Part I." In *Communications of the ACM,* Vol. 3, No. 4, pp. 185-195, April 1960.

McCarthy, J., Abrahams, P. W., Edwards, D. J., Hart, T. P., and Levin, M. I. (1962). *LISP 1.5 Programmer's Manual.* MIT Press, Cambridge, Massachusetts.

Meehan, J. R. (1979). *The New UCI LISP Manual.* Lawrence Erlbaum Associates, Hillsdale, New Jersey.

486

Moon, David. (1974). *MACLISP Reference Manual,* Version 0. Laboratory for Computer Science, MIT, Cambridge, Massachusetts, April 1974.

Rich, Elaine. (1983). *Artificial Intelligence.* McGraw-Hill, New York.

Siklossy, Laurent. (1976). *Let's Talk LISP.* Prentice-Hall, Englewood Cliffs, New Jersey.

Sussman, G., and Abelson, H. (1983). *The Structure and Interpretation of Computer Programs.* MIT Press, Cambridge, Massachusetts.

Teitelman, Warren. (1974). *INTERLISP Reference Manual.* Xerox Corporation, Palo Alto Research Center, Palo Alto, California, and Bolt Beranek and Newman, Cambridge, Massachusetts.

Touretzky, David S. (1983). *LISP: A Gentle Introduction to Symbolic Computation.* Harper and Row, New York.

Weinreb, Daniel L., and Moon, David. (1978). *LISP Machine Manual.* Artificial Intelligence Laboratory, MIT, Cambridge, Massachusetts.

Winston, P. H. (1977). *Artificial Intelligence.* Addison-Wesley, Reading, Massachusetts.

Winston, P. H., and Horn, B. H. (1981). *LISP.* Addison-Wesley, Reading, Massachusetts.

Index

Entries whose names contain non-alphabetic characters are sorted as if their names did not contain such characters. For example, *package* appears in the position it would if it were **package**. Entries without alphabetic characters in their names appear at the end of this index. Page numbers in italics refer to entries in the appendices.